The Science and Politics of Work Disability Prevention

The rising cost of illness and disability benefits is one of today's biggest social and labor market challenges. The promise of activation-oriented work disability policies was labor-market engagement for all people, regardless of illness, injury or impairment. However, the reality has been more complex.

This edited volume addresses social, political and economic contexts driving work disability policy reform in 13 countries. In this first attempt to explain the history and future of work disability policy, this pathbreaking book asks new questions about work disability policy design, focus, and effects. It details how work disability policies have evolved with jurisdictions, why these take their current shape, and where they are heading. The well-positioned authors draw on their insider knowledge and expertise in law, medicine, psychology, epidemiology and political and social sciences to provide detailed case studies of their jurisdictions.

This volume will be of interest to social security system policy makers, scholars, and students in the health and social sciences.

Ellen MacEachen, PhD, is Associate Professor with the School of Public Health and Health Systems at the University of Waterloo, Canada. She is an advisor to national and international labor market and health organizations. Her research focuses on work disability policy, precarious employment, and the future of work.

The Science and Politics of Work Disability Prevention

Edited by
Ellen MacEachen

NEW YORK AND LONDON

First published 2019
by Routledge
711 Third Avenue, New York, NY 10017

and by Routledge
2 Park Square, Milton Park, Abingdon, Oxon, OX14 4RN

Routledge is an imprint of the Taylor & Francis Group, an informa business

© 2019 Taylor & Francis

The right of Ellen MacEachen to be identified as the author of the editorial material, and of the authors for their individual chapters, has been asserted in accordance with sections 77 and 78 of the Copyright, Designs and Patents Act 1988.

All rights reserved. No part of this book may be reprinted or reproduced or utilised in any form or by any electronic, mechanical, or other means, now known or hereafter invented, including photocopying and recording, or in any information storage or retrieval system, without permission in writing from the publishers.

Trademark notice: Product or corporate names may be trademarks or registered trademarks, and are used only for identification and explanation without intent to infringe.

Library of Congress Cataloging-in-Publication Data
Names: MacEachen, Ellen, editor.
Title: The science and politics of work disability prevention / edited by Ellen MacEachen.
Description: 1 Edition. | New York : Routledge, 2019. | Includes bibliographical references and index.
Identifiers: LCCN 2018021029| ISBN 9781138335301 (hardcover) | ISBN 9781138335318 (pbk.) | ISBN 9780429443398 (ebk)
Subjects: LCSH: People with disabilities—Employment. | Industrial safety. | Social security.
Classification: LCC HD7255 .S35 2019 | DDC 363.11/7—dc23
LC record available at https://lccn.loc.gov/2018021029

ISBN: 978-1-138-33530-1 (hbk)
ISBN: 978-1-138-33531-8 (pbk)
ISBN: 978-0-429-44339-8 (ebk)

Typeset in Bembo
by Swales & Willis Ltd, Exeter, Devon, UK

To Patrick Loisel, for his vision and for building bridges between work disability communities.

Contents

List of Figures	x
List of Tables	xi
List of Contributors	xii
Acknowledgments	xviii

PART 1
Work Disability Policy Context   1

1 Work Disability Policy: Current Challenges and New Questions   3
ELLEN MACEACHEN

2 Reflections on the Sherbrooke Model and the Way Forward for Work Disability Prevention   18
PATRICK LOISEL

PART 2
Cause-Based Social Security Systems   29

3 Work Disability in the United States: A Fragmented System   31
ALLARD E. DEMBE

4 Strengths and Weaknesses of Regulatory Systems Designed to Prevent Work Disability After Injury or Illness: An Overview of Mechanisms in a Selection of Canadian Compensation Systems   50
KATHERINE LIPPEL

5 The Australian Work Disability Patchwork   72
GENEVIEVE GRANT

Contents

6 The New Zealand Universal Accident Scheme: Problems Solved and New Challenges 88
GRANT DUNCAN

7 An Overview of Work Disability Policies in China 103
DESAI SHAN

PART 3
Comprehensive Social Security Systems 123

8 Reforming Activation in Swedish Work Disability Policy 125
CHRISTIAN STÅHL AND IDA SEING

9 Work Disability Prevention in Finland: Promoting Work Ability Through Occupational Health Collaboration 141
KARI-PEKKA MARTIMO

10 Work Disability Prevention in France: Organizational and Political Challenges 158
JEAN-BAPTISTE FASSIER

11 Work Disability Policy in Germany: Experiences of Collective and Individual Participation and Cooperation 171
FELIX WELTI

12 Keeping People at Work: New Work Disability Prevention Measures in Switzerland 189
THOMAS GEISEN

13 Disability Prevention Policies in Belgium: Navigating Between Scientific and Socioeconomic Influences 205
PHILIPPE MAIRIAUX

14 Work Disability Prevention in the Netherlands: A Key Role for Employers 223
ANGELIQUE DE RIJK

15 The Rise and Fall of Income Replacement Disability
Benefit Receipt in the United Kingdom: What Are the
Consequences of Reforms? 242
BEN BARR AND PHILIP MCHALE

PART 4
Challenges and Opportunities for Work
Disability Policy 259

16 Science, Politics, and Values in Work Disability Policy:
A Reflection on Trends and the Way Forward 261
ELLEN MACEACHEN AND KERSTIN EKBERG

Index 284

Figures

3.1	Employer strategies for preventing and managing work disability.	41
9.1	Occupational health services in Finland.	145
9.2	The Work Ability House model.	147
10.1	Salary replacement of workers in case of sick leave.	160
13.1	Main components of the Belgian social security system for salaried workers and monthly deductions from workers' gross salaries for each component.	206
13.2	Pathway to be followed by sick-listed workers from the point of view of mandatory health insurance.	208
13.3	Change in the percentage of people remaining on sick-leave benefits during their first year of work incapacity.	213
13.4	Change in the number of disability benefits recipients among salaried workers, 1996 to 2015.	214
13.5	The new reintegration pathways introduced in health and disability insurance by Royal Decree on November 24, 2016.	218
14.1	Dutch sickness-absence scheme before 1996.	227
14.2	Dutch sickness-absence scheme since 2004.	231
14.3	Drop in sickness-absence and disability-pension expenditures, as a percentage of GDP.	234
15.1	Number of people receiving main earnings-replacement disability benefits, 1978 to 2016.	244
15.2	Percentage of men and women aged 20 to 59 reporting a health problem that limits the kind of paid work they can do, by educational group.	245
15.3	Trends in the disability/employment gap.	246
15.4	Policy changes regarding UK earnings-replacement benefits for disabled people and welfare-to-work programs, 1994 to 2016.	247
15.5	Trends in poverty among disabled and nondisabled people out of work, aged 20 to 59.	252

Tables

3.1	A summary of US disability-related programs	34
4.1	Quebec compensation systems for work disability, 2017	55
4.2	Workers' compensation rights in Quebec and Ontario	58
4.3	Determination of benefits after work injury for low earner and high earner	62
5.1	Australia's legal arrangements for work disability support and integration	77
7.1	Work-related injuries and disabilities (officially recognized), 2011–2015	107
7.2	Payments for medical treatment and rehabilitation	110
7.3	Rights to return to work after workplace injuries	111
7.4	Compensation standards for personal injuries	114
7.5	Medical leave for non-work-related injuries and diseases	115
13.1	Trends in the Belgian population 20 to 64 years old, 1996 to 2015	215
13.2	Prognostic categories used by social insurance physicians to classify sick-listed workers during the Quickscan procedure	218

Contributors

Ben Barr, PhD, FFPH, is a Senior Clinical Lecturer in Applied Public Health Research at the University of Liverpool, UK. His research focuses on evaluating the impact of social, welfare, health, and economic policies on health, and the social consequences of chronic illness. He has published extensively on the employment and health effects of welfare policies for people with disabilities. He is part of the World Health Organization (WHO) Collaborating Centre for Policy Research on Social Determinants of Health and has collaborated on a number of reports for the WHO. He advises the UK Department of Health on resource-allocation policy and was a panel member for the Inquiry on Health Equity in the North of England and key author for the Inquiry's report, *Due North* (2014). He has over 15 years' experience working as a senior manager in the National Health Service developing public health services. He studied anthropology as an undergraduate at University College London, trained and worked as a nurse, and undertook postgraduate studies in public health and epidemiology at the London School of Hygiene and Tropical Medicine. Ben held a National Institute for Health Research Doctoral Fellowship and was awarded a PhD from the University of Liverpool.

Allard E. Dembe, Sc.D., is a Professor at Ohio State University, College of Public Health. Dr. Dembe formerly held faculty positions at the University of Massachusetts Medical School, Harvard University, McGill University, and Northeastern University. He also served as Deputy Director of the Robert Wood Johnson Foundation's Workers' Compensation Health Initiative. Dr. Dembe's professional and scholarly interests include health policy, health-services research, workers' compensation, chronic disease, translational science, and work disability. He is the author of numerous articles and monographs, including *Occupation and Disease: How Social Factors Affect the Conception of Work-Related Disorders*, published by Yale University Press.

Grant Duncan, PhD, teaches political theory and New Zealand politics at Massey University's Albany campus in Auckland, where he is an

Associate Professor. He completed his PhD at the University of Auckland in 1989 and then worked for New Zealand's Accident Compensation Corporation (ACC) in injury prevention, before his appointment to Massey University in 1993. He has researched and published on the ACC scheme as well as social policy and public policy, and he frequently comments on political events in the media. His book, *Society and Politics: New Zealand Social Policy* (Auckland: Pearson), was first published in 2004. He has also published on topics in political theory and has a forthcoming book on political trust.

Kerstin Ekberg, PhD, is a certified psychologist and a Professor in Work and Rehabilitation at Linköping University, Sweden, where she was research leader of the National Centre for Work and Rehabilitation. She is a senior research leader at the multidisciplinary Helix Vinn Excellence Centre and was head of the Centre for Public Health at the County Council of Östergötland. She was appointed Professor of Excellence by the Vice Chancellor at Linköping University. The research group at the National Centre for Work and Rehabilitation (RAR) carries out research and development, education, and dissemination of information on health, work ability, and return to work. Dr. Ekberg has been principal investigator of a number of studies focusing on organizational and work-environment conditions for preventing work disability and promoting return to work. Research within RAR is multidisciplinary, in that it uses various theoretical starting points and research methods.

Jean-Baptiste Fassier, MD, PhD, is a medical doctor with qualifications in general medicine, pain medicine, and occupational medicine. Since completing his PhD in clinical sciences (community health) at the Université de Sherbrooke, he has been involved in work disability intervention research with a special interest in knowledge transfer. He has developed and tested an innovative model for assessing the feasibility of an intervention within new contexts of adoption, so as to facilitate its uptake and implementation. As an occupational physician, Dr. Fassier is in charge of medical follow-up, prevention of occupational hazards, and work disability prevention among healthcare workers at the Hospices Civils de Lyon, a consortium of public university hospitals. He is an associate researcher at the Université de Lyon and an Associate Professor at the Université de Sherbrooke.

Thomas Geisen, MA, PhD, is Professor for Workplace Integration and Disability Management at the University of Applied Sciences Northwestern Switzerland, School of Social Work in Olten, Switzerland. His fields of interest are work and migration. Recent research includes Aging Workforce and Low-Skilled Work (2015–2017) and Demographic Change and Private Sector Disability Management in Australia, Canada, China and Switzerland: A Comparative Study

(2013–2015). Recent publications include "Workplace Integration Through Disability Management" (2015, in Escorpizo, Reuben, et al. (Eds.), *Handbook of Vocational Rehabilitation and Disability Evaluation: Application and Implementation of the ICF* (pp. 55–72). Cham: Springer International); and *Disability Management and Workplace Integration* (2011, edited with Henry Harder).

Genevieve Grant, BA, LLB (Hons), PhD, is a Senior Lecturer in the Faculty of Law at Monash University in Melbourne, Australia, where she is Co-Director of the Australian Centre for Justice Innovation. Genevieve's experience includes practice as a personal injury lawyer, doctoral studies in law and public health, and completion of the Canadian Institutes of Health Research Work Disability Prevention training program. Her teaching and research interests include work disability, injury compensation systems, justice innovation, litigation and dispute resolution, and legal ethics.

Katherine Lippel, LLL, LLM, FRSC, is a Full Professor of law at the Faculty of Law (Civil Law Section) at the University of Ottawa and holds the Canada Research Chair in Occupational Health and Safety Law. She is also a member of the CINBIOSE research centre. She specializes in legal issues relating to occupational health and safety, workers' compensation, and return to work after work injury. She was a mentor in the CIHR-funded Work Disability Prevention Strategic Training Programme, led by Dr. Patrick Loisel between 2002 and 2015, and was responsible for training on disability insurance systems and their effects on return-to-work dynamics. She has received various awards for her research and was made a Fellow of the Royal Society of Canada in 2010. In 2017, she was awarded the Social Sciences and Humanities Research Council Gold Medal, the Council's highest award.

Patrick Loisel, MD, is an orthopedic surgeon, trained in Paris, France, who practiced at the Université de Sherbrooke Teaching Hospital in Quebec, Canada. He conducted research on work disability, demonstrating for the first time that an occupational intervention was effective for improving pain, function, and return to work while a clinical intervention alone was not. With his team, he published this new evidence as the Work Disability Paradigm. Subsequently, with a team of 25 researchers, he developed and led a Canadian Institutes of Health Research supported training program for researchers. This three-year part-time program, delivered initially from the Université de Sherbrooke and later the University of Toronto, rapidly became global, with Canadian and foreign mentors who trained 110 PhD students from more than 15 countries. Loisel is presently developing and teaching training programs for Return to Work managers.

Ellen MacEachen, PhD, is an Associate Professor and Associate Director of the School of Public Health and Health Systems at the University of Waterloo, Canada. Her research focuses on international work disability policy, precarious employment, and the future of work. In 2017, she was appointed to the Canadian Labour Market Information Experts panel. She is cofounder of the Centre for Research on Work Disability Policy, an associate editor with the *Journal of Occupational Rehabilitation*, an Advisory Board Member with the Centre for Critical Qualitative Health Research, and an invited international lecturer. She currently sits on the International Advisory Board for the Swedish HELIX Competence Centre for Sustainable Development in Organisations. Former roles include President of the Canadian Association for Research on Work and Health, and executive committee leadership of the internationally prominent CIHR Strategic Training Program in Work Disability Prevention (2003-2015).

Philippe Mairiaux, MD, PhD, is an occupational physician and ergonomist by training and until October 2016 was a full-time Professor at Liège University. During the last 10 years, he coordinated several studies and reports on return to work after long-duration sick leave. He is the Scientific Advisor to the task force coordinating the Belgian project for secondary prevention of low-back pain. He presently chairs the National College for Social Insurance Medicine, an expert body in charge of proposing standardized methods for work-incapacity assessment, and issuing recommendations for pathways to work reintegration within the various sectors of the social security system.

Kari-Pekka Martimo, MD, PhD, is a specialist in Occupational Health and Occupational Medicine. He is employed by the Finnish Institute of Occupational Health and by Elo, a pension insurance company. In addition to research related to work disability prevention, he develops collaborations between workplaces and occupational health services, especially related to work disability prevention. In addition to his doctoral dissertation in 2010, he has published scientific articles and given lectures on quality, ethics, and effectiveness of occupational health services and work disability prevention. He has also advised workplaces on issues related to occupational health and safety, disability management, and well-being at work.

Philip McHale, MFPH, is a Clinical Lecturer in Public Health and Policy at the University of Liverpool, UK and a public-health registrar in Cheshire and Merseyside, North West England. His research areas of interest include disability, with a particular focus on employment, and injuries, and he has published peer-reviewed articles about injuries, healthcare, public health, and health protection. He has also worked with the World Health Organization Collaborating Centre for Policy

Research on Social Determinants of Health on reports about health equity and working conditions. He studied medicine at the University of Liverpool and, as part of his registrar training in public health, undertook a Master's in Public Health.

Angelique de Rijk, PhD, is Full Professor in Work and Health, specializing in Reintegration into Work at the Department of Social Medicine, Maastricht University, the Netherlands. She holds a Master's and a doctorate in Work and Organizational/Health Psychology. Her research focuses on healthcare, employers, and (inter)national policy. She has contributed to over 100 publications, with over 2,000 citations. She coordinated the EU CANcer and WOrk Network study on employer perspectives (2014–2017). She is Co-Director of the Work, Health and Career Master's program at Maastricht University and faculty member for the Work Disability Prevention course at the Nordic Institute for Advanced Training in Occupational Health (NIVA).

Ida Seing, PhD, is a Senior Lecturer in Sociology at Linköping University in Sweden. Her research investigates social and labor-market policy, activation, welfare governance, and working-life issues. She has a special interest in issues related to sick leave, unemployment, and disability. Currently she is involved in a research project focusing on political and organizational governance in the Swedish Social Insurance Agency and the Public Employment Service, and its consequences for caseworkers' autonomy, professional identity, self, and subjectivity. Theoretically, she is inspired by governmentality, organizational governance, and the sociology of emotions. Seing uses qualitative methods, such as ethnography (participatory observations and shadowing) and interviews.

Desai Shan, PhD, LLB, is a postdoctoral research fellow at the Faculty of Law, University of Ottawa and associate research fellow with the Seafarers International Research Centre, Cardiff University. She is a Chinese lawyer and a sociolegal researcher. She is currently conducting a research project on occupational health and safety regulation and management on the Canadian Great Lakes and St. Lawrence River. Her research interests include occupational health and safety, workers' compensation, maritime labor, ocean governance, maritime law and policies, and Chinese law. Her studies were funded by the Social Sciences and Humanities Research Council through the On the Move Partnership, Nippon Foundation, and Chinese Scholarship Council. She has published in leading academic peer-reviewed journals, such as *Relations Industrielles/Industrial Relations*, and *Marine Policy*.

Christian Ståhl, PhD, is an Associate Professor in Work and Rehabilitation at Linköping University, Sweden. He leads a research group focusing on social insurance and work environment issues, with a specific focus on system perspectives and interorganizational dynamics. He is also a research leader in the HELIX Competence Centre, a multidisciplinary research milieu focusing on sustainable development in organizations. His studies are primarily framed by sociological theories and approaches, and have focused on stakeholder cooperation between public agencies and their relations with employers; the role of occupational healthcare services in rehabilitation; ethical issues in relation to work disability prevention; and contextual aspects in implementation of evidence-based practices.

Felix Welti, LLD, studied Law at the University of Hamburg from 1989 to 1993, where he also achieved his LLD in 1997. He worked as a legal intern in Hamburg with lawyers and at the courts from 1996 to 1998, when he passed his bar exam. From 1999 to 2005, he worked at the University of Kiel. He finished his habilitation (postdoctoral qualification) for Social and Health Law, European and Public Law in 2005. From 2007 to 2010, he worked as a Professor at the University of Applied Sciences Neubrandenburg, Department for Health, Long-Term Care and Management. Since 2010, he has been a Professor at the University of Kassel, Institute for Social Work. Felix Welti is an honorary judge at the Federal Social Court and the Constitutional Court of Schleswig-Holstein. He is Editor of www.reha-recht.de and a member of the board of the German Rehabilitation Association (DVfR).

Acknowledgments

This book could not have been assembled without the support of several people. I want to thank Dr. Margaret Oldfield for her stylistic and copy editing, graduate students Julia Goyal and Sonja Senthanar for helping with set up of the book, and post-doctoral fellow Jessica Carriere for her support with the initial author's workshop in Toronto. I would also like to acknowledge the funding for the development of this book from a Social Sciences and Humanities Research Council Partnership Research Grant.

Part 1

Work Disability Policy Context

Chapter 1

Work Disability Policy
Current Challenges and New Questions

Ellen MacEachen

After several decades of developing work disability policies (which encompass diverse but related workers' compensation, sickness and disability policy, and social security legal and regulatory frameworks), central questions remain about their design, focus, and effects. Within and across jurisdictions, work disability policies have been adjusted, formed, and reformed as policy makers strive to find the right balance of rules and inducements for agencies, employers, and workers to maximize labor-force participation. Despite this activity, a key and pressing question is why we have not been more successful at helping people to remain in the labor force. Indeed, an Organisation for Economic Co-operation and Development (OECD) report, *Sickness, Disability and Work: Breaking the Barriers*, described work disability as "one of the biggest social and labour market challenges for policy makers . . . [that] hinders economic growth as it reduces effective labour supply" (OECD, 2010, p. 9).

We have arrived at a point where it is time to reflect on the social security system changes made so far to stem work disability: their ideals, what worked, what did not, and why. Even more fruitful is to consider these issues by jurisdiction: Why did one jurisdiction take a particular route to improve work integration and another take a different route? What are relevant contexts that shaped the different pathways? Although a great deal of scientific research has been generated about work disability, interventions and policy are also confronted by the reality of implementation, budgets, and political favor. It is as important for analysts to reflect on the politics of work disability policy as it is to complete the science.

This chapter provides an overview of the field of work disability research and policy conditions and argues for the need to ask new questions about work disability policies, including why they are designed differently across jurisdictions and how well they function. It begins by describing social security challenges and shifts in understandings about health and activation that contributed to the growth of the field of work disability research and policy. Issues facing implementation of work disability policies are then examined, including aging populations and weakly coordinated work disability policies. The chapter then turns to approaches to understanding policy effectiveness and the need to consider work disability policies in their specific contexts; that is, what are the social, political, and economic conditions within individual countries that have led to their current configuration of work disability policies? The chapter concludes with overviews of the other chapters in the book.

Development of Work Disability Policy and Research

Policies, including those relating to work disability, are shaped by social contracts: social expectations and tolerance within a society that help to explain and justify its legal, political, and economic structures (Lessnoff, 1990; Paz-Fuchs, 2011). For work disability policy, social contracts shape how far citizens view the state as responsible for their employment and income security, whether employers see themselves as obliged to employ people with impairments or ill health, and how individuals understand their own responsibility for seeking and participating in employment. For instance, Americans have a different view of what is work limiting than do Europeans, and this is associated with more restrictive disability policies (Yin & Heiland, 2017).

Work disability policies emerged in advanced economies within a context of increased social security costs and emerging theories about work absence and health. Social security systems that developed after World War II to offer income security and healthcare to citizens began to shift in the 1990s, as spending on disability benefits began to be considered unsustainable (Organisation for Economic Cooperation and Development, 2010). At the same time, theory developed about the moral and health virtues of work activation and labor-force engagement (Bertram, 2013; Elbers et al., 2016; Martin, 2015). Work absence was now described as a social rather than a medical phenomenon (Waddell, Burton, & Aylward, 2008), and time away from work began to be considered psychologically harmful due to social exclusion (Shrey, 1996). These theories, together with a "cultural revolution" on how to manage back pain through activity rather than rest (Valat, 2005, p. 194; Waddell, 1998), spurred the growth of work disability prevention (MacEachen, Ferrier, Kosny, & Chambers, 2007), defined as management of health or impairments in conjunction with maintaining employment (Loisel & Côté, 2014).

The movement to integrate work-disabled people into the workforce coincided with and was buttressed by labor-market-activation strategies that emerged in the same era, such as workfare, a welfare system that required those receiving benefits to perform some work. This work-for-benefits approach emphasized a social contract of mutual obligation of citizens and the state: if citizens received state benefits then they should provide the state with something in return, that is, their labor (Martin, 2015). At the same time, successful disability-rights advocacy movements during the 1990s and 2000s prompted the creation of integration laws, including the Americans with Disabilities Act in the United States, and international conventions about the right of people with disabilities to participate fully in society (Putman, 2005). The labor-force integration goals of people with disabilities, who were fighting stigma and discrimination that prevented them from accessing employment, fit well with emerging work disability principles of social inclusion and labor-force engagement.

Broadly speaking, this activation movement shifted policy and programmatic emphasis away from income security and toward discourse on worker health, financial, and social issues. For example, income-support benefits that might passively encourage people to not work began to be depicted not only as expensive for insurers, but also unhealthy for workers (MacEachen et al., 2007). Across advanced economies, laws and policies were drafted to encourage workers and employers to implement return to work after injury or illness, and to reduce sick leave with innovations such as accommodations and modified duties for workers and financial incentives to employers. The last initiative includes financial penalties for worker absenteeism due to injury or illness (Clayton, 2012).

A new field of research on work disability prevention developed in the 1990s, concurrently with emerging labor-market-activation policies. Work disability prevention has focused on shifting injured workers from leaving work and dependence on state disability benefits to active recovery while working. It is focused on work accommodation, return to work, and social inclusion. Importantly, the term *work disability* refers primarily to employment situations; that is, being unable to stay at work or to access work.

Demographic and Policy-Coordination Challenges

Since the 1990s, many studies have investigated the health and fiscal effects of active labor-force engagement. Research has shown that unemployment is associated with ill health (Milner, LaMontagne, Aitken, Bentley, & Kavanagh, 2014; Orchard, 2015; Zhang & Bhavsar, 2013), that return to work reduces the duration of disability (Franche, Cullen et al., 2005; Viikari-Juntura, Kausto, Shiri, Kaila-Kangas, & Takala, 2012), and that return-to-work practices are cost-effective for employers (Bardos, Burak, & Ben-Shalom, 2015; Squires, Rick, Carroll, & Hillage, 2011). Yet, despite a burgeoning scientific-evidence base demonstrating that employment is healthy and that work reintegration is cost-effective for employers, work disability policy has been difficult to implement.

One challenge to work disability policy implementation may lie with the focus in research and policy on the health of workers, and the relative neglect of industrial relations. In research that focuses on workers, positive psychosocial and physical work environments are assumed; however, in reality these conditions are not always present in workplaces. For instance, when it adversely affects their business, employers may avoid implementing return-to-work policy (O'Grady, 2013; Seing, MacEachen, Ekberg, & Stahl, 2015). As well, a growing body of North American research shows that workers avoid reporting work injury because of their concerns about social stigma or employer reprisals (Kirsh, Slack, & King, 2012; Lewchuk, 2013; Lipscomb, Schoenfisch, & Cameron, 2015; Manapragada & Bruk-Lee, 2016). Poor work environments have been found to adversely affect health (Rueda et al., 2015) and return-to-work opportunities (Josephson, Heijbel, Voss, Alfredsson, & Vingård, 2008; Nyberg, 2012; St. Arnaud, Bourbonnais, Saint-Jean, & Rhéaume, 2007). Therefore, although research studies find that employment in general promotes health, it is realistic for policy designers to consider how work disability may be managed for individuals employed in less-than-ideal work environments (MacEachen, Kosny, Ferrier, & Chambers, 2010).

Aging populations and concerns about labor shortages and social security expenditures are an additional challenge in implementing work disability policy. These challenges have led to policy changes to encourage older workers to stay in the labor force; for instance, through delaying the start of old-age pensions (Börsch-Supan, 2000; Hering & Klassen, 2010; Turner, 2006). It is estimated that, by 2035, the over-65 population will double in advanced economies (Curry & Torobin, 2011; European Commission, 2015; Fields, Uppal, & LaRochelle-Côté, 2017). With a greater proportion of people aged 45 and over in the workforce, disability-benefit costs are expected to further increase (Beatty & Fothergill, 2015; Belin, Dupont, Oules, Kuipers, & Fries-Tersch, 2016; Burkhauser & Daly, 2012). Greater pressure will be placed on work disability systems to accommodate these older workers with increased healthcare needs and reduced ability to recover quickly from injury and illness (Berecki-Gisolf, Clay, Collie, & McClure, 2012; World Health Organization, 2015).

Changing workplaces pose further challenges for implementation of work disability policies. These policies expect employer accommodation of workers at a time when employers, in the face of intensely competitive global-trading conditions, have moved toward more flexible contracts with workers and fewer long-term responsibilities (Kalleberg, 2009; Stone, 2000). There has been a growth over recent decades of nonstandard businesses and precarious employment conditions, and increasing numbers of individuals are now self-employed or working on temporary contracts. The quickly growing *gig economy*, characterized by freelance work (Steinmetz, 2016) and automation (Brougham & Haar, 2017) further increases employment precariousness. In many jurisdictions, nonstandard forms of employment limit workers' access to income security and benefits coverage (Broughton et al., 2016; Fudge & Strauss, 2014).

System complexity is a further challenge for implementation of work disability policy, because this is not one single policy but rather a series of policies and initiatives that span areas of health, disability, employment, joblessness, and public health. Newer activation-oriented policies operate in conjunction with older systems developed at different times and for different reasons, and these various policies do not always coalesce to form coherent and consistent work disability policy (Belin et al., 2016; Prince, 2010; Stapleton, Tweddle, & Gibson, 2012). Indeed, lack of coordination between related work disability policies was identified as a key deterrent to effective policy implementation in a cross-jurisdictional analysis of European work disability policies (Belin et al., 2016). Particular challenges include cost shifting among programs; for instance, when tightening time limits or eligibility requirements for one program leads to shifting impaired workers to other programs, which can be the lowest-paying social assistance programs (LaDou, 2010; Mansfield et al., 2012; McInerney & Simon, 2012; Ståhl, Müssener, & Svensson, 2011; Stapleton et al., 2012).

Certainly, the social and legal environment of work disability is complex. The Work Disability Arena model, developed by Loisel et al. (2001), aptly situates work disability at the intersection of complex and interwoven personal, healthcare, workplace, and legislative systems. Each of these systems occurs within particular sociopolitical contexts (Franche, Baril et al., 2005) and involves a complex variety of stakeholders, each with their own institutional needs (MacEachen, Clarke, Franche, & Irvin, 2006; Ståhl, Svensson, Petersson, & Ekberg, 2010).

Interpreting Work Disability Policy Evidence

In trying to identify optimal work disability policies, it is tempting to compare policies and work disability outcomes across jurisdictions in order to distill core successful approaches. Indeed, systematic comparisons have yielded some interesting results, showing, for example, that (a) job characteristics and differences in eligibility criteria for long-term disability benefits are associated with differences in return-to-work rates (Anema et al., 2009) and (b) where spending on work activation policies is high, higher employment commitment and employment rates exist among people who are chronically ill or impaired (VanderWel & Halvorsen, 2015; Whitehead et al., 2008). Yet, policy-comparison studies are fraught with challenges. This is because it is difficult to compare evidence when underlying conditions that produce outcomes differ so much across jurisdictions. As noted by Campbell et al. (2007, p. 455), "context is all important." Population characteristics, how a problem is caused and sustained, existing policies and programs as well as cultural assumptions and socioeconomic conditions can affect health interventions. Indeed, studies of illness and injury in relation to employment often do not analyze the impact of the jurisdiction's social security system on its work disability policies (Lippel, Eakin, Holness, & Howse, 2016; Lippel & Lotters, 2014). As well, inconsistent use of outcome measures (e.g., in studies that equate cessation of benefits with being employed and that use differing criteria to determine return to work) undercuts the generalizability of studies that aim to compare policy efficacy across different systems (Clay, Berecki-Gisolf, & Collie, 2014; Vogel, Barker, Young, Ruseckaite, & Collie, 2011).

Essentially, principles of work activation that underlie work disability policies appear in different configurations and against different backgrounds. Existing social contracts, policy systems, beliefs, and the priorities of implementing agents, along with complex multiple layers of local and national governance, can offer more or less fertile terrain for new or revised work disability policy approaches (Cerna, 2013).

New Questions: Toward the Politics of Work Disability Policy

Policy researchers are increasingly turning toward approaches that allow for close consideration of interconnections and interdependencies, in order to understand policy change and adaption within complex systems (Pope, Robert, Bate, LeMay, & Gabbay, 2006; Stepputat & Larsen, 2015). Work disability has been discussed largely in terms of research evidence (Loisel & Anema, 2014; Schultz & Gatchel, 2016), but this approach becomes limited when researchers confront the politics of ethics, social expectations, and budgets.

A focus on both science and politics of work disability policy requires asking new questions about work disability systems. It is difficult to find coordinated collections of literature on how work disability policies have evolved within jurisdictions, why these take their current shape, and what failures as well as successes have occurred in implementation. It is also difficult to consider knowledge about a successful work disability system without knowing the climate required for it to thrive, including key social and political economic contexts driving state work disability reforms in different jurisdictions. As well, different jurisdictions face different demographic challenges. For instance, while aging populations pose an international concern for social security policy (Belin et al., 2016), other conditions, such as rising rates of mental illness (EU Joint Action on Mental Health and Wellbeing, 2016) or escalating opioid-addiction rates, can affect the focus of work disability policy in specific jurisdictions (Deyo, VonKorff, & Duhrkoop, 2015). Finally, existing social contracts need to be considered (Paz-Fuchs, 2011). What pressures and traditions are present? How far will change be tolerated by employers and citizens? Key policy decisions about when to help individuals integrate into the labor force or exit can vary. As well, there are questions about what kinds of pressure or inducements need to be applied, and to which parties.

The Chapters

The chapters in this volume reflect on the above-described political realities, which are key to understanding work disability policy change and implementation over the past 30 years. Jurisdictions in North America, Europe, and Australasia were leaders in forming work disability policies, and over recent decades they have revised and adjusted their programs. Work disability policies have now been taken up in middle-income jurisdictions, including China. This book contains analyses of work disability policy in 12 countries where these policies are well entrenched, and in China, where social security systems and activation strategies are emerging.

The chapters move beyond research evidence to include authors' insights into how and why policy changes have occurred. Positionality is an important issue in policy analysis that affects how researchers are able to access the policy environment and conduct meaningful research (Walt et al., 2008). It addresses how researchers are situated in relation to the topic at hand, their legitimacy within that field, and prior involvement in policy communities. This volume has drawn together a collection of well-positioned authors from across varying disciplines, including law, medicine and social science, who have had extensive direct interaction with key community and government stakeholders; for instance, through involvement with key committees and consultations.

The chapter authors extensively describe the context for the work disability systems within their countries. Covering the historical development of work disability policy in each jurisdiction provides readers with a view of national conditions and changes over time that led to current work disability policies. Against this background, the authors describe the design and implementation of present-day work disability policy, including incentives and inducements for different stakeholders. They also address social and demographic challenges in their jurisdictions. Finally, they provide recommendations for the future direction of work disability policy. The multidisciplinary nature of this book is reflected in the chapters. Depending on the expertise of the authors and their own academic and professional roles in work disability systems, the chapters vary in their tone and focus—from sociopolitical, to epidemiologic, to legal analyses.

Chapter 2 provides a framework for work disability policy. In this chapter, Patrick Loisel relays his first-person account of the political realities of building the Sherbrooke Model for return to work, which he and his team developed to foster labor-force reintegration of workers with complex health situations. The principles of this model, which addresses work disability in multiple domains, are evident in its adoption by successful scientific interventions (Cullen et al., 2017). It is notable that Chapters 10 and 13 in this volume, focused on France and Belgium, describe efforts to implement the Sherbrooke Model internationally.

A key difference among work disability systems is whether income and rehabilitation support are provided for injured or ill people regardless of their illness or injury's cause or their income; or rather, this support is tied to proof of work relatedness (Or et al., 2010). The remaining chapters, excluding the final synthesis chapter, are organized by cause-based or comprehensive social security system. In cause-based systems, coverage is occupational, and various groups in society are covered by different schemes. These systems often have separate workers' compensation systems, funded through employer levies. In comprehensive systems, such as those found in western Europe, the protection of social welfare regimes is universal, and the entire population is covered by one, largely tax-funded, regime (Bonoli, 1997; Lippel & Lotters, 2014).

Chapters 3 to 7 focus on cause-based systems. Chapters 3 to 5 address systems in the United States, Canada, and Australia, where social security policies exist at both national and provincial or state levels, forming a complex terrain. In Chapter 3, Allard Dembe explains how, despite many work disability policies in place in the United States that provide basic care, workers fall through the cracks in disjointed and sometimes adversarial systems. In Chapter 4, Katherine Lippel employs case studies to illustrate how disjointed work disability policies have led to uneven support provided by Canadian programs to claimants with different health situations. In Chapter 5, Genevieve Grant's analysis of the Australian work disability system focuses on complexity, reform, and reversal. She describes developments leading up to the 2016 National Disability Scheme and anticipates implementation challenges.

Chapters 6 and 7 describe cause-based systems in different contexts. In Chapter 6, the evolution of New Zealand's unique accident insurance is described by Grant Duncan, who considers the positive impacts of this reform as well as challenges of a dual system that provides different support for those who are work disabled for reasons other than accidents. In Chapter 7, work disability in China, now covered by a workers' compensation system requiring proof from workers and cooperation from employers, is described by Desai Shan. This chapter details the shift from communist-era full social security conditions to an economy with greater flexibility and accompanying new risks for population health and employment integration.

Chapters 8 to 15 focus on comprehensive systems across eight countries in Europe. Beginning with Scandinavia, in Chapter 8 Christian Ståhl and Ida Seing provide an analysis of policy changes in Sweden, as governments have worked to fine-tune labor-activation approaches with varying degrees of success. The authors draw attention to the shifting meaning of activation and to types of evidence used, and not used, by governments as they develop policy. Kari Pekka Martimo's review of Finnish work disability policy in Chapter 9 draws attention to policy integration. He describes how occupational health services in Finland are internationally unique, because they are integrated with primary healthcare services and are also a health and safety resource within workplaces. In Chapter 10, Jean Baptiste Fassier explains how in France there is no formal policy to improve employment reintegration for people who have had to leave their jobs because of illness or impairment. He identifies the need to address tensions associated with a lack of consensus among healthcare providers about medical job fitness, employer lobbying for fewer obligations, and government liberalization of legal constraints. In Chapter 11, Felix Welti describes the evolution of Bismarkian disability insurance in Germany, including reforms that have emphasized representation of disabled people at multiple levels, with workplace committees as emerging players in the political field. In Chapter 12, Switzerland's work disability policy is described by Thomas Geisen, who details policy developments that are now shifting to include not only employee needs but also ways to support workplaces in accommodating work-related health and disability issues. In Chapter 13, Philippe Mairiaux explains the development of Belgium's work disability policy in the context of a move from a passive to an active role for the state. Mairiaux interestingly situates Belgian policy changes in the context of political negotiations and personalities.

The Netherlands stands out, in Chapter 14, as a country with policies that impose strong responsibility on employers, who must pay the salaries of impaired or ill employees for two years. Angelique DeRijk describes how this policy developed incrementally, starting with identification of the "Dutch disease" and slowly integrating employers as the focus for solutions. Chapter 15 focuses on the United Kingdom, home of the well publicized Fit Note. Ben Barr and Philip McHale take a critical perspective on social security reforms geared to work ability. They remind researchers and policy makers of the complexity of implementation environments and how blunt reform measures, geared to encourage work ability, can have the perverse effect of increasing poverty.

Finally, in Chapter 16, Ellen MacEachen and Kerstin Ekberg synthesize the work disability policies described in this book. They consider policies that span both comprehensive and cause-based social security systems and reflect on activation strategies in relation to changing roles of the state, employers, healthcare providers, and workers. Their synthesis considers value assumptions embedded in work-activation policies as well as future directions for research and policy development.

Conclusion

Across jurisdictions, work disability policies increasingly focus on supporting individuals to participate in the labor force as a component of being active, engaged, and financially contributing members of society. The key issue is how to accomplish this active labor-market engagement in a way that is healthy for individuals as well as socially and economically inclusive. It is important to view work disability policy in the context of broad changes that have occurred in welfare states over recent decades, changes that have emphasized constraining public finances and labor-force activation. These fiscal and social influences come into play in different ways across different terrains, as social contracts and political conditions for work integration differ from country to country. By moving beyond scientific evidence about the health effects of work activation to the politics of how work disability systems have developed and evolved in different jurisdictions, we gain a deeper understanding of the logic and implementation of work disability policy. This book contains rich description of the development and evolution of work disability policy across 13 countries and provides a foundation for considering future developments in work disability policy.

References

Anema, J. R., Schellart, E. A., Cassidy, J. D., Loisel, P., Veerman, T. J., & van der Beek, A. J. (2009). Can cross country differences in return-to-work after chronic occupational back pain be explained? An exploratory analysis on disability policies in a six country cohort study. *Journal of Occupational Rehabilitation, 19,* 419–426.

Bardos, M., Burak, H., & Ben-Shalom, Y. (2015). *Assessing the costs and benefits of return-to-work programs.* Retrieved February 26, 2016 from www.dol.gov/odep/topics/pdf/RTW_Costs-Benefits_2015-03.pdf

Beatty, C., & Fothergill, S. (2015). Disability benefits in an age of austerity. *Social Policy & Administration, 49*(2), 161–181.

Belin, A., Dupont, C., Oulès, L., Kuipers, Y., & Fries-Tersch, E. (2016). *Rehabilitation and return to work: Analysis report on EU and Member States policies, strategies and programmes.* Retrieved February 26, 2016 from https://osha.europa.eu/en/tools-and-publications/publications/rehabilitation-and-return-work-analysis-eu-and-member-state

Berecki-Gisolf, J., Clay, F. J., Collie, A., & McClure, R. J. (2012). The impact of aging on work disability and return to work: Insights from workers' compensation claim records. *Journal of Occupational and Environmental Medicine, 54,* 318–327.

Bertram, E. (2013). Doors, floors, ladders, and nets: Social provision in the new American labor market. *Politics & Society, 41*(1), 29–72.

Bonoli, G. (1997). Classifying welfare states: A two-dimension approach. *Journal of Social Policy, 26*(3), 351–372.

Börsch-Supan, A. (2000). Incentive effects of social security on labor force participation: Evidence in Germany and across Europe. *Journal of Public Economics, 78*(1-2), 25–49.

Brougham, D., & Haar, J. (2017). Smart Technology, Artificial Intelligence, Robotics, and Algorithms (STARA): Employees' perceptions of our future workplace. *Journal of Management & Organization, 19.* doi:10.1017/jmo.2016.55

Broughton, A., Green, M., Rickard, C., Swift, S., Eichhorst, W., Tobsch, V., . . . Tros, F. (2016). *Precarious employment in Europe: Part 1, patterns, trends and policy strategy.* Retrieved February 26, 2016 from www.europarl.europa.eu/RegData/etudes/STUD/2016/587285/IPOL_STU(2016)587285_EN.pdf

Burkhauser, R. V., & Daly, M. C. (2012). Social security disability insurance: Time for fundamental change. *Journal of Policy Analysis and Management, 31*(2), 454–461.

Campbell, N. C., Murray, E., Darbyshire, J., Emery, J., Farmer, A., Griffiths, F., Guthrie, B., Lester, H., Wilson, P., & Kinmonth, A. L. (2007). Designing and evaluating complex interventions to improve health care. *BMJ, 334*(7591), 455–459.

Cerna, L. (2013). *The nature of policy change and implementation: A review of different theoretical approaches*. Paris: Organisation for Economic Co-operation and Development. Retrieved February 26, 2016 from www.oecd.org/edu/ceri/The%20Nature%20of%20Policy%20Change%20and%20Implementation.pdf

Clay, F. J., Berecki-Gisolf, J., & Collie, A. (2014). How well do we report on compensation systems in studies of return to work: A systematic review. *Journal of Occupational Rehabilitation, 24*(1), 111–124.

Clayton, A. (2012). Economic incentives in the prevention and compensation of work injury and illness. *Policy and Practice in Health and Safety, 10*(1), 27–43.

Cullen, K. L., Irvin, E., Collie, A., Clay, F., Gensby, U., Jennings, P. A., . . . Amick, B. C. (2017). Effectiveness of workplace interventions in return-to-work for musculoskeletal, pain-related and mental health conditions: An update of the evidence and messages for practitioners. *Journal of Occupational Rehabilitation, 28*(1), 1–15.

Curry, B., & Torobin, J. (2011, August 17). Canada's shrinking, aging work force poses economic problems: Statscan. *The Globe and Mail*. Retrieved February 26, 2018 from www.theglobeandmail.com/report-on-business/economy/jobs/canadas-shrinking-aging-work-force-poses-economic-problems-statscan/article590840/

Deyo, R. A., VonKorff, M., & Duhrkoop, D. (2015). Opioids for low back pain. *British Medical Journal, 350*, g6380.

Elbers, N. A., Collie, A., Hogg-Johnson, S., Lippel, K., Lockwood, K., & Cameron, I. D. (2016). Differences in perceived fairness and health outcomes in two injury compensation systems: A comparative study. *BMC Public Health, 16*. doi:10.1186/s12889-016-3331-3

EU Joint Action on Mental Health and Wellbeing. (2016, January 21). *European framework for action on mental health and wellbeing*. Paper presented at the EU Joint Action on Mental Health and Wellbeing Final Conference, Brussels.

European Commission. (2015). *The 2015 ageing report: Economic and budgetary projections for the 28 EU member states (2013–2060)*. Retrieved February 26, 2018 from http://ec.europa.eu/economy_finance/publications/european_economy/2015/pdf/ee3_en.pdf

Fields, A., Uppal, S., & LaRochelle-Côté, S. (2017). *The impact of aging on labour market participation rates* (Catalogue No. 75-006-X). Ottawa, Canada: Statistics Canada. Retrieved from www.statcan.gc.ca/pub/75-006-x/2017001/article/14826-eng.htm

Franche, R.-L., Baril, R., Shaw, W. S., Nicholas, M., & Loisel, P. (2005). Workplace-based return-to-work interventions: Optimising the role of stakeholders in implementation and research. *Journal of Occupational Rehabilitation, 15*(4), 525–542.

Franche, R.-L., Cullen, K., Clarke, J., Irvin, E., Sinclair, S., Frank, J., & the Institute for Work & Health (IWH) Workplace-Based RTW Intervention Literature Review Research Team. (2005). Workplace-based return-to-work interventions: A systematic review of the quantitative literature. *Journal of Occupational Rehabilitation, 15*(4), 607–631.

Fudge, J., & Strauss, K. (Eds.). (2014). *Temporary work, agencies and unfree labour: Insecurity in the new world of work*. New York, NY: Routledge.

Hering, M., & Klassen, T. R. (2010). *Is 70 the new 65? Raising the eligibility age in the Canada Pension Plan*. Toronto, Canada: Mowat Centre for Policy Innovation. Retrieved February 26, 2018 from https://mowatcentre.ca/wp-content/uploads/publications/13_is_70_the_new_65.pdf

Josephson, M., Heijbel, B., Voss, M., Alfredsson, L., & Vingård, E. (2008). Influence of self-reported work conditions and health on full, partial and no return to work after long-term sickness absence. *Scandinavian Journal of Work, Environment and Health, 34*(6), 430–437.

Kalleberg, A. L. (2009). Precarious work, insecure workers: Employment relations in transition. *American Sociological Review, 74*(1), 1–22. doi:10.1177/000312240907400101

Kirsh, B., Slack, T., & King, C. A. (2012). The nature and impact of stigma towards injured workers. *Journal of Occupational Rehabilitation, 22*, 143–154. doi:10.1007/s10926-011-9335-z

LaDou, J. (2010). Workers' compensation in the United States: Cost shifting and inequities in a dysfunctional system. *New Solutions, 20*(3), 291–302.

Lessnoff, M. H. (Ed.). (1990). *Social contract theory*. Oxford, UK: Basil Blackwell.

Lewchuk, W. (2013). The limits of voice: Are workers afraid to express their health and safety rights? *Osgoode Hall Law Journal, 50*, 789–812.

Lippel, K., Eakin, J. M., Holness, D. L., & Howse, D. (2016). The structure and process of workers' compensation systems and the role of doctors: A comparison of Ontario and Quebec. *American Journal of Industrial Medicine, 59*(12), 1070–1086. doi:10.1002/ajim.22651

Lippel, K., & Lotters, F. (2014). Public insurance systems: A comparison of cause-based and disability-based income support systems. In P. Loisel & H. Anema (Eds.) M. Feuerstein, E. MacEachen, G. Pransky, & K. Costa-Black (Co-Eds.), *Handbook of work disability: Prevention and management* [paperback] (pp. 183–202). New York, NY: Springer Science+Business Media.

Lipscomb, H. J., Schoenfisch, A. L., & Cameron, W. (2015). Non-reporting of work injuries and aspects of jobsite safety climate and behavioral-based safety elements among carpenters in Washington state. *American Journal of Industrial Medicine, 58*(4), 411–421.

Loisel, P. & Anema, H. (Eds.) Feuerstein, M., MacEachen, E., Pransky, G., & Costa-Black, K. (Co-Eds.). (2014). *Handbook of work disability: Prevention and management* [paperback]. New York, NY: Springer Science+Business Media.

Loisel, P., & Côté, P. (2014). The work disability paradigm and its public health implications. In P. Loisel & H. Anema, M. (Eds.) M. Feuerstein, E. MacEachen, G. Pransky, & K. Costa-Black (Co-Eds.), *Handbook of work disability: Prevention and management* [paperback] (pp. 59–67). New York, NY: Springer Science+Business Media.

Loisel, P., Durand, M.-J., Betrthelette, D., Vezina, N., Baril, R., Gagnon, D., . . . Tremblay, C. (2001). Disability prevention: New paradigm for the management of occupational back pain. *Disability Management Health Outcomes, 9*(7), 351–360.

MacEachen, E., Clarke, J., Franche, R.-L., & Irvin, E. (2006). Systematic review of the qualitative literature on return to work after injury. *Scandinavian Journal of Work Environment and Health, 32*(4), 257–269.

MacEachen, E., Ferrier, S., Kosny, A., & Chambers, L. (2007). A deliberation on "hurt versus harm" logic in early return to work policy. *Policy and Practice in Health and Safety, 5*(2), 41–62.

MacEachen, E., Kosny, A., Ferrier, S., & Chambers, L. (2010). The "toxic dose" of system problems: Why some injured workers don't return to work as expected. *Journal of Occupational Rehabilitation, 20*(3), 349–366.

Manapragada, A., & Bruk-Lee, V. (2016). Staying silent about safety issues: Conceptualizing and measuring safety silence motives. *Accident Analysis and Prevention*, *91*, 144–156. doi:10.1016/j.aap.2016.02.014

Mansfield, L., MacEachen, E., Tompa, E., Kalcevich, C., Endicott, M., & Yeung, N. (2012). A critical review of literature on experience rating in workers' compensation systems. *Policy and Practice in Health and Safety*, *10*(1), 3–25.

Martin, J. P. (2015). Activation and active labour market policies in OECD countries: Stylised facts and evidence on their effectiveness. *IZA Journal of Labor Policy*, *4*(4), 1–29.

McInerney, M., & Simon, K. (2012). The effect of state workers' compensation program changes on the use of federal social security disability insurance. *Industrial Relations: A Journal of Economy and Society*, *51*(1), 571–588.

Milner, A., LaMontagne, A. D., Aitken, Z., Bentley, R., & Kavanagh, A. M. (2014). Employment status and mental health among persons with and without a disability: Evidence from an Australian cohort study. *Journal of Epidemiology & Community Health*, *68*(11), 1064–1071.

Nyberg, D. (2012). "You need to be healthy to be ill": Constructing sickness and framing the body in Swedish healthcare. *Organization Studies*, *33*(12), 1671–1692.

O'Grady, J. (2013). *Workplace injury claim suppression: Final report*. Prepared for Workplace Safety and Insurance Board. Toronto, Canada: Prism Economics and Analysis. Retrieved February 26, 2018 from www.wsib.on.ca/cs/groups/public/documents/staticfile/c2li/mdex/~edisp/wsib011817.pdf

Or, Z., Cases, C., Lisac, M., Vrangbæk, K., Winblad, U., & Bevan, G. (2010). Are health problems systemic? Politics of access and choice under Beveridge and Bismarck systems. *Health Economics, Policy and Law*, *5*(3), 269–293.

Orchard, C. (2015). *Adult health in Great Britain, 2013*. London, UK: Office for National Statistics. Retrieved February 26, 2018 from www.ons.gov.uk/peoplepopulationandcommunity/healthandsocialcare/healthandlifeexpectancies/compendium/opinionsandlifestylesurvey/2015-03-19/adulthealthingreatbritain2013

Organisation for Economic Co-operation and Development. (2010). *Sickness, disability and work: Breaking the barriers. A synthesis of findings across OECD countries*. Paris, France: OECD.

Paz-Fuchs, A. (2011). *The social contract revisited: The modern welfare state*. Oxford, UK: The Foundation for Law, Justice and Society. Retrieved February 26, 2018 from www.fljs.org/files/publications/Paz-Fuchs-SummaryReport.pdf

Pope, C., Robert, G., Bate, P., Le May, A., & Gabbay, J. (2006). Lost in translation: A multi-level case study of the metamorphosis of meanings and action in public sector organizational innovation. *Public Administration*, *84*(1), 59–79.

Prince, M. J. (2010). Canadian disability policy: Still a hit-and-miss affair. In R. B. Blake & J. A. Keshen (Eds.), *Social fabric or patchwork quilt: The development of social policy in Canada* (pp. 435–454). Toronto, Canada: University of Toronto Press.

Putman, M. (2005). Developing a framework for political disability identity. *Journal of Disability Policy Studies*, *16*(3), 188–198.

Rueda, S., Smith, P., Bekele, T., O'Brien, K., Husbands, W., Li, A., . . . ECHO Study Team. (2015). Is any job better than no job? Labor market experiences and depressive symptoms in people living with HIV. *Aids Care*, 1–9. doi:10.1080/09540121.2015.1015479

Schultz, I. Z., & Gatchel, R. J. (Eds.). (2016). *Handbook of return to work: From research to practice*. New York, NY: Springer.

Seing, E., MacEachen, E., Ekberg, K., & Stahl, C. (2015). Return to work or job transition? Employer dilemmas in taking social responsibility for return to work in local workplace practice. *Disability and Rehabilitation, 37*(19), 1760–1769. doi: 10.3109/09638288.2014.978509

Shrey, D. E. (1996). Disability management in industry: The new paradigm in worker rehabilitation. *Disability and Rehabilitation, 18*(8), 408–414.

Squires, H., Rick, J., Carroll, C., & Hillage, J. (2011). Cost-effectiveness of interventions to return employees to work following long-term sickness absence due to musculoskeletal disorders. *Journal of Public Health, 34*(1).

St. Arnaud, L., Bourbonnais, R., Saint-Jean, M., & Rhéaume, J. (2007). Determinants of return-to-work among employees absent due to mental health problems. *Industrial Relations, 62*(4), 670–713.

Ståhl, C., Müssener, U., & Svensson, T. (2011). Implementation of standardized time limits in sickness insurance and return-to-work: Experiences of four actors. *Disability & Rehabilitation, 34*(16), 1404–1411.

Ståhl, C., Svensson, T., Petersson, G., & Ekberg, K. (2010). A matter of trust? A study of coordination of Swedish stakeholders in return-to-work. *Journal of Occupational Rehabilitation, 20*(3), 299–310.

Stapleton, J., Tweddle, A., & Gibson, K. (2012). *The "welfareization" of disability income programs in Canada. Where, how, and why?* Toronto, Canada: Metcalf Foundation. Retrieved February 26, 2018 from https://metcalffoundation.com/wp-content/uploads/2013/12/Welfareization-of-Disability-Incomes-in-Ontario.pdf

Steinmetz, K. (2016, January 6). Exclusive: See how big the gig economy really is. *Time*.

Stepputat, F., & Larsen, J. (2015). *Global political ethnography: A methodological approach to studying global policy regimes* (Working Paper 2015:01). Copenhagen, Denmark: Danish Institute for International Studies. Retrieved February 26, 2018 from www.diis.dk/files/media/publications/publikationer_2015/wp2015-01.pdf

Stone, K. V. W. (2000). The new psychological contract: Implications of the changing workplace for labor and employment law. *UCLA Law Review, 49*, 519.

Turner, A. (2006). Pension challenges in an aging world. *Finance and Development, 43*(3). Retrieved February 26, 2018 from www.imf.org/external/pubs/ft/fandd/2006/09/turner.htm

Valat, J. P. (2005). Factors involved in progression to chronicity of mechanical low back pain. *Joint Bone Spine, 72*(3), 193–195.

Van der Wel, K., & Halvorsen, K. (2015). The bigger the worse? A comparative study of welfare state and employment commitment. *Work Employment and Society, 29*(1), 99–118.

Viikari-Juntura, E., Kausto, J., Shiri, R., Kaila-Kangas, L., & Takala, E. (2012). Return to work after early part-time sick leave due to musculoskeletal disorders: A randomized controlled trial. *Scandinavian Journal of Work, Environment & Health, 38*(2), 134–143.

Vogel, A. P., Barker, S. J., Young, A. E., Ruseckaite, R., & Collie, A. (2011). What is return to work? An investigation into the quantification of return to work. *International Archives of Occupational and Environmental Health, 84*(6), 675–682.

Waddell, G. (1998). *The back pain revolution.* Toronto, Canada: Churchill Livingstone.

Waddell, G., Burton, A. K., & Aylward, M. (2008, May/June). A biopsychosocial model of sickness and disability. *The Guides Newsletter.*

Walt, G., Shiffman, J., Schneider, H., Murray, S. F., Brugha, R., & Gilson, L. (2008). "Doing" health policy analysis: Methodological and conceptual reflections and challenges. *Health Policy and Planning, 23*(5), 308–317.

Whitehead, M., Clayton, S., Holland, P., Drever, F., Barr, B., Gosling, R., . . . Chen, W. H. (2008). *Helping chronically ill or disabled people into work: What can we learn from international comparative analyses?* Liverpool, UK: Public Health Research Consortium. Retrieved February 26, 2018 from http://phrc.lshtm.ac.uk/papers/PHRC_C2-06_Short_Report.pdf

World Health Organization. (2015). *World report on ageing and health.* Geneva: World Health Organization. Retrieved February 26, 2018 from http://apps.who.int/iris/bitstream/10665/186463/1/9789240694811_eng.pdf

Yin, N., & Heiland, F. (2017). Disability policies and public views on work disability: A comparative analysis using anchoring vignette data. *International Journal of Population Studies, 3*(1), 42–63.

Zhang, S., & Bhavsar, V. (2013). Unemployment as a risk factor for mental illness: Combining social and psychiatric literature. *Advances in Applied Sociology, 3*(2), 131–136.

Chapter 2

Reflections on the Sherbrooke Model and the Way Forward for Work Disability Prevention

Patrick Loisel

In the 1980s, when I was practicing spine surgery, work disability resulting from low back pain (LBP) was considered a symptom of a specific medical disorder that had to correspond to a specific diagnosis. Without a precise diagnosis, malingering was suspected and the back-pain complaint was considered a forensic issue (Leavitt & Sweet, 1986). There was little doubt, until that decade, that bed rest was the best initial treatment and medical or surgical advances would hopefully solve the problem. However, during the 1980s across various countries, opinions about the management of LBP were changing. Gordon Waddell, an orthopedic surgeon from the United Kingdom who had developed a clinical method to detect patients simulating back pain in order to receive unwarranted benefits (Waddell, McCulloch, Kummel, & Venner, 1980), later advocated the need to apply Engel's Biopsychosocial Model (Engel, 1977) to LBP sufferers (Waddell, 1987). In the same decade, Alf Nachemson, an orthopedic surgeon from Sweden, after becoming known for trying to explain LBP by measuring intervertebral-disc pressure in different body postures (Nachemson, 1965), published a paper advocating not removing opportunities to work from workers with LBP (Nachemson, 1983). In Canada, the Research Institute of the Quebec Workers' Compensation Board (the IRSST[1]) commissioned a task force on the burden of LBP, chaired by Walter Spitzer. The main recommendations from this task force were:

- The ultimate goal of treatment of work-related spinal disorders should be returning the worker to his/her usual occupation or rehabilitation to appropriate work activity, with minimum delay.
- The attending physician should reassure the patient regarding the small risk of his/her condition when such is the case; encourage him/her to return to work with minimum delay; and monitor and participate in all stages of the management of the worker's spinal disorder and communicate with all management partners.
- If return to usual work activity on a full-time basis is not possible, return to light work or part time work during rehabilitation is recommended.

(Spitzer, LeBlanc, & Dupuis, 1987, pp. S37-S38)

These recommendations look like normal practice today but were revolutionary at the time. Deyo, Diehl, and Rosenthal (1986) published a randomized trial in the *New England Journal of Medicine* that compared two days and seven days of bed rest for acute LBP, and found two days were better.

As an orthopedic and spine surgeon, I was dissatisfied with the functional outcomes of many of my patients who had had lumbar spine surgery. It was clear that even excellent anatomical and imaging results of back-pain surgery might not lead to acceptable outcomes, including a return to functional life and work. How could I break this deadlock? Should I follow the treatment recommended during my training and written in then-current orthopedics textbooks, or should I adopt a new way of treating my patients that was not yet conceived? I suspected what not to do but had to decide what to do. Resolving this conundrum was the rationale for developing the Sherbrooke Model.

The Sherbrooke Model

I was fortunate that the stars aligned for innovation at the time, due to local circumstances. I was practicing at the University of Sherbrooke Teaching Hospital (CHUS)[2] in Quebec, Canada. This hospital had an above-average number of staff absent from work due to LBP, causing disruptions in personnel management and high compensation costs for the Quebec Workers' Compensation Board (the CSST[3]) at the time. My first star was the CSST asking the hospital's management to resolve this costly problem of work absenteeism. The hospital's management asked its occupational physician to address the problem, and he approached me due to my knowledge of back-pain issues and my previously expressed interest in developing a multidisciplinary team to address complex back-pain cases. Interestingly, this occupational physician had read the Spitzer task-force report and was developing a method of early, progressive return to work for the hospital's workers with back pain. Our discussions led to the underpinnings of a return-to-work program that included active participation of the workplace actors, including the worker. My second star came from the IRSST, who wanted to test the Spitzer task force's recommendations with an experimental approach. Applying these recommendations required a team that would be prepared to interact differently with stakeholders (employers, insurers, unions, and healthcare providers) while helping to vocationally rehabilitate workers with work-related LBP. The IRSST's international panel selected our team to take up this challenge. My third star was the support of the hospital's leaders, who were pleased to support a research project that responded to their mission as a teaching hospital and could also help to solve their worker-absenteeism problem. They decided to help the project by having their chief physiotherapist serve as the project's coordinator.

While some stars aligned to create this project, our team also made substantial efforts to "bring all the players onside," as was later advocated by Frank et al. (1998). Proposing joint arrangements between employers, insurers, unions, and healthcare providers remains a challenge even today but, at the time, it was close to unthinkable. I set out on a mission to develop our innovative scientific intervention and met these stakeholders separately to present our project, which we named the Sherbrooke Model (Loisel et al., 1996). Interestingly, employers were the easiest to persuade, perhaps because, in the small city of Sherbrooke, we were perceived as credible by being part of the University of Sherbrooke Teaching Hospital. Also, they were promised that all intervention costs would be absorbed by the research project. Unions were suspicious and more difficult to convince. They discussed every detail of the project including evaluation tools and team members. I directly experienced an ethical issue: The unions required that one important team member be excluded from the project. To support its success, this team member withdrew from the study but was still listed as a co-author in the final report and resulting article. General practitioners in the city area were informed of the research, and we did not face serious opposition to it among this group. The Quebec Workers' Compensation Board was concerned about possible additional costs associated with the intervention's work-rehabilitation and workplace activities, but the IRSST agreed to bear these costs as part of a research grant. Interestingly, at this time the CSST did not get involved in return to work until a year had passed since the work-related accident, and, following our research protocol and project philosophy, we promised to end our activity before this one-year period. This promise allowed us to create our own return-to-work approach, thus avoiding conflict with CSST about work-return-intervention decisions. Finally, for methodological reasons, I led the intervention team, but the project's co-principal investigator and methodologist, Lucien Abenhaim from McGill University, separately led the intervention-evaluation team. Following our research protocol, information about data collection and analysis was not shared with the intervention team until project completion (Loisel et al., 1997).

The evaluation showed that the Sherbrooke Model was successful. Compared with the usual-care intervention group (to whom care was prescribed by workers' attending physicians without any intervention from the Sherbrooke Model team), workers in the Sherbrooke-Model group returned to their regular duties with possible modifications accepted by the workers and their employers approximately two and a half times faster than workers in the usual-care intervention group. Also, one year after study entry, compared with the usual-care group, the mean of the Sherbrooke-Model group's Oswestry scores (measuring functional capacity) significantly improved ($p = 0.02$). The improvements in the means of their Sickness Impact Profile (SIP) and McGill-Melzack (MGM) pain scores were also statistically significant (for SIP $p = 0.052$, for MGM $p = 0.061$) (Loisel et al., 1997). The Sherbrooke Model, compared with the usual-care intervention, also financially benefited the CSST. After a six-year follow up, the

Sherbrooke Model saved CAN$18,585 [US$14,980] per patient (1991 value) (Loisel et al., 2002).

The Immediate Impact of the Sherbrooke Model

When we published our evaluation results, the Sherbrooke Model set the cat among the pigeons. I was surprised that the workplace intervention was so effective in improving return-to-work outcomes, when the clinical intervention was not. Combining the two, however, was the most effective. Even more surprised, and more doubtful, were the research community and most stakeholders. Interestingly, the unions, who had been the most doubtful about the Sherbrooke Model before it was tested, were the most enthusiastic about the results. They actively advocated for a general implementation of the Sherbrooke Model principles, even trying to persuade the Quebec government to impose legal changes, albeit with little success. Other stakeholders, including the CSST, were also difficult to convince. In fact, I think our success in implementing the Sherbrooke Model was in good part due to the control we had over return-to-work processes, which bypassed existing, outdated stakeholder practices, through our randomized-control-trial (RCT) research design. Our RCT applied very innovative return-to-work methods. As well, not only did we control the interventions, we also applied new early-intervention policies, as the Quebec-government agency responsible for work-related disorders declined to participate due to its own, delayed policies based on continuing conventional clinical treatments or undertaking legal actions.

Fortunately, researchers elsewhere were interested in replicating and testing the Sherbrooke-Model principles in other settings. The first one was Johannes Anema (Anema et al., 2007) from Vrije University in the Netherlands, who adapted the model to the Dutch context and obtained similar results on the outcomes of return to work and quality of life. He obtained even better results in return to work, quality of life, and savings in another Dutch RCT applied to a chronic-back-pain population (Lambeek, van Mechelen, Knol, Loisel, & Anema, 2010; Lambeek et al., 2011). These three studies, in two different social security systems, confirmed that medicine alone was insufficient to help work-related-back-pain sufferers get better and return to work, and that workplace and other social actors had to help this process. However, we lacked a comprehensive conceptual framework to explain this important shift in work disability management. Michael Feuerstein, a forerunner in the emerging work disability field, had published an innovative work disability framework in the opening paper of the first issue of the *Journal of Occupational Rehabilitation*, which he launched in 1991 (Feuerstein, 1991). That same year, while I was starting the Sherbrooke Model intervention, I had no knowledge of Feuerstein's framework, which I discovered later. In a similar theoretical venture, my research team and I described a new framework that emerged from the Sherbrooke intervention-study results. In the framework we used our basic assumptions, ways of thinking, and methodology to explain and manage work disability. We published our conceptual framework (Loisel et al., 2001) and later refined it (Loisel et al., 2005). Our framework has been applied globally by other researchers to causes of work disability besides back pain, such as other musculoskeletal disorders, cancer, and mental health conditions (Feuerstein, 1991; Loisel, 2009; Pomaki, Franche, Murray, Khushrushahi, & Lampinen, 2012).

Many researchers have since applied the Sherbrooke Model in return-to-work studies, mainly focusing on the link with the workplace and collaboration among stakeholders. A systematic review of workplace interventions in return to work for musculoskeletal, pain-related, and mental health conditions was recently published (Cullen et al., 2017). They found 36 good and high-quality studies published between 1990 and 2015 that applied the Sherbrooke Model to interventions in three domains: health, service coordination, and workplace modification. They found:

- strong evidence that time away from work for musculoskeletal disorders, pain-related conditions, and mental health conditions was significantly reduced by interventions encompassing at least two of the three domains; and
- moderate evidence that these multidomain interventions reduced costs.

Conversely, they found:

- strong evidence that cognitive behavioral therapy interventions that do not also include workplace modifications or service coordination are not effective in helping workers with mental health conditions return to work.

They concluded by recommending the "implementing [of] a multi-domain intervention (i.e. with health-focused, service coordination, and work modification components) to help reduce lost time from MSK [musculosketal], pain-related and MH [mental health] conditions" (Cullen et al., 2017, p. 12). This is exactly in line with what we learned from testing the Sherbrooke Model.

Policy, the Missing Link Between Science and Implementation

In an ideal world, practitioners should acquire new knowledge when it is confirmed by sufficient new evidence and apply appropriate interventions in the field. However, it is not always that simple. Take the example of a new medication with improved outcomes for some disorder. Prescribing a medicine is easy, but access to it depends on local availability and cost, which in turn depends on coverage under drug plans. The problem of availability due to policy, or the lack thereof, is not new if we look at the history of scurvy treatment (Milne & Chalmers, 2004). In the 18th century scurvy, rather than storms or wars, was killing half the sailors aboard oceangoing ships; these sailors were eating only preserved food. In 1747, James Lind, a Royal Navy surgeon, conceived and conducted the first recorded clinical trial involving supposed remedies for scurvy, and observed that sailors who had eaten citrus fruits were still alive and in good health after several months at sea. He published these results in a book, the *Treatise of the Scurvy* (Lind, 1753). The book was very successful and was republished in English (1757 and 1772) and translated into French (1756 and 1783), Italian (1766), and German (1775). However, it was only in 1794 that the English Admiralty finally ordered commanders to routinely issue citrus juice to Royal Navy sailors. This new policy had a dramatic effect, as scurvy disappeared from the whole fleet in two years. The history of scurvy tells us that "knowledge implementation" needs not only scientific knowledge but also implementation science to bring new knowledge to "knowledge consumers." As well, a third partner is needed: policy makers. The combination of science and policy is what this book is all about.

Returning to work disability, thinking that work-disability-prevention science and implementation efforts by scientists or knowledge brokers will allow general implementation of the new knowledge to prevent work disability is idealistic. If this were true, new-knowledge implementation would have lowered work disability rates and their financial burden. Unfortunately, it has not. The Association of Workers' Compensation Boards of Canada (2005) reported that the average benefit cost per lost-time claim was CAN$10,608 [US$8,706] in 2000, CAN$22,044 [US$18,091] in 2010, and CAN$26,262 [US$21,553] in 2015. As we discussed in Loisel et al. (2005), applying evidence in work disability prevention remains a challenge (Feuerstein, 1991). It depends on the institutional system, ambiguity, and conflict among actors; bounded rationality; and power relations among various stakeholders (Ståhl, Costa-Black, & Loisel, 2017). I think the main challenge of "get[ing] all the players onside," as Frank et al. (1998) perceived years ago, largely remains key to the solution. The systematic recent review by Cullen et al. (2017) confirms the key issues of service coordination, work modification, and health focus. Due to the multiple stakeholders involved—each with their differing interests, perceptions, knowledge and backgrounds—consensus on the appropriate strategies for each work disability situation is unlikely. This leads to the missing link: policy. Not only do interventions have to be evidence-based, but policies also should adapt to evidence so they can guide and unite stakeholders' actions and allow appropriate coordination between all players in the complex work disability-prevention arena (Feuerstein, 1991). Policy making is difficult, because policies, like medications, may have unexpected side effects.

Due to the very positive results of the Sherbrooke Model, the CSST decided to conduct an implementation trial in four rehabilitation centers in Quebec. To undertake this project, we formed the Quebec Work Rehabilitation Network (RRTQ)[4] and linked four rehabilitation centers in four cities: Montreal, Longueuil, Quebec City, and Rouyn-Noranda (Loisel et al., 2003). The RRTQ's work-rehabilitation teams in the four centers were functioning well under the same manager. However, after a good start, CSST staff became reluctant to refer clients to the RRTQ, as referral was not mandated by policy (Canadian Institutes of Health Research, 2011). This led the CSST to prematurely end the RRTQ project. Introducing new return-to-work practices did not bridge the gap between scientific evidence and quality implementation, even though we worked with the organization in charge of developing return-to-work practices.

Another reason for the failure to implement the Sherbrooke Model in Quebec may be the side effect of experience-rating policy developed and applied to employers by many workers' compensation boards, including Quebec's. This policy aims to incite employers to develop positive health and safety practices in order to avoid financial penalties linked to work disability absence among employees. However, this policy may instead incite employers to alter hiring practices or avoid reporting work accidents (MacEachen et al., 2012).

Science and policy worlds, due to their different objectives and methodologies, adhere to very different paradigms. Choi described the goal of scientists as searching for truth using a rational model. In contrast, he noted, "the goal of policy makers is to obtain popular support: they search for compromise, by using an intuitive model" (2005, p. 633). Policy makers have to adapt to the real world of people, and although theoretical models may be true, they may not yet be accepted by society. Policy processes are not usually linear and logical, as policy makers have to deal with multiple advice, opinions, values, and preconceived ideas. Findings from diverse studies that are conducted in controlled settings may not hold in real-world settings. Simply presenting research results to policy makers and expecting them to put the evidence into practice is very unlikely to work. As researchers, we have to find ways to consider the various rationales that are present in work disability practice: scientific, political, legal, and cultural. This variety was nicely described by Peter Gluckman in a document from the New Zealand Office of the Prime Minister's Science Advisory Committee:

> Quality evidence should be seen as base knowledge on which, in a democracy, multiple values and associated perspectives must be overlaid. However, where evidence is conflated with values, its power is diminished. Where evidence is not considered properly, the risk of less than desirable policy outcomes is inevitable
> (Prime Minister's Chief Science Advisor, 2013, p. 4)

Practices may look excellent but, as various actors have different understandings, training and interests, they may understand and apply them in different ways or find ways to escape their intended aim, as presented in the above-mentioned examples.

A Transdisciplinary Approach as a Proposed Solution

In my view, reconciling perspectives in science and policy requires a transdisciplinary approach, which involves bringing together the different disciplines involved. With this approach, scientists and policy experts would discuss implementation needs emerging from recent scientific evidence while sharing their knowledge and experience, and ensure that the resulting policies will be scientifically supported and effective for the targeted populations. Transdisciplinarity, a term coined by Piaget (1972) and then diffused by Nicolescu (1996), is the art and science of bringing together thinkers from various disciplines and experiences to address complex problems that cannot be solved by one discipline or a limited vision of reality (Bernstein, 2015). Our international training program in work disability prevention, supported by the Canadian Institutes of Health Research, trained high-level global trainees and young scientists (from health to law and policy) with this transdisciplinary perspective over 12 years (Loisel et al., 2008). More than 110 trainees and their 30 program mentors created myriads of transdisciplinary connections, and many continue to work together. I hope they will bridge scientific, political, legal, and cultural realities to match science and policy in ways that can best serve the needs of work disabled citizens globally.

Policy is a complex field that has to adapt not only to the topics at hand, but also to political issues, including diverse actors in a democratic society—much more complicated than an Admiralty decision in the scurvy case. Appropriate policies should facilitate agreement between the various actors of the work disability field as well as facilitate and even sometimes enforce evidence implementation. I think we now need to train "return-to-work managers," who will have the knowledge and skills of the science and politics related to work disability prevention and can guide disabled workers through the complex work disability prevention arena (Loisel et al., 2005). This is the only way that the individual and societal burdens of work disability will be actually reduced.

Notes

1 Institut de recherche Robert-Sauvé en santé et en sécurité du travail.
2 Centre hospitalier universitaire de Sherbrooke.
3 Commission de la santé et de la sécurité du travail.
4 Réseau en réadaptation au travail du Québec.

References

Anema, J. R., Steenstra, I. A., Bongers, P. M., Vet, H. C., Knol, D. L., Loisel, P., & Mechelen, W. V. (2007). Multidisciplinary rehabilitation for subacute low back pain: Graded activity or workplace intervention or both? *Spine*, *32*(3), 291–298. doi:10.1097/01.brs.0000253604.90039.ad

Association of Workers' Compensation Boards of Canada. (2005). *Detailed key statistical measures report*. Retrieved September 1, 2017 from http://awcbc.org/?page_id=9759

Bernstein, J. H. (2015). Transdisciplinarity: A review of its origins, development and current issues. *Journal of Research Practice*, *11*(1), Article R1.

Canadian Institutes of Health Research. (2011, November 30). *Moving population and public health knowledge into action*. Retrieved September 3, 2017 from www.cihr-irsc.gc.ca/e/30739.html

Choi, B. C. (2005). Can scientists and policy makers work together? *Journal of Epidemiology & Community Health*, *59*(8), 632–637. doi:10.1136/jech.2004.031765

Cullen, K. L., Irvin, E., Collie, A., Clay, F., Gensby, U., Jennings, P. A., . . . Amick, B. C. (2017). Effectiveness of workplace interventions in return-to-work for musculoskeletal, pain-related and mental health conditions: An update of the evidence and messages for practitioners. *Journal of Occupational Rehabilitation*. doi:10.1007/s10926-016-9690-x

Deyo, R. A., Diehl, A. K., & Rosenthal, M. (1986). How many days of bed rest for acute low back pain? A randomized clinical trial. *New England Journal of Medicine*, *315*(17), 1064–70. doi:10.1056/NEJM198610233151705

Engel, G. (1977). The need for a new medical model: A challenge for biomedicine. *Science*, *196*(4286), 129–136. doi:10.1126/science.847460

Feuerstein, M. (1991). A multidisciplinary approach to the prevention, evaluation, and management of work disability. *Journal of Occupational Rehabilitation*, *1*(1), 5–12. doi:10.1007/bf01073276

Frank, J., Sinclair, S., Hogg-Johnson, S., Shannon, H., Bombardier, C., Beaton, D., & Cole, D. (1998). Preventing disability from work-related low-back pain. New evidence gives new hope—if we can just get all the players onside. *Canadian Medical Association Journal*, *158*(12), 1625–1631.

Lambeek, L. C., Bosmans, J. E., van Royen, B. J., van Tulder, M. W., van Mechelen, W., & Anema, J. R. (2011). Effect of integrated care for sick listed patients with chronic low back pain: Economic evaluation alongside a randomised controlled trial. *British Medical Journal*, *341*. doi: 10.1136/bmj.c6414.

Lambeek, L. C., van Mechelen, W., Knol, D. L., Loisel, P., & Anema, J. R. (2010). Randomised controlled trial of integrated care to reduce disability from chronic low back pain in working and private life. *British Medical Journal*, *340*, 1–7.

Leavitt, F., & Sweet, J. J. (1986). Characteristics and frequency of malingering among patients with low back pain. *Pain*, *25*(3), 357–364. doi:10.1016/0304-3959(86)90239-3

Lind, J. (1753). *A treatise of the scurvy. In three parts. Containing an inquiry into the nature, causes, and cure, of that disease*. Edinburgh, UK: Printed by Sands, Murray & Cochran for A. Kincaid & A. Donaldson.

Loisel, P. (2009). Work disability: It is not just the "lesion." In M. Feuerstein (Ed.), *Work and cancer survivors* (pp. 93–104). New York, NY: Springer Science+Business Media. doi:10.1007/978-0-387-72041-8

Loisel, P., Abenhaim, L., Durand, P., Esdaile, J. M., Suissa, S., Gosselin, L., . . . Lemaire, J. (1997). A population-based, randomized clinical trial on back pain management. *Spine, 22*(24), 2911–2918. doi:10.1097/00007632-199712150-00014

Loisel, P., Buchbinder, R., Hazard, R., Keller, R., Scheel, I., Tulder, M. V., & Webster, B. (2005). Prevention of work disability due to musculoskeletal disorders: The challenge of implementing evidence. *Journal of Occupational Rehabilitation, 15*(4), 507–524. doi:10.1007/s10926-005-8031-210.1097/00043764-199606000-00004

Loisel, P., Durand, M., Berthelette, D., Vézina, N., Baril, R., Gagnon, D., . . . Tremblay, C. (2001). Disability prevention: New paradigm for the management of occupational back pain. *Disease Management and Health Outcomes, 9*(7), 351–360. doi:10.2165/00115677-200109070-00001

Loisel, P., Durand, M., Diallo, B., Vachon, B., Charpentier, N., & Labelle, J. (2003). From evidence to community practice in work rehabilitation: The Quebec experience. *The Clinical Journal of Pain, 19*(2), 105–113. doi:10.1097/00002508-200303000-00005

Loisel, P., Durand, P., Abenhaim, L., Gosselin, L., Simard, R., Turcotte, J., & Esdaile, J. (1996). Management of occupational back pain. *Occupational and Environmental Medicine, 38*(6), 567–568. doi:10.1097/00043764-199606000-0000410.1097/00043764-199606000-00004

Loisel, P., Hong, Q. N., Imbeau, D., Lippel, K., Guzman, J., MacEachen, E., . . . Anema, J. R. (2008). The Work Disability Prevention CIHR Strategic Training Program: Program performance after 5 years of implementation. *Journal of Occupational Rehabilitation, 19*(1), 1–7. doi:10.1007/s10926-008-9160-1

Loisel, P., Lemaire, J., Poitras, S., Durand, M. J., Champagne, F., Stock, S., Diallo, B., & Tremblay, C. (2002). Cost-benefit and cost-effectiveness analysis of a disability prevention model for back pain management: A six year follow up study [abstract]. *Occupational and Environmental Medicine, 59*(12), 807–815. doi:10.1136/oem.59.12.807

MacEachen, E., Lippel, K., Saunders, R., Kosny, A., Mansfield, L., Carrasco, C., & Pugliese, D. (2012). Workers' compensation experience-rating rules and the danger to workers' safety in the temporary work agency sector. *Policy and Practice in Health and Safety, 10*(1), 77–95. doi: 10.1080/14774003.2012.11667770

Milne, I., & Chalmers, I. (2004, October). Documenting the evidence: The case of scurvy. *Bulletin of the World Health Organization, 82*(10), 791–796. Retrieved September 3, 2017 from www.ncbi.nlm.nih.gov/pubmed/15643802

Nachemson, A. (1965). The effect of forward leaning on lumbar intradiscal pressure. *Acta Orthopedica Scandinavica, 35*(1–4), 314–328. doi: 10.3109/17453676508989362

Nachemson, A. (1983). Work for all. For those with low back pain as well. *Clinical Orthopaedics and Related Research, 179*(1). doi:10.1097/00003086-198310000-00012

Nicolescu, B. (2008). *Transdisciplinarity: Theory and practice*. Cresskill, NJ: Hampton Press.

Piaget, J. (1972). L'épistémologie des relations interdisciplinaires. In G. Berger, A. Briggs, & G. Michaud (Eds.), *L'interdisciplinarité: Problèmes d'enseignement et de recherche* (pp. 127–139). Paris, France: Organisation for Economic Co-operation and Development.

Pomaki, G., Franche, R., Murray, E., Khushrushahi, N., & Lampinen, T. M. (2012). Workplace-based work disability prevention interventions for workers with common mental health conditions: A review of the literature. *Journal of Occupational Rehabilitation, 22*(2), 182–195. doi:10.1007/s10926-011-9338-9

Prime Minister's Chief Science Advisor. (2013, September). *The role of evidence in policy formation and implementation.* Retrieved September 3, 2017 from www.pmcsa.org.nz/wp-content/uploads/The-role-of-evidence-in-policy-formation-and-implementation-report.pdf

Spitzer, W. O., LeBlanc, F. E., & Dupuis, M. (1987). Scientific approach to the assessment and management of activity-related spinal disorders: A monograph for clinicians. Report of the Quebec Task Force on Spinal Disorders. *Spine, 12*(7 Suppl), S1–S59.

Ståhl, C., Costa-Black, K., & Loisel, P. (2017). Applying theories to better understand socio-political challenges in implementing evidence-based work disability prevention strategies. *Disability and Rehabilitation, 40*(8), 952–959. doi:10.1080/09638288.2016.1277399

Waddell, G. (1987). 1987 Volvo Award in Clinical Sciences: A new clinical model for the treatment of low-back pain. *Spine, 12*(7), 632–644. doi:10.1097/00007632-198709000-00002

Waddell, G., McCulloch, J., Kummel, E., & Venner, R. (1980, March–April). Nonorganic physical signs in low-back pain. *Spine, 5*(2), 117–125. doi:10.1097/00007632-198003000-00005

Part 2

Cause-Based Social Security Systems

Chapter 3

Work Disability in the United States
A Fragmented System

Allard E. Dembe

A variety of approaches for addressing work disability are used in the United States. Each of the 50 states in the US has instituted workers' compensation (WC) laws to provide wage replacement and medical care to workers who sustain work-related injuries and illnesses on the job. Also, working people who are disabled for a prolonged period as a result of severe impairment and incapacity can qualify for benefits through the federal Social Security Disability Insurance (SSDI) program.

Numerous resources are available from governmental sources, employers, care providers, and disability-prevention specialists to help support the needs of disabled workers. Legislation has been enacted both at the state and federal levels to ensure the rights of affected individuals. Many successful programs have been established in the US to help integrate disabled workers back into productive employment. Laws are in place, such as the Americans with Disabilities Act of 2008, to protect the rights of people with disabilities.

The US has a well entrenched social security system that provides disability and income-protection benefits to people with low income and severe impairments. State-based workers' compensation benefits are typically available for the vast majority of workers who sustain work-related injuries or illnesses because of occupational hazards. Other federal laws have been devised to afford protection and compensation to particular populations, such as federal employees, railroad workers, and miners. In general, the US has substantial mechanisms in place to provide essential services to those who have the greatest need.

Despite these desirable features, the US faces continuing difficulties in addressing the everyday needs of people with work disabilities. Costs for disability services are continually mounting, outstripping the ability of agencies to fund programs sufficiently. The care provided is too often inadequate and fragmented. For disabled individuals who want to work, finding suitable employment is often difficult. Processes for establishing eligibility for benefits can be prolonged and frustrating. In some US disability programs—especially in the state-based workers' compensation system—relationships among doctors, compensation officials, employers, and injured workers are complicated and frequently adversarial in nature. The fragmented care arrangement in the US, with no central planning or authority, leads to confusion and inefficient care delivery.

In the SSDI program, which focuses on providing services to people with severe disabilities who are no longer able to work, eligibility rules are very strict, and denial rates are high (Vallas & Fremstad, 2014). SSDI benefits, on average, typically replace less than half of a disabled person's previous earnings. As a result, governmental programs are rarely able to provide the real support necessary for beneficiaries to live comfortably. At any time, about 14 million people are on work disability, representing 4.6% of the US working-age population (18–64) (Bureau of Labor Statistics, 2016). Benefit levels are relatively low. As of March 2013, the average monthly benefit for a disabled worker in the SSDI system was about US$1,129, with male workers averaging US$1,255 and females averaging US$993 per month (about US$14,000–15,000 per year) (Fremstad & Vallas, 2013).

Workers' compensation programs are relatively comprehensive, providing medical care and wage-replacement benefits, along with rehabilitation services, to workers harmed by activities performed on the job. The combination of medical care and wage replacement available through workers' compensation programs provides some level of structural cohesion in benefit design and adjudication. However, WC is divorced from other disability systems, particularly SSDI and the federal Supplemental Security Income (SSI) program (which provides income assistance for aged, blind, and disabled people who have little or no income), thereby hindering development of a coherent approach that spans the multiple needs faced by affected individuals and their families.

Workers' compensation is often characterized as a no-fault system, meaning that employers pay for the costs of work-related accidents in exchange for the injured workers giving up their rights to sue their employers for negligence. This arrangement is intended to constitute the exclusive remedy for work-related injuries and illness in the US. However, there is some crossover in practice, with work-related conditions sometimes being paid for by SSDI and other means, along with significant out-of-pocket costs borne by individuals. Despite the intended no-fault character of WC, the system is plagued by controversies about whether a worker's condition was caused occupationally, the inadequacy of benefit levels, and the overly litigious nature of determining whether a claim should be approved. As a result, administering WC claims is a complex undertaking, leading to delays and inefficiencies in the awarding of benefits.

Rising system costs jeopardize the continued integrity of the major disability programs in the US, including SSDI, SSI, and WC. Most of the nation's disability systems are significantly underfunded. It is estimated that total spending for SSDI was approximately US$144 billion in 2013 (DeHaven, 2013). SSI spending in 2017 was projected to be about US$56.2 billion in federal outlays, providing benefits for an estimated

8.2 million SSI recipients. In 2014, state and federal workers' compensation laws covered about 129.6 million employees. Employers' WC costs in 2014 were estimated to be US$91.8 billion, with approximately half of that amount used for medical care and half for cash benefits to beneficiaries (Baldwin & McLaren, 2016; Social Security Administration (SSA), 2016). To keep the system afloat, many politicians across the US are proposing to tighten eligibility requirements, which will further restrict recipients' ability to maintain a decent living standard.

Among 33 Organisation for Economic Co-operation and Development (OECD) member countries, the US has one of the least generous disability-benefit systems, ranking behind only Turkey, South Korea, Chile, Canada, and Japan (Organisation for Economic Co-operation and Development, 2017). SSDI disability benefits in the US typically replace less than half of a disabled worker's previous earnings. US workers' compensation benefits usually cover about two thirds of the worker's average weekly wages, although actual wage recovery can be significantly less because of underlying reductions in the state's ambient benefit levels, legal expenses, and other exigencies.

State-Based Workers' Compensation Plans

Workers' compensation insurance is the primary way that injured workers receive medical care and disability payments for occupational injuries and illnesses occurring on the job. Covered benefits include medical care, rehabilitation, and cash benefits for workers who are injured on the job or who contract work-related illnesses as the result of specific occupational disorders. No employee cost-sharing is required under workers' compensation. Each state develops its own WC laws and administrative procedures, independently of federal funding or oversight. System costs are borne primarily by employers. Each employer is experience rated, which means that the cost to a company for obtaining workers' compensation coverage is determined, in part, by how well the firm has done in preventing accidents and lowering costs.

Specific workers' compensation laws exist in every US state, each having its own specific rules regarding eligibility, benefit levels, and treatment of work disability. All employers must have workers' compensation coverage, provided by commercial insurance companies, state-operated insurance funds, or employers' self-insurance plans.

Through workers' compensation, employees are generally entitled to monetary benefits when injured at work, irrespective of who was at fault, in exchange for limits on employees' ability to file lawsuits against their employers. Medical providers are invested with the responsibility for determining whether a worker's injury or illness is actually caused by working conditions (i.e., whether it is work-related) and thus whether the worker is entitled to benefits.

There are several kinds of disability claims under WC, including claims for medical care only, temporary partial disability claims, temporary total disability claims, and permanent disability claims. The benefit amount is determined by the length of work disability and the prevailing benefit levels enacted in each state. Death benefits are also provided to dependents of those who died as the result of a work-related illness or injury.

In the US, medical professionals (physicians, therapists, and other authorized providers) are given the responsibility to determine whether the worker's condition is caused occupationally. Professionals' findings are then used as the basis for authorizing medical care and awarding disability benefits to injured workers. Determining eligibility can often be complicated and, consequently, there are frequently delays in obtaining initial care. In the best of circumstances, the process is handled in a straightforward way by workers' compensation insurers and claim administrators. However, in some cases, applicants are unable to obtain the benefits to which they are entitled.

Other Disability-Related Programs

Besides workers' compensation and SSDI, there is a wide assortment of other programs in the US that potentially address work disability. Some of the most notable programs are described in Table 3.1. Again, because of fragmentation among disability systems and the resulting lack of central coordination, particular programs are likely to be not particularly well coordinated, potentially leading to inefficiencies in care delivery. Many states have established their own disability programs, funded by federal grant programs or through other state-based initiatives.

Table 3.1 A summary of US disability-related programs

Program	Relevant Population	Programmatic Goal
Social Security Disability Insurance (SSDI)	People who cannot work because of a severe disability that is expected to last at least one year or result in death.	Replaces a portion of the worker's income and provides supports to regain work capacity.
Supplementary Security Income (SSI)	Disabled adults and children who have limited income and assets.	Provides stipends to low-income people who are either aged 65 or older, blind, or disabled.
Commercial (private) long-term and short-term disability coverage	Employed individuals who are temporarily unable to resume regular job duties.	Commercial insurance that provides a person with tax-free benefits until able to return to work.

The Americans with Disability Act (ADA) of 2008	Provides protections for people who, because of a disability, might suffer discrimination in employment, public services, public accommodations, telecommunications, and other facets of public life.	The ADA civil rights law prohibits discrimination against individuals with disabilities in all areas of public life, including jobs, schools, and transportation. The purpose of the law is to make sure that people with disabilities have the same rights and opportunities as everyone else.
The Family and Medical Leave Act (FMLA)	Fifty-nine percent of employees are covered and eligible to take leave under the FMLA. It applies to both women and men to help manage the dual demands of work and family.	The FMLA federal law requires covered employers to provide employees with job-protected and unpaid leave for qualified medical and family reasons.
Veterans Administration (VA) disability programs	Compensation benefits are paid to veterans who have injuries or diseases that occurred while on active duty, or were made worse by active military service.	VA disability compensation provides tax-free monetary benefits for veterans with disabilities that result from a disease or injury incurred or aggravated during active military service.
Disability coverage within the Medicaid program	Provides coverage for Medicaid applicants who are of low income, and who are considered legally blind, aged, or disabled, as classified by the SSA.	Medicaid disability recipients generally qualify for SSI, depending on state requirements. Some individuals are dually eligible.
Disability coverage within the Medicare program	It is necessary to collect Social Security disability benefits for at least 24 months to enroll in Medicare, although some people may enroll right away.	Besides regular Medicare disability coverage, Medicare also covers individuals under age 65 who have end-stage renal disease or amyotrophic lateral sclerosis.

(continued)

Table 3.1 (continued)

Program	Relevant Population	Programmatic Goal
Federal workers' compensation systems/ programs:		
Federal Employees Compensation Act	Provides compensation benefits to federal government employees for disability due to personal injury sustained on the job or due to employment-related disease.	Provides benefits for federal employees, with benefits similar to those used in state-based WC plans.
Energy Employees Occupational Illness Compensation Program Act (EEOICPA)	Provides disability compensation benefits to federal employees potentially exposed to radiation-induced cancer, beryllium, uranium, and nuclear weapons employees.	This federal Act has specific eligibility requirements specific to workers potentially exposed to those hazards.
Longshore and Harbor Workers' Compensation Act (LHWCA)	Provides disability benefits to workers in maritime or longshore occupations, and any harbor workers, including ship repairers.	This federal Act has specific eligibility requirements specific to workers potentially exposed to those hazards.
Black Lung Benefits Act	Provides benefits to coal miners totally disabled from pneumoconiosis (black lung disease) arising from employment in or around coal mines.	This federal Act has specific eligibility requirements specific to coal miners exposed to black lung disease.
Asbestos-related disability (generally handled through products liability tort actions)	Provides disability benefits related to asbestos exposure, often handled through product liability litigation.	There is no federal disability program related to asbestos exposure, but a considerable amount of disability-related tort actions.

Disability Determination

Almost all U.S. disability systems require specific criteria to decide whether a person is disabled and qualifies for disability benefits. In the SSDI system, there is a five-step test to decide whether the claimant is qualified:

1 Is the applicant working?
2 Is the person's medical condition deemed to be severe, and does it significantly limit functionality?[1]
3 Does the person have particular qualifying impairments?[2]
4 Is the applicant unable to do the work previously performed?
5 Is the person unable to perform other kinds of work?

Medical personnel and disability specialists conduct a qualifying assessment to summarize their findings in the five-step test. Based on those criteria, only about 32% of SSDI applicants were awarded disability status in 2016 (SSA, 2016). The low acceptance rate reflects inadequate government funding and concerns about possible inappropriate overuse of benefits.

In workers' compensation systems also, physicians conduct qualifying examinations to determine whether a particular injury or illness was caused by work that arose out of and in the course of employment, and is therefore eligible for coverage. Perhaps the biggest impediment to administering workers' compensation claims is the need to definitively ascertain whether an injury was caused by occupational conditions within a workplace. However, advances in epidemiology have shown that most injuries have numerous underlying causes; these can include an occupational component along with other factors, such as heredity, behavioral choices, and environmental considerations. Uncertainties about the precise contribution of distinct causes for an injury seriously complicate the handling of claims for preexisting conditions and aggravation of existing injuries. Debates rage in some states (especially Florida, Oregon, and Illinois) about whether to award compensation only when a predominant major contributing cause of the injury can be identified (Burton, 2015).

During America's early industrial period, many serious traumatic injuries occurred, and so it was relatively easy to verify whether an injury resulted from working conditions. Today, however, most WC claims involve common medical problems such as routine back pain, muscle strains, repetitive motions of the hands and wrists, and chronic diseases. Consequently, doctors now have a very difficult time deciding whether a particular condition is caused by work activities, and whether eligibility for compensation benefits should be conferred. These ambiguous situations introduce considerable uncertainty and thus can erode trust in the processes used to award benefits.

Other Complexities Regarding Work Disability in the US

There is considerable complexity regarding American work disability practices, owing to the nation's decentralized approach, which features both federal and state disability programs and extensive private-sector involvement. Multiple system goals apply to work disability, including access to healthcare services, short- and long-term income replacement, rehabilitation and return to work, employment support, reintegration, and disability management. Sometimes the overlap is confusing. The goal of SSDI is to provide long-term wage replacement to individuals with a significant work history who can no longer gainfully work because of a severe, prolonged, chronic medical impairment. Benefits are only available to those who have accumulated a sufficient number of work credits[3] as a result of previous employment. By contrast, workers' compensation provides short- and long-term benefits for workers who are injured or contract an illness as a result of performing employment activities at a workplace. Medical benefits are provided to workers starting from the day of injury (after an initial waiting period of 3–7 days in most states) until they are medically able to return to work.[4] Long-term medical payments, covering a portion (typically two thirds) of the injured workers' wages, are provided for short-term as well as prolonged disability.

The crossover effects between systems can be confusing. For example, recent studies indicate that there may be considerable cost-shifting between WC, SSDI, and Medicare programs. Evidence suggests that recent cuts in WC benefit levels in some states might induce workers, especially older ones, to file claims instead through SSDI or Medicare to pay for long-term medical conditions. Data from New Mexico indicate that 7% of new SSDI claims in that state were actually due to workplace injuries. If this percentage is extrapolated to the entire country, this results in an additional cost to the SSDI program of about US$23 million (Buffie & Baker, 2015).

As a result, American disability programs are fraught with complexities that may not be fully recognized by program designers, workers, and policy makers. For example, there are often lengthy appeal processes in each of those programs, which can drag on for months or years. At least in SSDI, few beneficiaries qualify for benefits, and only a small proportion are actually able to successfully return to work (Vallas, Fremstad, & Ekman, 2015).

Trying to rationalize existing US disability programs is a difficult undertaking, given this complexity. Eligibility is determined by convoluted procedures that can be frustrating and time-consuming. This can lead prospective beneficiaries to drop out of the application process. The overlapping complexity of the multiple systems can foster an environment for waste generated inside the programs themselves, as well as potential fraud and abuse stemming from external influences. The resulting confusions and lack of clarity about how the system works can undermine confidence in the US disability system.

Especially in WC, injured workers bear the brunt of the deficiencies, both financially and psychologically. Workers in both the WC and SSDI systems face substantial obstacles in obtaining appropriate recompense for their medical problems. Many injured or sick workers incur substantial financial losses that are not adequately recovered by the available statutory benefits. Employees frequently have difficulty establishing the legitimacy of their injuries. Additionally, studies have shown that a significant proportion of workers fear employer retribution if they file claims. Physicians are often caught in the middle of arguments about whether the claimant's injury or illness is medically legitimate and should be compensated. So-called "independent medical examinations"—typically ordered by private insurers and paid for by employers—further aggravate workers and cloud the decisions made about compensability of specific injuries.

Although experience rating provides employers with an incentive for accident prevention and lower costs, some companies attempt to subvert the system by failing to report accidents and threatening retribution to workers who file claims, in order to save the company money. Another emerging threat to the US workers' compensation system is the use of so-called "independent contractors" or "gig" workers. By classifying them as "contractors" rather than "employees," the employer can avoid the employment taxes that are normally required. However, the workers face the loss of labor law protections that a conventional employment arrangement provides.

Issues Concerning Short-Term Disability

Another problem in the US work disability system is the lack of any standardized approach for dealing with short-term disability (STD) that is medically judged not to have resulted from a workplace injury. For example, consider the plight of a working person who has a mild stroke that causes temporary work incapacity for a few weeks or months (typically 12–24 weeks or less). No federal laws ensure that the worker will be able to obtain wage-replacement income during that period of infirmity. However, the Americans with Disabilities Act (ADA) does protect the employee's job during the disability leave. A few states—notably California, New York, New Jersey, Hawaii, and Rhode Island—provide state-sponsored, STD insurance coverage (Morley, 2017).

In general, most American workers experiencing short-term work incapacity must rely either on employer-sponsored STD insurance or purchase a commercial STD policy themselves. Also, some employees use accrued vacation days or sick-time allowances authorized by employers, rather than STD-insurance benefits from their employers. The former option is more often offered by larger, self-insured employers, who have sufficient resources to offer that kind of assistance to their workers. Of course, in the event of temporary incapacity, many workers would merely forgo having insurance, leaving them without any means of income protection. The US Bureau of Labor Statistics has estimated that only 39% of private-sector employers provide STD insurance to their workers (Monaco, 2015).

Most short-term insurance arrangements pay for about 40% to 60% of the employees' gross income during the period of convalesce (Nathan, 2016). The reason that a greater proportion of income is not replaced is moral-hazard effects. Moral hazard provides an incentive for people to accrue more benefits than they would otherwise in the absence of insurance coverage. The American approach to dealing with STD is not ideal. The main problems are that commercial STD coverage is often not provided to workers by their employers, benefits are modest, and federal and state governmental entities are not heavily involved in ensuring coverage for STD.

Disability Management and Return to Work

Perhaps the most pressing concern in US disability policy is how to most effectively prevent disability and enhance return-to-work outcomes. The goals of these efforts should be to increase the recruitment, hiring, retention, and promotion of people with disabilities; enhance their economic status; and more fully integrate individuals with disabilities into productive employment. To achieve these goals, it will be necessary to go beyond the initial protections and accommodations that were established through the Americans with Disabilities Act of 1990. It is important to determine whether people with disabilities are working to their full potential, and additional research is necessary to answer that question.

In the US, employers have considerable authority for how to set up work arrangements in their facilities. This presents a significant opportunity for forward-thinking managers to develop meaningful programs that can substantially benefit the workforce, especially employees who need assistance as the result of a disability. Of course, some management officials are reluctant to establish recruitment and retention programs for disabled workers, because of the possible effect on productivity or other considerations. Indeed, in one recent survey, 20% of management officials were of the opinion that the greatest barrier to hiring disabled workers was officials' own prejudicial attitudes and discrimination (Dixon, Kruse, & Van Horn, 2003). Other reasons for low job retention include the inability of employees with disabilities to sustain adequate work performance; changes in work duties or working conditions; health complaints; and individual employer policies or practices that discourage continued employment. In addition, many people with disabilities work in relatively small companies, with correspondingly lower wages, education, and household income compared with people working for larger companies.

Despite these concerns, many successful initiatives have been developed to help disabled workers secure well-paying jobs that match their skills and education. There are various strategies that employers can adopt to help design and implement successful employment programs to support better employment for workers with disabilities. Figure 3.1[5] portrays some of the measures that can be introduced at specific points in time, related to medical conditions or disabilities that might exist within a company.

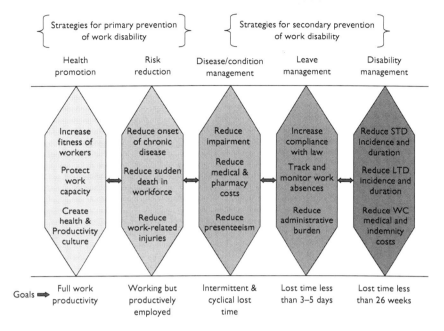

Figure 3.1 Employer strategies for preventing and managing work disability. STD = Short-term disability, LTD = Long-term disability, workers' compensation. Source: Tingus, Pledger, Horne, & Johnson (2007).

An employer can choose to implement retention-support programs in a variety of ways: for example, by developing a transitional return-to-work policy; providing reasonable accommodations; performing ergonomic evaluations to address workers' abilities and limitations; regular on-the-job analysis of suggested strategies; undertaking disability-management education; or instituting flexible work schedules that can be customized to accommodate employees with disabilities.

Model programs for employing people with disabilities have been established in the US by state and federal agencies, employer groups, and disability-related organizations. One example of such programs is EARN (The Employer Assistance and Resource Network on Disability Inclusion), which is an initiative of the US Office of Disability Employment Policy. EARN aims to help employers recruit, hire, retain, and promote people with disabilities. In addition, it hosts education programs and disseminates information through a national website.

Many private-sector-employer associations and individual companies have developed guidelines for effective disability management. A notable example is the collaboration between Cornell University's Employment and Disability Institute and the Disability Management Employer Coalition (von Schrader, Malzer, & Bruyère, 2014). In this program, disability-management practices are introduced through an integrated approach that strives to combine an organization's functional needs in areas such as workers' compensation, short- and long-term disability, family medical leave, and health-and-wellness programing. Dyck (2014) describes specific features of an integrated disability-management approach that can include:

> development of supportive policies (e.g. flexible work options), manager and employee education, supportive benefit programs, a coordinated approach to addressing injury and illness, communication plans to share information about programming, a return to work program, performance measurement for programming, and workplace wellness interventions.

Workplace disability-management programs are also being developed to address key specific health conditions, such as mental health disorders and the inappropriate use of opioid medications. According to recent estimates from the Congressional Research Service, between 26.2% and 32.4% of US adults have a 12-month prevalence of mental illness (Bagalman & Cornell, 2016). Depression among working adults is a particular problem, affecting as many as 16 million American adults (6.9%) (National Alliance on Mental Illness, 2017). Approximately 30% to 45% of all new disability-benefit claims are attributed to mental disorders.

Mental health disability is a very significant and growing issue in US health policy. Because of its importance, substantial efforts are being made at the federal, state, and private-sector levels to devise disability-management programs for people with mental health conditions, such as depression, anxiety, and other serious mental illnesses. At the federal level, the Substance Abuse and Mental Health Services Administration (SAMHSA) is the primary US agency responsible for policy and programing related to behavioral health. SAMHSA also give states Mental Health Block Grants to provide community-based mental health services. State and local agencies conduct a variety of interventions involving clinical treatment outside the workplace, workplace-based psychological interventions, and employer-sponsored counseling, often as part of Employee Assistance Programs (EAPs).

Along with mental health issues, the US is experiencing an epidemic in the use and abuse of opioid pain medications. Drug overdoses have now become the leading cause of death among Americans under 50. In 2016 alone, more than 59,000 lives were lost as the result of opioid addiction and substance abuse (Katz, 2017). The rate of drug overdose is rising sharply; in fact, drug overdoses in the US are now more common than motor-vehicle-crash deaths. Long-term use of opioids significantly prolongs disability and reduces the likelihood for successful return to work.

According to the US Centers for Disease Control and Prevention, long-term use of opioids is significantly more acute among injured workers. In 2016, 50.9% of injured workers had an opioid-prescription claim, and 25% of injured workers used opioids for 30 days or more in that year (Esola, 2017). In many states, lawmakers are taking action to curb overuse and abuse of opioid medications. Numerous states have introduced legislation to limit prescription doses of opioids to a maximum duration; for instance, an initial dose of 7 to 30 days.

Rehabilitation and Return to Work

Most authorities agree that early intervention is key to preventing disability.[6] Especially in the workers' compensation context, there is considerable evidence that the first two months after a disabling injury are the most critical for intensive treatment and rehabilitation. If therapeutic measures are delayed past that point, the odds for a good outcome are significantly reduced. The public health model involves three types of disability prevention:

1. Primary: avoiding workplace injuries and illnesses.
2. Secondary: mitigating the impact of disease or injury that has already occurred.
3. Tertiary: managing and alleviating the long-term deleterious effects of work injury.

In addition to disability prevention, programs should be established that promote employee health through wellness and disability management. In this vein, ergonomic job re-engineering and restructuring can create positive outcomes for both employers and employees. Support from senior managers is critical in facilitating effective disability management. People with disabilities often prefer flexible work schedules, teleworking, job sharing, and nonstandard work arrangements. Evidence-based early intervention programs can help workers stay in the labor force and avoid applying for government disability benefits.

Workers' compensation systems are designed to help injured employees return to work safely and productively following work accidents. Indeed, many workers obtain helpful assistance from employer personnel and vocational-rehabilitation specialists. However, a variety of barriers can undermine employers' efforts to help employees successfully recover and resume job activities. Some employers may refuse to facilitate suitable transitional work. Treating physicians and claims administrators may fail to inform employers about different jobs that could be assigned to a worker while recovering. There is evidence that some employers try to bring back employees as soon as possible, to avoid paying STD benefits or providing reasonable accommodations. In addition, there can be legal conflicts between WC rehabilitation programs and provisions of the Americans with Disabilities Act and the federal Family Medical Leave Act.

Difficulties in Obtaining Appropriate Benefits

Legislation in most states requires employers to provide workers' compensation coverage to their employees. Employers pay the costs of the coverage as a mandated payroll tax. On a deeper level, a significant portion of the employers' WC costs are offset by paying workers lower wages. As a result, workers indirectly end up funding much of the system's expenditures. Doctors are paid by workers' compensation insurers. Employers hire third-party insurance companies and claims administrators to investigate claims and administer payments. Lawyers, administrative courts, and rehabilitation specialists (e.g., physical and occupational therapists) all derive profit from the WC compensation system. Self-interest can motivate insurers to deny claims and minimize workers' benefits.

Since 2010, employer funding for the workers' compensation system has steadily increased (per $100 of covered wages) (McLaren & Baldwin, 2017). However, during that same period compensation paid to injured workers has steadily declined. In many states, tighter restrictions are being placed on benefit eligibility. For example, states are imposing more stringent time limits to secure indemnification. Cutbacks in benefit levels are also encouraging workers to shift costs onto public tax-supported programs. Some states are even considering allowing employees to pursue tort actions, if the prevailing benefits available through WC become so diluted as to not permit viable and sufficient remuneration to injured workers.

Injuries resulting in permanent partial impairment account for most costs in the WC system. In most states, impairment ratings are determined by medical doctors, based on the *AMA Guides to the Evaluation of Permanent Impairment* (AMA) or similar impairment rating systems, such as *The Official Disability Guidelines* (ODG). Impairment calculations are converted into permanent disability awards using those standards. However, there is considerable controversy about considering the AMA or ODG guidelines as the "gold standard" for determining impairment ratings. Although disability payments are typically distributed to recipients over a set number of weeks, lump-sum settlements are also common. Unfortunately, some claimants may be persuaded to accept lump-sum settlements that are far lower than total benefits paid over the long run.

Prevention and Safety in the Workplace

The actual incidence of workplace injuries throughout the US has been declining for years. That may indicate that safety conditions in American workplaces are improving. Alternatively, it could indicate that workers are sustaining job-related injuries but not reporting accidents, perhaps because they fear employer reprisals. Research studies have generally found that occupational injuries and illnesses are significantly underreported. Some states provide premium discounts to employers that certify their workplaces as drug-free, based on mandatory drug and/or alcohol tests for employees. Except for exclusive-fund states (e.g., Ohio, Washington),[7] there is little effective coordination between state workers' compensation programs and employers' workplace-safety programs.

Disability prevention is a key concept that needs to be infused throughout the therapeutic process. Studies have shown that early intervention following workplace injury can decrease overall claim costs and lead to better functional outcomes. Early therapeutic intervention can lower claim costs for back pain and other musculoskeletal complaints. For example, a 2015 study of claims for lower-back pain found that early referral to guideline-adherent physical therapy was associated with significantly lower utilization of healthcare services for all physical-therapy outcomes and 60% less back-pain-related costs (Childs et al., 2015).

Improving Work Disability Systems: What Changes Are Possible?

In the US, there is little political interest in significantly altering the fundamental structures of the SSDI and WC systems, with the exception of employers and insurers who hope to further reduce or restrict benefits. Some authorities have advocated creating an entirely federalized system to help unite and standardize work disability programs across states. However, the current shared arrangement of federal disability programs and state-based workers' compensation systems appears to be entrenched as the predominant current paradigm for dealing with issues of work disability. Since the ascendance of more conservative state and federal governments in 2017, there has been accelerated movement toward further limiting social insurance programs and public assistance (US Department of Labor, 2016). This movement has spurred interest in potentially privatizing certain aspects of work disability programs, especially in the workers' compensation system. For example, proposals have been made in some states, such as Oklahoma, to opt out of traditional workers' compensation and move to more of a private market approach for dealing with work-injury and compensation issues.

By contrast, many progressive voices hope for a more integrated approach to work disability, whereby certain components of the US workers' compensation system and federal SSDI are more closely coordinated. For example, common processes could be established for medical evaluation of disability determination. A combination of employer-sponsored and commercial short- and long-term disability insurance plans, supplemented by SSDI for employees with serious disabilities, could be used to provide workers with needed protection against temporary job interruption and long-term work disability. Additional financial incentives, in the form of tax credits or subsidies, could be provided to ensure that work disability needs are effectively addressed.

The US workers' compensation system continues to provide a basic level of protection for many Americans who are hurt on the job. However, there are many injured workers who fall through the cracks and are denied care and appropriate benefits. Employer control over the WC system is becoming stronger, creating additional obstacles for many workers. A new patient-oriented paradigm is needed: one in which workers have a meaningful voice, and injured workers are treated as "clients" rather than "claimants." The system needs to be harmonized with other existing healthcare and social insurance programs, to achieve coordination and efficiency of functions. Benefits have to be able to replace a more substantial proportion of income. Most importantly, the reliance on determining the work-relatedness of a medical condition as the primary eligibility test for conferring WC wage-replacement benefits should be replaced with processes that make it easier to obtain services and medical care without prolonged arguments about the underlying cause of work injury.

Notes

1 According to the Social Security Administration website, "To be awarded Social Security disability or Supplemental Security Income (SSI) disability, you must have a condition, or combination of conditions, that have prevented you from working for twelve continuous months, or that you expect to prevent you from performing any kind of 'substantial and gainful work activity' for twelve continuous months."
2 This depends on the degree of impairment, which varies by what the medical assessment shows.
3 Generally an SSDI applicant will have had to have worked at least 40 quarters full-time. According to the SSA website, "To be eligible for Social Security retirement benefits, a worker born after 1928 must have accumulated at least 40 quarters of work in 'covered employment'. A 'quarter of coverage' generally means the three-month calendar quarter. In addition, you must earn at least $1,260 in a quarter (in 2016) for it to count."
4 The worker has the physical capability to perform the job or not perform the job. This can be as ascertained in many ways. A doctor makes the first assessment, but the insurance company and its doctors, independent medical evaluations, and/or other challenges may be made to the workers' status.
5 Primary prevention involves preventing an illness or disease from occurring, secondary prevention involves reducing the severity and impact of the problem, and tertiary prevention involves addressing the long-term effects so that it will not recur.
6 There are many similar articles, but virtually all focus on addressing a specific disease, such as back pain or rheumatoid arthritis (see, for example, Frank et al., 1996; Frank et al., 1998; Gatchel et al. (2003); Quinn & Cox, 2005; Ramey & Ramey, 1998).

7 A few states have a system in which the state government (and self-insurance) are the only options. Other states have commercial (private) workers' compensation. Many states have a combination of state funds, commercial insurance, and self-insured companies.

References

Bagalman, E., & Cornell, A. S. (2018, January). *Prevalence of mental illness in the United States: Data sources and estimates.* Washington, DC: Congressional Research Service. Retrieved February 21, 2018, from https://fas.org/sgp/crs/misc/R43047.pdf

Baldwin, M. L., & McLaren, C. F. (2016, October). *Workers' compensation: Benefits, coverage, and costs.* Washington, DC: National Academy of Social Insurance. Retrieved July 3, 2017, from www.nasi.org/research/2016/workers-compensation-benefits-coverage-costs

Buffie, N., & Baker, D. (2015). *Rising disability payments: Are cuts to workers' compensation part of the story?* Washington, DC: Center for Economic and Policy Research. Retrieved from http://cepr.net/publications/reports/rising-disability-payments-are-cuts-to-workers-compensation-part-of-the-story

Bureau of Labor Statistics. (2016, June 21). *Persons with a disability: Labor force characteristics (Economic News Release).* Retrieved June 14, 2017, from https://www.bls.gov/news.release/disabl.nr0.htm

Burton, J. F. (2015, May 5). *Workers compensation: Recent developments in Illinois and in the nation.* Brief presented to the Committee of the Whole before the Illinois House of Representatives.

Childs, J. D., Fritz, J. M., Wu, S. S., Flynn, T. F., Wainner, R. S., Robertson, E. K., . . . George, S. Z. (2015). Implications of early and guideline adherent physical therapy for low back pain on utilization and costs. *BMC Health Services Research, 15*, 150. Retrieved from https://bmchealthservres.biomedcentral.com/articles/10.1186/s12913-015-0830-3

DeHaven, T. (2013, August 6). *The rising cost of Social Security Disability Insurance* (Policy Analysis No. 733). Washington, DC: CATO Institute. Retrieved July 3, 2017, from www.cato.org/publications/policy-analysis/rising-cost-social-security-disability-insurance

Dixon, K. A., Kruse, D., & Van Horn, C. E. (2003). *Restricted access: A survey of employers about people with disabilities and lowering barriers to work.* New Brunswick, NJ: Rutgers University, John J. Heldrich Center for Workforce Development.

Dyck, D. (2014). *Disability management programs: Employer challenges turned opportunities.* Working paper, Employment and Disability Institute, Cornell University, Ithaca, NY.

Esola, L. (2017, May 1). States grapple with opioid restrictions. *Business Insurance.* Retrieved from www.businessinsurance.com/article/20170501/NEWS08/912313149/States-grapple-with-workers-compensation-reform-opioid-restrictions

Frank, J. W., Kerr, M. S., Brooker, A. S., DeMaio, S. E., Maetzel, A., Shannon, H. S., . . . Wells, R. P. (1996). Disability resulting from occupational low back pain. Part I: What do we know about primary prevention? A review of the scientific evidence on prevention before disability begins. *Spine, 21*(24), 2908–2917.

Frank, J., Sinclair, S., Hogg-Johnson, S., Shannon, H., Bombardier, C., Beaton, D., & Cole, D. (1998). Preventing disability from work-related low-back pain. New evidence gives new hope—if we can just get all the players onside. *Canadian Medical Association Journal, 158*(12), 1625–1631.

Fremstad S., & Vallas, R. (2013, May 30). *The facts on Social Security Disability Insurance and Supplemental Security Income for workers with disabilities*. Washington, DC: Center for American Progress. Retrieved February 21, 2018, from www.americanprogress.org/issues/poverty/reports/2013/05/30/64681/the-facts-on-social-security-disability-insurance-and-supplemental-security-income-for-workers-with-disabilities/

Gatchel, R. J., Polatin, P. B., Noe, C., Gardea, M., Pulliam, C., & Thompson, J. (2003). Treatment-and cost-effectiveness of early intervention for acute low-back pain patients: A one-year prospective study. *Journal of Occupational Rehabilitation, 13*(1), 1–9.

Katz, J. (2017, June 5). Drug deaths in America are rising faster than ever. *The New York Times*. Retrieved July 7, 2017, from www.nytimes.com/interactive/2017/06/05/upshot/opioid-epidemic-drug-overdose-deaths-are-rising-faster-than-ever.html

McLaren, C. F., & Baldwin, M. L. (2017, October). *Workers' compensation: Benefits, coverage, and costs*. Washington, DC: National Academy of Social Insurance. Retrieved February 21, 2018, from www.nasi.org/research/2017/workers-compensation-benefits-coverage-costs

Monaco, K. (2015). *Disability insurance plans: Trends in employee access and employer costs*. Washington, DC: US Bureau of Labor Statistics. Retrieved December 31, 2017, from www.bls.gov/opub/btn/volume-4/disability-insurance-plans.htm

Morley, T. (2017). *Temporary disability insurance requirements by state*. Society for Human Resource Management. Retrieved February 21, 2018, from www.shrm.org/resourcesandtools/legal-and-compliance/state-and-local-updates/xperthr/pages/temporary-disability-insurance-requirements-by-state.aspx

Nathan, S. (2016, October 19). Short-term disability basics. *The Balance*. Retrieved from www.thebalance.com/short-term-disability-basics-1177839

National Alliance on Mental Illness. (2017). Mental health by the numbers. Retrieved from www.nami.org/Learn-More/Mental-Health-By-the-Numbers

Organisation for Economic Co-operation and Development. (2017). *Public spending on incapacity*. Retrieved from https://data.oecd.org/socialexp/public-spending-on-incapacity.htm

Quinn, M. A., & Cox, S. (2005). The evidence for early intervention. *Rheumatic Diseases Clinics of North America, 31*(4), 575–589.

Ramey, C. T., & Ramey, S. L. (1998). Early intervention and early experience. *The American Psychologist, 53*(2), 109–120.

Social Security Administration. (2016). *Annual statistical supplement to the Social Security Bulletin*. Retrieved from www.ssa.gov/policy/docs/statcomps/supplement/2016/supplement16.pdf

Tingus, S. J., Pledger, C., Horne R., & Johnson, E. (2007, September). *Employer perspectives on workers with disabilities: A national summit to develop a research agenda*. Report prepared for Interagency Committee on Disability Research, Interagency Subcommittee on Employment. Washington, DC: US Department of Labor. Retrieved February 22, 2018, from www2.ed.gov/rschstat/research/pubs/ise-report--employer-perspectives.pdf

US Department of Labor. (2016, October 6). *Does the workers' compensation system fulfill its obligations to injured workers?* Retrieved from www.dol.gov/asp/WorkersCompensationSystem/WorkersCompensationSystemReport.pdf

Vallas, R., Fremstad, S., & Ekman, L. (2015, January 28). *A fair shot for workers with disabilities.* Center for American Progress. Retrieved June 14, 2017, from https://cdn.americanprogress.org/wp-content/uploads/2015/01/WorkersDisabilities.pdf

Vallas, R., & Fremstad, S. (2014, July 8). *Social Security Disability Insurance: A bedrock of security for American workers.* Retrieved June 14, 2017, from https://cdn.americanprogress.org/wp-content/uploads/2014/07/SSDIBrief.pdf

Von Schrader, S., Malzer, V., & Bruyère, S. (2014). *Research brief: Absence and disability management practices for an aging workforce.* Presented on behalf of the Cornell University Employment and Disability Institute and the Disability Management Employer Coalition at the State of the Science Conference, October 22–23, 2013, Washington, DC. Retrieved February 22, 2018, from https://digitalcommons.ilr.cornell.edu/cgi/viewcontent.cgi?referer=https://www.bing.com/&httpsredir=1&article=1329&context=edicollect

Chapter 4

Strengths and Weaknesses of Regulatory Systems Designed to Prevent Work Disability After Injury or Illness

An Overview of Mechanisms in a Selection of Canadian Compensation Systems

Katherine Lippel

In Canada, fewer than half (47%) of 15-to-64-year-olds with disabilities reported they were employed in 2012, compared with 74% of those not reporting disability in that age group (Statistics Canada, 2017a). Although Statistics Canada is currently revising its methodology to measure disability in light of international discussions on the UN Convention on the Rights of Persons with Disabilities, regardless of the measurement tools applied almost 25% of Canadians aged 15 or over report a disability (Statistics Canada, 2017b), so the access to employment of these Canadians is clearly a key policy issue.

The Organisation for Economic Co-operation and Development (OECD) has published numerous studies ranking programs for supporting disabled workers in different countries around the world, including Canada (OECD, 2010). However, their study overlooks most disability support systems, including workers' compensation (WC), as they fall under provincial jurisdiction, despite Canadian WC programs being the providers of disability insurance with the highest payouts. Although the Canada Pension Plan paid out CAN$4.2 billion [US$3.4 billion] to disabled workers and their children in the year 2014–2015 (Government of Canada, 2015), in 2014 benefits paid to workers who were injured or diseased because of their work, and their survivors, on behalf of assessable employers by Canadian workers' compensation boards (WCBs), came to CAN$8.6 billion [US$7.1 billion] (Association of Workers' Compensation Boards of Canada, 2017). Like WC, disability policies fall, for the most part, under provincial jurisdiction, and there are 13 territories and provinces in Canada, each with their own regulatory frameworks, in addition to the federal government.

The Canadian Constitution divides legislative powers between the federal and provincial parliamentary authorities, and each is sovereign within its respective jurisdiction. Under federal-provincial agreements, there is universal access to healthcare everywhere in Canada, regardless of the cause of the illness or injury. However, Employment Insurance (EI), the only short-term publicly managed sickness insurance, is federally regulated and accessible only to those who have sufficiently contributed through employment. EI replaces only 50% of maximum insurable earnings for those who are eligible and only for 15 weeks in cases of absence for health reasons. The Canada/Quebec pension plans provide disability benefits to those who are "incapable regularly of pursuing any substantially gainful occupation," which is the official criterion for eligibility as defined in s. 42(2) of the Canada Pension Plan Act, R.S.C. 1985, c C-8. The maximum monthly benefit is low, set at CAN$1,313.66 [US$1078.13] in 2017 (Government of Canada, 2017). If these sources of income replacement are inaccessible, each province has some form of income support that is available to claimants as a last resort. These programs are means-tested based on family income and provide a very low level of support. There are, however, various cause-based compensation systems: workers' compensation exists in all provinces and territories, replacing employer liability for damages with a no-fault system, and no-fault compensation for motor-vehicle accidents exists in a few provinces. No two provincial systems are identical, although the workers' compensation systems are similarly structured (Lippel, 2012).

For those whose disability is not attributable to a specific cause, state support is uneven, often means-tested, and inadequate. The impact of this fragmented support on the social inclusion, health, and well-being of people with disabilities has been documented in Quebec (Fougeyrollas et al., 2008) and elsewhere in Canada.[1] This chapter will not explore these programs, and thus the findings in this chapter cannot be generalized to work disability prevention mechanisms available to those with disabilities who are not targeted by the programs discussed.

This chapter focuses on the design of regulatory systems for compensation related to injury in two Canadian provinces in order to shed light on the importance of system design to the experience of the person who is injured or ill. It also seeks to show that, in countries such as Canada that do not have universal disability insurance systems regardless of cause, an injury can generate very different return-to-work supports and experiences, depending not on the nature of the injury but on its cause. This, in turn, determines the extent to which an injury or illness can lead to work disability.

Clay, Berecki-Gisolf, and Collie (2014), in a systematic review of the scientific literature on return to work, concluded that there was a dearth of information on the regulatory and sociopolitical contexts in which studies on return to work were rooted. As a result, studies that seek to measure the effectiveness of specific interventions to reduce work disability fail to take into consideration key factors that will affect the outcomes of the interventions. They may misunderstand the role of key players, such as doctors, in the system studied (Lippel, 2008b), or they may misunderstand economic incentives affecting employers and workers—incentives that vary extensively between jurisdictions and, as we shall see, within jurisdictions.

In previous studies, we have shown that the nature of a benefit system, be it based on specific causes of injury or universally accessible, affects the experiences of workers and the extent to which return-to-work supports are made available to them (Lippel & Lötters, 2013). We have also documented the impact of compensation systems on the experience of health professionals, showing that differences between two workers' compensation systems in Canada shape the experience of healthcare providers and, by extension, the experience of injured workers (Lippel, Eakin, Holness, & Howse, 2016). System design influences the environment in which the injured or disabled individual attempts to return to his or her preinjury employment or to re-enter the labor market. Aside from the compensation system itself, it is also necessary to consider other regulatory protections relating to job security, discrimination, and other social security systems, including healthcare systems. Together, these protections may, or may not, provide a universal safety net for people experiencing short- or long-term work disability.

A first basic question is whether the injured person, given the circumstances that produced the injury and the nature of that injury, is eligible for benefits under a wage-replacement system, as opposed to a system of last resort. The latter is a means-tested system that usually evaluates the family's resources rather than those of the individual who is injured or ill. If he or she is eligible, it then becomes important to examine the specific rules of the wage-replacement system: What level of benefits are available and for how long? What vocational-rehabilitation services are available, and to whom and by whom are they offered? Who comes to the table in the return-to-work process? Is the employer a party to the compensation process? Can the employer dispute eligibility for benefits? What incentives, either positive (carrots) or negative (sticks) apply to the injured worker or to the employer, and how are these incentives applied to different categories of workers?

This chapter relies on classic legal methodology analyzing legislation and policy, as interpreted by administrative tribunals in two Canadian provinces. The legal rules are then applied to five case studies designed to tease out similarities and differences in the application of compensation systems, a method often applied to studies of comparative regulation (Bradshaw & Finch, 2002). The similarities and differences in outcomes depend on the factual situation leading to the injury or illness, the sociodemographic characteristics of the individual claimant, and the province in which the injury or illness occurs. The illustrative composite cases are detailed in the box below.

Case Studies

Marie

Marie was injured when she was hit by a car while on her bicycle. She was 15 years old and in Grade 10 at the time and hoped to study engineering in college.

As a result of the accident, she is paraplegic and uses a wheelchair for mobility. Marie lost a year of schooling but can return to an accessible school at the age of 16 if she is provided with the necessary support. She still hopes to work in the field of engineering. At the time of her injury, she was working part-time doing deliveries for a grocery store, earning $60 per week.

Omar

Omar arrived in Canada in 2016 as a landed immigrant, selected because of his ability to speak English and French and his education level. He is single. He was a surgeon in his home country and had practiced medicine for 10 years. His qualifications were not recognized when he arrived in Canada and he eventually found a manual-labor job. He works for a temporary employment agency that offers him, on average, enough work to earn $120 per week at minimum wage. Omar's hands were seriously burned in a car accident, and he will never be able to return to his profession as a surgeon; nor will he be able to do any heavy lifting or repetitive manual labor.

Marc

Marc was working as a traveling salesman earning $80,000 per year when he was injured. A car accident left him with back problems that prevent him from driving long distances. He was 55 at the time of the accident and an employee of a major producer of agricultural products. He had no dependents at the time of the accident. Marc will be able to occupy a desk job when he recovers but will no longer be able to work on the road.

Joanne

Joanne, 35, was working as a home-care nurse and earning $49,000 per year when she was sexually assaulted on the street near her last client's house. She was heading home at the end of her shift. The assault left her with chronic major depression and agoraphobia.

Stephanie

Stephanie works in a factory where she has been harassed and bullied by her supervisor and her colleagues for over a year. At first, the mistreatment was barely perceptible. However, it escalated over time and, in her final weeks at the factory, she was no longer capable of working because she had become chronically depressed. She is being treated by a psychiatrist who confirms that she is unable to work because of the bullying and harassment that occurred in her workplace.

These case studies were chosen to tease out specific demographic and employment characteristics and specific categories of health problems:

- visible (Marie and Omar) versus invisible injuries (Marc, Joanne, and Stephanie);
- physical (Marie, Omar, and Marc) versus psychological injuries (Joanne and Stephanie); and
- injury sustained during standard employment (Marc, Joanne, and Stephanie, who all worked full-time under an indeterminate contract at the time of their accidents) versus injury sustained by a full-time student working part time (Marie) or a precarious employee of a temp agency (Omar).

The people in the case studies vary in age from 15 to 55.

This chapter is also informed by interviews that took place in 2016 and 2017 with nine key informants, specialized in the application of workers' compensation legislation in their respective jurisdictions.[2]

For each of the five cases, we compared what compensation and rehabilitation programs Marie, Omar, Marc, Joanne, and Stephanie would receive if they lived in Quebec and were injured either at work, in a non-work related motor-vehicle accident, or as a result of the commission of a crime, when applicable. We also compared the outcomes of those injured at work in Quebec and in Ontario. These two Canadian provinces have different coverage and regimes. Quebec has a public, no-fault, wage-replacement compensation system for work-related injuries and disease, motor-vehicle accidents, and crime victims. Ontario has a public workers' compensation system but does not have public, no-fault, wage-replacement systems for victims of motor vehicle accidents or crime. Our Quebec portrait thus applies three regulatory regimes (work, motor-vehicle, and crime compensation) to our five case studies, while our Ontario portrait is based solely on the workers' compensation system.

Access to Compensation and Return-To-Work Support in Quebec: Overview of Regulatory Protections

In Table 4.1, we provide an overview of the three compensation regimes applicable in Quebec. Although the level of benefits is comparable across the three regimes (90% of net earnings), there are minimum benefit levels (floor benefit) for those injured at work, and the duration of benefits and the calculation of benefits differ depending on the regime. Those injured at work are provided with wage replacement until they are judged capable of returning to preinjury employment. If they cannot return to their previous job, the injured worker will be provided with a rehabilitation

Table 4.1 Quebec compensation systems for work disability, 2017

		Cause of injury/illness		
		Work-related[a]	Not work-related Motor-vehicle injury[b]	Crime-related injury[c]
Nature of benefits	Short-term benefits	90% of net earnings Floor = minimum wage × 40 hours = $23,463.20 Maximum insurable earnings: $72,500 Students: $104/week (minimum wage for 40 hours, as of age 18)	90% of net earnings Students receive special benefits Precariously employed: 90% of net earnings No floor for first 6 months	90% of net earnings Floor = 90% of minimum wage[d]
	Duration	Until deemed able to earn preinjury earnings Benefits reduced at age 65, cease at age 68	Until deemed able to earn preinjury earnings Benefits reduced at age 65, cease at age 68	Temporary disability
	Permanent impairment	Lump sum payment, based on % of impairment and age Maximum: $106,513 for 100% impairment and 18-year-old worker[e]	Lump sum payment, based on % of impairment Maximum: $242,311	90% of net income X% of permanent impairment Lifetime pension (indexed)

(continued)

Table 4.1 (continued)

		Cause of injury/illness		
		Work-related[a]	Not work-related	
			Motor-vehicle injury[b]	Crime-related injury[c]
Process of return to work	Modified work	If employer chooses to offer suitable modified work approved by physician, worker must accept or appeal	No	No
	Rehabilitation	Physical, social, and vocational rehabilitation is a right if functional limitations or permanent impairment	At discretion of compensation authority	At discretion of compensation authority
	Players	Employers and compensation authority	Compensation authority	Compensation authority
	Right to return to work	1 year or 2 years, depending on firm size	Workers cannot be fired for illness during first 26 weeks in a 12-month period, unless the employer can show just cause for terminating the contract given the consequences of the injury[f]	104 weeks of authorized absence[g]

Note. [a]Quebec, Industrial Accidents and Occupational Disease Act, CQLR c. A-3.001. [b]Quebec, Automobile Insurance Act, CQLR c. A-25. [c]Quebec, Crime Victims Compensation Act, CQLR, c. I-6. [d]//www.ivac.qc.ca/IND_inctotale.asp (retrieved July 14, 2017). [e]www.csst.qc.ca/employeurs/accidents-maladies-lesions/indemnites/Pages/prejudice-corporel.aspx. [f]Quebec, Labour Standards Act, CQLR c. N-1.1, s. 79.1. [g]Quebec, Labour Standards Act, CQLR c. N-1.1, s. 79.1.

program and when it is completed they will be deemed to be capable of earning the salary associated with the "suitable employment" targeted by the rehabilitation program. Twelve months after, they will see their benefits reduced by the amount they are deemed capable of earning, regardless of whether they are actually working or earning that amount. The residual benefit is re-evaluated every five years for the purpose of reducing the benefit (it cannot be increased). Those with a high residual loss have a financial incentive to work, as their work income will not affect their residual benefit unless they surpass the preinjury earnings, which are indexed to the cost of living. The application of these rules is illustrated in Table 4.3.

Workers have a right to rehabilitation if they have functional limitations or permanent impairment resulting from work-related injury or disease. The quality of the rehabilitation program, whether or not they receive training, the nature of that training, and the quality of support provided will vary depending on the gap between their preinjury earnings and their residual earning ability. The greater the gap, the better the rehabilitation program, as a dominant objective of the compensation board is to reduce the level of benefits payable to the worker after the rehabilitation program, and the law favors the most cost-effective solution. Thus, a worker who is a high earner at the time of injury and who will subsequently only be able to earn minimum wage without rehabilitation support, will be entitled to greater rehabilitation investment than a worker earning minimum wage at the time of injury. For minimum wage earners at the time of injury, any residual working ability will allow the compensation board to conclude there is no long-term wage loss. Employers have the right, but no obligation, to propose modified work for an injured worker, but it is the worker's physician who decides whether the proposed work meets the legal criteria including the requirement that the work benefits the worker's rehabilitation. There is an important economic incentive for employers to offer modified work, because the experience-rating system in Quebec is the most reactive in Canada. Large employers may see a fourfold increase in their future premiums for every dollar spent on an injured worker, be it for benefits, healthcare or rehabilitation services.

In contrast, those injured in motor-vehicle accidents have no minimum benefits. For the first six months after injury, their benefits will be based on 90% of net actual earnings, although students and caregivers do have immediate access to benefits even if they are not earning at the time of the accident. Victims of crime do have a minimum benefit as well as the right to a lifetime pension based on preinjury earnings, regardless of whether they return to work. Employers are not involved in either of these compensation systems, although there is a possibility that claimants may be offered rehabilitation at the discretion of the compensation board.

Table 4.2 Workers' compensation rights in Quebec and Ontario

	Short-term benefits[a]	Duration	Modified work	Rehabilitation[b]	Players	Right to return to work
Quebec All injuries or illnesses arising out of or in the course of employment are covered	90% of net earnings Minimum wage X 40 hours = floor benefit Maximum insurable earnings: $72,500 Students receive $104/week (minimum wage for 40 hours as of age 18)	Until deemed able to earn preinjury earnings Benefits reduced at age 65, cease at age 68	If employer chooses to offer suitable modified work that is approved by treating physician, worker must accept or appeal	Physical, social, and vocational rehabilitation is a right if functional limitations or permanent impairment	Employers and compensation authority	1 or 2 years, depending on firm size (more than 20: 2 years)[c] No other duty to accommodate prior to February 2018
Ontario Chronic stress excluded from compensation between 1999 and 2017	85% net No floor benefit Maximum insurable earnings: $88,500	Until deemed able to earn preinjury earnings or age 65[d]	Both worker and employer must cooperate. Appropriate modified work must be offered and accepted.	Yes	Employers and compensation authority	None in small firms of fewer than 20 employees. One year for larger firms.[e] Duty to accommodate

Note. [a]Information drawn from legislation or from the Association of Workers' Compensation Boards of Canada (AWCBC), http://awcbc.org/wp-content/uploads/2013/12/Maximum_Earnings_and_Methods_of_Adjustment.pdf. [b]Information drawn from legislation or from AWCBC. [c]Quebec, Industrial Accidents and Occupational Disease Act CQLR c. A-3.001, ss. 235 and 251. [d]Ontario, Workplace Safety and Insurance Act, 1997, S.O. 1997, c. 16, s. 43. [e]Ontario, Workplace Safety and Insurance Act, 1997, S.O. 1997, c. 16, s. 41.

Application to Case Studies in Quebec

Workers' Compensation

In Quebec, Marie, Omar, and Marc will have coverage for their injuries, irrespective of whether their car accidents occurred while performing work-related activities. If they were performing work-related activities, they have no choice but to apply for workers' compensation. They cannot file for compensation under the other regimes if their accidents arise out of or in the course of employment. Joanne and Stephanie will have access to workers' compensation if the assault or the harassment is found to have arisen out of or in the course of employment. In the five cases, if coverage under workers' compensation is available, the workers will have access to wage replacement and lump-sum, permanent disability benefits. Support for return to work will be made available if the claimants incur a permanent impairment or functional limitations that prevent them from doing their jobs at the time of injury. They have a right to return to work, if they are capable of doing the same job, for 12 months if they work for a firm with fewer than 20 employees or for 2 years if the firm is larger. However, unlike the situation in Ontario, the Charter of Human Rights and Freedoms provisions regarding the duty to accommodate disabled workers did not clearly apply to workers covered by workers' compensation, although they do apply to all others with disabilities that are not recognized as compensable work injuries. This issue was settled by the Supreme Court of Canada in February 2018, and the Court confirmed that the duty to accommodate disabled workers applies to all situations, regardless of the cause of disability.[3]

Cost-benefit analyses dictate the quality of the rehabilitation plan and the return-to-work support provided by the Quebec compensation board. Omar is likely to receive minimum support, as his earning capacity was undervalued at the time of his injury, so that the board need only assist him to earn the equivalent of full-time work at minimum wage. As we shall see, in Ontario the incentive to rehabilitate Omar is even lower, as there is no minimum weekly benefit.

Workers like Marc, who are high earners, lose quite a bit under the workers' compensation regime in Quebec, so Marc would have an economic incentive to accept modified work, if it is offered by his employer. However, if his doctor refuses to authorize modified work, he is not obliged to accept the work proposed.

Compensation for Victims of Car Accidents or Crime

If the accidents incurred by Marie, Omar, and Marc were not related to work, they will all have coverage under Quebec's public automobile insurance program. Since Marie is under 16 and a student, she will receive CAN$5,500 [US$4,514] for every school year missed (Québec Automobile Insurance Act, henceforth AIA, s. 36), in addition to 90% of her net salary (AIA, s. 37). When she resumes her studies, she will continue to receive her wage replacement. If she is forced to leave school because of her injury, her new income-replacement rate will be based on 90% of the average weekly earnings of the Industrial Composite in Quebec, as established by Statistics Canada (AIA, s 32(2)). This means that she will be presumed to have a much higher earning capacity than her actual earnings at the time of the injury. This system provides an important economic incentive for the Quebec Automobile Insurance Corporation[4] (SAAQ), the public, not-for-profit automobile insurer, to invest in her rehabilitation, and it is likely the insurer will support her throughout her studies if she passes her courses. She may even be funded for advanced postsecondary education if she is judged to require high level skills because of her disability. She will also have access to physical rehabilitation, as she would have had if her accident had been work-related. This will include home modifications and other supports that are not available to those disabled from birth, for example (Lippel, 2005). Omar will not be so lucky. For the first six months, his benefits will equal about CAN$103 [US$85] per week, representing 90% of his actual earnings after taxes. After six months, his income replacement will be based on equivalent full-time earnings for a job he is deemed to have been capable of holding at the time of the injury. However, nothing in the law requires him to be considered capable of earning more than his hourly wage at the time of injury. He will quickly be deemed to again be able to earn minimum wage, so the SAAQ has no economic incentive to invest in his rehabilitation, even though the injury made it impossible for Omar to resume his medical career, or even resume his manual employment. Marc, on the other hand, had a high income at the time of his injury, earning more than the maximum insurable earnings. If he does not return to work, he will receive full wage replacement benefits for three years, after which he will receive wage replacement equal to the difference between his previous earnings and the earnings of the desk job that he will be deemed capable of performing. Because of his age (55), payment of the wage loss will have a limited impact on the SAAQ, as benefits cease when he turns 68.

If Joanne's sexual assault is not considered to have arisen out of or in the course of employment,[5] she will have the right to benefits under the Quebec Crime Victims' Compensation Act. These include payment of temporary benefits, and a lifetime pension based on preinjury earnings and the level of permanent impairment. This pension is payable regardless of whether she returns to work, and she can keep both the pension and her salary if she does return to work, an important economic incentive to return. While employers are not actively involved in the crime victims' compensation process, human rights legislation provides that employers have a duty to accommodate people with physical or psychological disabilities. In addition, the Quebec Labour Standards Act gives crime victims who are seriously injured the right to be absent from work for up to 104 weeks without reprisal.

However, harassment is not included in the crime-victims' compensation regime, so Stephanie would not have the right to benefits, should her workers' compensation claim be denied for whatever reason. Without coverage, she would have no access to paid psychological care beyond the very limited services provided in the public healthcare system and no wage replacement beyond the 15 weeks of employment insurance at 50% of her salary, available to those who have sufficiently contributed to the EI program. After the 15 weeks of employment insurance benefits, she would be eligible for social assistance if her family income and property value were sufficiently low. No formal support for return to work would be provided.

Access to Compensation and Return to Work after Work Injury: Comparing Quebec and Ontario

An overview of rights and obligations under workers' compensation in Quebec and Ontario is provided in Table 4.2. When these rights and obligations are applied to the case studies, we find that everyone except Stephanie will theoretically have coverage in Ontario. In Ontario, coverage for chronic stress was recognized only in 2017, despite several appeal-tribunal decisions declaring the exclusion to be unconstitutional.[6] Benefits would be lower in Ontario than in Quebec for everyone, as the wage-replacement level is only 85% of net income. There are no minimum benefits in Ontario, so Omar will be compensated on the basis of 85% of his real salary at the time of the injury (see Table 4.3), which may be adjusted in the long term and possibly lowered. This would also determine the investment that will be made in his rehabilitation. Because Mary was a student at the time of the accident, her average earnings will be recalculated, using the average earnings of a worker employed in a job in which Mary would likely be employed or the average industrial wage for the year in which her work injury occurred (Workplace Safety and Insurance Board [WSIB], 2013). Policy also addresses the determination of her rehabilitation (work reintegration) program, as there are special, more favorable, rules that apply to workers aged 15 to 24 (WSIB, 2012). So, unlike Omar, in Ontario Mary's deemed earning potential will likely significantly exceed her earnings at the time of her injury. For Marc, because his salary is less than the maximum insurable earnings, he would not be penalized as a high earner in Ontario, unlike in Quebec.

Contrary to Quebec, Ontario employers of all workers covered under the Workplace Safety and Insurance Act (WSIA) have a legal requirement to cooperate in the return-to-work process or else subject themselves to penalties, specified in Section 40 of the WSIA. They are obliged to offer modified work.

Table 4.3 Determination of benefits (in CAN$) after work injury for low earner and high earner

	Quebec	Ontario
Omar		
Presumed gross earnings, 2017 **Single, no dependents**	$23,463.20[a] (Quebec minimum support = full-time minimum wage)	$6,240 (Ontario has no minimum support. This is the amount of actual wages earned.)
Benefits	90% net = $17,878.86[b]	100% net = $6,002.36[c]
"Suitable employment": **In Quebec, a full-time sedentary job could pay at least minimum wage = deemed earnings** **In Ontario, a full- or part-time[d] sedentary job could pay at least minimum wage = deemed earnings**	$23,000.00 gross or $19,539.60 net[e]	Minimum wage of $11.60/hour. If he is deemed able to work 15 hours/week, he is deemed able to earn $9,048.00
Postinjury wage loss after maximum medical recovery, if suitable employment possible without retraining	$0. He will be deemed able to perform an unskilled minimum-wage job full-time, and 100% of deemed net earnings will be subtracted from his benefits.	$0. He will be deemed able to perform an unskilled minimum-wage job part-time or full-time, depending on his situation at the time of the injury.
Benefits payable during search for suitable employment	$17,878.86 for 12-month search, starting after rehabilitation	None guaranteed
Marc		
Presumed gross earnings, 2017 **Single, no dependents**	$72,500 (Quebec has a lower ceiling on wages than Ontario)	$80,000
Full benefits	$45,182.01 (90% of net as per regulation[b])	$80,000 gross = $60,166 NAE 85% NAE = $51,141[f]
"Suitable employment": **Full-time sedentary job using skills = deemed net earnings**	$44,897.97[e]	$45,000 NAE

Postinjury wage loss after maximum medical recovery, if suitable employment possible without retraining	$284.04[g]	85% of the difference between NAE before ($60,166) and after ($45,000) 85% of $15,166 = $12,891[f]
Benefits payable during job search to find suitable employment	$45,182.01 for 12-month search, starting after rehabilitation to do suitable employment[g]	none guaranteed

Note. Omar's average preinjury earnings are $120/week = $6,240/year. Marc's average preinjury earnings are $1,538/week = $80,000/year.[a]Quebec, Industrial Accidents and Occupational Disease Act, CQLR c. A-3.001, ss. 6 and 65, www.csst.qc.ca/employeurs/accidents-maladies-lesions/indemnites/Pages/remplacement-revenu.aspx. [b]Regulation respecting the table of income replacement indemnities payable under the Act respecting industrial accidents and occupational diseases and of indemnities payable under the Workers' Compensation Act for 2017, CQLR c. A-3001, r. 15 (2017). [c]Exceptionally, Ontario allows for loss of earnings benefits up to 100% of net average earnings for those earning less than $15,312.51 in 2017. Sources: Workplace Safety and Insurance Act, 1997, s. 43(2); Workplace Safety and Insurance Board (2013).[d]Workplace Safety and Insurance Board (2012). [e]Regulation respecting the table of gross annual income from suitable employment for 2017, CQLR c. A-3.001, r.16 (2017), www.canlii.org/en/qc/laws/regu/cqlr-c-a-3.001-r-16-2017/latest/cqlr-c-a-3.001-r-16–2017.html; Quebec, Industrial Accidents and Occupational Disease Act, CQLR c. A-3.001, s. 50. [f]Workplace Safety and Insurance Board (2011); WSIB net average earnings (NAE) calculator. [g]Quebec, Industrial Accidents and Occupational Disease Act, CQLR c. A-3.001, s. 49.

Workers who fail to accept that work, for reasons not approved by the Workplace Safety and Insurance Board (WSIB), will be penalized and may see their benefits terminated. Also, the opinion of their healthcare professional about the acceptability of modified work is not binding on the WSIB, contrary to the situation in Quebec (Lippel et al., 2016). Despite the penalties provided for in the legislation, in our interviews, two key informants with much experience in representing Ontario employers and workers, respectively, told us that they had never seen a case in which an employer was actually sanctioned for failing to cooperate. However, experience-rating rules in Ontario provide economic incentives to employers to offer workers modified work (MacEachen et al., 2012). In Ontario, employers have always had a legal duty to accommodate workers with disabilities, unlike the situation in Quebec, where the obligation has applied only since February 2018. Although Ontario employers have the right to dispute workers' compensation claims, they are far less likely to do so than their Quebec counterparts (Lippel et al., 2016).

Discussion

Our results clearly demonstrate that, in Canada, access to support in preventing work disability depends on both the cause of the injury or illness and the geographic location in which it occurs. First we discuss the systems in Quebec and then we turn to a comparison of workers' compensation in Quebec and Ontario.

The cause of a worker's disability is a key factor in determining the supports available and the incentives provided to encourage return to work. In Quebec, where three public compensation systems provide benefits based on previous earnings, the return-to-work process in each is very different. Employers are not active participants in compensation for motor-vehicle accidents or crime, and the compensation boards do not have leverage to force employers to take a claimant back under those systems. Yet participation of the employer and other stakeholders in the return-to-work process is key to successful reintegration (Loisel & Côté, 2013).

Although the duty to accommodate employees who are injured outside work applies under human-rights legislation in Quebec, it is a complaint-based system and its application does not fall within the powers of the boards managing disability insurance. On the other hand, if a claimant is injured at work, until the Supreme Court ruling of February 2018 in the Caron case, the employer's duty to accommodate the worker's disability up to the point of undue hardship was not applied by the Quebec workers' compensation board (CNESST).[7] The employer has, in workers' compensation cases, a huge economic incentive to provide modified work to the worker as early as possible because experience-rating rules, especially in the case of large employers, can impact future premiums by up to four times the cost of the injury compensation (Lafond, Lussier, & Mercier, 2008). However, until 2018 the employer had no legal obligation to offer modified work or to create suitable employment under the workers' compensation system in Quebec.

Workers are the subjects of economic incentives to return to work in all three Quebec systems. Under workers' compensation, failure to accept modified work that is approved by the worker's doctor will lead to a suspension of benefits. Those injured at or by work have the *right* to rehabilitation services if they have functional limitations or impairments that prevent return to the job they were performing at the time of injury. Access to such services for victims of motor-vehicle accidents or crimes is at the *discretion* of the compensation board. Incentives for workers to return to work are associated with the deeming process,[8] applied as part of the rehabilitation program for those injured at work and after three years of benefits for victims of motor-vehicle accidents. Deeming is particularly unfair to people like Omar who earn less than their real earning capacity at the time of their injury. In Quebec, the automobile-accident-compensation system acknowledges that young workers who are injured while in school are not yet at their true earning capacity, and it presumes they could have earned the average industrial earnings. This favorably affects their benefits and the quality of the rehabilitation provided, as its goal is to enable them to sustain employment generating the average industrial earnings, not minimum wage. However, no such provision exists for people underemployed for reasons other than age, such as newcomers to Canada who are limited in their access to the labor market because of language skills, lack of Canadian experience, or simply discrimination (Côté, 2014; Dubé & Gravel, 2014; Premji & Shakya, 2017).

The deeming process linked to workers' compensation rehabilitation programs was critiqued in a recent report examining the workers' compensation system in Alberta. The review panel stated:

> Equally important is the need to flip the process around so that the deeming of earnings is a by-product of the [rehabilitation] process, rather than a driver of the process. Right now, the deeming process appears to be premised on targeting a certain level of earnings for the worker and then identifying a job profile that achieves this level. Instead, the deeming process should be premised on identifying an occupation that realistically exists in Alberta's labour market and for which the worker would be suited given an assessment of their training, experience and capabilities. Once a suitable occupation has been identified, the income that could realistically be earned from that occupation should be assessed and used to adjust the worker's benefits.
> (Alberta Workers' Compensation Board Review Panel, 2017, p. 77)

This criticism applies in many respects to practices in Quebec and Ontario, whereby the goal of a deemed earning ability appears to eclipse the more tangible goal of returning the worker to employment.

Although the deeming process is not applied to victims of crime, this is not to say crime victims have no incentive to return to work. They have a pension that will not be affected by subsequent earnings, thus making work an attractive option if they are capable of working. The same holds true for those injured at work who are provided with a residual pension due to ongoing wage loss attributable to their injury. Thus, they can earn up to their preinjury earnings without affecting their wage replacement. This carrot approach encourages claimants to seek work to supplement their pensions. This contrasts with the stick approach where workers are penalized if they do not accept modified work. In Quebec, employers are less likely to be encouraged to rehire car-accident or crime victims than workers sustaining work injuries. However, return to work remains a priority in all three systems. This is not necessarily the case in the other provinces, where no public wage-replacement system exists for victims of crime or motor-vehicle accidents.

Now, we compare the Quebec and Ontario workers' compensation systems. Workers with mental health problems, particularly those related to chronic stress, have experienced unequal access to coverage in Canada for decades (Lippel & Sikka, 2010), with Quebec but not Ontario (prior to 2018) providing coverage. Young workers who are earning less than minimum wage will have their earning capacity re-evaluated in Ontario but not in Quebec.

Quebec, however, is the only province to guarantee wage replacement based on minimum wage for full-time work, regardless of the hours or earnings of the worker at the time of injury. This guarantee benefits not only young workers but also precariously employed people like Omar, who have the right to benefits until they reach the ability to earn minimum wage for a 40-hour week. In Ontario, as soon as Omar is deemed capable of earning CAN$120 [US$98] a week, he will lose his wage replacement. Therefore, there is little incentive for the WSIB to retrain him and little incentive for his employer to rehire him. His workers' compensation benefits will not cost much, and his employer's experience-rated insurance premiums will not likely increase, reducing the likelihood that Omar's employer will have an economic incentive to take him back. The stick approach is used in Ontario to encourage employers and workers to cooperate with the return-to-work process. The stick approach has been found in many studies to lead to inappropriate practices that include returning workers to demeaning or meaningless tasks for as long as necessary to avoid sanction by compensation systems (Eakin, 2005; MacEachen, Kosny, Ferrier, & Chambers, 2010; MacEachen et al., 2011). Experience-rating incentives can lead to similar abusive return-to-work practices (Lippel, 2008a) and can drive legal disputes that reduce the possibility of sustainable work return. The disability-management process itself, when controlled by compensation boards using coercive incentives to obtain employer cooperation, has also been found to lead to alienating experiences whereby workers feel like objects with price tags, rather than active players in the process (Lippel, 2007; Roberts-Yates, 2003).

The design of a system determines the stakeholders who come to the table. When employers are not involved, this can reduce the contentious nature of the process, as there is no economic incentive for an employer to contest a claim. On the other hand, if neither carrots nor sticks are applied to the preinjury employer by the compensation system, then, in the absence of protections in collective agreements or labor standards, there is no reason for the employer to actively participate in the return-to-work process. This lack of participation makes rehabilitation interventions less effective (Loisel & Côté, 2013).

One final point relates to the stigmatization of injured workers in the return-to-work process. This has been well documented in the literature (Francis, Cameron, Kelloway, Catano, & Day, 2014) and linked by some to the coercive mechanisms that force employers to bring workers back before they are fully capable of doing the job. This can lead to resentment and sometimes an increased burden on colleagues. Returning workers to meaningless tasks can also lead to stigmatization by coworkers (Lippel, 2008a).

Conclusion

Clearly, the landscape of regulatory protection driving support for people with disabilities is hugely fragmented in Canada, both by reason of the dichotomy of federal and provincial jurisdictions, which allow 14 different workers' compensation systems to operate, and because of the political economy of compensation. Compensation and rehabilitation supports vary depending on the cause of a disability in Canada. Those injured by crime, motor vehicles or work have more protections, at least in some provinces, than those who are disabled at birth or by disease. Industry accepts their role of funding workers' compensation because the system protects employers from economic liability for its workers, who may not sue the employer regardless of their negligence. However, there is less appetite in Canada for a universal disability system funded by employers, or by all taxpayers, in a context in which deregulation and diminished state intervention is the dominant discourse. There is a certain irony in the fact that Canadians are so proud of their universal healthcare system, a product of the 1960s and 1970s, yet are less compelled to entertain a universal disability system. In contrast, New Zealanders, who are no strangers to neoliberal policies, are nonetheless staunchly proud of their universal accident-compensation system introduced in the early 1970s (see Duncan, this volume). This suggests that familiarity with a good system allows for its survival even in neoliberal times, when social innovation is no longer entertained without a compelling business case and is resisted by private insurers and employers.

In an ideal world, a universal disability system would provide support for all people with disabilities regardless of their cause, and would engage all employers, healthcare providers, unions, workers, and insurance systems in a supportive and positive return-to-work process, while guaranteeing disability benefits to allow an adequate standard of living for people with disabilities and to avoid destitution attributable to work disability. Elsewhere, we have described such a system (Lippel, 2012); however, it is unlikely that the political will to provide universal access to wage replacement linked to preinjury earnings and rehabilitation support for workers with disabilities, or to provide guaranteed annual income to those who have never worked, would be politically acceptable in the current Canadian political climate. There is the danger that a harmonization process could reduce the quality of the best systems, such as the Quebec workers' compensation system, and provide minimal support to all. Such a proposal could further divide communities of people with disabilities, unless those eligible for no-fault compensation (which replaced victims' rights to sue) maintain their coverage (Blais, Gardner, & Lareau, 2005).

Compensation systems should be designed to provide organized institutional support and economic incentives to promote successful and sustainable return to work, and in many cases they achieve these goals and should be applauded. The way each system is designed in light of the realities of different subgroups of people with disabilities, as well as the nature of the practices promoted by the design of each system, are key factors in determining the system's effects on those who are injured, and those who employ them. Disability insurance systems are echo chambers for structural inequalities in the labor market that leave large pockets of workers disproportionately affected by injury and disability, notably the young, those belonging to racialized and ethnic minorities, new migrants to Canada, precariously employed workers, and others who experience income inequities, such as those in predominantly female, service-industry jobs (Cox & Lippel, 2008).

Notes

1 See the various reports available from the Council of Canadians with Disabilities on its website: www.ccdonline.ca/en/socialpolicy/poverty-citizenship/income-security-reform/poverty-reduction-strategies
2 These interviews are part of an ongoing study funded by the Canadian Institutes of Health Research and the Social Sciences and Humanities Research Council (Grant No. 890–2016-3016), *Policy and practice in return to work after work injury for the precariously employed or geographically mobile workforce: A four province study.*
3 Commission des normes, de l'équité de la santé et de la sécurité du travail (the Quebec Workers' Compensation Board or CNESST) v. Caron et al., 2018 SCC 3. In *CNESST v. Caron et al.*, 2015, QCCA 1048, the Quebec Court of Appeal held that the duty to accommodate a person with a disability under the Quebec Charter of Rights and Freedoms (CQLR, c. C-12) applied to injured workers. The court changed its previous position, which had exempted employers from the duty to accommodate injured workers who receive workers' compensation. The CNESST appealed that judgment to the Supreme Court of Canada and lost in February 2018. The duty to accommodate now applies to injured workers in Quebec.
4 Société de l'assurance automobile du Québec.
5 Accidents or incidents occurring at the end of shifts as the worker is returning home fall into a gray zone that may not meet the criteria for coverage under workers' compensation.
6 In 2017, Ontario adopted the Stronger, Healthier Ontario Act (Budget Measures), which includes chronic stress within the purview of the Workplace Safety and Insurance Act. The Act came into force on January 1, 2018. The Stronger, Healthier Ontario Act responded to the Workplace Safety and Insurance Appeals Tribunal decisions 2157/09, 1945/10, and 665/10, which found that the mental stress limitation was unconstitutional.
7 Commission des normes, de l'équité, de la santé et de la sécurité du travail.
8 The deeming process in workers' compensation systems refers to the process by which the compensation board determines suitable jobs for workers, in light of their abilities and limitations. Once workers are judged capable of doing their deemed jobs, potential earnings from that job are subtracted from the benefits, regardless of whether the worker has a job. Systems vary as to the immediacy of the deemed-earnings calculation; for example, Quebec provides 12 months of job-search benefits before deducting the deemed earnings, while Ontario deducts the amount much sooner.

References

Alberta Workers' Compensation Board Review Panel. (2017). *Working together: Report and recommendations of the Alberta Workers' Compensation Board (WCB) Review Panel.* Retrieved September 30, 2017 from www.alberta.ca/assets/documents/WCB-Review-Final-Report.pdf

Association of Workers' Compensation Boards of Canada. (2017). *Detailed key statistical measures report for 2014.* Retrieved from http://awcbc.org/?page_id=9759

Blais, F., Gardner, D., & Lareau, A. (2005). Un système de compensation plus équitable pour les personnes handicapées. *Santé, Société et Solidarité, 2,* 105–114. doi:10.3406/oss.2005.1059

Bradshaw, J., & Finch, N. (2002). *A comparison of child benefit packages in 22 countries.* Norwich, UK: Department for Work and Pensions.

Clay, F. J., Berecki-Gisolf, J., & Collie, A. (2014). How well do we report on compensation systems in studies of return to work: A systematic review. *Journal of Occupational Rehabilitation, 24*(1), 111–124. doi:10.1007/s10926-013-9435-z

Côté, D. (2014). La réadaptation au travail des personnes issues de l'immigration et des minorités ethnoculturelles: Défis, perspectives et pistes de recherche. *Perspectives interdisciplinaires sur le travail et la santé, 16*(2). Retrieved from http://journals.openedition.org/pistes/3633

Cox, R., & Lippel, K. (2008). Falling through the legal cracks: The pitfalls of using workers' compensation data as indicators of work-related injuries and illnesses. *Policy and Practice in Health and Safety, 6*(2), 9–30.

Dubé, J., & Gravel, S. (2014). Les pratiques préventives auprès des travailleurs d'agences de location de personnel temporaire ou permanent: Comparaison entre les travailleurs immigrants et non immigrants. *Perspectives interdisciplinaires sur le travail et la santé, 16*(2). Retrieved from http://journals.openedition.org/pistes/3911

Eakin, J. M. (2005). The discourse of abuse in return to work: A hidden epidemic of suffering. In C. L. Peterson & C. Mayhew (Eds.), *Occupational health and safety: International influences and the "New" Epidemics* (pp. 159–174). Amityville, NY: Baywood Publishing.

Fougeyrollas, P., Beauregard, L., Gaucher, C., & Boucher, N. (2008). Entre la colère... et la rupture du lien social: Des personnes ayant des incapacités témoignent de leur expérience face aux carences de la protection sociale. *Service social, 54*(1), 100–115.

Francis, L., Cameron, J. E., Kelloway, E. K., Catano, V. M., & Day, A. (2014). The working wounded: Stigma and return to work. In P. Y. Chen & C. L. Cooper (Eds.), *Work and wellbeing: A complete reference guide* (Vol. 3, pp. 339–356). Chichester, UK: John Wiley & Sons.

Government of Canada. (2015). *Annual report: Canada Pension Plan 2014–2015.* Retrieved from www.canada.ca/en/employment-social-development/programs/pensions/reports/annual-2015.html

Government of Canada. (2017). *Canada Pension Plan—How much could you receive.* Retrieved from www.canada.ca/en/services/benefits/publicpensions/cpp/cpp-benefit/amount.html

Lafond, R., Lussier, M., & Mercier, G. (2008). *Réduire ses cotisations de la CSST par transferts et partages de coût: Mode d'emploi—Collection Le Corre en bref* (Vol. 5). Cowansville, QC: Éditions Yvon Blais.

Lippel, K. (2005). Does Quebec law recognize collective responsibility for the economic consequences of impairments, disabilities or handicaps? Could it do so? *Human Development, Disability and Social Change, 14*(2–3), 6–19.

Lippel, K. (2007). Workers describe the effect of the workers' compensation process on their health: A Quebec study. *International Journal of Law and Psychiatry, 30*(4–5), 427–443.

Lippel, K. (2008a). 'L'intervention précoce pour éviter la chronicité': Enjeux juridiques. In Barreau du Québec (Ed.), *Développements récents en droit de la santé et sécurité au travail* (Vol. 284, pp. 137–187). Cowansville, QC: Éditions Yvon Blais.

Lippel, K. (2008b). La place des juristes dans la recherche sociale et la place de la recherche sociale en droit: Réflexions sur la «pratique de la recherche» en matière de droit à la santé au travail. In P. Noreau & L. Rolland (Eds.), *Mélanges Andrée Lajoie* (pp. 251–284). Montréal, QC: Éditions Thémis.

Lippel, K. (2012). Preserving workers' dignity in workers' compensation systems: An international perspective. *American Journal of Industrial Medicine, 55*(6), 519–536. doi:10.1002/ajim.22022

Lippel, K., Eakin, J. M., Holness, D. L., & Howse, D. (2016). The structure and process of workers' compensation systems and the role of doctors: A comparison of Ontario and Québec. *American Journal of Industrial Medicine, 59*(12), 1070–1086. doi:10.1002/ajim.22651

Lippel, K., & Lötters, F. (2013). Public insurance systems: A comparison of cause-based and disability-based income support systems. In P. Loisel & J. R. Anema (Eds.), *Handbook of work disability: Prevention and management* (pp. 183–202). New York: Springer Science+Business Media.

Lippel, K., & Sikka, A. (2010). Access to workers' compensation benefits and other legal protections for work-related mental health problems: A Canadian overview. *Canadian Journal of Public Health, 101*(S1), S16–S22.

Loisel, P., & Côté, P. (2013). The work disability paradigm and its public health implications. In P. Loisel & J. R. Anema (Eds.), *Handbook of work disability: Prevention and management* (pp. 59–67): New York: Springer Science+Business Media.

MacEachen, E., Kosny, A., Ferrier, S., & Chambers, L. (2010). The "toxic dose" of system problems: Why some injured workers don't return to work as expected. *Journal of Occupational Rehabilitation, 20*(3), 349–366. doi:10.1007/s10926-010-9229-5

MacEachen, E., Kosny, A., Ferrier, S., Lippel, K., Neilson, C., Franche, R.-L., & Pugliese, D. (2011). The "ability" paradigm in vocational rehabilitation: Challenges in an Ontario injured worker retraining program. *Journal of Occupational Rehabilitation, 20*(4), 1–13. doi:10.1007/s10926-011-9329-x

MacEachen, E., Lippel, K., Saunders, R., Kosny, A., Mansfield, L., Carrasco, C., & Pugliese, D. (2012). Workers' compensation experience-rating rules and the danger to workers' safety in the temporary work agency sector. *Policy and Practice in Health and Safety, 10*(1), 77–95.

Ontario. The Stronger, Healthier Ontario Act (Budget Measures), S.O. 2017, c. 8.

Ontario. Workplace Safety and Insurance Act, S.O. 1997, c. 16, ss. 41, 43.

Organisation for Economic Co-operation and Development. (2010). *Sickness, disability and work: Breaking the barriers—Canada: Opportunities for collaboration*. Paris: OECD.

Premji, S., & Shakya, Y. (2017). Pathways between under/unemployment and health among racialized immigrant women in Toronto. *Ethnicity and Health, 22*(1), 17–35.

Quebec. Automobile Insurance Act, CQLR c. A-25.

Quebec. Crime Victims Compensation Act, CQLR, c. I-6.

Quebec. Industrial Accidents and Occupational Disease Act, CQLR c. A-3.001, ss. 6, 49, 50, 65, 235, 251.

Quebec. Labour Standards Act, CQLR c. N-1.1, s. 79.1.

Quebec. Regulation respecting the table of gross annual income from suitable employments for 2017, CQLR c. A-3.001, r.16 (2017). Retrieved from www.canlii.org/en/qc/laws/regu/cqlr-c-a-3.001-r-16-2017/latest/cqlr-c-a-3.001-r-16-2017.html

Quebec. Regulation respecting the table of income replacement indemnities payable under the Act respecting industrial accidents and occupational diseases and of indemnities payable under the Workers' Compensation Act for 2017, CQLR c. A-3001, r. 15 (2017).

Roberts-Yates, D. C. (2003). The concerns and issues of injured workers in relation to claims/injury management and rehabilitation: The need for new operational frameworks. *Disability & Rehabilitation, 25*(16), 898–907.

Statistics Canada. (2017a). *A profile of persons with disabilities among Canadians aged 15 years or older, 2012.* Retrieved from www.statcan.gc.ca/pub/89-654-x/89-654-x2015001-eng.htm#a4

Statistics Canada. (2017b). Disability statistics: Canadian experience. *Presentation to United Nations Expert Group Meeting on the Guidelines and Principles for the Development of Disability Statistics*, New York, July 12–14, 2017. Retrieved from https://unstats.un.org/unsd/demographic-social/meetings/2017/new-york--disability-egm/Session%204/Canada.pdf

Workplace Safety and Insurance Board. (2011). *WSIB policy manual: Payment and reviewing LOE benefits (prior to final review)* (Document 18-03-02). Toronto, ON: Workplace Safety and Insurance Board.

Workplace Safety and Insurance Board. (2012). *WSIB policy manual: Determining suitable occupation* (Document 19-03-03). Toronto, ON: Workers' Safety and Insurance Board.

Workplace Safety and Insurance Board. (2013). *WSIB policy manual: Determining average earnings—Exceptional cases* (Document 18-02-08). Toronto, ON: Workplace Safety and Insurance Board.

Chapter 5

The Australian Work Disability Patchwork

Genevieve Grant

The estimated cost of work injury and illness to the Australian community exceeds AUS$61 billion [US$46 billion] annually (Safe Work Australia, 2015). Efforts to prevent and manage work disability are concentrated in a network of workers' compensation (WC) schemes, spanning state, territory and federal jurisdictions. These schemes provide compensation in the form of income benefits, medical and treatment expenses, return-to-work support and lump-sum awards. For those with work disability incurred outside WC-eligible employment, a far less generous federal social security system is available. The Australian WC and social security arrangements operate in a broader context of laws, policies, and programs relevant to work disability. These include healthcare, antidiscrimination law, employment law, disability care and support, private income-protection insurance, other injury compensation systems (beyond WC), and common-law damages claims for negligently inflicted injury.

The Australian legal landscape of WC is notoriously varied, with 11 distinct schemes providing benefits to eligible workers among the nation's 12.3 million employees (Australian Bureau of Statistics (ABS), 2017). In recent years, impetus for comparative analysis of scheme performance has grown, with the emergence of large claim-based datasets, harmonization projects, minimum-benchmarking activities, and broader national reviews of disability care and support, discrimination, economic productivity, and competition. A series of inquiries have decried the inequities and inefficiencies of the state of Australian WC, highlighting the disparate levels of coverage, support, and outcomes across subnational jurisdictions and schemes (Howe, 2015; Productivity Commission, 2011; Purse, Meredith & Guthrie, 2007).

This chapter identifies diversity as the hallmark of Australian work disability law and policy and explains the influential role of the legal system's structure in this state of affairs. It begins by setting out relevant economic, industrial, and demographic trends, before providing an account of the characteristics of the legal and political systems that shape the field. The chapter identifies the key elements of the Australian patchwork and explains the resultant challenges of performance measurement, inequity, and access.

In examining the Australian response to the challenge of work disability and reintegration, the chapter adopts a sociolegal approach. It explores the law's sources, organization, and structure, and the differential access and impacts experienced by community members (Cotterell, 2002). This approach is well suited to understanding work disability policy, as it calls attention to the diverse mechanisms used to promote health, prevent chronic disability, and improve workers' quality of life "through the organized efforts of society" (Loisel & Côté, 2013, p. 59). In particular, the approach involves examining the wide range of legal measures used to address work disability in Australia.

Trends Relevant to Work Disability: An Australian Snapshot

The chief demographic and economic trends relevant to work disability include employment and labor-force participation; industrial and economic change; and health, disability, and aging in the community. Australia's employment participation rate (the proportion of people aged 15 and older in the labor force) sits at 65%, with unemployment at 5.6% as of August 2017 (ABS, 2017). From 2007 to 2017, labor-force participation was relatively stable: Although unemployment remained low during the global financial crisis of 2007–2008, it increased slightly from 2011 to 2015, before stabilizing in 2017 (Organisation for Economic Co-operation and Development (OECD), 2017a). The steadiness of these employment indicators is said to reflect the resilience of the Australian labor market (OECD, 2017a).

Still, the benefits of these trends have been received unevenly across the community. Women, young people, indigenous Australians, and people with disability and mental ill-health continue to experience disadvantage in labor-market outcomes (OECD, 2017b). There was little change in the rate of labor-force participation of people with disability aged 15–64 years from 1993 (55%) to 2012 (53%) (ABS, 2015), a period in which the participation rate of people without disability increased from 77% to 83% (ABS, 2015). Importantly, this means the gap in employment levels between people with and without disability has increased in the past 15 years, from 22% to 30% (ABS, 2016). By 2017, Australia ranked behind only the United States among OECD countries in terms of the disability employment gap (OECD, 2017b).

Like other nations, Australia is feeling the effects of globalization, increasing automation, and associated industrial change. Locally, these developments are occurring in conjunction with the continued decline of manufacturing. Flexible forms of employment engagement are now entrenched in the Australian labor market and broader economy (Forsyth, 2016). Digital disruption, the growth of the "gig" economy, and the expansion of precarious work are attracting growing media, policy, and research attention.

Existing legal protections are typically based on a model of the employment relationship that is not present in more insecure forms of work (Stewart & Stanford, 2017). For example, WC systems typically apply to employees, only as understood in a traditional sense. Workers engaged in newer, less secure forms of employment may be excluded from the most prominent work disability prevention and management arrangements (Purse et al., 2007; Quinlan & Mayhew, 1999). Trends in health, disability, and aging in the Australian population also make a significant contribution to the work disability landscape. Chronic disease is the predominant cause of ill-health in Australia, with 50% of the population reporting that they have at least one of eight chronic conditions (arthritis, asthma, back problems, cancer, chronic obstructive pulmonary disease, cardiovascular disease, diabetes, or a mental or behavioral condition) (Australian Institute of Health and Welfare, 2016). After adjusting for population aging, however, the overall burden of disease (measured in Disability Affected Life Years) decreased by 10% from 2003 to 2011 (Australian Institute of Health and Welfare, 2016). The proportion of the population aged 65 or older rose from 13% in 2009 to 15% in 2015, and projections suggest this group will grow to represent 18% to19% of the population in 2031 and 22% to 25% by 2061 (ABS, 2013). The number of Australians living with a disability, defined by the ABS (2016) as "a limitation, restriction or impairment, which has lasted, or is likely to last, for at least six months and restricts everyday activities," has remained stable over the last decade at around one in five (ABS, 2015).

Measured Work Disability in Australia

Evidence of an Australian work disability profile is captured in multiple sources, including WC and social security claims, surveys about work-related injury and illness, and hospital admission and health service utilization data. Each source represents a different dimension of the work disability landscape (Lane, Collie, & Hassani-Mahmooei, 2016; McInnes et al., 2014). For example, comparative analysis of data sources has shown that, for surveillance of work-related injury, emergency department data reflect a greater proportion of injuries sustained by younger workers; whereas, WC claims data better capture musculoskeletal injury (McInnes et al., 2014). The appropriate evidence to focus on depends on the way work disability is understood; for example, with a limited focus on compensable injury or illness sustained in the course of employment, or a more holistic understanding of work disability as a product of a range of societal, community, industrial, and person-level factors. Below we strike a balance by reviewing Australian WC claims trends; survey evidence related to the experience of work-related injury and disease, and the impact of disability on employment; and social security benefit uptake for health-related work incapacity.

Data from Workers' Compensation Claims

Reports from Australia's WC schemes depict a slice of what should be understood as "work-sustained" disability, charting the injuries and illnesses workers incur in the course of their employment and for which compensation has been paid (Lane et al., 2016). Trends in these data include a decline in the number of serious claims (involving a week or more of work absence) but increases in the associated incapacity and costs. Over the period 2000–2001 to 2013–2014, the frequency rate of serious claims declined by 33%, from 9.5 to 6.3 serious claims per million hours worked, but the median time lost increased from 4.2 to 5.6 working weeks (Safe Work Australia, 2017). Although men remained more likely than women to make a serious claim, the gap in the frequency rates by gender fell from 40% to 17% (Safe Work Australia, 2017). The workers' compensation profile has also shifted in terms of the nature of the injury or disease giving rise to claims: over the same period, there was a 15% drop in the number of claims arising from injury and musculoskeletal disorders. Those associated with diseases also fell, by 11%. Mental health disorders were the only major conditions for which serious claims rose (by 1%). In 2013–2014, serious claims arising from mental disorders resulted in a median lost time of 15.4 working weeks, the highest for any condition group, and nearly three times the median time lost for all serious claims (5.6 working weeks).

Survey Evidence of Work Disability and its Employment Impacts

Broader evidence of work-sustained injury and illness comes from self-reports in population-level surveys conducted by the Australian Bureau of Statistics (ABS). In 2013–2014, 4.3% of the 12.5 million people who worked in the previous 12 months (531,800) reported experiencing a work-related injury or illness in that period, and of those 61% reported having some time off work (ABS, 2014). This finding represents a decline: In 2013–2014, 43 out of 1,000 people who had worked in the previous 12 months reported experiencing a work-related injury or illness, compared with 52 per 1,000 people in 2009–2010 (ABS, 2015).

An alternative picture of longer-term work disability is provided by survey evidence about employment experiences of people living with disability. In 2015 among the working-age population (aged 15 to 64) living in households, there were 2.1 million Australians living with disability, of whom 1 million were in employment and 114,900 were looking for work. This amounted to 53% of working-age people with disability being in the labor force. Of the 1 million Australians with disability who were employed, 53% experienced employment restrictions, such as needing time off work because of their disability (ABS, 2016).

Uptake of Social Security Benefits for Work Incapacity

Longer-term work disability is reflected in the uptake of the Disability Support Pension (DSP), a flat-rate, means-tested social security benefit for people who, due to a permanent medical condition, are assessed as unable to work for at least the next two years. Recipients include those who have exhausted their WC entitlements, did not claim, or were never eligible for WC. The share of the working-age Australian population in receipt of the DSP rose from 3.9% in 1995 to 5.4% in 2011, before falling to 4.7% in 2016 (Whiteford, 2017).

However, particular care is required in interpreting apparent trends in DSP claiming rates. As Whiteford (2017) identified, although the share of the Australian population claiming the DSP has largely increased over time, the growth is at least partly explained by the contribution of demographic and policy factors, including the aging of the population; the increase in the qualifying age for the Age Pension for women (which was associated with growth in DSP claims); and the movement of recipients of phased-out social security programs onto the DSP. The recent tightening of eligibility rules for the DSP is also likely to be reducing claiming rates (McVicar & Wilkins, 2013).

Legal Responses to Work Disability in a Federal System of Government

Australia's arrangements for the prevention and management of work disability are best understood as comprising a complex, uneven, and ever-changing patchwork. The structure of the prevailing legal system plays a central role in dictating the composition of the patchwork. Australia is a parliamentary democracy with a legal system based on English common law. The legal tradition is received rather than indigenous, having been inherited from the colonial power (Parkinson, 2013). Below the level of the national government, there are eight subnational jurisdictions (six states and two territories), each with its own laws, regulations, policies, politics, priorities, and legal culture. Australia has a federal system of government, enshrined by a national constitution that sets the exclusive law-making powers of the Commonwealth [national] government and areas of concurrent lawmaking power of the states and territories, with residual legislative powers left to the states and territories. This structure effectively stands in the way of the national government acting unilaterally to establish a single system of WC or work disability reintegration.

The dominant and most recognizable features of the Australian work disability arrangements are WC, with 11 separate schemes providing benefits for eligible workers who experience injury or illness in the course of their employment, and a social security safety net. Although prominent, these mechanisms are part of a wider landscape of legal measures, policies, and programs. A number of justifications exist for taking a wide-angle view of work disability measures in the Australian context. First, a wide-angle view highlights the multiple fields of policy development, implementation, and responsibility relevant to work disability, and the associated enhanced likelihood of change. Second, it makes clear the range of opportunities for poor interaction of the elements of the work disability patchwork, and the resultant potential for negative impacts on work reintegration. Finally, it most accurately represents the complicated picture of protections, benefits, and supports relevant to work disability, and the roles and obligations of the various actors involved.

The Australian Work Disability Patchwork

By its nature, work disability implicates a range of fields of law, policy, and practice. The Australian patchwork spans:

- healthcare;
- employment law;
- disability care and support;
- antidiscrimination law;
- private income-protection insurance;
- tortious damages claims for negligently inflicted injury;
- no-fault, cause-based injury compensation schemes (including WC); and
- social security benefits.

The key elements of this patchwork, and the parliaments primarily responsible for making the relevant laws, are summarized in Table 5.1.

Table 5.1 Australia's legal arrangements for work disability support and integration

Element	Government with primary responsibility
Universal healthcare and tax-incentivized private health insurance	National
Employment law standards and protections	National, state/territory
Anti-discrimination law and human rights protections	National, state/territory
National Disability Insurance Scheme	National
Private income protection and disability insurance	National
Damages claims for negligent injury (statutory modifications to common law)	State/territory
No-fault, cause-based injury compensation schemes	State/territory
Social security benefits for work incapacity	National

In addition to the development of legislation by the relevant parliaments, Australia's courts and tribunals play an important role in shaping the law through their review and application of laws, both in terms of government decision making and in private disputes. Beyond making and interpreting the law, in a number of areas responsibility is shared between multiple levels of government for the delivery of services, implementation of programs, and associated enforcement activities.

In the provision of healthcare in Australia, "law is used to determine what and how services are funded, organised, regulated, managed, operated and governed" (White, McDonald, & Willmott, 2014, p. 70). These arrangements impact the nature, quality, and cost of healthcare accessed by people with work disability. The national government funds primary and other clinical care, while the state and territorial governments fund public hospitals, with a significant contribution from the national government. There is little explicit reference to healthcare in the lawmaking powers divided up by the Australian Constitution. Accordingly, the national parliament has made extensive use of its powers to provide assistance in relation to pharmaceutical, sickness, hospital, and health services and to make conditional grants to the states and territories to fund and shape health services (Wheelwright, 1995; White, McDonald, & Willmott, 2014). The Medicare system, in particular, facilitates universal access to specific health services, with tax incentives used to encourage the uptake of additional private health insurance.

In terms of employment law standards and protections, most enterprises and employees are covered by the federal workplace relations system, which sets out minimum National Employment Standards (NES). Enterprise bargaining operates as a basis for the negotiation of agreements that supplement or exceed the terms and conditions provided in the NES or modern industrial awards (Howe, Hardy, & Cooney, 2013). Of relevance to work disability prevention and integration, the NES entitles employees to 10 days per year of paid personal or carer's leave, including sick leave. Additionally, federal employment law enables employees who have exhausted their accumulated leave to utilize unpaid leave for health-related reasons for up to three months, during which their employment cannot be terminated (Fair Work Act, 2009; Fair Work Regulations, 2009). Importantly, these provisions apply only to part-time and full-time workers and not to casual employees. Unlike many other countries where quotas are stipulated for the employment of people with disability in the public and private sectors (World Health Organization, 2011), Australia does not have any such quotas in place as a matter of state, territorial, or federal law.

Sitting alongside employment law provisions, Australia has antidiscrimination laws relevant to work disability. There is no national bill of human rights, although there are limited protections for specific freedoms implied in the national constitution and protections in the common law. A nationwide network of antidiscrimination laws and investigatory bodies seeks to protect community members from discrimination on the basis of a range of characteristics, including disability and work-related injury. Enforcement of these mechanisms mostly relies on action being taken by victims of discrimination, and the provisions have been relatively underutilized in connection with work disability concerns. As the OECD (2017b) noted, Australia's highly developed antidiscrimination laws have not helped to address the disability employment gap. Citizen action in relation to discrimination may also be constrained by access-to-justice barriers, with the obtaining of information and the high cost of legal action the major impediments to the enforcement of such rights (Parkinson, 2013).

Another emerging area of relevance to work disability in Australia is the development of the National Disability Insurance Scheme (NDIS). Established with trial sites in 2013, the NDIS is a "once-in-many-generation reform" (Productivity Commission, 2017, p. 8) intended to integrate what were highly fragmented national and state disability policies and services (Hemphill & Kulik, 2016). Its purpose is to fund care and support for Australians with permanent and significant disability, including supports reasonable and necessary to facilitate engagement in employment (Productivity Commission, 2017). The case for the NDIS was made on the basis of the economic benefits of advancing the welfare, employment, and social participation of people with disability (Productivity Commission, 2011). In 2017 a cost review found that the scheme was behind schedule and that the responsible agency had focused on getting participants enrolled at the expense of the quality of the support plans it developed (Productivity Commission, 2017). The boundaries of the scheme are being tested through litigation about participants' entitlements, and one of the most high-profile such cases involved a dispute about scheme funding for transport to a participant's place of employment (*McGarrigle v. National Disability Insurance Agency*, 2017; *National Disability Insurance Agency v. McGarrigle*, 2017).

Other sources of financial support potentially relevant to people experiencing work disability in Australia are private income protection and disability insurance, and damages claims for negligently inflicted injury. Australians are able to purchase private insurance to provide income benefits in the event of short- or long-term work incapacity and lost income. Many people have a built-in benefit available to them as part of their superannuation or retirement savings. Insurance products of this kind are regulated at the national level. Claims for damages for economic and noneconomic losses (or pain and suffering) in the event of negligently inflicted, permanent injury may also provide financial support for some people experiencing permanent work disability. In most Australian states and territories, workers injured in the course of their employment as a result of their employer's negligence may be able to claim damages. Such claims may also be possible against negligent parties where workers sustain injury in vehicle collisions, in public places, in the course of medical treatment, or as the result of defective products.

Since the early 2000s, these claims have been increasingly regulated by state and territorial legislation setting minimum levels of injury and maximum levels of damages that can be claimed (Luntz, Hambly, Burns, Dietrich, Foster, Grant & Harder, 2017). In theory, the availability of such claims has a deterrent or preventative impact on injury and resultant work disability. Empirical evidence suggests that the benefit of any such deterrence is likely outweighed by the transaction costs associated with fault-based compensation mechanisms (Luntz, 2013; Luntz et al., 2017; Productivity Commission, 2011).

The measures described above operate in addition to the major sources of financial and work reintegration support for Australians experiencing work disability: no-fault, cause-based injury compensation schemes, and social security. Social security is legislated and managed at the federal level. The network of no-fault schemes provides benefits for eligible people who experience work-related injury and illness (WC schemes), vehicle-collision injury, and criminally inflicted injury. These schemes predominantly operate at the state and territory levels, and there is wide variation among jurisdictions in the nature and extent of the benefits provided.

Workers' Compensation

Within Australia, there are 11 WC schemes providing support and benefits for eligible employees who sustain injury or illness in the course of their employment. There is one scheme for each of the eight state and territorial jurisdictions and three additional federal schemes for government employees (and some national, self-insured enterprises), defence-force personnel, and seafarers. Recent analysis indicates that, in the 2014 financial year, there were 241,700 accepted workers' compensation claims across all Australian schemes (Lane et al., 2016). Although each scheme has its own legislative purposes, the common objectives are the provision of adequate financial compensation, rehabilitation and return to work, affordable insurance premiums, and full funding by employers (Gunningham, 2012). The core benefits typically include:

- weekly income-replacement payments, which are capped based on earnings, and time-limited;
- medical and rehabilitation costs (including preferential access to services, as privately insured patients would receive);
- return-to-work support;
- lump-sum compensation for permanent impairment; and
- death and dependency benefits for dependents of deceased workers.

Despite their apparent similarity, there is an enormous degree of variation in the finer detail of the Australian WC schemes and the benefits they provide (Lippel & Lötters, 2013; Luntz et al., 2017). Additionally, this is an area of law in which controversies and reforms are constant. Each year, Safe Work Australia publishes a very valuable comparison of the Australian schemes, highlighting key changes and scheme characteristics (Safe Work Australia, 2017).

A range of explanatory categories can be used to understand the key differences between the Australian schemes (see, for example, Clay, Berecki-Gisolf, & Collie, 2014; Collie, Lane, Hassani-Mahmooei, Thompson, & McLeod, 2016; Lippel & Lötters, 2013). Some differences are structural, including whether work health and safety and compensation functions are performed by the same organization. Others relate to the nature and degree of coverage provided (e.g., which workers are eligible to claim; health conditions for which workers may be eligible for compensation; the level and duration of benefits, including step-downs in income benefits over time), and the period within which a worker must instigate a claim. A further category of variations relates to the management of claims (particularly whether private insurers or agents are involved), and associated mechanisms for resolving disputes, including the role of lawyers in such processes.

Promoting return to work is a primary focus of WC schemes across Australian jurisdictions (Collie, 2016), and they provide support for work reintegration, vocational rehabilitation, and retraining. Workers are obliged to participate in return-to-work planning and activities, though there is considerable diversity as to when a return-to-work plan is required, what its content should be, and who is responsible for the plan (Safe Work Australia, 2017). Legislation typically obliges an employer to attempt to reintegrate a worker with a disability in the event the worker is able to return to suitable duties within one to two years, depending on the jurisdiction (Guthrie, 2002; Purse, 2000; Safe Work Australia, 2017). Guthrie (2002) describes these "employment protection" provisions as "generally lame and without adequate remedy for workers" (p. 557), in that they mostly fail to facilitate reinstatement where the employer breaches the provisions. The decisions of industrial tribunals and courts on these matters have delivered inconsistent results, and enforcement remains critical to ensuring the promise of the legislation is achieved (Guthrie, 2002; Purse, 2000).

Social Security for Health-Related Work Incapacity

Australian social security benefits take the form of a minimum safety net and include Sickness Allowance (for temporary work incapacity) and the Disability Support Pension (DSP) (for longer-term incapacity). The DSP is the chief form of health-related social security, and in 2016 there were 736,000 people of working age in receipt of the pension (Whiteford, 2017). To be eligible, claimants must be assessed as having work incapacity of 15 hours per week or more that will endure for at least two years, and have either a severe condition warranting a Manifest Grant or be certified as having a requisite level of impairment in a Job Capacity Assessment. It is likely that, after injured workers' time-limited income benefits are exhausted in the WC scheme, many will transfer into the social security system, although the degree of this movement is not measured or tracked. Importantly, it is estimated that movement off the DSP amounts to less than 10% of recipients in a given year (including deaths and transfer to other benefits) (Cai, Vu & Wilkins, 2008).

In 2012, the DSP eligibility criteria were tightened with the intention of reducing the perceived growth in pension uptake. Granting of the DSP to applicants declined from 53% in July 2011 to 39% in June 2014 (Australian National Audit Office, 2016). From 2015, an additional step was introduced into the DSP qualification process, in which applicants are required to undergo a Disability Medical Assessment, performed by a government-contracted doctor. In May 2017, ongoing concerns about the administration of the DSP resulted in a parliamentary-committee inquiry recommending the responsible government departments conduct an end-to-end review (Parliament of the Commonwealth of Australia, 2017).

The Patchwork in Practice: Performance and Key Challenges

The high watermark of Australian work disability data is evidence of accepted claims in the WC schemes. Through these data, a reliable picture of work injury for which compensation has been successfully claimed is accessible. Rates of compensated work-related injury declined in recent years, from 31 injuries per 1,000 eligible workers in 2009 to 22 in 2014 (Lane et al., 2016). Return-to-work rates among compensated workers are another commonly cited indicator of system performance. These indicators are published annually by Safe Work Australia in a report comparing the WC schemes. The latest such report indicates that, in both 2014 and 2016, the national return-to-work rate among workers with a claim in the previous nine months involving 10 or more days of compensation was 83%, with scheme-specific rates varying from 65% (for the seafarers' scheme) to 90% (for the federal Comcare scheme) (Safe Work Australia, 2017).

Pulling together the threads of the Australian approach remains a complex task. WC claims data do not provide a reliable proxy for work disability (Spieler & Burton, 2012), and the patchwork nature of Australia's response to work disability creates challenges for assessing the success of the measures in place. This difficulty is driven by the sheer variety of systems and supports relevant to work disability and the multiple jurisdictions across which they operate. Recent research has optimistically highlighted the diversity of schemes as an opportunity for comparative research exploring the most effective policy approaches (Collie et al., 2016). Nonetheless, there are three persistent complexities that create significant barriers to a better understanding of system performance in this field.

The first complexity is the challenge of tracking work disability outcomes across programs administered at different levels of government. As discussed, the states and territories have the lion's share of responsibility for WC schemes in Australia; whereas, the federal government administers the social security system. In the Australian context, the disparate levels of management and systems of data collection associated with key work disability measures have to date meant that there has been little effort to track the transition of injured workers from WC to social security. Accordingly, little is known about the longer-term outcomes of these workers. The siloed nature of reforms in programs administered by different governments also perpetuates the problem of people who experience work disability falling between the cracks of eligibility and coverage rules.

Second, it is clear that there is a high degree of unprincipled within- and between-jurisdiction inequity in the supports available to Australians experiencing work disability. Access to benefits depends on the nature of an individual's condition, and the geographical location and circumstances in which they were injured or developed their incapacity. Claimants in Australian WC schemes "find that their entitlements and benefits are determined by sometimes arbitrary differences between the provisions of different jurisdictions," and "very little of this variation can be justified in terms of any overall principle" (Gunningham 2012, p. 277). Additional inequities are created by the differential treatment of workers within one scheme or jurisdiction, whether because of the definition of a work-related injury or changes arising as part of reforms over time. The combined effect of the variations between schemes and frequency of reforms is both intra- and inter-scheme inequity in the coverage of injured workers and the outcomes they experience. This inequity is borne out by recent analysis suggesting that the state or territory in which a WC claim is made has a "substantial and independent impact" on work disability duration (Collie et al., 2016, p. 8) and that jurisdiction-level differences in the design and management features of WC schemes may play a role in this finding.

A third and perhaps most underappreciated source of complexity relates to benefit uptake and enforcement of rights across the multiple work disability prevention and management programs. The number of work-related injuries in Australia is estimated at twice the number of accepted workers' compensation claims (Lane et al., 2016). This gap between injuries and claims raises important questions about why injured workers may not benefit from the nation's most prominent arrangements for work disability prevention and management.

There are many reasons why a person experiencing work disability may not claim WC. More than half (57%) of the 477,900 employees who self-reported experiencing work-related injury in 2013–2014 did not claim compensation, because they perceived their injuries as minor, believed they were not eligible, did not want to prejudice their employment, or because of another reason (ABS, 2014). Informed underclaiming (i.e., where an injured worker consciously elects not to claim) may be a rational response to minor injury. Of greater concern, however, is nonclaiming because of an injured worker's impaired legal capability or understanding about the available mechanisms (McDonald & People, 2014). The growth of precarious employment may increase the number of workers who are ineligible to claim WC, or who are reluctant to do so for fear of adverse consequences for their employment. The extent of more active claims suppression in Australia is unknown. The lack of clear evidence about whether people experiencing work disability are readily able to access the intended supports impedes our ability to determine whether the broader Australian patchwork and its constituent elements are functioning in optimal ways.

Conclusion

Broadly viewed, the Australian approach to preventing and managing work disability appears comprehensive, with WC and social security functioning as the dominant means of support. Evidence of declining rates of serious workers' compensation claims may create cause for comfort in the performance of the local systems. There are good reasons to retain a healthy skepticism, however. On closer inspection, Australia's work disability arrangements are a legal and policy patchwork, in multiple senses. The sheer variety of schemes and programs makes it difficult to assess what is working, both in terms of the extent to which people with work disability are able to access equitable support and the outcomes achieved. These challenges reflect the realities of work disability as a transdisciplinary phenomenon, and the federal nature of the legal system in which Australia develops and implements its strategies for responding to the problem. Improved understanding of the successes and failures of the Australian approach requires better coordination between programs administered by different levels of government as well as monitoring of the longer-term outcomes of people experiencing work disability.

References

Australian Bureau of Statistics. (2013). *Population projections, Australia, 2012 (base) to 2101* (Cat. No. 3222.0). Canberra, Australia: Australian Bureau of Statistics.

Australian Bureau of Statistics. (2014). *Work-related injuries, Australia* (Cat. No. 6324.0). Canberra, Australia: Australian Bureau of Statistics.

Australian Bureau of Statistics. (2015). *Disability and labour force participation, 2012* (Cat. No. 4433.0.55.006). Canberra, Australia: Australian Bureau of Statistics.

Australian Bureau of Statistics. (2016). *Disability, ageing and carers, Australia: Summary of findings, 2015* (Cat. No. 4430.0). Canberra, Australia: Australian Bureau of Statistics. Retrieved from www.abs.gov.au/ausstats/abs@.nsf/mf/4430.0

Australian Bureau of Statistics. (2017). *Labour force, Australia, Aug 2017* (Cat. No. 6202.0). Canberra, Australia: Australian Bureau of Statistics.

Australian Institute of Health and Welfare. (2016). *Australia's health 2016* (Australia's Health Series No. 15, Cat. No. AUS 199). Canberra, Australia: Australian Institute of Health and Welfare.

Australian National Audit Office. (2016). *Qualifying for the disability support pension.* (Report No. 18 of 2015–16). Canberra, Australia: Australian National Audit Office.

Cai, L., Vu, H., & Wilkins, R. (2008). The extent and nature of exits from the Disability Support Pension. *Australian Bulletin of Labour, 34*, 1–27.

Clay, F. J., Berecki-Gisolf, J., & Collie, A. (2014). How well do we report on compensation systems in studies of return to work: A systematic review. *Journal of Occupational Rehabilitation, 24*(1), 111–124.

Collie, A. (2016). Australian workers' compensation systems. In E. Willis, L. Reynolds, & H. Keleher (Eds.), *Understanding the Australian health care system* (3rd ed.) (pp. 195–206). Chatswood, Australia: Elsevier.

Collie, A., Lane, T. J., Hassani-Mahmooei, B., Thompson, J., & McLeod, C. (2016). Does time off work after injury vary by jurisdiction? A comparative study of eight Australian workers' compensation systems. *BMJ Open, 6*(5), e010910.

Cotterrell, R. (2002). Subverting orthodoxy, making law central: A view of socio-legal studies. *Journal of Law and Society, 28*, 632.

Fair Work Act (Australia, federal), Sections 351, 352, 385 (2009).

Fair Work Regulations (Australia, federal), Regulation 3.01 (2009).

Forsyth, A. (2016). *Victorian inquiry into the labour hire industry and insecure work.* Melbourne, Australia: Victorian Government.

Gunningham, N. (2012). Asbestos-related diseases and workers' compensation. *Sydney Law Review, 34*, 269.

Guthrie, R. (2002). The dismissal of workers covered by return to work provisions under workers compensation laws. *Journal of Industrial Relations, 44*(4), 545–561.

Hemphill, E., & Kulik, C. T. (2016). Shaping attitudes to disability employment with a national disability insurance scheme. *Australian Journal of Social Issues, 51*(3), 299–316.

Howe, J. (2015). Possibilities and pitfalls involved in expanding Australia's national workers' compensation scheme. *Melbourne University Law Review, 39*, 472–506.

Howe, J., Hardy, T., & Cooney, S. (2013). Mandate, discretion, and professionalisation in an employment standards enforcement agency: An Antipodean experience. *Law & Policy, 35*, 81–108.

Lane, T., Collie, A., & Hassani-Mahmooei, B. (2016). *Work-related injury and illness in Australia, 2004 to 2014.* Melbourne, Australia: Institute for Safety, Compensation and Recovery Research.

Lippel, K., & Lötters, F. (2013). Public insurance systems: A comparison of cause-based and disability-based income support systems. In P. Loisel & J. R. Anema (Eds.), *Handbook of work disability prevention and management* (pp. 183–202). New York, NY: Springer Science+Business Media.

Loisel, P., & Côté, P. (2013). The work disability paradigm and its public health implications. In P. Loisel & J. R. Anema (Eds.), *Handbook of work disability prevention and management* (pp. 59–67). New York, NY: Springer Science+Business Media.

Luntz, H. (2013). Compensation recovery and the National Disability Insurance Scheme. *Torts Law Journal, 20*, 153–207.

Luntz, H., Hambly, D., Burns, K., Dietrich, J., Foster, N., Grant, G., & Harder, S. (2017). *Torts: Cases and commentary*. Chatswood, Australia: LexisNexis Butterworths.

McDonald, H. M., & People, J. (2014). Legal capability and inaction for legal problems: Knowledge, stress and cost. *Updating Justice, 41*, 1–11.

McGarrigle v. National Disability Insurance Agency (Australia), FCA 308 (2017).

McInnes, J. A., Clapperton, A. J., Day, L. M., MacFarlane, E. M., Sim, M. R., & Smith, P. (2014). Comparison of data sets for surveillance of work-related injury in Victoria, Australia. *Occupational and Environmental Medicine, 71*(11), 780.

McVicar, D., & Wilkins, R. (2013). Explaining the growth in the number of recipients of the Disability Support Pension in Australia. *Australian Economic Review, 46*(3), 345–356.

National Disability Insurance Agency v. McGarrigle (Australia), FCAFC 132 (2017).

Organisation for Economic Co-operation and Development. (2017a). *How does Australia compare? Employment outlook 2017*. Retrieved from www.oecd.org/australia/Employment-Outlook-Australia-EN.pdf

Organisation for Economic Co-operation and Development. (2017b). *Connecting people with jobs: Key issues for raising labour market participation in Australia*. Retrieved from http://dx.doi.org/10.1787/9789264269637-en

Parkinson, P. (2013). *Tradition and change in Australian law*. Pyrmont, Australia: Lawbook.

Parliament of the Commonwealth of Australia, Joint Committee of Public Accounts and Audit. (2017). *Commonwealth risk management—Inquiry based on Auditor-General's report 18 (2015–16)*. Retrieved from www.aph.gov.au/Parliamentary_Business/Committees/Joint/Public_Accounts_and_Audit/CRM

Productivity Commission. (2011). *Disability care and support: Inquiry report* (Report No. 54). Canberra, Australia: Productivity Commission.

Productivity Commission. (2017). *National Disability Insurance Scheme (NDIS) costs: Study report*. Canberra, Australia: Productivity Commission.

Purse, K. (2000). The dismissal of injured workers and workers' compensation arrangements in Australia. *International Journal of Health Services, 30*(4), 849–871.

Purse, K., Meredith, F., & Guthrie, R. (2007). Neoliberalism, workers' compensation and the Productivity Commission. *Journal of Australian Political Economy, 54*, 45–66.

Quinlan, M., & Mayhew, C. (1999). Precarious employment and workers' compensation. *International Journal of Law and Psychiatry, 22*(5), 491–520.

Safe Work Australia. (2015). *The cost of work-related injury and illness for Australian employers, workers and the community: 2012–13*. Canberra, Australia: Safe Work Australia.

Safe Work Australia. (2017). *Comparative performance monitoring report: Comparison of work health and safety and workers' compensation schemes in Australia and New Zealand* (18th ed., rev.). Canberra, Australia: Safe Work Australia.

Spieler, E. A., & Burton, J. F. (2012). The lack of correspondence between work-related disability and receipt of workers' compensation benefits. *American Journal of Industrial Medicine, 55*(6), 487–505.

Stewart, A., & Stanford, J. (2017). Regulating work in the gig economy: What are the options? *The Economic and Labour Relations Review, 28*, 420–437.

Wheelwright, K. (1995). Commonwealth and state powers in health—A constitutional diagnosis. *Monash University Law Review, 21*, 53–83.

White, B., McDonald, F., & Willmott, L. (Eds.). (2014). *Health law in Australia* (2nd ed.). Pymont, Australia: Thomson Reuters/Lawbook.

Whiteford, P. (2017). Social security and welfare spending in Australia: Assessing long-term trends (Policy Brief 1/2017). Retrieved from https://taxpolicy.crawford.anu.edu.au/publication/12584/social-security-and-welfare-spending-australia-assessing-long-term-trends

World Health Organization. (2011). *World report on disability.* Geneva, Switzerland: World Health Organization.

Chapter 6

The New Zealand Universal Accident Scheme

Problems Solved and New Challenges

Grant Duncan

As an island nation of 4.8 million people, New Zealand does not often stand out in international comparative studies. In disability law and administration, however, its universal no-fault accident compensation scheme (ACC) makes it a special case. So, a brief history of this scheme is called for, to explain its basic legal and social rationale. ACC covers disability within its statutory definition of personal injury. Other forms of short- and long-term work disability are covered by the social security system on a less generous basis. And, although ACC has led the way in vocational rehabilitation and work-capacity assessment, its current statutory basis falls short of best practice. This chapter therefore identifies areas for improvements in work disability policy in New Zealand.

Demographically, New Zealand is growing, diversifying, and aging. The population is projected to increase by about 21% between 2017 and 2037. Those self-identifying as indigenous Māori represented about 15% of the population in 2013. But Māori and other ethnic-minority groups (notably those of Asian and Pacific Island origins) are projected to grow more rapidly than those of settler-British or European descent (Statistics New Zealand, 2017).

The median age of New Zealanders rose from 35.9 years in 2006 to 38 in the 2013 census, while the proportion of those aged 50 to 69 rose from 20.2% to 23.3%. The proportion of the population aged 65+ was 15% in 2016 and has a 90% probability of increasing to 21%–26% in 2043 (Statistics New Zealand, 2016). This poses challenges for the future of work disability policy, as the prevalence of disability rises steadily with age. Overall, the most recent estimates are that one in four New Zealanders experiences disability due to physical, sensory or psychological impairment (Statistics New Zealand, 2014).

An estimate of the working-age population receiving public income support for disability can be gained from social security and accident-compensation statistics. In March 2017, 84,417 people received the Supported Living Payment (for a health condition or disability). The large majority of these were for durations of more than one year, as the eligibility criterion is permanently and severely restricted ability to work. Just over one third (34.3%) of them had a psychological or psychiatric disorder. Largely due to the aging of the population, the numbers receiving this category of social security entitlement have gradually increased over the years; whereas, the total number of working-age welfare beneficiaries has decreased. People who temporarily stop work, or work reduced hours, due to a health condition or disability may also be eligible for a work-tested benefit. In March 2017, 55,460 people were receiving the work-tested Jobseeker Support for a health condition or disability—25,670 (46.3%) for psychiatric or psychological conditions. So, a total of 138,887 people received social security income support for health conditions and disability, or about 4.8% of the working-age population (Ministry of Social Development, 2017).

In the 12 months before June 2016, by comparison, 97,600 people received weekly income-replacement compensation from the ACC scheme, although 93% of them returned to work within nine months of the accident. When minor treatment-only claims are counted, however, ACC reported that 30.8% of New Zealanders benefited from its services in the 2015–2016 financial year (Accident Compensation Corporation, 2016). New Zealanders normally qualify for a universal public pension at age 65, and those on ACC or health and disability benefits can transfer to that.

Historical Background

In 1900, New Zealand followed the examples of Germany and Britain and passed a Workers' Compensation Act, putting an end to the old employer-liability regime. This remained in place, with significant modifications, until 1974. In the meantime, the social security system, which includes support for health and disability, also developed. The Social Security Act of 1938 introduced improved pensions for sickness and disability, free public hospitals, and subsidized private healthcare.

A major turning point arrived in 1967, however, with the report of the Royal Commission on Compensation for Personal Injury, commonly known as the "Woodhouse Report" after its chairperson, the late Sir Owen Woodhouse (Royal Commission of Inquiry, 1967). This report is so influential, even to this day, that no public debate on accident compensation in New Zealand can ignore its five main principles: community responsibility; comprehensive entitlement; complete rehabilitation; real compensation; and administrative efficiency.

Woodhouse reasoned that a certain rate of personal injury caused by accidents is statistically inevitable, and arises from activities that are socially and economically valuable. He also realized that the costs of accidents fall on employees, employers, families, and communities. Hence, the community should share the responsibilities of prevention, rehabilitation and compensation. He pointed out that the same costs and consequences arising from personal injury are incurred regardless of the circumstances of the incident, be it at work, at home, on the road, or elsewhere. Hence, he saw no reason why work-related and off-the-job injuries should be treated differently in terms of compensation for economic loss and vocational rehabilitation. He also recognized the social and economic value of unpaid labor, although he described this in terms of the role of "housewives" (Royal Commission of Inquiry, 1967, p. 21), assuming a gendered division of labor considered normal at that time. Hence, he recommended a comprehensive, or universal, entitlement to compensation for noneconomic loss and to social rehabilitation. Of particular relevance are his comments about rehabilitation:

> [The rehabilitation process] begins with the earliest treatment of the injury or disease. It does not end until everything has been done to achieve maximum social and economic independence. The aim is that this should be achieved in a minimum of time.
> (Royal Commission of Inquiry, 1967, p. 141)

Woodhouse rightly understood the importance of early intervention. Financial compensation should support rehabilitation, rather than be the primary focus of attention; legal-administrative processes should be efficient and not obstruct rehabilitation. Hence, Woodhouse boldly concluded that "there could be no point in retaining any form of adversary system in regard to the assessment of compensation" (Royal Commission of Inquiry, 1967, p. 125). He recommended the cessation of torts: the termination of the civil-legal right to sue for compensation for personal injury in the courts.

By 1972, the New Zealand parliament had passed legislation that largely (although not entirely) implemented Woodhouse's recommendations. The ACC scheme came into force in 1974, and, since then, all personal injuries caused by accident (including off-the-job and in medical treatment) or by work-related gradual process, disease, or infection were covered on a no-fault basis. As well, everyone (including visitors to the country) with a personal injury covered by ACC, regardless of severity or cause, is barred from suing for compensation for that injury in any New Zealand court (Campbell, 1996). Although the ACC scheme radically limits individuals' legal rights, in return for 24-hours-a-day, 7-days-a-week, no-fault compensation, it is warmly regarded by international observers (Gaskins, 2004; Luntz, 2004). Voices in favor of a return of the right to sue have been rare (e.g., Thomson, Begg, & Wilkinson, 1998), and there is no significant parliamentary support for it.

In spite of several legislative overhauls, the ACC scheme has remained basically intact as a state monopoly. Beginning in 1992, employers' levies have been experience rated, introducing an insurance-based model. For a brief period (1999–2000), competitive provision of employers' accounts by private-sector insurers was required, but this was reversed following a change of government, and the state monopoly was restored (Duncan, 2002). In 2011, the government again proposed competitive private-sector provision of personal-injury insurance, but this idea was quietly shelved, implicitly acknowledging the relative efficiency of a state monopoly. Nonetheless, larger employers can undertake to act on behalf of ACC by managing in-house their employees' work-related claims, provided they can demonstrate financial stability and have health and safety, rehabilitation, and claims administration systems in place. Up to agreed limits, these so-called "accredited employers" assume responsibility for the costs and management of claims, in return for reduced levies, on the same statutory basis. ACC has thus been surprisingly robust, retaining its monopoly in an era of neoliberal reform. The Woodhouse principles are holding up, albeit with significant compromises.

ACC does not, however, apply to disability that is congenital or caused by non-work-related illness. Disability not covered by ACC may be addressed through the public health and social security systems, but only on a needs-related and means-tested basis. This compares poorly with the loss-based, income-related entitlements of the ACC scheme. Hence, the accident-compensation law creates horizontal inequity between two classes of disability: those caused by personal injury covered by ACC and those caused by illness or congenital disorder.[1] This was foreseen by Woodhouse:

> It may be asked how incapacity arising from sickness and disease can be left aside. In logic there is no answer. A man overcome by ill health is no more able to work and no less afflicted than his neighbour hit by a car. In the industrial field certain diseases are included already.
> (Royal Commission of Inquiry, 1967, p. 26)

While he was unwilling, at that stage, to recommend a scheme that would cover incapacity caused by all forms of disability, he did suggest that the way should be left open for that in due course. However, this has yet to happen.

Moreover, Section 27 of the Accident Compensation Act 2001 excludes "mental injury" (defined as "clinically significant behavioral, cognitive, or psychological dysfunction") unless it is caused by a physical injury that is covered. Mental injury without physical injury may be covered only when it is caused by criminal acts of a sexual nature, such as sexual violation or indecent acts on a child. In addition, Section 30(5) of the Act excludes "non-physical stress," even if work related. Hence those with chronic stress, anxiety, or other psychological or psychiatric conditions that are severe enough to result in incapacity for work can only apply for means-tested social security benefits.

Discrimination

If not covered by ACC, a person with a disability is entitled to public health subsidies for treatment and rehabilitation, including prostheses and the like. These entitlements are set by the Ministry of Health and provided through 20 District Health Boards. If the person is of working age and is permanently and severely incapacitated, there is a needs-based, means-tested welfare benefit. If the work incapacity is temporary, income support is also work-tested. These welfare entitlements are provided by the Ministry of Social Development and its delivery agency, Work and Income New Zealand.

But the public health and social security entitlements are significantly less than ACC's income-related compensation[2] and its vocational- and social-rehabilitation provisions. ACC entitlements are funded by a special levy, and they are substitutes for what would have been heads of damages in the common-law claims barred since 1974. Social security is a taxation-funded, redistributive program, regarded as a safety net for the purpose of poverty alleviation. The difference between the public health and social security systems is acutely felt, due to more generous provisions for home and vehicle modifications under ACC.

This horizontal inequity has been investigated from time to time since the 1970s. Incorporation of illness into the ACC model—possibly offset by restrictions of ACC entitlements to mitigate extra costs—was repeatedly considered, notably by the Royal Commission on Social Policy of 1988. Subsequently, a bill was introduced into the House of Representatives that would have reconstituted ACC to cover incapacity for employment regardless of how it arose. This legislation was repealed by the incoming government in 1990, however. The issue of costs has always been the major hurdle (Campbell, 1996; Duncan, 2008; Oliphant, 2004; Stephens, 2004).

In *Trevethick v. Ministry of Health* (2008), it was claimed that the discrepancy caused by ACC amounted to discrimination on grounds of disability. Trevethick, a woman with multiple sclerosis who uses a wheelchair and has severe impairments, received significantly less support than an ACC claimant with similar needs. The Ministry challenged her right to have her case heard, however, arguing that cause of disability is not the same as "disability," one of the prohibited grounds covered by the Human Rights Act 1993, and hence there was no case to answer. The High Court agreed, but the Court of Appeal did accept that there is prima facie discrimination. Nevertheless, it was also found that such discrimination was justifiable under Section 5 of the New Zealand Bill of Rights Act 1990, which provides that fundamental human rights "may be subject only to such reasonable limits prescribed by law as can be demonstrably justified in a free and democratic society." The ACC legislation was intended to replace the right to sue with various no-fault entitlements, but the costs of illness were to continue to be provided by the public health system and/or private insurance. Although this results in disadvantage, the Court found it was reasonable and justified (Duncan, 2009).

So, the inequity between ACC and social security entitlements has remained in place. Expanding ACC to cover incapacity caused by illness would have cost-and-revenue implications. But New Zealanders are paying taxes for illness-related disability anyway, through social security: over

NZ$1.5 billion [US$1.1 billion] a year to support people with permanent disabilities alone. There are many more who are disabled due to illness and yet eligible for neither ACC nor social security (due to means testing of spouses' incomes), but arguably the community stands to benefit from addressing the rehabilitation needs of these citizens, too. ACC expenditure, and hence levies, would rise if it were to cover illness-related incapacity—but not the employers' levy, as work-related illness is already covered. As social security sickness-related benefits costs are reduced, and as ACC picks up more of the public health expenses, there would be off-setting savings on the government's budget. To deal with a lengthy transition period, ACC reserves are large enough (NZ$34.8 billion [US$25.5 billion] as of June 30, 2016) to absorb cost fluctuations. At the end of 2017, though, there was no political push for the extension of ACC and the removal of the discrimination between different causes of disability.

Disputes over Causation

The cause of personal injury and disability, rather than the legal test of negligence, becomes the critical factor in disputes about coverage in no-fault schemes. A founding goal of ACC law was to minimize disputes and appeals, and it has achieved this goal. In Australian workers' compensation schemes, formal appeals (such as to a review officer or mediation service, but excluding common-law actions) occur, on average, in over 6% of active claims a year. In New Zealand, the comparable rate is 1% or lower, declining to 0.6% in 2014–2015 (Safe Work Australia, 2017, p. 31). ACC's own figures of 3.3% of all entitlement claims going to formal reviews in 2013–2014, and 2.5% in 2015–2016 (Accident Compensation Corporation, 2016) are based on a different denominator, but are still relatively low.

Nonetheless, disputes are common, and the resolution processes are often negatively experienced by claimants (Forster, Barraclough, & Mijatov, 2017). Complex legal criteria concerning the causes of personal injury define coverage. Scientific knowledge (and debate) on etiologies, medical opinions about individual cases, and difficulties in finding clear diagnostic evidence lead to disputes between ACC and claimants over applications for coverage or entitlements, especially elective surgery.

Two key conditions that exclude personal injury from coverage (under Section 26, Accident Compensation Act 2001) are "personal injury caused wholly or substantially by the ageing process" and "personal injury caused wholly or substantially by a gradual process, disease, or infection"—although the latter has important exceptions, notably when work-related. Differentiating between accident and aging, or between accident and gradual process, as causes of a physical impairment, can be complicated in many cases, and the phrase "caused wholly or substantially by" does not make it easier.

In cases of personal injury caused by a work-related gradual process, disease, or infection, the criteria for coverage become even more complicated, as the relevant causative properties of the job tasks or environment must not be "found to any material extent in the non-employment activities or environment of the person," and the risk of having the condition must be "significantly greater" for people in that occupation than for others (Accident Compensation Act, 2001, Section 30). Hence there is often disagreement between claimants' common-sense understandings of personal injury or occupational disease and the statutory definitions and medical assessments that inform ACC's decision-making. The claimant who appeals a decision is disadvantaged, due to the disparity of access to information and medical knowledge, and the costs of legal advice. ACC's decisions are upheld in administrative reviews[3] 84% of the time.

One principal reason for ACC's existence is the minimization of disputes over fault, or over causation or circumstances of injury, and the universal, 24/7 coverage does assist this. But there are still disputes about the boundaries of the scheme, especially concerning work-relatedness (for occupational diseases), and injury versus illness or aging. The extension of ACC to cover all causes of disability and work incapacity would further reduce disputes and appeals.

Work-Capacity Assessment

In 1991, New Zealand's unemployment rate reached a peak of 10.3%. The following year saw a major overhaul of ACC's governing legislation, including new provisions for work-capacity assessment. A relatively open-ended entitlement to weekly compensation for lost earnings had contributed to a rapid rise in expenditure, and the government wanted to rid the scheme of so-called "hidden unemployment." Then, in 1995, a review of sickness and invalids' benefits (as the social security benefits for disability were then known) led to stricter medical assessments in social security, including the use of designated doctors. Then, in 1998, after much delay, ACC implemented a work-capacity assessment (Duncan, 1999). The new Accident Compensation Act 2001 redefined capacity for work as "vocational independence," and an assessment process was firmly integrated into the provisions for rehabilitation.

Work-capacity assessment can be a valuable tool for rehabilitation. With multidisciplinary input and direct observation of the person in a work trial, assessment plays a positive role in safely integrating or reintegrating a person with a disability into productive employment. This is not an exact science, however. Subjective symptoms and psychological impairments need to be considered carefully. The work environment should be taken into account, and modifications to the workplace may be as important as training. An assessment in a consulting room may lack relevance to the workplace, and so disability "should be interpreted in functional terms and in the context of the job requirements" (Cox & Edwards, 1995, p. 3).

Two perennial problems arise, however. First, assessment for the aims of vocational rehabilitation may be conflated with, or supplanted by, a test of eligibility for (or termination of) income-support entitlements. Second, the authority that determines eligibility may rely too heavily on physicians' assessments of impairment, rather than seeking well-rounded, real-world evaluations of job-person fit. Both of these problems affect the validity of work-capacity assessment in ACC.

Within 13 weeks of a claim for compensation being submitted, ACC is required to initiate a plan for social or vocational rehabilitation, in consultation with the claimant, if a plan is likely to be needed. The purpose of vocational rehabilitation is to help a claimant to maintain or obtain employment, or to regain or acquire vocational independence. The achievement of vocational independence, therefore, does not necessarily mean that the claimant actually returns to paid employment. It does, however, mean that the claimant loses entitlement to weekly compensation with three months' notice. Once excluded from the scheme, ACC has no obligation to monitor the claimant's well-being or employment status; for example, to ensure that the claimant is not working in any occupation that could exacerbate a pre-existing impairment.

The assessment of vocational independence occurs in two steps. First, an occupational assessment considers the claimant's progress in vocational rehabilitation, whether the types of work that were considered in the rehabilitation plan are still suitable for the claimant (regardless of job vacancies), and whether they "match the skills that the claimant has gained through education, training, or experience" (Accident Compensation Act, 2001, Section 108). The occupational assessor may (not "shall") take into account the claimant's previous earnings.

The second step is a medical assessment. This considers all of the types of work identified as suitable in the occupational assessment, and provides an opinion on the claimant's capacity to undertake any of them, having regard to the claimant's personal injury but not taking into account any other impairment not covered by ACC. Based on this medical opinion on the claimant's capacity for work in suitable occupations, ACC may determine that a claimant is vocationally independent, and income-replacement compensation ceases within three months.

Hence, the vocational-independence assessment conflates the assessment of work capacity in particular occupations with the test of continued eligibility for compensation. And, although the medical assessor should take into account work trials undertaken since the injury occurred, this assessment may be conducted without reference to actual job vacancies, and without validation in the context of either a work environment or the demands of observable tasks. It may be only a theoretical opinion formed in the consulting room.

In cases where return to the previous job, or transition to a job of similar skill and income, has not been achieved,[4] vocationally independent may mean, in practice, that the claimant is deemed fit for a lower-skilled occupation based on past experience. If no such suitable job is actually available, the outcome could be unemployment. In such cases, the goal of complete rehabilitation has not been met, when judged by Woodhouse's standard that the rehabilitation process "does not end until everything has been done to achieve maximum social and economic independence" (Royal Commission of Inquiry, 1967, p. 141).

How Effective is ACC?

As the ACC model is unique, it is worth considering evidence of its performance in returning injured people to work (RTW). Using basic economic logic, a universal no-fault scheme with 80% income-replacement looks like an incentive not to return to work. Entitlements are not open-ended, however. Indeed, an injured worker could be deemed vocationally independent and left without employment or income at all. Neither ACC nor the Ministry of Social Development publicly reports the numbers of former recipients of ACC weekly compensation who transfer onto social security benefits after being found vocationally independent. But an unpublished study (cited in Duncan, 2004) found that about 12% of such people transferred to sickness or invalids' benefits within three months. Many of those, however, may have done so due to illness or impairment that was not covered previously by ACC. A further 10% went on to claim working-age social security benefits unrelated to health or disability.

There is evidence (using matched samples from the records of the tax authority) "that injuries have long-term effects on individual labor market outcomes and that the institutional arrangements in place in New Zealand fail to compensate for this" (Crichton, Stillman, & Hyslop, 2011, p. 784). One negative outcome that can be expected following a serious injury is thus a decline in income and reduced work capacity. If ACC does not fully compensate for this, to what extent does it at least mitigate it compared with other models?

Regular monitoring reports compare the ACC employers' account (covering workers injured at work) with the workers' compensation schemes in the Australian states. New Zealand has lower rates of long-term claims (12 weeks' compensation or more) than the Australian schemes. In addition, employers' levies are lower in New Zealand, in part because ACC does not directly cover mental conditions such as stress (Safe Work Australia, 2017). The employers' levy has dropped to an average of 80¢ per $100 of payroll, and the employers' account is fully funded (Accident Compensation Corporation, 2016).

A survey of injured workers in Australia and New Zealand who had 10 or more days off work, and whose claims were submitted seven to nine months earlier, showed that, in 2013–2014, over three quarters (77%) had returned to work following their injury and were still working at the time of interview. The rate in New Zealand was closely comparable to the average from the Australian states (Social Research Centre, 2016).

However, when a broader sample of New Zealand injured workers were interviewed, including those with at least one day off work due to either work-related or non-work-related accidents, then the "durable" (three-month stable) RTW rate in New Zealand is 54%. This compares with 69% in Australia, although the Australian sample did not include any non-work-related claimants (Social Research Centre, 2016). The lower comparative performance of the wider New Zealand sample, however, indicates that the RTW rate under ACC must be lower for those whose injuries were incurred off the job than for those whose injuries were incurred at work. This may be due to experience rating: Employers are more motivated to reintegrate workers injured in their own workplaces, as the claims costs may reduce bonuses or increase penalties. Injuries sustained off the job are not a priority. Or, some employers may illegitimately persuade injured workers to tell the medical practitioner who first registers the claim that the accident happened off the job. In that case, due to the 24-hour coverage in New Zealand, the worker still gets ACC coverage, while the employer evades accountability under experience rating. It is not, however, possible to estimate the frequency of this behavior. Also, employers may be covertly discriminating against job applicants with pre-existing ACC claims arising from other workplaces or off the job, again due to experience rating and/or safety-related risk (Harcourt, Lam, & Harcourt, 2007). Those covered by ACC whose claims do not directly affect their employers' experience rating may thus be getting less support to reintegrate into the workforce. And hence the RTW rates for workers injured off the job are poorer than for those with work-related injuries. Further research into these issues is called for.

We can be confident, though, that workers injured on the job and covered by the ACC scheme are being reintegrated at rates that compare well with Australian states. There are far fewer disputes in New Zealand, and employers are paying relatively low levies.

Two studies have compared outcomes for ACC-covered and non-ACC-covered incapacity. Although the two groups differ in significant ways, both studies took measures to match the samples. One matched age, sex, and functional impairment (McAllister, Derrett, Audas, Herbison, & Paul, 2013), and the other compared samples with the same kind of impairment (spinal-cord injury) (Paul, Derrett, Herbison, & Beaver, 2013). People covered by ACC were less likely to have inadequate incomes than those not covered, and were significantly more likely to have returned to work. A simplistic economic logic would suggest that ACC's higher rate of income replacement (80% of previous income, compared with flat-rate, needs-based social security benefits) would incentivize so-called "malingering," but this appears not to be the case. ACC's relatively generous income replacement supports RTW and reduces poverty and further ill-health compared to social security. In a less optimistic light, the labor-market outcomes for people who receive long-term ACC are poorer than those who are not injured (Crichton et al., 2011), but people disabled by sickness who rely on social security are worse off. ACC's relatively good outcomes are aided by the low levels of disputes over coverage and the elimination of lawsuits, reducing barriers to prompt and effective rehabilitation.

A comparison of six developed countries (Denmark, Germany, Israel, the Netherlands, Sweden, and the United States) found that a greater focus on work interventions and less strict policies on eligibility for long-term and partial disability benefits (shifting attention away from compensation and towards rehabilitation) led to more sustainable RTW rates (Anema et al., 2009). High levels of stress related to dealing with the compensation system itself, moreover, is correlated with poorer long-term health and disability status (Grant, O'Donnell, Spittal, Creamer, & Studdert, 2014).

Empirical evidence, therefore, supports Woodhouse's argument that the goals of the injury compensation scheme should be to prioritize rehabilitation above compensation, while applications for coverage and entitlements should be administratively efficient and minimize all causes of disputes (Royal Commission of Inquiry, 1967). The prompt acceptance of claims, and relatively generous financial support, allow for a less stressful experience for the injured person, and hence greater motivation and opportunity to return to work. In practice, however, the ACC scheme is not providing the full level of compensation that Woodhouse would have envisaged in return for the loss of the right to sue.

Experience Rating

The use of experience rating in ACC since 1992 was intended to incentivize employers to prevent accidents and to return injured workers to work. In fact, though, it may not have aided vocational rehabilitation overall, and ACC no longer makes strong claims to that effect. It generally justifies experience rating on the grounds of fairness among levy-payers; that is, that employers who make more frequent and more costly claims pay more. Research evidence on experience rating is mixed, suggesting a need for critical analysis of the economic logic that supported it. Although some employers may find that experience rating encourages and rewards good in-house occupational health and rehabilitation practices, others may suppress the submission of claims and/or put pressure on claimants to return to work prematurely (Mansfield et al., 2012). As suggested above, there is indirect evidence that experience rating may create obstacles to RTW for those covered by ACC for off-the-job injuries.

Experience rating has reintroduced an element of fault into the ACC scheme, moreover, by encouraging employers to dispute work relatedness (Duncan, 2008), and it has undermined ACC's foundation as a social program, in favor of an insurance-based approach (Lamm, McDonnell, & St John, 2012). Nonetheless, the evidence shows ACC compares well in RTW rates with Australian workers' compensation schemes (with a caveat regarding ACC claimants injured off the job), and those on ACC have better occupational and economic outcomes than those with comparable levels of disability who rely on means-tested disability support. If experience rating does have positive effects for RTW, these may be restricted to claims that are registered as work related, while those injured off the job get less support from employers to reintegrate.

Improvements

Occupational and economic outcomes for those with a permanent incapacity for a previous skilled occupation are likely to be negative, and ACC's statutory provisions for vocational rehabilitation set a fairly low bar of vocational independence when an injured person cannot return to the same or a similar job. A transfer from the scheme to unemployment or into a lower skilled occupation is lawful under the Accident Compensation Act 2001. But this falls short of Woodhouse's principle of complete rehabilitation. It also falls short of the ILO [International Labour Organization] Vocational Rehabilitation and Employment (Disabled Persons) Convention 1983, which regards the purpose of vocational rehabilitation as "to enable a disabled person to secure, retain *and advance* in suitable employment and thereby to further such person's integration or reintegration into society" [italics added] (see Duncan, 2004). New Zealand has yet to ratify this convention, however.

Some excellent research on the costs and consequences of personal injury and on vocational-independence outcomes has been conducted in New Zealand (Adams et al., 2002; Armstrong & Laurs, 2007; Crichton et al., 2011; Department of Labour, 2004; Langley, Lilley, Samaranayaka, & Derrett, 2014; O'Dea & Wren, 2010). However, this research has not stimulated legislative reform to raise the standard of rehabilitation for people permanently incapacitated for skilled occupations under ACC.

Further work is needed to eliminate the discrimination between personal injury covered by ACC and the sickness-related or congenital disabilities that fall under the public health and social security systems. Given ACC's better RTW outcomes, it makes no sense to expand the latter to cover all disability—and certainly not without returning the right to sue. Repeated proposals and efforts to extend the ACC model to all work incapacity in New Zealand have been unsuccessful so far.

Coverage under ACC does not normally include conditions that are solely psychological or psychiatric. But 39% of those receiving social security benefits for "health condition or disability" (as defined by the Ministry of Social Development) have a psychological or psychiatric disorder. An extension of ACC to cover sickness could create a new discriminatory distinction between people with physical disorders and those with psychological or psychiatric disorders. Any future proposal to extend ACC to all forms of work disability should avoid creating any new cause of discrimination.

Conclusion

New Zealand faces challenges similar to those facing other developed nations: a diversifying and aging population; rising rates of disability; rising healthcare costs; rapid technological and economic change; and the rise of precarious employment. There are genuine pressures to upskill workforces in order to respond to rapid technological change and to make workplaces open to diversity, including to those with differing levels of ability. Disability policy needs to play its part in that effort, rather than laying a pathway towards lower-skilled occupations and economic stress.

Hence, the Woodhouse principles could make a renewed contribution to public policy. The principles of community responsibility, comprehensive entitlement, complete rehabilitation, real compensation, and administrative efficiency—adapted to the social and technological changes over the intervening five decades—could reinvigorate disability policy, leading to reforms that will assist people with disability to enjoy prosperity and to contribute to their communities and economies. New Zealand's policy makers have yet to see this opportunity. If they were to grasp it, however, they would set another world-leading example.

Notes

1 People may also purchase private insurance.
2 On ACC, normally 80% of preinjury, before-tax earnings are treated as taxable.
3 Disputes are initially taken to an administrative review, which then may be appealed to the courts.
4 If the nature and/or permanence of the disability mean that the employee is unable to return to work with the previous employer, New Zealand law permits termination of employment on medical grounds.

References

Accident Compensation Act 2001 (New Zealand), Sections 26, 27, 30, 108.
Accident Compensation Corporation. (2016). *Annual report 2016*. Wellington, New Zealand: ACC.
Adams, M., Burton, J., Butcher, F., Graham, S., McLeod, A., & Rajan, R. (2002). *Aftermath: The social and economic consequences of workplace injury and illness*. Wellington, New Zealand: Department of Labour/Accident Compensation Corporation.
Anema, J., Schellart, A., Cassidy, J., Loisel, P., Veerman, T. J., & van der Beek, A. J. (2009). Can cross country differences in return-to-work after chronic occupational back pain be explained? An exploratory analysis on disability policies in a six country cohort study. *Journal of Occupational Rehabilitation, 19*(4), 419–426.

Armstrong, H., & Laurs, R. (2007). *Vocational independence: Outcomes for ACC claimants.* Wellington, New Zealand: Department of Labour.
Campbell, I. B. (1996). *Compensation for personal injury in New Zealand: Its rise and fall.* Auckland, New Zealand: Auckland University Press.
Cox, R., & Edwards, F. (1995). Introduction. In R. Cox, F. Edwards, & R. McCallum (Eds.), *Fitness for work: The medical aspects* (pp. 1–24). Oxford: Oxford University Press.
Crichton, S., Stillman, S., & Hyslop, D. (2011). Returning to work from injury: Longitudinal evidence on employment and earnings. *ILR Review, 64*(4), 765–785.
Department of Labour. (2004). *Measuring the costs of injury in New Zealand.* Wellington, New Zealand: Department of Labour.
Duncan, G. (1999). The assessment of residual capacity for work: Easier said than done. *Social Policy Journal of New Zealand* (12), 35–52.
Duncan, G. (2002). Workers' compensation. In M. Lloyd, *Occupational health and safety in New Zealand: Contemporary social research* (pp. 19–42). Palmerston North, New Zealand: Dunmore.
Duncan, G. (2004). Advancing in employment: The way forward for vocational rehabilitation. *Victoria University of Wellington Law Review, 35*(4), 801–809.
Duncan, G. (2008). Boundary disputes in the ACC scheme and the no-fault principle. *New Zealand Law Review* (1), 27–36.
Duncan, G. (2009). The achievements of New Zealand's Labour-led government in social security, 1999–2008. *Zeitschrift für ausländisches und internationales Arbeits- und Sozialrecht, 23*(3), 231–247.
Forster, W., Barraclough, T., & Mijatov, T. (2017). *Solving the problem: Causation, transparency and access to justice in New Zealand's personal injury system.* Dunedin, New Zealand: New Zealand Law Foundation and the University of Otago.
Gaskins, R. (2004). New dymanics of risk and responsibility: Expanding the vision for accident compensation. *Victoria University of Wellington Law Review, 35*(4), 951–968.
Grant, G. M., O'Donnell, M. L., Spittal, M. J., Creamer, M., & Studdert, D. M. (2014). Relationship between stressfulness of claiming for injury compensation and long-term recovery: A prospective cohort study. *JAMA Psychiatry, 71*(4), 446–453.
Harcourt, M., Lam, H., & Harcourt, S. (2007). The impact of workers' compensation experience-rating on discriminatory hiring practices. *Journal of Economic Issues, 41*(3), 681–699.
Human Rights Act (New Zealand) (1993).
Lamm, F., McDonnell, N., & St John, S. (2012). The rhetoric versus the reality: New Zealand's experience rating. *New Zealand Journal of Employment Relations, 37*(2), 21–40.
Langley, J., Lilley, R., Samaranayaka, A., & Derrett, S. (2014). Work status and disability trajectories over 12 months after injury among workers in New Zealand. *New Zealand Medical Journal, 127*(1390), 53–60.
Luntz, H. (2004). The Australian picture. *Victoria University of Wellington Law Review, 35*(4), 879–903.
Mansfield, L., MacEachen, E., Tompa, E., Kalcevich, C., Endicott, M., & Yeung, N. (2012). A critical review of literature on experience rating in workers' compensation systems. *Policy and Practice in Health and Safety, 10*(1), 3–25.

McAllister, S., Derrett, S., Audas, R., Herbison, P., & Paul, C. (2013). Do different types of financial support after illness or injury affect socio-economic outcomes? A natural experiment in New Zealand. *Social Science and Medicine, 85*, 93–102.

Ministry of Social Development. (2017). *Benefit fact sheets*. Retrieved May 29, 2017 from www.msd.govt.nz/about-msd-and-our-work/publications-resources/statistics/benefit/index.html

O'Dea, D., & Wren, J. (2010). *New Zealand estimates of the total social and economic cost of "all injuries" and the six priority areas respectively, at June 2008 prices*. Wellington, New Zealand: Accident Compensation Corporation.

Oliphant, K. (2004). Beyond Woodhouse: Devising new principles for determining ACC boundary issues. *Victoria University of Wellington Law Review, 35*(4), 915–936.

Paul, C., Derrett, S. M., Herbison, P., & Beaver, C. S. (2013). Socioeconomic outcomes following spinal cord injury and the role of no-fault compensation: Longitudinal study. *Spinal Cord, 51*(12), 919–925.

Royal Commission of Inquiry. (1967). *Compensation for personal injury in New Zealand*. Wellington, New Zealand: R.E. Owen, Government Printer.

Safe Work Australia. (2017). *Comparative performance monitoring report: Comparison of work health and safety and workers' compensation schemes in Australia and New Zealand* (18th ed., rev.). Canberra, Australia: Safe Work Australia.

Social Research Centre. (2016). *Return to work survey 2016: Summary research report (Australia and New Zealand)*. Canberra, Australia: Safe Work Australia.

Statistics New Zealand. (2014, June 17). *Disability survey: 2013*. Retrieved May 22, 2017 from www.stats.govt.nz/browse_for_stats/health/disabilities/DisabilitySurvey_HOTP2013.aspx

Statistics New Zealand. (2016, October 19). *National population projections*. Retrieved May 22, 2017 from www.stats.govt.nz/browse_for_stats/population/estimates_and_projections/NationalPopulationProjections_HOTP2016.aspx

Statistics New Zealand. (2017, May 18). *National ethnic population projections*. Retrieved May 22, 2017 from www.stats.govt.nz/browse_for_stats/population/estimates_and_projections/NationalEthnicPopulationProjections_MR2013-2038.aspx

Stephens, R. (2004). Horizontal equity for disabled people: Incapacity from accident or illness. *Victoria University of Wellington Law Review, 35*(4), 783–800.

Thomson, C., Begg, S., & Wilkinson, B. (1998). *Accident compensation: Options for reform*. Wellington, New Zealand: New Zealand Business Roundtable.

Trevethick v. Ministry of Health, High Court of New Zealand, CIV-2007-485-2449 (2008).

Chapter 7

An Overview of Work Disability Policies In China

Desai Shan

This chapter provides an overview of work disability policies in China. Work disability occurs when a worker is unable to stay at work or return to work because of an injury or disease (Loisel & Côté, 2013). Although there is no corresponding term for work disability in the Chinese legal framework, the state has adopted legal instruments aiming to integrate people with disabilities into the labor market and to provide remedies to victims of occupational accidents and diseases. Current work disability policy in China comprises policies on employing people with disabilities, work-related disability compensation, and non-work-related injury and disease benefits.

China has the world's largest population, 1.38 billion, and 66.3 % of the population are of working age (15–59) (United Nations Department of Economic and Social Affairs, Population Division, 2015). In 2016, China's gross domestic product (GDP) was US$11.2 trillion, ranking second in the world after the United States (World Bank, 2017a). Since the global financial crisis of 2008, China has become the largest contributor to world economic growth. However, China remains a developing country; in 2016 its GDP per capita ranked 76th in the world, at US$8,132 (World Bank, 2017b). China's economic development is imbalanced among its 34 provincial jurisdictions. In nine eastern provinces, the 2016 provincial GDP per capita was about US$10,000 (National Bureau of Statistics of China, 2016). However, in the inland provinces and territories (e.g., Gansu, Guizhou, Yunnan, and Tibet), the regional GDP per capita was below US$5,000 (National Bureau of Statistics of China, 2016). The income gap between rural and urban residents is also significant. In 2015, the annual disposable per-capita income of urban residents was US$4,789—about three times that of rural residents, which was US$1,754 (National Bureau of Statistics of China, 2016). The disparities in Chinese economic development are significant.

From 1949 to 1979, both China's political and economic regimes were socialist. The capitalist regime had been abolished, and the working class became the ruling class (Howell & Pearce, 2002; Taylor, Kai, & Qi, 2003). Under the socialist planned economy, all enterprises were state-owned or collective-owned, and, usually, urban residents were assigned permanent full-time jobs in a practice called the "iron rice bowl"[1] (J. Li, 2008; Zhu & Dowling, 2002). Workers' welfare was covered by government regulations and implemented by enterprises. After 1957, the state set uniform compensation standards for work-related injuries and illnesses, and enterprises made compulsory payments for industrial-injury damages directly to injured workers. Meanwhile, people with disabilities (work-related or not) in urban areas were organized by all levels of government to work for various welfare enterprises, which were set up by the local government to create jobs for people with disabilities. In rural areas, residents with disabilities obtained farming land, so they could produce food to sustain themselves.

Under the planned economy, workers' welfare (including pensions, healthcare, and compensation for occupational injuries and death) was supposed to be fully provided for by state- or collective-owned enterprises, according to the standards set by the state (Mao & Zhang, 2007). However, continuous political movements, especially the Cultural Revolution from 1966 to 1976, so greatly disturbed development of the economy that, by the end of the 1970s, most Chinese people lived in poverty (Yao, 2000). In 1978, the Reform and Opening-Up policy was agreed to at the Third Plenum of the Central Committee of the Chinese Communist Party (Zhu, 1996). 'Reform' refers to the program of economic reforms termed "Socialism with Chinese characteristics." These reforms were initiated by reformists within the Communist Party of China, led by Deng Xiaoping. In urban areas, one major reform was privatizing state-owned enterprises and introducing market competition. According to the Reform and Opening-Up policy, in 1992 a new socialist market economy, adapted to the Chinese context, was implemented (Zhu, 2002). As private property and market-oriented businesses were gradually restored, these policies profoundly changed the direction of the country.

The last three decades have witnessed the tremendous social and economic transformation of China—from a command economy to a relatively free market economy. Meanwhile, free and independent workers and labor markets have come into existence, and traditional industrial relationships have greatly changed (Lu, 2001). The iron rice bowl is no longer the common employment mechanism in the newly emerging labor markets. Instead, widely adopted labor contracts establish fixed-term employment relationships (Zhu, 2002). Enterprises can freely hire employees without too much intervention from government in relatively free labor markets, and employers need not be completely responsible for their employees' pensions, healthcare, and work-related injuries (Wu, 2008). Protections of workers' rights from the previous socialist planned economy are no longer universally applied, and the newborn labor force, including migrant workers and college graduates, is no longer entitled to the previous welfare schemes (Mao & Zhang, 2007). In the relatively free market economy, Chinese work disability policies can no longer rely on government controls and arrangements by state-owned enterprises. In the 1990s and 2000s, a series of reforms to policies on employing people with disabilities and workplace disability compensation were introduced to address work disability problems in the context of the Chinese market economy.

This chapter is divided into three sections. The first describes the development of policies on employing people with disabilities in China. The second section describes the scope and standards of China's workers' compensation system and criticisms of it. The third section describes the limited financial supports employers provide for workers with non-work-related injuries and diseases.

Policies on Employing People with Disabilities

China has the world's largest disabled population: 82.96 million in 2006. Of this population, 25% lived in urban areas and 75% in rural areas. Among people with disabilities over age 15, 44% were illiterate, which restricted their participation in the labor market (National Bureau of Statistics of China, 2007). Only about 21% of people with disabilities participate in paid work. As reported by the China Disabled Persons' Federation, by the end of 2015 4.3 million people with disabilities in urban areas and 13.2 million in rural areas were either employed or involved in agricultural work (China Disabled Persons' Federation, 2016).

The Law of the People's Republic of China (PRC) on the Protection of Disabled Persons of 2008 (Section 2) defines a disabled person as "one who suffers from abnormalities or loss of a certain organ or function, psychologically or physiologically, or in anatomical structures and has lost wholly or in part the ability to perform an activity in the way was considered normal." As defined in this statute, disabilities include visual, hearing, speech, physical, developmental, mental disorder, multiple, and/or other. The state promises to support the rehabilitation, education, and employment of people with disabilities. They may apply to the local Disabled Persons' Federations for "identity of disabled people" status. After medical assessment,[2] people with this status can be certified and claim disability benefits (China Disabled Persons' Federation, 2007).

Under the Law on the Protection of Disabled Persons, all levels of governments are obliged to create opportunities for the employment of people with disabilities, including concerted and dispersed arrangements. Concerted arrangements are those in which governments set up social-welfare enterprises where more than 25% of the staff are disabled. Dispersed arrangements are those in which the state requires public institutions, enterprises, companies, and organizations to employ a certain proportion of people with disabilities in appropriate jobs (Law of the PRC on the Protection of Disabled Persons (2008), Sections 29–30). In addition, the state encourages people with disabilities to become self-employed, open individual businesses, and apply for tax deductions or exemptions (Law of the PRC on the Protection of Disabled Persons of 2008, Section 33). In 2007, the State Council of the People's Republic of China passed the Regulation on the Employment of the Disabled. It requires all employers to ensure that employees with disabilities comprise no less than 1.5% of total staff. Employers who fail to achieve this proportion must pay the disability-employment tax. Small enterprises, employing no more than 20 employees, are exempted for the first three years after the date of company registration (Regulation on the Employment of the Disabled of 2007, Section 16).

The Law on the Protection of Disabled Persons (2008) and the Regulation on the Employment of the Disabled (2007) promote a set of policies to support the employment of Chinese people with disabilities, and also protect them from discrimination in employment. According to these laws, all level of governments should provide preferential treatment to people with disabilities in taxation and training. However, China's transition from a planned to a market economy has significantly impacted the employment of people with disabilities. During the planned-economy period, social-welfare enterprises and arranging concerted employment of people with disabilities were the major work disability policies. In the 1980s, social-welfare enterprises developed rapidly, due to tax deductions and exemptions (Liao, 2015). For example, in Shanghai, social-welfare enterprises employed 50% of the city's people with disabilities who had work capacity. However, in the 1990s, social-welfare enterprises could not survive in the competitive market economy, and most of them went bankrupt (Liao, 2015). Concerted employment could not create sustainable jobs for people with disabilities, and dispersed employment became the alternate mode. Public institutions, organizations, and enterprises are now required to hire people with disabilities. However, instead of doing so, many employers prefer to pay the disability-employment tax (Shang & Liang, 2011).

Drawing on 2001–2013 data from the Chinese Household Income Project, Liao (2015) reported that, despite the enforcement of the Disabled People Employment Regulation (2007), the employment rate of people with disabilities is unchanged and significantly lower than employment of people without disabilities. Liao (2015) pointed out that, in 2007, the Ministry of Finance[3] decreased the tax benefits for social-welfare enterprises. From 2007 to 2014, the number of registered social-welfare enterprises dropped from 25,969 to 17,876, which reduced concerted-employment opportunities for people with disabilities tremendously. In recent years, e-commerce and online shops have increased opportunities for people with disabilities to become self-employed. However, current disability-employment benefits do not cover self-employed workers, so many are not able to claim tax deductions and exemptions.

Work-Related Injuries and Disabilities

Of China's population with disabilities, 3.4% sustained work injuries (Dai et al., 2011). Every year in China, more than 500,000 workers are disabled in

Table 7.1 Work-related injuries and disabilities (officially recognized), 2011–2015

Year	Injuries	Disabilities	Disability rate (%)
2011	1,200,000	510,000	42.50
2012	1,174,000	513,000	43.70
2013	1,183,000	512,000	43.28
2014	1,147,000	558,000	48.65
2015	1,076,000	542,000	50.37

Note. Ministry of Human Resources and Social Security (2012, 2013, 2014b, 2015, 2016).

workplace accidents, and the disability rate of injured workers keeps increasing (see Table 7.1). About 80% of workers disabled by industrial injuries are from rural areas (Yin & Tian, 2016).

The Workers' Compensation System in China

In the 1990s, the social security system in China's socialist market economy had not been established, and contract workers' rights and welfare were ambiguous. Within the emerging private sector, workers with occupational injuries had very limited access to compensation and medical care (Sun & Zhu, 2009). Although some state regulations provided some benefits for injured workers, there were no effective measures forcing private employers to comply with the law (Mao & Zhang, 2007). However, at that time, tort litigation was problematic as well. Injured workers could neither receive defined compensation under a workers' compensation system, nor could they claim sufficient damages through tort litigation. Moreover, in China healthcare was paid for by individual patients.[4] Under these circumstances, private-sector injured workers became huge burdens on their families, since it was difficult for injured workers to obtain compensation from employers or benefits from the social insurance fund (Sun & Zhu, 2009).

Economic and social transformation demands the improvement of legal frameworks to ensure the stability of society and the sustainability of development (Zhu, 2002). In order to regulate employment relationships and protect workers' rights, the Labor Law was enacted in 1994 and the Labor Contract Law in 2008 (Labor Law of the PRC, 2009; J. Li, 2008). On January 1, 2004, the Regulation on Work-Related Injury Insurance came into force. This regulation covers all categories of enterprises in mainland China and provides procedures for the official recognition of work injuries, application for work-injury compensation, arbitration rules for labor disputes, and appeal procedures (Mao & Zhang, 2007). Through this regulation, public work-injury-insurance funds have been established nationwide, and they are managed by the provincial governments (Z. Li, 2008). Employers are obliged to pay work-injury-insurance premiums for their employees.

If employers fail to pay the premiums and their employees are injured at work, they must pay the full amount of compensation, according to the standards in the Regulation on Work-Related Injury Insurance (2011, Art. 62).

The workers' compensation system enables Chinese workers to claim no-fault-based compensation from the work-related injury insurance fund (WIIF) and also against their employers.[5] Meanwhile, the WIIF also obliges all Chinese employers to pay social insurance premiums for their employees. In 2010, the Standing Committee of the National Congress[6] passed the Social Insurance Law, which incorporated the work-related injury insurance regime. In 2011, the Regulation on Work-Related Injury Insurance (2003) was revised to include protection of precarious workers, particularly migrant workers from rural areas.

Whether WIIF should cover temporary-agency workers and freelancers has been debated for many years. Many agencies or labor-supply companies have argued that these workers should not be categorized as employees under WIIF. In 2014, the Ministry of Human Resources and Social Security promulgated the Interim Provisions on Labor Dispatch (Ministry of Human Resources and Social Security, 2014a). In this regulation, temporary agencies and labor-supply companies are liable for work-related-injury insurance premiums. Agencies and employers are jointly liable for compensating agency workers for work-related injuries and disabilities.

Scope of Work-Related Injuries, Compensation Standards, and Sources of Payment

According to the Regulation on Work-Related Injury Insurance (2011), in order to qualify for compensation, workers' injuries must fulfill one of the following three conditions. First, in principle, the injury should be relevant to work tasks, including work preparations, after-work conclusions (e.g., commuting to and from work), and business trips. Second, the injury should happen at the workplace, or death should occur within a limited period due to sudden disease (e.g., a heart attack). Third, the injury could be caused while protecting the public interest (e.g., voluntary rescue during natural disasters) or during military service. Injuries incurred in certain circumstances are excluded (Regulation on Work-Related Injury Insurance of 2011, Art. 16).[7]

WIIR only broadly defines work-related injuries. Unless they are caused by workers' own illegal, criminal behavior or deliberate self-harm, any injuries relevant to work and injuries occurring at the workplace or on the way to or from work qualify as work-related injuries. Injuries caused by traffic accidents during work commutes are also covered by Work-Related Injury Insurance, unless injured workers are mostly at fault.

Compensation Standards and Sources of Payment

According to the Regulation on Work-Related Injury Insurance (2011), when a workplace accident occurs, the employer should immediately report the accident to the local social insurance administration authority, so it can create an official record. Within 30 days, the employer should submit a workplace-injury-recognition application to the local social insurance administration authority. However, there is little incentive for employers to comply with these directives. One reason employers do not report accidents is that they want to avoid their partial-compensation liabilities. When employers refuse to report accidents, then the social insurance administration will reject any claims they make for work-related injury insurance. In this situation, injured workers have to apply for workplace-injury recognition on their own. To receive compensation from the work-related injury insurance fund (WIIF), this should be done within one year of the workplace accident.

Once workers' injuries have been officially recognized as work-related, the trauma of their impairments is stabilized, and they do not need further treatment, employers, employees, or employees' close relatives need to file an application for work-capacity assessment with the Work Capacity Assessment Committee (WCAC), which is affiliated with the local labor administration. The WCAC assesses the level of work-related disability within 90 days; levels range from Grade 10, the least severe, to Grade 1, the most severe. According to their work-capacity assessments, workers are entitled to a certain amount of disability compensation, from both WIIF and their employers, including payments for medical treatment and rehabilitation. If their injuries are assessed as disabling, lump-sum disability payments, monthly disability allowances, and/or nursing allowances should be paid by WIIF. These payments vary by degree of disability (see Table 7.2).

Rights to Return to Work

According to their degree of disability, some workers are entitled to return to work (see Table 7.3). Workers with disabilities of Grades 1 to 4 (70%–100% work-capacity loss) are entitled to leave their jobs and receive 70% to 90% of their former salaries from the Work-Related Injury Insurance Fund (WIIF) until they reach retirement age (Regulation on Work-Related Injury Insurance, 2011). Employers of workers with Grades 1 to 4 disabilities are exempted from their obligation to arrange return to work. However, employers are obliged to provide return-to-work opportunities for workers with disabilities of Grades 5 to 10. If jobs cannot be arranged for these workers, their employers are obliged to replace their wages. Employers are not allowed to terminate the employment relationship even if the fixed-term labor contract has expired. If employers do not arrange other jobs for workers with disabilities Grades 5 to 10, the workers are still entitled to 60% to 70% of their salaries every month. However, workers with disabilities of Grade 5 and 6 can choose to terminate their employment relationships. If they do, they are entitled to claim re-employment

110 Desai Shan

Table 7.2 Payments for medical treatment and rehabilitation

Costs	Standard for payment calculation	Schedule of payment	Source of payment
Fees for hospital registration, hospitalization, medical treatment, and medicine	Work-related injury insurance diagnosis and treatment catalogue of fees	Reimbursed according to standard, as needed	Work-Related Injury Insurance Fund
Transportation costs, including meals and housing	Same standard as cost reimbursements for business trips	Reimbursed according to standard, as needed	Employer
Cost of meals while hospitalized	Same standard as cost reimbursements for business trips	Reimbursed according to standard, as needed	Employer
Prosthetics, rehabilitation equipment (e.g., wheelchair, crutches), rehabilitation fees	National regulations	Reimbursed according to standard, as needed	Work-Related Injury Insurance Fund
Nursing during rehabilitation	As needed	As needed	Employer
Wages while undergoing treatment and rehabilitation	Workers' original wages and benefits	Monthly	Employer

Note. Work-Related Injury Insurance Regulation (2011), Articles 30–33.

subsidies from their employers, equal to 48–60 months of their average salaries over the past 12 months. Employers of workers with disabilities of Grades 7 to 10 (10%–40% work-capacity loss) whose employment contracts expire are no longer obliged to arrange return to work. Nonetheless, these disabled workers are entitled to claim re-employment subsidies equal to 6–26 months of salary.

In addition to paying Work-Related Injury Insurance premiums (0.5–2% of workers' salaries), Chinese employers also have to contribute to workers' medical treatment and rehabilitation costs, disability payments, and severance payments. Therefore, some employers are reluctant to help their employees claim social insurance compensation. To address the problem of employers refusing to pay work-related-injury compensation, an advanced-payment scheme was added to the Social Insurance Law adopted in 2010. If employers fail to pay work-related injury insurance premiums and also refuse to

Table 7.3 Rights to return to work after workplace injuries

Grade of injury	Labor capacity loss	Employment relationship	Right to terminate	Liability for paying wage replacements	Disability re-employment subsidy	Medical subsidy
Grades 1–4	70–100%	Retained	N/A	Work-Related Injury Insurance Fund	N/A	N/A
Grades 5–6	50–60%	Can be terminated	Employees	Employer (if alternative job cannot be arranged)	Employer	Work-Related Injury Insurance Fund
Grades 7–10	10–40%	Can be terminated	Employers and employees	Employer (until the labor contract expires)	Employer	Work-Related Injury Insurance Fund

Note. Work-Related Injury Insurance Regulation (2011), Articles 34–37.

pay work-related injury compensation, the WIIF should compensate their injured employees (Social Insurance Law, 2011 Art. 41).

Criticism of China's Workers' Compensation System

The State Council passed the Regulation on Work-Related Injury Insurance (2004) to create uniform procedures for handling work-related injuries throughout the country (except for the two Special Administrative Regions, Hong Kong and Macao). There are at least five problems with this regulation. First, enforcing it and establishing social insurance funds for workplace injuries in the 32 provinces of mainland China is a complicated task (Z. Li, 2008). Although the regulation provides uniform standards for calculating compensation of work-related injuries and deaths, the power to award compensation belongs to local governments. As a consequence of differences in economic development among regions, coverage of work-related injuries and compensation practices varies.

Second, domestic migrant workers are not sufficiently protected against occupational injuries (Zhao, 2005). Until now, China has restricted domestic migration through the relatively strict registration of households. Migrant workers do not automatically acquire official residential identity in the cities where they work. Because the workers' compensation system greatly depends on regional budgets, local governments are not willing to spend extra money to protect workers registered in other regions. Therefore, a significant number of migrant workers in China cannot access workers' compensation through governments where their workplaces are located (Sun & Liu, 2014; Zhao, 2005).

The third problem is insufficient supervision by the labor administration of private-sector employers. The regulation obliges all employers to purchase insurance against work injuries for their employees (Regulation on Work-Related Injury Insurance, 2011, Art. 2). Otherwise, employers are obliged to pay injured workers compensation equivalent to the amount that is supposed to be paid by WIIF. Although this seems to be an effective way to ensure workers' rights, in the Chinese market with large amounts of surplus labor, private-sector employers are able to use their position of power to exploit employees (Sun & Liu, 2014; Sun & Zhu, 2009; Zhao, 2005). Without effective supervision of private-sector employers, it is extremely difficult for individuals in an oversupplied labor market to gain access to WIIF (Sun & Liu, 2014).

Fourth, the Regulation on Work-Related Injury Insurance (2011) identifies two types of compensation liability: One requires WIIF to cover disability damages and medical expenses, and the other requires employers to cover workers' sick pay. Li (2014) criticizes this regime as a mixed model of self-insurance and social security insurance, which reduces the compulsory nature of work-related injury insurance. Employers' motivations are decreased if contributing to the injury-insurance scheme does not exempt them from liability for compensation. In addition, WIIF intentionally limits

its own liability, which weakens the social security function of work-related injury insurance. As a result, this mixed model of self-insurance and social security insurance makes Chinese workers confront two parties, both of whom are eager to reduce their compensation liability.

Fifth, Chinese trade unions do not actively fight for workers' rights and welfare in the workers' compensation system. As Chen (2003) argued, the All-China Federation of Trade Unions (ACFTU) (the only association of trade unions with legal status in China) cannot represent Chinese workers' interests and rights in the market economy, as trade unions are under the control of the Chinese Communist Party (CCP). The chief task of ACFTU is to enforce the CCP's policies, rather than promote workers' interests. In this situation, official Chinese trade unions can provide little support to workers in claiming damages for work injuries.

During China's transition from planned to market economy, the previously socialist worker-welfare regime ended, and a Western-style social security system, to ensure labor rights and well-being in the market economy, was recently introduced on a trial basis. Work-related injury insurance is one of the core features of the new social security system. The process for claiming workers' compensation may bring some additional negative outcomes for injured workers. In the Chinese context, the imbalance between regions, strict limits on domestic migration, and the lack of independent trade unions have already created considerable operational difficulties for this new workers' compensation system.

Compensation Schemes for Disabilities Caused by Non-Work-Related Injuries and Diseases

In China, compensation schemes for disabilities caused by non-work-related injuries and diseases include tort litigation, governed by the Tort Law (2010), and benefits paid by employers, governed by the Interpretation of the Supreme People's Court of Some Issues Concerning the Application of Law for the Trial of Cases on Compensation for Personal Injury (2004) (see Table 7.4). Currently, these laws apply to personal and workplace injuries that cannot be officially recognized under workplace-injury insurance. Due to the limitations and restrictions of this insurance, many noncompensable claims are arising from workplace accidents. For example, many claims from maritime-transport workers arising from workplace accidents at sea are covered by tort law rather than WIIR (Shan, 2017). This is because maritime-workplace accidents occur outside China, and maritime workers have precarious, rather than formal, employment agreements. If injured maritime workers litigate to claim compensation, their employers are not obliged to arrange their return to work. The rationale of the tort-law approach is to remedy injured workers' losses, including medical expenses, loss of earnings, disability, and death. However, the civil-law approach does not support injured workers' return to work or re-employment.

Table 7.4 Compensation standards for personal injuries

	Coverage and calculation formula		
Medical fee	Actual expense incurred, based on hospital invoices		
Disability rehabilitation equipment	Reasonable expense incurred		
Disability compensation	Urban resident	Degree of disability × 20 years × Annual disposable income per capita of the urban area where the court entertained the claim	
	Rural resident	Degree of disability × 20 years × Net annual income per capita of the rural area where the court entertained the claim	
Dependents' living allowance[a]	Urban resident	Dependent < 18 years old	Degree of disability × Urban consumption expenditure per capita × (18 years minus actual age)
		Dependent > 18 years old, no work capacity, no income	Degree of disability × Urban consumption expenditure per capita × 20 years[b]
	Rural resident	Dependent < 18 years	Disability degree × Per capita rural consumption expenditure × (18 years minus actual age)
		Dependent > 18, no work capacity, no income	Per capita rural consumption expenditure × 20 years[c]
Damages for emotional distress	Amount determined by the judge, according to the situations of tort, local living expenses, and the compensation capacity of the party at fault		
Other property damages	Amount determined by the judge, according to evidence provided by the claimant		

Note. Supreme People's Court (2004).

[a] If the dependent can be supported or raised by any other person, the party obliged to compensate the claimant may only compensate the proportion that the victim bears. If there is more than one dependent, the total annual compensation amount cannot exceed the average per-capita consumption expenditure of urban/rural residents in the previous year. [b] If the dependent is over 60, the formula is as follows: Per-capita urban consumption expenditure × [20 − (actual age − 60)]. If the dependent is over 75, the formula is as follows: Per-capita urban consumption expenditure × 5. [c] If the dependent is over 60, the formula is as follows: Per-capita rural consumption expenditure × [20 − (actual age − 60)]. If the dependent is over 75, the formula is as follows: Per-capita rural consumption expenditure × 5.

Table 7.5 Medical leave for non-work-related injuries and diseases

Years in the workforce	Length of service at current employer	Medical leave
< 10 years	< 5 years	3 months
	≥ 5 years	6 months
≥ 10 years	< 5 years	6 months
	5–10 years	9 months
	10–15 years	12 months
	15–20 years	18 months
	≥ 20 years	24 months

Note. Ministry of Labor (1994), Articles 3–4.

Return to Work After Non-Work-Related Injuries

Employers' liabilities to workers are much lower for non-work-related injuries or diseases than for work-related ones. In 1994, the Ministry of Labor promulgated the Rules Regulating Medical Periods for Non-Occupational Injuries and Diseases. The rules provide medical leave for workers, during which employers cannot unilaterally terminate employment relationships. Medical leave is determined by the employee's years in the workforce and length of service at the current employer (see Table 7.5).

During their allotted medical leave, workers are entitled to return to work. If they cannot recover within the allotted leave, their work capacity should be assessed. If their degree of disability is assessed as between Grades 1 and 4 (100%–60% work-capacity loss), their employers should arrange retirement, which entitles workers to collect pensions. If their degree of disability is assessed as between Grades 5 and 10, employers are entitled to terminate their employment contracts after medical leave, with 30 days' notice. Under the Labor Contract Law (issued 2008, revised 2012), workers are entitled to severance pay equivalent to one month's salary for each year they worked for their employers, up to a maximum of 12 months' salary (Labor Contract Law of the PRC, 2012). If employees with non-work-related disabilities and diseases do not return to work after medical leave, their employers are entitled to unilaterally terminate the employment relationships.

Discussion

Following implementation of the Reform and Opening-Up policy, the Chinese work disability system was restructured. Its focus changed from concentrated employment of disabled workers in social-welfare enterprises to dispersed employment in the free labor market. With regard to work-related disability, compensation by social insurance has replaced the liability of state-owned enterprises. Governments gradually withdrew their direct intervention in work disability policy and, instead, tended to adopt market-oriented measures, including the disability-employment tax and work-related injury insurance.

Chinese work disability policy takes a cause-based approach to disability. To access work disability benefits, people with disabilities need to be certified either by a local Disabled Persons' Federation or WCAC. The system does not recognize work-related mental disabilities. The right of workers with non-work-related disabilities to keep their jobs is only protected within medical leave. Compared with China's general policy on employing people with disabilities and non-work-related disability policy, its work-related disability policy is more comprehensive, and workers can claim benefits both from Work-Related Injury Insurance Fund and employers.

China's work disability policy differs in rural and urban areas. Most people with disabilities in China are rural residents, and most injured workers are migrants from rural areas. For rural people with disabilities, work disability policy focuses mainly on supporting farming, planting, animal breeding, and handicraft industries. However, rural migrants to cities no longer engage in these activities. Following work-related injuries, they may need rehabilitation and want to return to industrial jobs rather than agriculture. In the current policy context, it is almost impossible for them to access supports for returning to urban industry. Following industrial accidents, most injured migrant workers have to return to rural areas, since they can no longer afford to live in cities. As a result, the challenges of dealing with work disabilities have shifted from urban to rural areas, which may exacerbate poverty there.

Current measures to remedy work-related and non-work-related disabilities focus on financial compensation rather than rehabilitation or return-to-work supports. Employers' obligations are limited to maintaining employment relationships and sick pay. Only when workers have Grade 5 or 6 work-related disabilities are employers liable for arranging alternative jobs. In the case of more serious (Grades 1–4) or less serious (Grades 7–10) disabilities, employers can either transfer their liability for compensation to the Work-Related Injury Insurance Fund or terminate employment relationships with injured workers once their fixed-term employment contracts expire. Except for financial compensation, Chinese employers do not have much involvement in supporting injured workers during return to work or rehabilitation.

Occupational rehabilitation is still at the pilot stage in China. In 1996, the Ministry of Labor proposed a plan for an occupational-rehabilitation service (Chan & Tang, 2008). In 2004, the Work-Related Injury Insurance Fund began to reimburse the costs of occupational-rehabilitation therapy. In 2009, the Ministry of Human Resources and Social Security launched a pilot occupational-rehabilitation service in Guangdong. Sun and Mao (2007) pointed out that, if injured workers are asked to choose between low compensation for rehabilitation plus return to work and high compensation for return to work without rehabilitation, many would choose the latter. To develop China's work disability policy, in addition to promoting occupational rehabilitation it is also important to improve understanding and awareness of occupational rehabilitation among workers, employers, and other stakeholders (Costa-Black, Cheng, Li, & Loisel, 2011).

Every year, 16 million new workers enter the Chinese labor market. With a significant labor surplus, integrating people with disabilities into the highly competitive labor market is even more challenging. Although China's work-related disability policy is comprehensive, enforcement challenges are still tremendous. By the end of 2014, 206.4 million workers were covered by work-related injury insurance, and coverage of migrant workers increased to 73.7 million. However, in some sectors, such as maritime transport, Work-Related Injury Insurance covers fewer than 50% of workers (Chen, Zhu, & Hao, 2014). The enforcement of advance payment of compensation is highly problematic. According to a survey of work-related injury insurance funds in 283 cities, only 28 made advance payments of work-related-injury compensation if injured workers' employers had refused to take responsibility for compensation. More than 90% of the funds expressly refused workers' applications for advance payment (Yu, 2013).

Chinese work disability policy faces two challenges. The first is giving employees with work injuries and occupational diseases sufficient compensation and support for return to work. The second is promoting the employment of people with disabilities in a highly competitive labor market. Meanwhile, every year the Work-Related Injury Insurance Funds accumulate a significant surplus. By the end of 2015, that surplus had reached CNY 120.5 billion [US$18.82 billion]. Yu (2013) argued that the huge surplus should be invested in initiatives to prevent work disability and promote occupational rehabilitation.

Conclusion

From liberalizing planned-economy enterprises in the 1980s and 1990s to ensuring workers' rights in the 2000s through new legislation, Chinese work disability policy has undergone significant reform. With regard to employing people with disabilities, concentrated employment in social-welfare enterprises declined under market-economy competition. An alternative policy now requires employers to either ensure that 1.5% of their employees are disabled or pay a disability-employment tax. Instead of offering alternate jobs to newly disabled workers, employers may be more inclined to pay the tax. In the long term, job opportunities for disabled workers will keep declining. As for injured workers, work-related injury insurance has removed some compensation liability from enterprises.

These policy efforts aim to free employers from direct liability for work disabilities and, instead, establish a social security system to support people with disabilities and occupational illnesses, and injured workers. However, work disability policy confronts significant enforcement challenges. Since the Regulation on the Employment of the Disabled (2007) came into force, the employment rate of China's urban disabled population has not significantly increased. More than 10 years after the Work-Related Injury Insurance Regulation came into force in 2003, many precarious, rural migrant, and mobile transport workers (e.g., seafarers) are still not fully covered by social insurance. Occupational rehabilitation and return-to-work programs are still underdeveloped. On one hand, Work-Related Injury Insurance coverage still needs to be expanded. On the other hand, China needs to further develop financial compensation and other supports for disabled workers, including occupational rehabilitation and return-to-work programs.

Notes

1 This term refers to lifelong employment relationships in the context of a planned economy.
2 Medical assessments are conducted at hospitals or special medical assessment institutions. Under the statute, there are six types of disability: vision impairment, hearing impairment, speech disorder, physical disability, mental disability, and intellectual disability. Within each type of disability, there are various degrees. Taking physical disability as an example, a thumb loss (or loss of four fingers except the thumb) is a Grade 4 disability, according to the Disability Standards of the Second National Survey.
3 Ministry of Finance is the official English translation of 财政部.
4 In China, public medical care is not free, and patients have to pay deposits before receiving any treatment.
5 This is because (a) employers are obliged to pay a certain percentage of the damages even though work-related injury insurance is arranged and (b) if employers have refused to purchase the insurance, then injured workers are entitled to claim compensation against their employers.
6 Standing Committee of the National Congress is the official English translation of 全国人民代表大会常务委员会.
7 The following are not considered work-related injuries:

 (1) Injuries incurred while employees are drunk or under the influence of illegal drugs.
 (2) Injuries incurred while employees are knowingly committing crimes.
 (3) Cases in which employees deliberately harm themselves or commit suicide.

References

Chan, C. C. H., & Tang, D. (2008). Work rehabilitation in Mainland China: Striving for better services and research. *Work*, *30*(1), 3.
Chen, F. (2003). Between the state and labour: The conflict of Chinese trade unions' double identity in market reform. *The China Quarterly*, *176*, 1006–1028.

Chen, G., Zhu, X., & Hao, Y. (2014). *The application of Maritime Labour Convention (2006) in China and standard employment contractual remedies.* Wuhan: Wuhan University of Technology & Fujian: Maritime Safety Administration.

China Disabled Persons' Federation. (2007). *Administrative rules of disabled persons' identity cards.* Retrieved January 19, 2018, from www.cdpf.org.cn/ywzz/zzjs_199/cjrz/200711/t20071114_26266.shtml

China Disabled Persons' Federation. (2016). *The development report of Chinese disabled persons.* Retrieved from www.cdpf.org.cn/zcwj/zxwj/201604/t20160401_548009.shtml

Costa-Black, K. M., Cheng, A. S., Li, M., & Loisel, P. (2011). The practical application of theory and research for preventing work disability: A new paradigm for occupational rehabilitation services in China? *Journal of Occupational Rehabilitation, 21,* 15–27.

Dai, J., Wang, S., Dong, S., Wang, C., Zhao, G., & Dong, X. (2011). Current situation on disabilities caused by work-injury in China and its prevention strategy. *Disabled People, 3,* 41–45.

Howell, J., & Pearce, J. (2002). *Civil society and development: A critical exploration.* London: Lynne Rienner.

Labor Contract Law of the People's Republic of China. (2012, December 18). Issued by the Standing Committee of the National People's Congress 2008, revised 2012. Retrieved January 19, 2018, from www.lawinfochina.com/display.aspx?id=13222&lib=law&SearchKeyword=&SearchCKeyword=%c0%cd%b6%af%ba%cf%cd%ac%b7%a8

Labor Law of the People's Republic of China. (2009, August 27). Issued by the Standing Committee of the National People's Congress 1995, revised 2009. Retrieved January 19, 2018, from www.lawinfochina.com/display.aspx?id=22793&lib=law&SearchKeyword=&SearchCKeyword=%c0%cd%b6%af%b7%a8

Law of the People's Republic of China on the Protection of Disabled Persons. (2008, July 1). *Issued by the Standing Committee of the National People's Congress 2008.* Retrieved January 19, 2018, from www.lawinfochina.com/display.aspx?id=7015&lib=law

Li, J. (2008). China's new labor contract law and protection of workers. *Fordham International Law Journal, 32,* 1083–1132.

Li, M. (2014). *Mandatory work-related injury insurance and its implementation path.* Beijing: Law Press.

Li, Z. (2008). Realistic options for the work injury rehabilitation system in China. *Work, 30*(1), 67–71.

Liao, J. (2015). The evaluation of disability employment policies. *Population and Economics, 209*(2), 68–77.

Loisel, P., & Côté, P. (2013). The work disability paradigm and its public health implications. In P. Loisel & J. R. Anema (Eds.), *Handbook of work disability: Prevention and management* (pp. 59–67). New York: Springer.

Lu, X. (2001). Transition, globalisation, and changing industrial relations in China. In C. Candland & R. Sil (Eds.), *The politics of labor in a global age: Continuity and change in late-industrializing and post-socialist economies.* New York: Oxford University Press.

Mao, Q., & Zhang, G. (2007). On China's industrial injury insurance system. *Journal of Lanzhou University (Social Sciences), 35,* 107–112.

Ministry of Human Resources and Social Security. (2012). *The statistics of the development of the human resources and social security of 2011*. Retrieved January 19, 2018, from www.mohrss.gov.cn/SYrlzyhshbzb/zwgk/szrs/ndtjsj/tjgb/201206/t20120605_69908.htm

Ministry of Human Resources and Social Security. (2013). *The statistics of the development of the human resources and social security of 2012*. Retrieved January 19, 2018, from www.gov.cn/guoqing/2014-04/21/content_2663699.htm

Ministry of Human Resources and Social Security. (2014a, March 1). *Interim Provisions on Labor Dispatch*. Retrieved January 19, 2018, from www.lawinfochina.com/display.aspx?id=16484&lib=law&SearchKeyword=&SearchCKeyword=%c0%cd%ce%f1%c5%c9%c7%b2

Ministry of Human Resources and Social Security. (2014b). *The statistics of the development of the human resources and social security of 2013*. Retrieved January 19, 2018, from www.mohrss.gov.cn/SYrlzyhshbzb/dongtaixinwen/buneiyaowen/201405/t20140528_131110.htm

Ministry of Human Resources and Social Security. (2015). *The statistics of the development of the human resources and social security of 2014*. Retrieved January 19, 2018, from www.mohrss.gov.cn/SYrlzyhshbzb/dongtaixinwen/buneiyaowen/201505/t20150528_162040.html

Ministry of Human Resources and Social Security. (2016). *The statistics of the development of the human resources and social security of 2015*. Retrieved January 19, 2018, from www.mohrss.gov.cn/SYrlzyhshbzb/dongtaixinwen/buneiyaowen/201605/t20160530_240967.html

Ministry of Labor. (1994, December 1). *Rules regulating medical periods for non-occupational injuries and diseases*. Issued by the Ministry of Labor. Retrieved January 19, 2018, from www.mohrss.gov.cn/gkml/xxgk/201407/t20140717_136132.htm

National Bureau of Statistics of China. (2007). *The second national survey of the disabled people*. Beijing: National Bureau of Statistics of China. Retrieved June 28, 2017, from www.stats.gov.cn/tjsj/ndsj/shehui/2006/html/fu3.htm

National Bureau of Statistics of China. (2016). *China statistical yearbook 2015*. Beijing: China Statistics Press. Retrieved June 28, 2017, from www.stats.gov.cn/tjsj/ndsj/2015/indexch.htm

Regulation on the Employment of the Disabled. (2007, May 1). *Issued by the State Council*. Retrieved January 19, 2018, from www.lawinfochina.com/display.aspx?id=5906&lib=law&SearchKeyword=&SearchCKeyword=%b2%d0%bc%b2%c8%cb%be%cd%d2%b5

Regulation on Work-Related Injury Insurance. (2011, January 1). Issued by the State Council 2004, revised 2011. Retrieved January 19, 2018, from www.lawinfochina.com/display.aspx?id=8627&lib=law&SearchKeyword=&SearchCKeyword=%b9%a4%c9%cb%b1%a3%cf%d5

Shan, D. (2017). *Seafarers' claims for compensation following workplace injuries and death in China*. (Unpublished doctoral thesis). Cardiff University, UK.

Shang, K., & Liang, T. (2011). *The disability employment in the new economy of China*. Beijing: China Labor and Social Security Press.

Social Insurance Law. (2011, July 1). Issued by the Standing Committee, National People's Congress. Retrieved January 19, 2018, from www.lawinfochina.com/display.aspx?id=8328&lib=law&SearchKeyword=&SearchCKeyword=%c9%e7%bb%e1%b1%a3%cf%d5%b7%a8

Sun, L., & Liu, T. (2014). Injured but not entitled to legal insurance compensation: Ornamental institutions and migrant workers' informal channels in China. *Social Policy & Administration, 48*(7), 905–922.

Sun. S., & Zhu, L. (2009). Occupational injury insurance system of China: Development and changes in the last sixty years (1949–2009). *Hebei Academic Journal, 29*, 1–6.

Sun, S. H. H., & Mao, A. L. (2007). Problems and resolutions for work injury rehabilitation. *Journal of Beijing Vocational College of Labour Social Security, 1*(4), 9–13.

Supreme People's Court. (2004). *Interpretation of the Supreme People's Court of some issues concerning the application of law for the trial of cases on compensation for personal injury*. Retrieved January 19, 2018, from www.lawinfochina.com/display.aspx?id=3416&lib=law

Taylor, B., Kai. C, & Qi, L. (2003). *Industrial relations in China*. Cheltenham: Edward Elgar Publishing.

Tort Law. (2010, July 1). *Issued by the Standing Committee, National People's Congress*. Retrieved January 19, 2018, from www.lawinfochina.com/display.aspx?id=7846&lib=law

United Nations Department of Economic and Social Affairs, Population Division. (2015). *World population prospects: The 2015 revision, key findings and advance tables* [Working Paper No. ESA/P/WP.241]. Retrieved January 19, 2018, from https://esa.un.org/unpd/wpp/publications/files/key_findings_wpp_2015.pdf

World Bank. (2017a). *Gross domestic product 2016*. Retrieved January 18, 2018, from http://databank.worldbank.org/data/download/GDP.pdf

World Bank. (2017b). *GDP per capita (current US$)*. Retrieved January 18, 2018, from https://data.worldbank.org/indicator/NY.GDP.PCAP.CD?end=2016&start=2015&year_high_desc=true

Wu, B. (2008). *Vulnerability of Chinese contract workers abroad: A case of the working conditions and wages of Chinese seafarers*. Nottingham: University of Nottingham, China Policy Institute.

Yao, S. (2000). Economic development and poverty reduction in China over 20 years of reforms. *Economic Development and Cultural Change, 48*, 447–474.

Yin, J., & Tian, L. (2016). Work-related disability and rural migrant workers' "leaving the city and returning to the country." *Journal of Social Security Studies, 1*, 72–78.

Yu, X. (2013). Ten years of Work-Related Injury Insurance: Development, challenges and the future. *Chinese Social Security, 6*, 39–41.

Zhao, L. (2005). An analysis of five contradictions in the matter of social security for migrant workers from rural areas. *Journal of Shenzhen University (Humanities and Social Sciences), 22*, 69–72.

Zhu, C. J., & Dowling, P. J. (2002). Staffing practices in transition: Some empirical evidence from China. *International Journal of Human Resource Management, 13*, 569–597.

Zhu, Y. (1996). Economic reform and the challenge of transforming labour regulation in China. *Labour and Industry, 7*, 29–50.

Zhu, Y. (2002). Economic reform and labour market regulation in China. In S. Cooney, T. Lindsey, R. Mitchell, and Y. Zhu (Eds.) *Law and Labour Market Regulation in East Asia*, (pp. 157–184). London: Routledge.

Part 3

Comprehensive Social Security Systems

Chapter 8

Reforming Activation in Swedish Work Disability Policy

Christian Ståhl and Ida Seing

Sweden is regularly characterized as one of the world's most generous welfare states, with high benefits and low thresholds for entering the social security system. In recent decades, this generosity has gradually changed, especially regarding the sickness insurance system, which has become more restrictive. In this chapter, we analyze the development of Swedish work disability policy in the 2000s, giving special attention to the introduction of new activation policies and how these policies have been influenced by scientific knowledge and political pressure. The chapter provides an overview of the Swedish sickness insurance system and the social and political issues that have driven its development in recent decades. Swedish work disability policy is constructed and governed by policy makers who are concerned not only with the design of the compensation system but also with matters related to preventing or reducing sick leave, strategies for promoting return to work (e.g., promotion of healthcare interventions), and strategies for promoting labor-market reintegration after sick leave.

This chapter draws on two influential government reports in order to illustrate developments in work disability policy. Both reports have led to significant changes in policy. We analyze how reforms were advocated in these reports, with special attention to how policy makers used research in building their arguments, and how the interpretation of activation and the incorporation of activation components into policies has changed over time. The chapter uses critical and interpretive policy analysis, where policy is regarded as a dynamic, powerful tool for the state to signal its political goals to citizens. The analysis draws on two theoretical concepts from political science: bounded rationality (limitations on decision makers in terms of information, cognitive capacity, and attention) and path dependency (how current decisions are limited by decisions made in the past or by system design). The chapter concludes with a discussion about the adequacy of Swedish policies in relation to work disability prevention research, and of prospects for recently introduced policy changes that have not yet been evaluated.

The Swedish Sickness Insurance System

Swedish sickness insurance offers income protection for claimants with work disability due to illness or disease, regardless of cause. Benefits are provided if the individual has a work disability of at least 25%, and may be granted for 25%, 50%, 75%, or 100%. The benefit level is approximately 80% of previous wages, up to a ceiling. After a two-week period of sick pay paid by the employer, the Swedish Social Insurance Agency[1] (SSIA) pays out benefits, which are financed through taxes. Additional benefits may be provided by unions or employers, depending on the availability of collective agreements. There is also a separate work-injury insurance system, which applies in cases of workplace accidents or occupational diseases. In this system, future earnings and costs associated with the injury may be compensated. The sickness insurance system is, however, the main income-replacement system and is therefore the focus of this chapter.

While the Swedish sickness insurance system primarily replaces lost income, it also promotes and enforces return to work and job transitions. The SSIA has formal responsibility for coordinating the actors involved in return to work, and the Social Insurance Act[2] defines the responsibilities of employers and healthcare providers. Apart from the financial responsibilities, employers are obliged to accommodate workers as far as possible. Accommodation is also regulated by the Work Environment Act[3]. Physicians are responsible for issuing the medical certificates that the SSIA uses in assessing individuals' work ability. Specialized clinics also carry out extended medical assessments, if required. The Public Employment Service[4] may offer vocational rehabilitation in cases where return to work is not possible, or for the unemployed.

Although employers are legally responsible for both prevention and return to work, much of the responsibility is placed on individual employees and government agencies to manage the sick-leave process (Ståhl, Müssener, & Svensson, 2012). Furthermore, the process is designed primarily for traditional employment contracts, leaving employees in nontraditional employment worse off with respect to compensation and return to work. Self-employed individuals generally have worse income protection from the sickness insurance system, and temporary workers are loosely connected to the workplace, which may complicate return to work processes.

One of the major developments in recent years is an increase of mental health problems. These are now the most common cause for sick leave, and more prevalent among women than men. Municipal workers, such as those working in elder care and schools, belong to the occupational sector with the highest rate of sick leave, and it is also a sector where women are over-represented. Hence, the structure of the Swedish labor market, with its rather strong division between male- and female-dominated jobs (with female-dominated jobs often having stressful work conditions), causes structural discrimination against women with regard to sick leave

(Lidwall, Bergendorff, Voss, & Marklund, 2009). Furthermore, increasing mental health problems among younger workers pose future challenges for the sickness insurance system.

Activation Policies in Swedish Sickness Insurance

Reducing the economic burden on societies of sick leave has been a critical task for policy makers in most Western welfare states in recent decades. Policies to promote labor-market participation are common tools for reducing this economic burden. In these policies, sickness absence is considered a problem in terms of societal costs as well as individuals' health and financial situation. Activation policies have been strongly promoted by international organizations such as the Organisation for Economic Co-operation and Development (OECD) and the European Union (EU) (e.g., Organisation for Economic Co-operation and Development (OECD), 2003, 2010) as well as national governments (e.g., Seing, 2014). Although there is considerable variation in the design and intensity of activation policies across national models, a common objective is to quickly reintegrate people without jobs into the labor market: moving them from inactivity into working life. Research has highlighted both "enabling" (focusing on investment in individuals' skills and abilities) and "demanding" (focusing on financial work incentives by reducing social benefits) aspects of activation policies, which may be balanced differently (Eichhorst & Konle-Seidl, 2008).

In line with this broad international shift towards activation, Swedish work disability policy has undergone substantial changes over recent decades, with a number of reforms introduced by governments with different political party majorities (Björnberg, 2012; Hetzler, 2009; Seing, Ståhl, Nordenfelt, Bülow, & Ekberg, 2012; Ståhl et al., 2012). The first activation policies targeting sickness insurance were introduced in the early 1990s.

During this time the so-called "work principle," a long-standing tenet of Swedish labor-market policies, was used to argue for activation elements within the sickness-insurance system in order to counter long-term sickness absence. For instance, part-time sick leave, work training, and work accommodation were promoted, while the statutory responsibility of employers for their workers on sick leave was expanded to include requirements to assess workers' rehabilitation needs, make adjustments in order to stimulate return to work, and pay benefits during the first 14 days of sick leave. These changes were designed to increase employers' incentives to reduce and prevent sick leave, and to invest in the work environment. In 2007, the responsibility for employers to produce rehabilitation plans was abolished. However, the responsibility for workplace accommodations remains.

The activation trend is illustrated by the introduction of the rehabilitation chain, which is analyzed in the next section. This activation approach was discussed in a report from the OECD, where it was presented as a positive reform due to its focus on activating individuals on sick leave and making them responsible for changing their situations:

> One of the more striking features of Sweden's revised sickness benefits policy and its corresponding rehabilitation-chain model is that recipients are being seen for the first time as actively responsible for adapting to their changed circumstances and staying in whatever work they are able to perform. In the past, these individuals were considered as incapacitated and essentially passive recipients of assistance from the [S]SIA and their employer.
>
> (OECD, 2009, p. 24)

The activation trend in Swedish sickness insurance is also illustrated by an emphasis on work ability rather than work disability, a rhetoric promoted through media campaigns, summarized by the slogan, "We don't ask how sick you are, but what work ability you have." In recent decades, activation policies have led to a more restrictive sickness insurance system, where eligibility criteria have been restrained and the possibilities of being granted a permanent disability pension have been limited. Some of these changes will be analyzed in more detail in the following sections.

Activation Policies 2006–2008: Activating the Individual

Although activation policies were introduced in sickness insurance during the 1990s, regulations for sick-leave entitlement changed more dramatically in the 2000s. In 2008, the center-right government introduced the rehabilitation chain, a policy that set separate eligibility criteria at different times in a sick-leave case. The reform consisted of a fixed schedule for assessing individuals' work ability, where assessments broadened over time, with the intention of restricting access to benefits and thereby promoting and enforcing work reintegration. During the first 90 days of sick leave, work ability was assessed in relation to the job from which the person was sick-listed and then, between Day 91 and Day 180, for any job that the employer may offer. After this, work ability for any job normally available on the labor market was assessed, meaning that sickness benefits could end if a person was considered able to work in another job, regardless of its availability. Another feature of the 2008 reform was a limit on how long benefits may be granted, which was initially set to 365 calendar days and later extended to 915 days, depending on the severity of the condition and the claimant's prognosis. After the time limit, the person on sick leave had to enroll in a work-reintegration program through the public employment service and could not apply for renewed sickness benefits during a waiting period of three months. In addition to these changes, access to permanent disability benefits was restricted.

Although the 2008 reforms were introduced by a center-right government, most of the details were described in a report, *More insurance and more work*[5], issued by a social-democratic government in 2004 and published in 2006 (Swedish Government, 2006). The following section presents an analysis of the arguments in this report, and the proposals made by the center-right government prior to their implementation.

Sickness Insurance as Transition Insurance

In the 2006 report, the social-democratic government argued that the sickness insurance system functioned poorly and that reforms were necessary in order to facilitate early return to work and increase the transition of sick-listed people from sick leave back into the labor market. The report explicitly stated that the sickness insurance was too soft, and that this was the reason why an increasing number of people left working life following an illness. Furthermore, the proposed solution to this problem was to increase the insurance principles in the system; that is, the relationship between individual risk and compensation. The report criticized the sickness insurance system with reference to moral-hazard theories, in which social insurance was seen as providing disincentives for engagement in gainful employment. According to the report, the system should, therefore, be reformed to offer time-limited benefits, in order to shorten sick-leave spells and promote return to work and/or job transitions. Transition was described in positive terms, and changing jobs was seen as a solution to the problem of sickness absence. Through job transition, a better match between the individual's work ability and jobs on the labor market was expected:

> It is important that sick leave becomes the start of a transition process. In successful cases, there can be a direct transition from sick leave to a new job, and in other cases, a period of unemployment may be required before the goal is reached. In all cases, transition is preferable to continued sick leave and ultimately disability pension.
> (Swedish Government, 2006, p. 62)

This understanding of sickness insurance as a support system for job transitions, rather than income replacement, can be traced back to discussions about social-protection systems as "re-adjustment insurance," advocated by the European Commission in the 1990s (Commission of the European Communities, 1997). The above quotation illustrates how the purpose of the sickness insurance system is defined as promoting return to work, work reintegration, or even unemployment, rather than sustaining people on sickness benefits. The Swedish government's report also argued that transition measures should be developed so that people can manage to find new jobs within a year of being granted sick leave. The report emphasized that, for those who cannot find new jobs, unemployment is preferable to continued sickness benefits.

Hence, in the government's report, sick leave was considered to be problematic in itself. The insurance system should therefore aim to initiate transition to another job as soon as possible if the person cannot, due to their disease, return to their current job. The report also concluded that the sickness and unemployment insurance systems needed to be harmonized, and that supports for sick-leave recipients to find new jobs needed to be improved. Furthermore, the report argued that both time limits and more formalized assessments of work ability at various intervals were needed in the sickness insurance system. These arguments were later translated into the rehabilitation chain and incorporated into policy by the center-right government in 2008.

Work as an Obligation and an Individual Responsibility

The focus of the reforms was on employment promotion, in contrast to the earlier, more traditional emphasis on social security and income protection. This focus reflected a belief that employers and the labor market can solve the problem of sickness absence by better matching people's abilities with job requirements. Simultaneously, the reform bill placed much of the responsibility for this transition on the individual:

> The insured person should have greater responsibility than previously for taking care of his or her work ability, and should take the initiative and ask for measures at the workplace, which may result in him/her being able to return to work.
> (Swedish Government, 2007, p. 64)

The report and the government's reform emphasized the responsibilities of individuals towards society, including the need to have a job and stay active. This individualized interpretation of activation—and the responsibility for it—articulated a new, more demanding direction in policy. The conceptualization of the work principle, in this case, emphasized people's duty to return to work. Although the government's report suggested the development of transition-support measures, its actual policies focused mostly on providing financial incentives to individuals to return to work by restricting their eligibility for sickness insurance benefits and the number of days on sick leave; that is, sticks rather than carrots. Support measures primarily took the form of a work-reintegration program offered to those reaching the end of their sick leave, while there was less focus on reintegration earlier in the sick leave. A program offering rehabilitation for those with musculoskeletal disorders and common mental disorders (called the "rehabilitation guarantee") was introduced, but this program focused on individual, medically oriented interventions and only briefly involved workplaces (Riksrevisionen, 2015).

During the same period, several government agencies involved in the sick-leave process, such as the SSIA, underwent reorganization and centralization.

Insurance-medicine guidelines were developed that suggested sick-leave times for different diagnoses. As a result, the sick-leave process became increasingly standardized.

Before the time limit for how long sickness benefits can be paid out was abolished in 2016, over 100,000 individuals lost their benefits because they reached the limit. Most of these people were transferred from the sickness insurance system to the work-reintegration program. A year later, most of them had returned to the sickness insurance system, after being deemed unemployable due to work disability.

Activation Policies from 2015 to 2017: Activating the System

We now jump forward to 2015, a year after the center-right government was replaced by a center-left government. At this time, a second influential government report, entitled *More security and better insurance*[6] (Swedish Government, 2015), presented conclusions from a cross-parliamentary committee that was established to recommend revisions to the social insurance system. The report was 1,195 pages long (not counting 11 preparatory reports) and took a broad perspective on many topics. These covered general income-replacement policies across different insurance systems and specific considerations in relation to the unemployment, work-injury, and sickness insurance systems. Regarding the sickness insurance system, specific chapters focused on rehabilitation, return to work, and the different roles of various actors in these processes. The report emphasized that broad political support was necessary to secure what it called "stability" and "trust" in the systems. This is why the committee that produced the report was set up to include all parties in the parliament. In this report, we can find much of the rationale that inspired policy development in subsequent years.

Activation and Return to Work as a Shared Responsibility

The interpretation of the activation concept had developed in the decade after the 2006 report. The 2015 report used a slightly softer touch to describe activation and how it is proposed to be translated into policy. While the earlier report and its subsequent reforms emphasized individual responsibility for activation, the 2015 report began by stating that there is a strong public support for a general welfare system, and that it was crucial to maintain public legitimacy and trust by continuing to offer adequate income replacement. This statement represented a change of tone; although the report still emphasized individual responsibility for financial support, it contained a broader discussion of measures necessary to make this possible. The report maintained the notion of sickness insurance as transition support rather than income replacement, although it described these functions as complementary rather than opposing:

> The sickness insurance is both an income replacement and a transition insurance. In short-term absences, it is primarily an income insurance. In long-term absences, the transition features increase. In these cases, the insurance shall create conditions so that the work ability of the insured person can be utilized as much as possible.
>
> (Swedish Government, 2015, p. 480)

The 2015 report's emphasis on security contrasted to the earlier report's more one-sided focus on activation and transition. The 2015 report stated that the government ought to make sickness insurance effective and predictable, offering individuals the security that they had a right to expect and measures to promote return to work. The work principle, previously discussed mostly in terms of individual responsibility, was now viewed as a joint responsibility of individuals and society:

> The work principle means that the individual has a duty to contribute to working life, according to his/her ability. Each and every one has a responsibility to contribute, even if the ability is temporarily or more permanently limited. Society has a responsibility to provide early and well-functioning support for people in need of help. Measures must be adapted to each person's individual needs. Security is dependent on the societal actors having efficient systems for early identification of people in need of support, and for providing help quickly. Long periods of passivity and waiting for support severely decrease individuals' chances of returning to work.
>
> (Swedish Government, 2015, p. 269)

Return to work was now defined as a multistakeholder endeavor and, hence, a societal responsibility. The 2015 report referred to rehabilitation research and emphasized its finding that the probability of returning to work decreases over time on sick leave, and that it is therefore important to engage multiple actors in the rehabilitation process. The report stressed that this recent research provided guidance for promoting return to work and that rehabilitation may enhance people's recovery and self-efficacy, even before their work ability is fully restored. Early return to work was described as desirable for most conditions, and the report argued that responsibility for return to work lies with the healthcare system and employers:

> A disillusioned picture has spread over several years, questioning whether job transitions and work-oriented rehabilitation can actually work. The committee wants to stress that international reviews and research in recent years give good guidance to how good measures for return to work should be designed. . . . Return to work is dependent on a work-oriented health care system and responsible employers.
>
> (Swedish Government, 2015, p. 269)

The report also discussed time limits within the sickness insurance system and stressed that all measures should be taken to restore individuals' work ability before they have to leave the system. Furthermore the healthcare system should play a key role in restoring work ability; for example, by taking responsibility for coordinating the stakeholders involved.

This system-oriented perspective was a notable change from the 2006 report's purely individual incentive structure (withdrawing benefits at specific times). While the 2006 report described return to work as an individual obligation, the 2015 report described it as both an obligation and a right. Although still acknowledging individual responsibility, the focus had moved toward providing relevant support for individuals to enable them to return to work. In other words, the work principle was expanded from changing individual behavior to making the entire work disability system (involving healthcare and employers) more supportive and work-oriented.

The 2015 report's new multistakeholder approach was translated into rhetoric, as illustrated by a media campaign by the SSIA, called Team Sweden. Here is an excerpt:

> Sweden is facing a great challenge where sick leave is steadily increasing. In the long term it will affect our [social] security system. The trend must be reversed. In order to succeed, the Swedish Social Insurance Agency, other government agencies, employers, health care and individuals must help each other.
> (Swedish Social Insurance Agency, 2016)

A Reconciled Approach to Social Insurance

Where the 2006 report and the 2008 reforms emphasized individual responsibility and restricting the welfare system's generosity, the 2015 report displayed a more nuanced approach that reconciled the basic principles of the traditional Swedish welfare model (income replacement and state responsibilities) with individual responsibility for participating in their rehabilitation process. The 2015 report recommended that both the sickness and unemployment insurance systems be designed to support the work principle, promote transition, and ensure that individuals' income is protected. However, echoing earlier policies, the report added that it should be more profitable to work than to receive benefits. Job transition was still emphasized but as a shared responsibility:

> [Transition] can mean other work tasks, transition to a job at another employer, or even a change of careers. It means a responsibility for the individual. But a transition is also needed in the social insurances, and the society as a whole. It must become more obvious that also those with problems related to health, competence or availability should be able to find their place in the labor market.
> (Swedish Government, 2015, p. 253)

The report also emphasized that the sickness insurance system plays a key role in ensuring that (a) no one stays on benefits longer than necessary and (b) people's abilities are made use of as much as possible, both from the individual and societal perspectives. It was argued that feeling useful benefits individuals, since it helps the recovery process and promotes participation. This reinforces the need to keep work incentives in the system design. Furthermore, this is thought to lead to sustainable state finances.

To secure a sustainable sickness insurance system, the report suggested that a reference level for sickness absence be established (i.e., the mean number of days of sick leave per individual and year that should be considered preferable). The level was proposed to be similar to the mean level of comparable countries, and the report suggested using the Swedish sickness absence level of 2013 as the reference, since it was close to the EU15 mean level at that time:

> A broad political agreement should define a sustainable level for sickness absence. The overarching goal of the government related to sickness absence is that it should be stable and low in a long term. The goal should be developed and it should be made clear which actors that are responsible for reaching it, and in what way.
> (Swedish Government, 2015, p. 489)

The new center-left government chose to implement different suggestions from the 2015 report. One of the government's first actions was to abolish the end date of the rehabilitation chain, as discussed above. Another action translated the recommended sick-leave reference level into a policy goal to reduce the sickness absence level, which the government stated should not exceed nine days per individual and per year in 2020. Furthermore, the government stressed that the number of newly granted disability pensions should not exceed 18,000 per year from 2016 to 2020. In achieving these targets, the SSIA and its frontline staff were identified as key actors, both by being gatekeepers of sickness benefits and by promoting rehabilitation measures among the other stakeholders. The multistakeholder approach to return to work, promoted by the report, was also translated into policy by assigning a coordinating function to healthcare, and by recommending an increase in employers' financial responsibility for long-term sick leave. The latter suggestion was withdrawn, however, after employers criticized increasing costs and administration, and unions feared that this policy would discourage employers from hiring people with disabilities.

Discussion

In this section, we discuss the changing understanding of activation over time, factors that have influenced these changes, and consequences for policy.

Different Times, Different Evidence

Our comparison of the understanding of activation in the 2006 and 2015 reports shows how use of the concept changed over the decade that separated them. This change could be interpreted as an evolution of the concept, or as a change of paradigm. Historical research shows that the work principle, a central concept in Swedish welfare policies since the 1930s, has had different connotations in different time periods, depending on the political environment and the parties in power (Junestav, 2004). This suggests that the reason for the different understandings of activation is to be found in contextual conditions, rather than in a linear development of the concept itself.

One similarity between the reports and the reforms they inspired is that they cross political lines. The 2006 report was commissioned by a social-democratic government and led by a person who previously served as the Swedish social insurance minister (1994–1996) and as director general at the SSIA (1996–2004). The report's recommended reforms did not obviously align with traditional social-democratic values, as they emphasized restricting welfare provision and increasing individual responsibility. The reforms, implemented by a center-right government, were heavily criticized for being right-wing (particularly by the opposition party, which commissioned the report). Similarly, the 2015 report crossed political lines, being authored by a cross-parliamentary committee that aimed to propose reforms with broad political support.

A striking difference between the two reports can be found in the type of scientific knowledge underpinning their arguments. When we examined the background chapters and the research that was cited, it became clear that the two reports were built on different traditions of thought and, hence, cited research from different scientific disciplines. The 2006 report was built on economic perspectives about individuals' motivations, norms, and attitudes, and almost exclusively cited economic research. In this context, designing social insurance became an issue of regulating moral hazards, and the work principle became a moral issue. Although the 2015 report also referred to economic theories, it was framed by an equality perspective and argued that the financial resources are unevenly distributed throughout society and that too much risk was placed on the individual. While the 2006 report described social insurance as problematic because it gives people incentives to not work, the 2015 report described it as a beneficial and efficient way of managing risks. The 2015 report was also broader, citing research from multiple scientific disciplines, such as rehabilitation research, especially regarding return to work. Consequently, the 2015 report described return to work as a multistakeholder issue, for which responsibility cannot be placed solely on the individual.

Although scientific evidence related to work disability and return to work evolved after 2006, it did not change in ways that would explain the different understandings of activation in the two reports. Neither did these understandings result from different political ideologies. Rather, the reports reflect how different times gave emphasis to different types of research and where the policy conclusions from these research traditions substantially differed. Although the reasons for citing one type of research over another may have varied, the difference between the two reports may have had more to do with changing national and international political agendas. The 2006 report was written when several international organizations (such as the OECD) were advocating that policies increase activation and reduce the use of passive benefits. This understanding of activation aligned with economic research focusing on individual behavior. In 2015, this focus was not as strong, and policies were informed more by research promoting system perspectives on issues of sick leave and return to work.

Sociopolitical Factors Influence Policy Implementation

As argued in a previous article (Ståhl, Costa-Black, & Loisel, 2017), the 2008 policy changes could be seen as a major political reform, because they challenged fundamental assumptions in the Swedish welfare model about the responsibility of the state versus the individual. The reforms were path-dependent (Pierson, 2000) in the sense that, although they did not change the basic system principles, they implied a change in core policy beliefs (Sabatier & Weible, 2007)—especially for social democrats. Further, the political debate following the 2008 reforms was largely disconnected from the nearly unanimous political support for them, as they were proposed by social-democratic politicians but implemented by a center-right government (Ståhl et al., 2017). Criticism following the reforms' implementation was harsh. The opposition (social democrats and the left party) excoriated the reforms as being inhumane, drawing on their core policy beliefs. The reforms were characterized as a "devil shift" (Sabatier, Hunter, & McLaughlin, 1987), a tendency of political actors to demonize their opponents. However, the reforms could be supported by governments of different political inclinations, illustrating the bounded rationality of political decision making (Jones & Baumgartner, 2005), where decisions are made under pressure of budgets and political priorities. The political use of evidence is, therefore, contextually determined and related both to the agendas at the time and to the political ideologies of policy makers in a complex interplay (Greenhalgh & Russell, 2009).

In the two cases we examined, the government reports and the subsequent reforms highly correlate, although many aspects of the reports failed to make it into policy. For politicians, choices about which report recommendations to enact depend on various factors, and the political party in power may play a role. For instance, although the rehabilitation chain developed out of the 2006 report, the resulting policy focused more on financial incentives for individuals to work than on measures to support job transitions. One possible interpretation of this individual focus is that the center-right government chose the report features that were best aligned with its ideology. Another perhaps more reasonable interpretation (given that much of the report already aligned with right-wing ideology) is that measures to support job transitions were more complicated to implement. It is considerably easier (albeit unpopular) to restrict individuals' eligibility for benefits, compared to changing complex rehabilitation systems. Similarly, although the multistakeholder perspective underlies the rhetoric of policies developed after the 2015 report, this perspective is difficult to implement in actual policy making, because the report's recommendation implied significant changes to rehabilitation actors' responsibilities and interactions. Some stakeholders, such as employer organizations, also lobbied to prevent these changes. Hence, there was pressure to maintain the status quo. Taking the multistakeholder perspective seriously in policy making would challenge long-established relationships among actors and, given the path-dependent restrictions of policy development (Pierson, 2000), dramatic changes in such relationships are difficult to pursue.

Another important political change during the period we examined was increased instability in the Swedish parliament due to the growth of the Sweden democrats, a far-right party focused mainly on cutting immigration. Members of this party were first elected in 2010, receiving 5.7% of the vote. In 2014 the party increased its share of votes to 12.9%, becoming the third largest party in parliament. Sweden has had minority governments since 2010, because none of the other parties wanted to form a coalition with the Sweden democrats, and because the other parties did not deviate from the traditional left-right blocs. Hence, government proposals can be voted down in parliament if the opposition and the Sweden democrats oppose them. The unstable minority-government situation means that it is more difficult for the center-left government to get contentious reforms passed in parliament.

The 2015 report provided arguments for the government to promote a more system-oriented agenda. In their policies, however, this agenda was combined with a political goal of reducing sickness absence levels. This goal has, a couple of years later, resulted in stricter assessments by the SSIA, contrary to the broader societal responsibility that the report emphasized, as the way to combat sickness absence; again, this is a consequence of restricting eligibility being easier than changing complex systems. Hence, policies and political goals can be regarded as powerful tools for governments to steer public agencies as well as citizens. In an ongoing study (Seing, 2017), results show how the government uses a numerical target for sickness absence to steer the SSIA and its frontline staff, and how this target shapes SSIA caseworker subjectivity and emotions. The target itself (nine sick days per individual per year in 2020) has spurred positive emotions among SSIA frontline staff (e.g., a sense of achievement, pride, and belonging) and also negative emotions (e.g., anxiety and ambivalence because of the risk that stricter assessments will increase rejections of sickness benefits applications). Governing by a numerical target illustrates the SSIA's effort to induce common goals among SSIA case workers as well as to maintain the work principle in the sickness insurance system and reduce the number of people on sickness benefits. The target, therefore, becomes an effective managerial tool for strengthening the agency's work of attaining policy goals (Seing, 2017).

Conclusions

In this chapter, we analyzed the contents of two influential Swedish government reports that had considerable impact on work disability policy. We conclude that both reports were concerned with the concept of activation but in different ways. The 2006 report, and the reforms it inspired, emphasized increasing individual responsibility for sick leave, while the 2015 report presented a broader system perspective on activation that promoted joint societal and individual responsibility for return to work after sick leave. Our analysis shows how these reports were built on different types of knowledge. This illustrates how different evidence may be used to solve similar policy problems and that policies are contingent and subject to a variety of influences. Thus, policies may not always align with the core beliefs of political parties in power.

Moving forward, in 2017 the development of the Swedish sickness insurance system was guided by a broader and more nuanced evidence base than in the previous decade. However, anecdotal evidence of recent policy implementation within local agencies points to a continued focus on reducing sick leave numbers through restrictive work-ability assessments, rather than system-oriented measures to improve return to work processes. For the system to move toward sustainable compensation and return to work services, policy makers need to be aware of the power of numbers and not resort to using numerical targets to guide policy development.

Notes

1 Försäkringskassan.
2 Socialförsäkringsbalken.
3 Arbetsmiljölagen.
4 Arbetsförmedlingen.
5 *Mera försäkring och mera arbete.*
6 *Mer trygghet och bättre försäkring.*

References

Björnberg, U. (2012). Social policy reforms in Sweden: New perspectives on rights and obligations. In B. Larsson, M. Letell, & H. Thörn (Eds.), *Transformation of the Swedish welfare state: From social engineering to governance?* Basingstoke, UK: Palgrave.

Commission of the European Communities. (1997). M*odernising and improving social protection in the European Union (COM(97)102)*. Brussels, Belgium: Commission of the European Communities.

Eichhorst, W., & Konle-Seidl, R. (2008). *Contingent convergence: A comparative analysis of activation policies.* IZA Discussion Paper No. 3905. Bonn, Germany: Institute for the Study of Labor.

Greenhalgh, T., & Russell, J. (2009). Evidence-based policymaking: A critique. *Perspectives in Biology and Medicine, 52*(2), 304–318.

Hetzler, A. (2009). Labor market activation policies for the long-term ill—A sick idea? *European Journal of Social Security, 11*(4), 369–403.

Jones, B., & Baumgartner, F. (2005). *The politics of attention.* Chicago, IL: University of Chicago Press.

Junestav, M. (2004). *Arbetslinjer i svensk socialpolitisk debatt och lagstiftning 1930–2001 [Work principles in Swedish social political debate and legislation 1930–2001]* Uppsala, Sweden: Uppsala University.

Lidwall, U., Bergendorff, S., Voss, M., & Marklund, S. (2009). Long-term sickness absence: Changes in risk factors and the population at risk. *International Journal of Occupational Medicine and Environmental Health, 22*(2), 157–168.

Organisation for Economic Co-operation and Development. (2003). *Transforming disability into ability: Policies to promote work and income security for disabled people.* Paris, France: OECD.

Organisation for Economic Co-operation and Development. (2009). *Sickness, disability and work: Breaking the barriers. Sweden: Will the recent reforms make it?* Paris, France: OECD.

Organisation for Economic Co-operation and Development. (2010). *Sickness, disability and work: Breaking the barriers. A synthesis of findings across OECD countries.* Paris, France: OECD.

Pierson, P. (2000). Increasing returns, path dependence, and the study of politics. *American Political Science Review, 94*(2), 251–267.

Riksrevisionen. (2015). *Rehabiliteringsgarantin fungerar inte—tänk om eller lägg ner [The rehabilitation guarantee does not work—rethink or discontinue].* Stockholm, Sweden: Riksrevisionen.

Sabatier, P. A., Hunter, S., & McLaughlin, S. (1987). The devil shift: Perceptions and misperceptions of opponents. *The Western Political Quarterly, 40*(3), 449–476.

Sabatier, P. A., & Weible, C. M. (2007). The advocacy coalition framework: Innovations and clarifications. In P. A. Sabatier (Ed.), *Theories of the policy process.* Boulder, CO: Westview Press.

Seing, I. (2014). *Activating the sick-listed: Policy and practice of return to work in Swedish sickness insurance and working life.* Linköping, Sweden: Linköping University.

Seing, I. (2017). *The activation regime and emotions in welfare bureaucratic work: Organizational shaping of the "ideal" caseworker in the Swedish Social Insurance Agency.* Paper presented at the 10th International Critical Management Studies (CMS) Conference, Liverpool, UK.

Seing, I., Ståhl, C., Nordenfelt, L., Bülow, P., & Ekberg, K. (2012). Policy and practice of work ability: A negotiation of responsibility in organizing return to work. *Journal of Occupational Rehabilitation, 22*(4), 553–564.

Ståhl, C., Costa-Black, K., & Loisel, P. (2017). Applying theories to better understand socio-political challenges in implementing evidence-based work disability prevention strategies. *Disability and Rehabilitation, 40*(8), 1–11. doi:10.1080/09638288.2016.1277399

Ståhl, C., Müssener, U., & Svensson, T. (2012). Implementation of standardized time limits in sickness insurance and return-to-work: Experiences of four actors. *Disability and Rehabilitation, 34*(16), 1404–1411.

Swedish Government. (2006). *Mera försäkring och mera arbete* [More insurance and more work]. Stockholm, Sweden: Swedish Government.

Swedish Government. (2007). Prop. 2007/08:136 En reformerad sjukskrivningsprocess för ökad återgång i arbete [A reformed sick leave process for increased return on work] Stockholm, Sweden: Swedish Government.

Swedish Government. (2015). *Mer trygghet och bättre försäkring* [More security and better insurance]. Stockholm, Sweden: Swedish Government.

Swedish Social Insurance Agency. (2016). Team Sweden media campaign. Retrieved September 2017 from www.forsakringskassan.se/lagetsverige

Chapter 9

Work Disability Prevention in Finland
Promoting Work Ability Through Occupational Health Collaboration

Kari-Pekka Martimo

Social security systems in Finland developed differently than in other Nordic countries. Agriculture dominated the Finnish economy for a longer time, industrialization happened later, and many reforms were first made after Finland gained its independence in 1917. Between the two world wars, the Finnish social security did not develop as much as those in other western European countries (Niemelä & Salminen, 2006).

Traditionally in Finland, the trade unions and employer organizations have been strongly involved in the evolution of social security. For example, as labor-market organizations considered that the means-tested, flat-rate national pension scheme enacted in 1956 was no longer able to ensure adequate employee pensions, in 1961 they pressured the government to enact earnings-related pension acts (Niemelä & Salminen, 2006).

Another significant sociopolitical reform was the introduction of compulsory sickness insurance in 1963. The Health Insurance Act (Finland Ministry of Justice, 2004a) includes medical-care insurance that reimburses costs incurred by illness, pregnancy, and childbirth. In addition, it includes a daily allowance that compensates for loss of earnings due to medical conditions. This system will be described in more detail below.

Occupational health (OH) services emerged in the 19th century, when factory owners in rural Finland arranged medical services for their employees and their families. With increasing knowledge about work-related hazards following World War II, more prevention initiatives were added to OH services in order to protect employees from health risks at work. The Finnish Institute of Occupational Health, established in 1948, has played a crucial role in the development of and support to OH services.

The management of work disability in Finland stems from a tradition of rehabilitation. Until the 1940s, rehabilitation chiefly concerned tuberculosis sanatoria and certain hospitals. After World War II, the sizeable veteran population increased demand for invalid care and, consequently, rehabilitation services. Once the number of veterans started to decline, the services and resources used for their rehabilitation were redirected to the working-age population in order to support and improve their work capacity.

As a result of tripartite collaboration, the Occupational Health Care Act (Finland Ministry of Justice, 2001) was introduced in 1978 and revised in 2001. The Act requires all employers to arrange OH services for their employees, irrespective of the size or type of workplace. In this chapter, the role of OH services in work disability prevention is described together with the concept of work ability and its collaborative promotion within workplaces.

In 2016, the population of Finland was 5.5 million, with a life expectancy of 78.4 years for men and 84.1 years for women. The size of the labor force was 2.7 million, with an unemployment rate of 8.8%. Full-time work is most prevalent, with only 16% of employees working part-time. Most enterprises are small; 89% of private companies employ fewer than five people (Statistics Finland, n.d.). In 2015, healthcare expenditure comprised 9.4% of the gross domestic product (National Institute for Health and Welfare, n.d.)

One in five Finns is 65 years of age or older. The population is aging more rapidly in Finland than in most Organisation for Economic Co-operation and Development (OECD) countries (Organisation for Economic Co-operation and Development (OECD), 2013), and this is exerting growing pressure on public finances and labor resources. Faced with the challenge of an increasing old-age-dependency ratio, the Finnish government committed to extending work careers and increasing the employment rate from 69% to 72% (Finnish Government, 2014). This mandate will be achieved by (a) providing students with incentives to enter the labor market earlier; (b) taking actions to reduce unemployment; (c) increasing employment among people with disabilities; and (e) gradually raising the age of eligibility for old-age pensions from the current 63 years.

With prolonged work disability, the role of pension insurance companies has become central. This system is described below, along with the incentives for work disability prevention embedded in pension insurance premiums. Vocational rehabilitation is mostly the responsibility of pension insurance companies, and this is described in relation to the tradition of medical rehabilitation. At the end of this chapter, the system of insurance for work accidents and occupational diseases is described, before the chapter concludes with a discussion of challenges related to work disability prevention in Finland.

The Healthcare System and Temporary Work Disability

Every Finn is covered by general health insurance. This includes not only medical care and rehabilitation, but also the right to sickness allowance if the employee is unable to perform regular work due to any medical condition. In order to receive the benefit, the employee must present a doctor's certificate, first to the employer and later to the Social Insurance Institution of Finland (SII). The waiting period for benefits is 10 business days, during which the employer pays the worker's salary. Some employers will accept a nurse's certificate or the employee's own notification for the first few sickness days.

The sickness certificate, indicating length of absence and diagnosis, is required for salary payment and later for sickness allowance. This policy was adopted because, while the employee receives a salary, the employer receives the sickness allowance from the SII, and for this application a physician's statement with diagnosis is required. According to the Act on the Protection of Privacy in Working Life (Finland Ministry of Justice, 2004b), this sensitive information about the worker's diagnosis has to be restricted to those who need this information at the workplace, and these individuals are obliged to maintain confidentiality. The most common maximum length of salary payment during work disability, defined in private-sector collective agreements, is 56 work days, depending on the length of employment. In the public sector, the salary is paid for much longer but is gradually reduced over time.

The amount of sickness allowance received by workers depends on their annual earnings. The allowance is 70% of the salary up to €30,000 [US$35,829] a year, with an additional 20% of earnings exceeding that level of income. No income can be earned while a full sickness allowance is being paid. Self-employed and unemployed citizens are also entitled to sickness allowance with the same criteria and waiting period; however, the waiting period for entrepreneurs is shorter. The right to full sickness allowance ends after 300 compensated days (Finland Ministry of Justice, 2004a).

A part-time alternative to full-time sick leave was made available in 2007. Employees and self-employed workers who work 30 hours or more per week are eligible for this part-time leave. The employee has to be absent from work during the waiting period (10 business days). After that, the employee's work hours can be reduced to 40% to 60% of the average number of hours on a daily or weekly basis. Part-time sickness allowance is 50% of the full-time benefit for not more than 120 compensated days (Finland Ministry of Justice, 2004a). Studies based on SII registers (Kausto et al., 2014; Viikari-Juntura et al., 2017) have shown that, compared with full-time sick leave, partial sick leave reduces the risk of a worker going on a full disability pension. Even if the risk for partial disability pension is increased, the result is increased work participation.

Occupational Health Services

The role of voluntary OH services was strengthened in 1963 by the implementation of general sickness insurance that reimburses employers for part of the costs of organizing OH services (Finland Ministry of Justice, 2004a). First, the costs of medical care, and later also preventive services, became partially refundable. OH services became mandatory in 1979 when a duty was imposed on employers to arrange preventive services for all of their employees, including part-time and temporary staff. In order to improve the availability of OH services, the Primary Health Care Act (Finland Ministry of Justice, 1972), as amended in 1978, obligated the primary healthcare centers all over Finland to offer OH services to local employers.

The OH Care Act (Finland Ministry of Justice, 2001) was revised in 2001 to oblige employers, employees (or their representatives) and OH professionals to collaborate in several ways. Together they must promote (a) prevention of work-related diseases and work accidents; (b) health and safety in work environments; (c) health, work ability, and functional capacity of employees at all stages of their careers; and (d) activities at workplace. The development of OH services is supported by the Finnish government's commitment to the principles of International Labour Organization (ILO) Convention No. 161 (International Labour Organization (ILO), 1985a) and Recommendation No. 171 (ILO, 1985b), which Finland ratified in 1986. The role and functions of OH services also meet the requirements of the EU Framework Directive 391 (European Agency for Safety and Health at Work, 1989).

According to the OH Care Act, the main OH services that employers must arrange are (a) risk assessments; (b) health surveillance; (c) maintenance of first-aid preparedness at the workplace; (d) informing employees and counseling them about topics related to health and safety at work; and (e) participation in activities promoting work ability. In addition, OH services are intended to support employees with disabilities at the workplace, including employees who receive treatment outside OH services. Therefore, collaboration with other healthcare, social security, employment, and social services is necessary.

In addition to the above-mentioned legally required OH services, employers may arrange medical care as part of OH services. Accordingly, their employees may use these medical services, including all necessary laboratory tests and imaging, for any health problem free of charge. The costs to the employer caused by both legally required services and medical care as part of OH services (excluding specialist care) are partially reimbursed by the SII, at a rate of 50%. If the employer has a written policy on attendance management due to illness, up to 60% of employers' costs for legally required services are reimbursed (Finland Ministry of Justice, 2004a). However, there is a maximum compensation amount per employee per year, which is verified annually.

Despite Finland's well developed public healthcare system, OH services continue to play an important role in employees' primary healthcare, especially in the prevention of work disability. Major concerns are temporary workers, whose access to OH services is continuously changing, and the unemployed, who do not have access to OH services.

Before reimbursing part of employers' costs for OH services, the SII assesses their appropriateness. In addition, the Regional State Administrative Agencies oversee employer compliance with legally required OH services.

Every employer must have a valid and open contract with the OH services provider, as well as an annual OH action plan with targets based on risk assessments carried out at the workplace (Finland Ministry of Justice, 2001).

The role of Finland's OH services is internationally unique. Not only are they part of primary healthcare services, they also provide professional OH resources to workplaces (Figure 9.1). Information on employees' health and work ability at a group level collected by OH services may be used at individual workplaces for making decisions that influence occupational health and safety. In addition, OH services have taken on the role of bridging healthcare and workplaces in case management of employees with disabilities. OH services also mediate between rehabilitation-service providers and workplaces (Finland Ministry of Justice, 2001).

About 90% of employees have access to OH services (Social Insurance Institution, 2017). The 10% who do not has remained constant since 2003. The smaller the workplace, the more often OH services are not provided. Around 90% of employees with OH services also have access to medical services as part of OH services. Especially in situations where the health problem is related to work (symptoms are partly caused or exaggerated by work, or work ability is reduced by the health condition), early access to OH services enables work-related interventions in addition to individual medical treatments.

The role of OH services in work disability prevention has been strengthened by recent legislative changes. Since part-time sick leave was introduced in 2007, this disability benefit is approved only with a certificate of an occupational physician, who has knowledge of the employee's job and working conditions. Since 2010, employers have been encouraged, through higher reimbursement of the costs incurred for preventive OH services, to collaborate with those services in developing a model for early support.

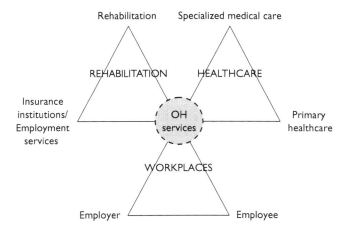

Figure 9.1 Occupational health services in Finland.

This model should include a system to monitor sickness absences, indicating which collaborator has primary responsibility for what at which stage of work disability, and how work-related interventions will be applied in addition to disease management (Finland Ministry of Justice, 2001).

The 2012 amendment to the Health Insurance Act obliges all employers to notify their OH services when an employee has been on sick leave for 30 days. Under the same amendment, all employees who have been on sickness benefit for 90 days (about four months) are obliged to undergo assessments by occupational physicians concerning their remaining work ability and the possibilities of returning to work. This assessment must be discussed with the workplace, usually the supervisor. The statement given by an occupational physician and sent to the SII is required for the continuation of sickness benefits (Finland Ministry of Justice, 2004a).

Physicians, nurses, physiotherapists, and psychologists are the main healthcare professionals working in OH services, provided that they have relevant training. Since 2013, OH teams can be complemented by professionals in rehabilitation and social services (Finnish Government, 2013). This change has contributed to demedicalizing work disability and to finding solutions outside medicine. Rehabilitation and social-services professionals become more involved if work disability is prolonged, and vocational rehabilitation should be considered.

The occupational physician's sickness-absence certificate with diagnosis can be sent to the employer's OH service, which creates an opportunity to contact and support even employees on sick leave who receive their treatment outside OH services. Strategies used by OH services include (a) collaboration with supervisors; (b) suggestions for work accommodations; and (c) collaboration with pension or accident insurance companies and the SII in matters related to rehabilitation. The duty of the supervisor is to keep in contact with the absent worker, discuss the need for support at return to work, and participate in finding solutions for modifying the returning employee's work.

Work Ability and its Promotion

Based on research by the Finnish Institute of Occupational Health in the 1980s, the concept of work ability (WA) was introduced. The Work Ability Questionnaire was first applied to screen public-sector employees in order to identify those eligible for early retirement (Gould, Ilmarinen, Järvisalo, & Koskinen, 2006). Later, the tool was often used to screen for employees in need of support because of future work disability risk, as indicated by a low Work Ability Index (WAI) score (Jääskeläinen et al., 2016). However, the validity of the WAI in early detection has been criticized, because of its strong focus on medical conditions. Despite high scores, employees might still have difficulties related to work ability (Gould et al., 2006). In addition, the WAI does not measure interpersonal dimensions of work.

Theoretically, the concept of WA was first described as a triangle, with individual health and functional ability, work tasks with work environment, and work community as the three corners. Later, the model grew to accommodate professional skills as the fourth corner. Presently, WA is most often described as the roof of a four-story house (Figure 9.2). Health and functional capacities make up the basement, while the other three floors are (1) competence; (2) values, attitudes, and motivation; and (3) work, work community, and leadership (Ilmarinen, 2009). This more comprehensive model also incorporates other components: the external operational environment, immediate social environment, and family.

As part of a general collective agreement in 1990, labor organizations recommended WA promotion in workplaces. In 2001, WA promotion was included in the revised OH Care Act, which legally mandated collaboration between workplaces and OH services. WA promotion is defined as a systematic and target-oriented collaboration focused on work tasks, work environments, and employees; whereas, OH services' role is to promote and support employees' work and functional ability. Despite the comprehensiveness of the WA model, most workplace-related interventions have focused on individual health and lifestyle risks. Other areas of WA have received less attention.

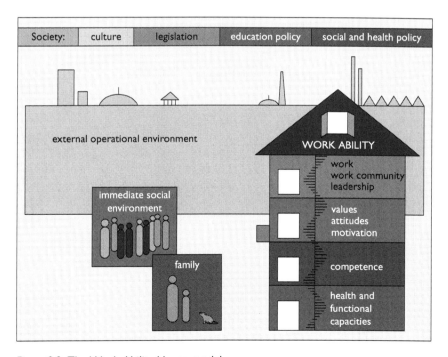

Figure 9.2 The Work Ability House model.

However, the WA concept has increased interest and created a shared language between workplaces and their OH services. In practice, this shared language has helped stakeholders consider not only individual health but also work-related factors as targets for collaborative interventions. In addition to the cost-saving potential for employers of preventing sickness absence and disability pensions, the work ability concept emphasizes the possibility to promote employee commitment and innovativeness by improving health and safety at work. This background facilitated the introduction and implementation of the concept of work disability prevention in Finnish workplaces.

The Pension Insurance System and Prolonged Work Disability

Earnings-related pension insurance constitutes one element of statutory social security in Finland. The money needed to pay pensions is collected from employers (about 18% of payroll) and employees (about 7% of salary). In addition to the old-age pension, pension benefits include full and partial disability pensions, the rehabilitation benefit, and vocational rehabilitation (Finnish Centre for Pensions, 2017). The SII provides the same benefits, except partial disability pensions, to those not eligible for earnings-related pensions.

According to the Employee Pensions Act (Finland Ministry of Justice, 2006), once the sickness-allowance period ends, an employee may be eligible for a full or partial disability pension. A full disability pension is paid if the employee's work ability (income-earning capacity) falls permanently by at least 60%, and a partial disability pension is paid if work ability falls by at least 40%, but less than 60%. The partial disability pension pays half of the full disability pension.

The rehabilitation benefit (formerly known as the "temporary disability pension") is paid if the work ability is expected to improve with treatment and rehabilitation. The other eligibility criteria for the rehabilitation benefit are the same as those for the disability pension. The rehabilitation benefit, which amounts to the disability pension, is always granted for a specific period, during which the insured person is assumed to be unable to work due to the disability. However, there is no time limit for this temporary benefit, and it is renewable.

When a pension company evaluates eligibility for a disability pension, the employee's capacity to earning a living through any type of work, even outside the current workplace, is taken into account. Other evaluation criteria include the employee's formal training, employment history, age, and place of residence. The vocational impact of the disability is taken into account when evaluating entitlement to a disability pension of employees older than 60 years and is always considered for employees in the public sector.

When employees receive full disability pensions and rehabilitation benefits, they cannot earn more than 40% of their previous incomes. When they receive partial disability pensions, on the other hand, they can earn up to 60% of their previous incomes. In the event that a claimant's income exceeds these limits, the full benefit can be changed to a partial benefit or temporarily removed.

To assess the eligibility of an applicant for disability benefits, the pension insurance company's medical adviser consults medical reports provided by the applicant's physicians. Through this process, the overall framework, general decision-making practice, and legal requirements of the work disability pension system are applied to the individual case (Finnish Pension Alliance, n.d.). The final decision on eligibility is made together with lawyers and other pension experts within the company. Pension insurance companies have also set up advisory boards that monitor and guide the handling of disability pension claims and decision making. These advisory boards include representatives of employers' and employees' organizations.

Altogether, 214,000 Finns (about 8% of the labor force) received disability pensions in 2016 (Finnish Centre for Pensions, 2017). Most disability pensions are granted for musculoskeletal (34%) and mental (28%) disorders. Since 2008, the annual number of new disability pensions has declined, while the proportions of both partial and temporary disability pensions compared with full permanent pensions have increased. The average rejection rate was 28% in 2016. If an applicant is not satisfied, an appeal for reassessment can be made to an independent body outside the pension insurance company. In 2011, rejections were reversed in 11% of appeals. If an applicant is still not satisfied with the result, an appeal can be made to the insurance court. In 2011, 14% of the decisions were changed at this stage.

The disability pension fee makes up one portion of the premium that employers pay for pension insurance. The amount of this fee is experience rated in relation to the total payout of disability pensions to company employees. Each individual disability pension has a theoretical cost, which depends on the age and salary of the employee. Total costs for disability pensions related to one employer are compared annually with those of other enterprises, and the payment (or risk) level is determined accordingly.

There are a total of 11 disability pension payment levels, and there is a 55-fold difference in cost to the employer between the lowest and highest levels. Therefore, larger employers (with payrolls of more than €33 million [US$39 million] per year) with full liability have an incentive to prevent permanent disability. The smaller the company, the less possible it is to reduce these costs, because the portion of experience rating drops with the size of the company. Companies with payrolls of less than €2 million per year [US$2.4 million] pay a fixed disability pension fee and therefore have no liability related to disability pensions.

A change in the number of disability pensions and related theoretical costs does not affect an employer's premium for two years, but afterwards the effect lasts for two consecutive years. In addition, disability retirement of an individual who is no longer employed by the company has an effect on theoretical disability pension costs for at least two years after termination of employment. This has been a concern for many companies, because they have a limited possibility to support individuals when they are no longer employed by the company.

The implementation model of the Finnish earnings-related pension system differs from models used elsewhere in the EU. Private-sector pensions are managed by several pension insurance companies, while the public sector has its own pension-provision agencies. One reason for decentralizing pension provision in the private sector was to promote competition between companies and thereby improve efficiency and keep the system's operating costs low (Finnish Pension Alliance, n.d.). There is ongoing debate about whether this has actually happened.

Pension insurance companies have adopted an important work disability prevention role in their clients' workplaces. Pension companies' competing work disability prevention services, including how vocational rehabilitation is managed, have gained more attention in recent years. The goals and contents of these so-called "well-being services" have not been defined by law. The Finnish Financial Supervisory Authority has, however, issued more detailed guidelines concerning the costs of these services. These guidelines outline that the services must focus on employee groups with an elevated risk of work disability, the methods applied and interventions have to be effective, and the employer has to pay half the cost.

From Medical to Vocational Rehabilitation

Rehabilitation in Finland is presently organized by various actors aiming to support individuals with disabilities to maintain or improve their physical, psychological, and social functional abilities (Kuntoutuksen uudistamiskomitea, 2017). The main responsibility of medical rehabilitation lies within the primary healthcare system. The SII is responsible for arranging rehabilitation for individuals with severe disabilities, as well as specific rehabilitation related to musculoskeletal and mental disorders. Social rehabilitation is the responsibility of public social service agencies and employment services; whereas, vocational rehabilitation belongs to pension insurance companies and the SII. In the case of disability due to traffic and work accidents, insurance companies are responsible for both medical and vocational rehabilitation.

Since the 1980s, rehabilitation of working-age individuals has been a key part of work disability prevention. A multiprofessional rehabilitation team collaborates closely with OH services, supervisors, and employers throughout the process, from the selection of employees for rehabilitation to the rehabilitation itself. Although the rehabilitation approaches focus mainly on physical exercise and individual lifestyle habits, individuals' work tasks are also seen as a significant part of rehabilitation.

The effectiveness of this rehabilitation has, however, been criticized. A study by Saltychev (2012) showed that the risk of long-term work disability related to musculoskeletal or mental disorders did not differ between employees who participated in rehabilitation and their propensity-score-matched controls who did not participate in rehabilitation. These results suggest that the recognition of employees in need of rehabilitation, which mainly takes place in OH services, may fail to identify those with a higher risk of work disability. Recently, the SII launched a new work-rehabilitation program with a stronger emphasis on psychosocial determinants of work disability and closer collaboration with workplaces and their OH services.

The most important reform of rehabilitation legislation in recent years was the 2004 amendment to the earnings-related pension acts, which enshrined the right of employees to vocational rehabilitation. This reform also expanded earnings-related pensions to enable applicants to receive rehabilitation in order to restore their work capacity and/or improve their work and earnings capacity. If applicants' functional abilities do not meet the requirements of their occupations, the pension insurance company or the SII determines whether applicants would be able to do other jobs, if necessary with the help of vocational rehabilitation.

Pension insurance companies must ensure that applicants are provided with options for rehabilitation before decisions are made about their eligibility for disability pensions. If the pension application is rejected, the pension provider must confirm that the applicant was given information about rehabilitation options and referred to a suitable rehabilitation that met his or her needs. Medical rehabilitation is not compensated by pension insurance companies, as it is the responsibility of other authorities.

Most commonly, vocational rehabilitation includes a work trial (gradually increasing work hours during the three months after returning to either previous or new work tasks) or retraining for an occupation without inappropriate exposures and strain. From a pension insurance point of view, investing in vocational rehabilitation is desirable; it reduces future costs related to disability pensions because work disability is either postponed or prevented. During vocational rehabilitation, employees receive a rehabilitation benefit that is 33% higher than their disability pension, at no cost to their employers.

Vocational rehabilitation has increased in popularity in recent years. In 2016, the number of employees undergoing rehabilitation approached the number of employees receiving new disability pension benefits. The results of this shift are encouraging. A report by the Finnish Center for Pensions (Saarnio, 2017) shows that, at the end of their rehabilitation, 60% returned to work, 15% received a disability pension, and 8% were unemployed or continued studying. The results are even better if the applicant applied for vocational rehabilitation instead of receiving the benefit when applying for a disability pension. Fewer than 20% of applications for vocational rehabilitation are rejected by pension insurance companies. The main reasons for rejection are a lack of sufficient income or length of employment, or that the medical condition does not increase the risk of receiving a permanent disability pension. If employees are not deemed eligible for vocational rehabilitation by pension insurance companies, they may receive it through the SII.

Work-Accident Insurance

According to the Occupational Accidents, Injuries and Diseases Act (Finland Ministry of Justice, 2015), employers are obliged to insure their employees against work-related accidents and occupational diseases. The insurance premium includes fees that are based on company-specific risks of occupational accidents and disease and related treatment expenses. Compulsory work-accident insurance applies to work performed both in the private and public sectors. For self-employed individuals who have pension insurance coverage, work-accident insurance is voluntary.

Work accidents comprise any sudden, unexpected incident caused by factors external to the worker that leads to an injury at the workplace or in an adjacent area, or while commuting between home and work. In addition, consequences of short-term exposure to hazards such as gases, fumes, and radiation may be considered work injuries, even if the exposure does not cause occupational disease. Even significant aggravation of an injury or illness originally not caused by work is considered compensable, if the consequent deterioration is likely to be caused by work-related factors. In such cases, compensation is paid for as long as the injury- or illness-related deterioration persists.

Occupational disease is defined by this law as a medical condition that has been probably and principally caused by a physical, chemical, or biological hazard at work. A causal connection between the disease and the hazard can be established, if other diseases have been excluded, and the exposure to the hazard has been significant enough to cause the disease. Diagnosis of occupational disease requires cause and effect relationship assessed at two levels. First, there has to be scientific evidence that the exposure can cause the disease. Second, there has to be evidence that the patient's condition is mainly caused by a work-related exposure that has been verified at the workplace. The determination is based on medical findings, how the injury occurred, and previous injuries and diseases.

The Occupational Accidents, Injuries and Diseases Act (Finland Ministry of Justice, 2015) contains a list of physical, chemical, and biological hazards and the diseases they cause. This list is not exhaustive, and medical conditions caused by other hazards can also be recognized as occupational diseases after a cause-and-effect relationship has been confirmed in an individual case.

In 2012, 4,404 cases of possible occupational disease were identified; that is, almost 18 cases per 10,000 employed individuals (Oksa et al., 2014). The most common diagnoses were hearing loss, repetitive-strain injuries, allergic respiratory diseases, skin diseases, and asbestos-induced diseases. Of all identified cases, 40% were compensated by insurance companies as occupational disease. Only a few musculoskeletal and mental disorders are recognized as occupational diseases. Tenosynovitis and epicondylitis may be compensated if the employee was engaged in repetitive, monotonous, or unfamiliar movements before the symptoms appeared. Carpal tunnel syndrome is compensated if the employee was exposed over time to strenuous, non-neutral wrist movements. The only mental disorder that has sometimes been compensated is post-traumatic stress disorder.

Compensation during inability to work related to a work accident or occupational disease is higher than that for other medical conditions. This difference applies to both short- and long-term disability, as well as to permanent partial- or full-disability (accident) pensions. Compensation for an injury or illness caused by a work accident or occupational disease is also more comprehensive than that related to other injuries and illnesses. It covers medical examinations and public or private treatment, a daily allowance, rehabilitation, and medical aids. In the case of a fatal accident, the survivor's pension and funeral allowance are also covered.

The daily allowance during a period of inability to work equals the injured employee's regular salary for the first year. After that, the maximum annual accident pension drops to 85% of the employee's annual earned income until the employee turns 65, after which it drops to 70% of the annual earned income. By comparison, the pension for disability not related to work is lower, at about 50% of previous annual earned income.

Vocational rehabilitation compensated by work-accident insurance can be arranged in the same manner as that compensated by pension insurance. However, there are two main differences between vocational rehabilitation provided by a pension- or accident-insurance company. First, after an occupational injury, accident insurance companies must maintain the income level of injured workers after vocational rehabilitation; whereas, pension insurance companies aim solely at retaining employment. Second, the costs of vocational rehabilitation increase the employer's work-accident-insurance premium after an occupational injury; whereas, vocational rehabilitation in the pension insurance system does not.

Future Challenges

According to OECD (2005), access to physicians in Finland is inequitable across income groups, after adjusting for needs. Currently, employed citizens with access to OH services are in a better position than those outside the workforce, who can only access under-resourced public healthcare if they cannot afford private healthcare or insurance. In 2017, the government proposed a major reform of health and social services (Finnish Government, 2017). This reform will establish new counties in Finland, reform the structure, services, and funding of health and social services, and transfer new duties to the counties. The reform is due to come into force gradually, starting on January 1, 2021.

The reform is intended to drastically change the organization and provision of healthcare services, especially primary healthcare. Its goal is equal access to health services regardless of employment or place of residence. OH services have been left out of the reform, mainly because trade unions and employer organizations do not support major changes. Funding for reimbursement of employers' OH-services costs is collected from employers and employees, and, therefore, their organizations need to participate in deciding how that funding is used.

Trade unions particularly appreciate the medical care provided by OH services. They see this as a key benefit that should not be reduced. The challenge is that resources in OH services are limited and, with easy access to the services, medical care takes up a major part of OH-services professionals' resources. In addition, the need for access to OH services among people who are precariously employed and unemployed has been acknowledged (Finnish Government, 2017). According to another OECD report (OECD, 2008), Finland should make it mandatory for self-employed people to organize OH services for themselves, and organize an OH-services-like system for unemployed people. In 2017, the Health Insurance Act and Occupational Health Care Act were revised, giving employees of larger companies the right to use OH services up to six months after dismissal.

There is no specific legislation concerning injured workers' right to return to work. According to the Criminal Code of Finland as well as the Non-Discrimination Act (Finland Ministry of Justice, 2014), it is illegal to discriminate against an employee on the basis of health or disability. The employer must, where necessary, take any reasonable steps to help people with disabilities gain access to work or training, cope at work, and advance in their careers. However, what is reasonable has not been explicitly defined.

According to a survey (Liukko, Polvinen, Kesälä, & Varis, 2017), 60% of large employers agree that experience rating in the pension insurance system encourages them to invest in activities to maintain employees' work ability, despite the fact that one third of employers find the system difficult to understand. In addition, experience rating has led to a situation where some large companies avoid recruiting people at risk of work disability in order to keep disability pension costs low.

The OECD recommends (OECD, 2008) that Finland consider some form of experience rating for small and medium-sized enterprises as well, at least for a limited number of years of disability-benefit payment. To counterbalance hiring disincentives arising from experience rating, measures such as targeted payroll-tax reductions could be introduced. In Finland, there is no legal obligation to employ a quota of individuals with disabilities.

The rehabilitation system in Finland is complex, managed through various laws and by various agencies. To address these issues, the government established a task force in 2017 to build a cost-effective and equitable rehabilitation system that supports employees with disabilities in every phase of their lives. The task-force report (Kuntoutuksen uudistamiskomitea, 2017) emphasizes clarifying the roles of responsible actors and organizing rehabilitation as an efficient process.

The OECD (2008) urged Finland to simplify its support systems, as the country has several agencies that serve working-age people with illness or disability. The Public Employment Service helps jobseekers with disabilities, while general healthcare and OH services serve those with long-term illness, and the SII assists people with insufficient work history. These are only a few of the multiple support providers. It is not entirely clear to clients, or to the agencies, who is supposed to serve whom.

Finally, in order to prevent the complex social-benefit system from discouraging employment, the government began a two-year experiment providing a basic income in 2017 (Social Insurance Institution, n.d.). Two thousand participants receive €560 [US$669] a month, with no restrictions on other income. Opinions about the ideology behind basic income vary. Some regard it as "freedom to work", whereas others consider it as "freedom from work." Results are expected in 2019.

References

European Agency for Safety and Health at Work. (1989). *EU framework directive 89/391/EEC*. Retrieved from https://osha.europa.eu/en/legislation/directives/the-osh-framework-directive/1

Finnish Centre for Pensions. (2017). *Earnings-related pension system in graphs and figures*. Retrieved from www.etk.fi/en/about-us/image-gallery/earnings-related-pension-system-in-graphs-and-figures/

Finnish Government. (2013). *Asetus hyvän työterveyshuoltokäytännön periaateista, työterveyshuollon sisällöstä sekä asiantuntijoiden ja ammattihenkilöiden koulutuksesta* [Government decree on the principles of good occupational health practice, contents of OH services, and training of professionals and experts]. Retrieved from www.finlex.fi/fi/laki/alkup/2013/20130708#Pidp452637952

Finnish Government. (2014). *Hallituksen päätös rakennepoliittisen ohjelman toimeenpanon vahvistamisesta* [Government's decision on validating the implementation of structural policy programme]. Retrieved from http://valtioneuvosto.fi/documents/10184/1043904/hallituksen-paatos-280814.pdf/d886dc21-4fa5-4583-949f-c2c32fccf8c0

Finnish Government. (2017). *Työterveys 2025—yhteistyöllä työkykyä ja terveyttä* [Health at work 2025—collaboration for work ability and health]. Helsinki, Finland: Ministry of Social Affairs and Health.

Finland Ministry of Justice. (1972, amended 1978). *Primary health care act*. Retrieved from http://finlex.fi/en/laki/kaannokset/1972/en19720066?search%5Btype%5D=pika&search%5Bpika%5D=primary%20health%20care

Finland Ministry of Justice. (2001). *Occupational health care act.* Retrieved from http://finlex.fi/en/laki/kaannokset/2001/en20011383?search%5Btype%5D=pika&search%5Bpika%5D=occupational%20health

Finland Ministry of Justice. (2004a). *Health insurance act.* Retrieved from http://finlex.fi/en/laki/kaannokset/2004/en20041224.pdf

Finland Ministry of Justice. (2004b). *Act on the protection of privacy in working life.* Retrieved from www.finlex.fi/fi/laki/kaannokset/2004/en20040759.pdf

Finland Ministry of Justice. (2006). *Employee pensions act.* Retrieved from http://www.finlex.fi/fi/laki/kaannokset/2006/en20060395.pdf

Finland Ministry of Justice. (2014). *Non-discrimination act.* Retrieved from http://finlex.fi/en/laki/kaannokset/2004/en20040021.pdf

Finland Ministry of Justice. (2015). Occupational accidents, injuries and diseases act [in Swedish]. Retrieved from http://finlex.fi/sv/laki/ajantasa/2015/20150459

Finnish Pension Alliance. (n.d.). *Grounds for the earnings-related pension system.* Retrieved from www.tela.fi/en/grounds_for_the_pension_system

Gould, R., Ilmarinen, J., Järvisalo, J., & Koskinen, S. (2006). *Työkyvyn ulottuvuudet* [Dimensions of work ability]. Helsinki, Finland: ETK, Kela, KTL, TTL. Retrieved from www.julkari.fi/bitstream/handle/10024/129155/Tyokyvynulottuvuudet.pdf?sequence=1

Ilmarinen, J. (2009). Work ability—A comprehensive concept for occupational health research and prevention [editorial]. *Scandinavian Journal of Work, Environment and Health, 35*(1), 1–5. doi:10.5271/sjweh.1304

International Labour Organization. (1985a). *Convention no. 161—Occupational health services.* Retrieved from http://blue.lim.ilo.org/cariblex/pdfs/ILO_Convention_161.pdf

International Labour Organization. (1985b). *Occupational health services recommendation no. 171.* Retrieved from www.ilo.org/dyn/normlex/en/f?p=NORMLEXPUB:12100:0::NO::P12100_ILO_CODE:R171

Jääskeläinen, A., Kausto, J., Seitsamo, J., Ojajärvi, A., Nygård, C.-H., Arjas, E., & Leino-Arjas, P. (2016). Work ability index and perceived work ability as predictors of disability pension: A prospective study among Finnish municipal employees. *Scandinavian Journal of Work, Environment and Health, 42*(6), 490–499. doi:10.5271/sjweh.3598

Kausto, J., Viikari-Juntura, E., Virta, L. J., Gould, R., Koskinen, A., & Solovieva, S. (2014). Effectiveness of new legislation on partial sickness benefit on work participation: A quasi-experiment in Finland. *BMJ Open, 4*(12). Retrieved from https://doi.org/10.1136/bmjopen-2014-006685

Kuntoutuksen uudistamiskomitea [Committee to revise rehabilitation]. (2017). *Ehdotukset kuntoutusjärjestelmän uudistamiseksi* [Proposals to improve the rehabilitation system]. Helsinki, Finland: Ministry of Social Affairs and Health. Retrieved from http://urn.fi/URN:ISBN:978-952-00-3891-5

Liukko, J., Polvinen, A., Kesälä, M., & Varis, J. (2017). *Effectiveness and incentive effects of experience rating in disability insurance: A questionnaire study on employers' views [English summary, full report in Finnish].* Retrieved from www.etk.fi/wp-content/uploads/Summary_Tyokyvyttomyyselakkeiden_maksuluokkamallin_toimivuus_ja_kannustinvaikutukset.pdf

National Institute for Health and Welfare. (n.d.). *Health expenditure and financing 2015.* Retrieved from www.thl.fi/en/web/thlfi-en/statistics/statistics-by-topic/finances-in-the-health-and-social-services-sector/health-expenditure-and-financing

Niemelä, H. & Salminen, K. (2006). *Social security in Finland.* Retrieved from www.kela.fi/documents/12099/12170/socialsecurity.pdf

Oksa, P., Palo, L., Saalo, A., Jolanki, R., Mäkinen, I., Pesonen, M., & Virtanen. S. (2014). *Occupational diseases in Finland in 2012. New cases of recognized and suspected occupational diseases.* Helsinki, Finland: Finnish Institute of Occupational Health. Retrieved from www.julkari.fi/bitstream/handle/10024/131563/Occupational_diseases_2012.pdf?sequence=1

Organisation for Economic Co-operation and Development. (2005). *Reviews of health systems: Finland 2005.* Retrieved from www.oecd-ilibrary.org/social-issues-migration-health/oecd-reviews-of-health-systems-finland-2005_97892 64013834-en

Organisation for Economic Co-operation and Development. (2008). *Sickness, disability and work: Breaking the barriers (Vol. 3)—Denmark, Ireland, Finland and the Netherlands 2008.* doi:10.1787/9789264049826-en

Organisation for Economic Co-operation and Development. (2013). *Highlights from A good life in old age? Monitoring and improving quality in long term care.* Retrieved from www.oecd.org/els/health-systems/Finland-OECD-EC-Good-Time-in-Old-Age.pdf

Saarnio L. (2017). *Työeläkekuntoutus vuonna 2016 [Work pension rehabilitation, 2016].* Helsinki, Finland: Eläketurvakeskuksen tilastoja [Statistics, Finnish Centre for Pensions]. Retrieved from www.etk.fi/wp-content/uploads/Tyoela kekuntoutus-vuonna-2016.pdf

Saltychev M. (2012). *The effectiveness of vocationally oriented medical rehabilitation (Aslak) amongst public sector employees.* Turku, Finland: University of Turku. Retrieved from www.utupub.fi/bitstream/handle/10024/76643/AnnalesD1007Saltychev.pdf?sequence=1&isAllowed=y

Social Insurance Institution. (n.d.). *Basic income experiment 2017–2018.* Retrieved from www.kela.fi/web/en/basic-income-experiment-2017-2018

Social Insurance Institution. (2017). *Kelan työterveyshuoltotilasto 2015 [Statistics on OH services by social insurance institution, 2015].* Retrieved from https://helda.helsinki.fi/bitstream/handle/10138/212975/Kelan_tyoterveyshuoltotilasto_2015.pdf?sequence=6

Statistics Finland. (n.d.). *Finland in figures 2016.* Retrieved from www.stat.fi/tup/julkaisut/tiedostot/julkaisuluettelo/yyti_fif_201600_2016_16182_net_p2.pdf

Viikari-Juntura, E., Virta, L. J., Kausto, J., Autti-Rämö, I., Martimo, K. P., Laaksonen, M., Leinonen, T., Husgafvel-Pursiainen, K., Burdorf, A., & Solovieva, S. (2017). Legislative change enabling use of early part-time sick leave enhanced return to work and work participation in Finland. *Scandinavian Journal of Work, Environment and Health, 43*(5), 447–56. doi:10.5271/sjweh.3664

Chapter 10

Work Disability Prevention in France
Organizational and Political Challenges

Jean-Baptiste Fassier

Work disability prevention in France sits at the crossroads of the social security system, employers, the occupational health system, and the healthcare system. In the first part of this chapter, the actors and the responsibilities of each system are described. In the second part, current measures for work disability prevention are detailed, with a focus on the legal status "disabled worker"[1] in France. Finally, recent reforms and current challenges are presented with their political, financial, and demographic drivers.

Overview of Social Security in France

Social security in France is characterized by various inherited schemes. The largest one is the "general social security scheme" in the private sector, which covers 18 million workers (Chevreul, Berg Brigham, Durand-Zaleski, & Hernández-Quevedo, 2015). The other main schemes cover (a) employees at the state and regional levels and within public hospitals (5.6 million); (b) agricultural workers (5.4 million); and (c) independent workers (2.8 million). Other social security schemes cover employees of the national railways, miners, and several other sectors or administrations (e.g., Banque de France [the French national bank], National Assembly). Consequently, numerous codes and their component laws and regulations (i.e., labor code, social security code, civil-servant code) apply to work disability prevention across these different schemes. This creates a very complex system for all stakeholders involved. In order to provide an overview of the French work disability context, this chapter will address only the general scheme that covers all private-sector, salaried workers (Centre of European and International Liaisons for Social Security, 2017).

The compulsory general scheme is managed by a network of local, regional, and national institutions and organized by risk category. It is administered by representatives of employers and employees under the supervision of the different ministries in charge of social security (i.e., the Ministry of Labor, the Ministry of Health, and the Ministry of Finance and Public Accounts) and is financed mainly by employer contributions and taxes deducted from workers' earnings. The scheme covers wage earners in the private industrial, trade, and service sectors as well as their families. The French healthcare system is mix of types: structurally based on a Bismarckian approach with a Beveridge-type, single-payer, public model. The latter model reflects the currently increasing importance of tax-financed healthcare and strong state intervention (Chevreul et al., 2015). Contributions are made by both employers and employees. The healthcare system is organized into five branches (Centre of European and International Liaisons for Social Security, 2017), of which two are involved in work disability prevention. The health, maternity, paternity, disability, and death branches are universal and tax-based. The industrial-accident and occupational-illness branches are financed by employer premiums, and employees are the beneficiaries. A noteworthy aspect of the French healthcare system is the important role played since 1946 by social-insurance physicians (SIPs) and occupational physicians (OPs). The latter are directly employed by large firms. Small and medium-sized companies contract with occupational health services, which include OPs.

The Occupational-Health System

The General Social Security Scheme and the Role of Social-Insurance Physicians

In France's general social security scheme, social-insurance physicians are employed by the National Salaried Workers' Health Insurance Fund,[2] which runs the health branch of the social security system. SIPs are important actors in the worker-recovery trajectory. When workers report illness, they must send their sickness certificates, issued by a general practitioner or specialist, to the local health-branch administration. Depending on sick-leave durations, frequency of sickness absences, and workers' illnesses, SIPs may be obliged to ask workers to attend medical examinations in order to verify the necessity of their sickness certificates, which may then be confirmed or rejected. For example, sick-leave prescriptions for back pain are usually from 45 to 90 days. The amount and conditions of salary replacement depend on the work-relatedness of the medical condition (see Figure 10.1). If sick leave is caused by a work-related condition (work accident or occupational disease), salary replacement is provided without a waiting period, time limit, or conditions. It is also capped at a higher level than salary replacement for sick leave attributable to a non-work-related condition (Social Security Code,[3] Art. L433–1 to L433–4). In the latter case, salary replacement is provided after a waiting period of three days, for a maximum duration of three years, and under certain conditions.[4]

The role of SIPs is paramount, both medically and administratively, in the so-called "stabilization assessment." This is the time point after which no

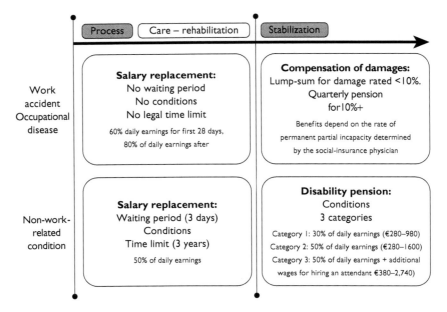

Figure 10.1 Salary replacement of workers in case of sick leave.

further improvement nor aggravation of the medical condition is expected. Although the stabilization assessment should be made by the treating physician (general practitioner or specialist), who has the best knowledge of the medical condition and the therapeutic process, it can be done by the SIP. In this case, the SIP's assessment overrides the treating physician's. Nonetheless, the worker can challenge the SIP's assessment, first to the amicable settlement board[5] and then to the social security court.[6] The main consequence of the stabilization assessment is termination of salary-replacement benefits, which forces workers to meet with their occupational physicians to plan a return to work. Although work resumption may be facilitated by job accommodations, the abruptness of the return to work in these circumstances rarely allows time to plan and implement these accommodations.

If a medical condition is work-related, financial compensation based on body-part damage can be provided. The compensation amount depends on the rate of partial permanent incapacity assessed by the SIP. Partial permanent incapacity is assessed according to a fixed scale, expressed as a percentage, and then converted into a compensation amount (Social Security Code, Art. L434–1, L434–2). If the rate is over 10%, injured workers receive a quarterly pension; if not, they receive a lump-sum payment. However, this lump sum does not compensate for harm to workers' careers in the event of termination. For example, a worker with chronic low back pain resulting from a work accident could have a 9% rate of partial permanent incapacity, resulting in a lump-sum payment of €4,110 [US$4,909]. If the worker lost her job, she would receive no further compensation. If a medical condition is not work-related, the SIP may recommend that the worker be granted a disability pension, depending on the worker's earning capacity and the fulfillment of different conditions.[7]

When sick leaves exceeds three months, the SIP and the treating physician may ask workers to consult their occupational physicians for a pre-return-to-work medical checkup. Although these visits are not mandatory, in recent years the social security system has actively promoted them to healthcare practitioners and workers. Pre-return-to-work medical consultations are very important in identifying barriers and formulating return-to-work strategies.

Beyond its historical role as a public insurer, the French social security system has recently taken a more active role in work disability prevention and reintegration. In 2009, work disability committees were created within the national network of local social security agencies. These local committees each comprise an SIP, a social worker, and a case manager, who are expected to facilitate return to work and job retention of workers who are on long-term sick leave and at risk of losing their jobs. However, some of these committees have been criticized by other stakeholders for not coordinating their actions and decisions with other stakeholders (employers, occupational physicians, family physicians). Furthermore, neither the committees' coverage of the target population nor their effectiveness has been systematically evaluated. In the same vein, a pilot case-management program was developed in 2014 to improve return to work of seriously injured workers. This pilot is still underway. An ongoing process evaluation of a separate case-management program for workers with low-back pain found important communication problems between social security system actors (SIPs, case managers), occupational health services, and rehabilitation centers. In addition, general practitioners were not clearly integrated into the pilot. Perhaps as a consequence of the process evaluation, the number of workers with low-back pain included in the pilot program was lower than expected. Despite the mitigating effect of these two programs, they clearly illustrate the French social security system's intent to take a more active role than before in work disability prevention. The two examples also highlight the importance of addressing intersectoral barriers among insurance, occupational health, and healthcare organizations that may impede the management of workers' cases.

The Occupational Health System and the Role of Occupational Physicians

All French employers in the private, public, and association sectors must subscribe to an occupational health service, to which they pay an annual per-employee fee. Only self-employed workers do not have to comply with this obligation. For companies with more than 1,500 employees, the occupational health service is within the firm.[8] Small and medium-sized companies share occupational health services.[9] All occupational health services must be approved by the regional office of the Ministry of Labor. Occupational health practitioners comprise OPs and allied professionals, such as occupational health nurses, ergonomists, psychologists, toxicologists, and social workers. Since its development in 1946, the French occupational health system has centered on OPs, according to the "medicalized prevention" model (Matsuda, 2012). This model assigns two main roles to OPs. First, they give workers regular medical checkups, from their hiring until the end of their contracts. In addition to scheduled checkups, other types of legally required visits to OPs may be scheduled. For example, return-to-work visits to OPs are mandatory after any sick leave exceeding one month, and pre-return-to-work consultations are organized when sick leaves exceed three months. Eventually, visits may be organized at the request of workers, employers, or OPs. Second, at least one third of OPs' work time must be spent carrying out preventive actions in the workplace. Workplace actions may be part of collective initiatives, such as occupational-risk assessment, information provision, training, and research, or individual initiatives by OPs, such as job assessment and recommending accommodations for injured or ill workers.

The notion of OPs medically assessing job fitness is a cornerstone of work disability prevention in France. Job fitness is defined as the ability of a worker to perform a specific job in its context (i.e., workplace or department) without risk to the worker's health (Labor Code, Art. L4622–2, L4622–3). The OP performs the job-fitness assessment and is expected to evaluate the match between individuals' work capacity and their job requirements. For example, the medical fitness of a geriatric nurse's aide is assessed according to the physical requirements of the job (e.g., heavy lifting of patients), which would not be required of a nurse's aide in a day-care center.

When a risk to the worker's health is identified due to a mismatch between the job requirements and the worker's capacities, the OP is expected to formulate recommendations for the employer, either suitable job accommodations or training for another job assignment. In turn, employers are expected to follow these recommendations, although they can object if it can be proven that such OPs' recommendations are not possible at the company level. Employers' liability goes only so far as their ability to accommodate, and workers can be fired for medical reasons on the basis of poor job fitness, as assessed by OPs. In the case of refusal, employers must justify their reasons in writing to workers and their occupational physicians.

The job accommodations that OPs recommend may pertain to work hours, job tasks, and job equipment. In order to formulate these recommendations, OPs must perform job analyses in the workplace and may request collaboration from allied health professionals within their occupational health services (e.g., ergonomists). OPs are also required to discuss, first with workers and then their employers, job modifications that could be implemented to accommodate the workers. In the case of specific occupational diseases (e.g., asthma or allergies), OPs may refer workers to specialists in occupational-disease departments of university hospitals. Eventually, OPs may take an active role in the job-accommodation process. Although employers must implement OPs' recommendations, Grataloup, Massardier-Pilonchery, Bergeret, & Fassier (2016) observed that OPs' direct involvement in the process is important from a social point of view as regards acceptance by accommodated workers' colleagues and supervisors.

In addition to recommending job accommodations, the other major role of OPs in work disability prevention is performing pre-return-to-work checkups (Petit et al., 2015). According to the labor code, these visits are mandatory when sick leave exceeds three months. Paradoxically, neither employers nor OPs are allowed to initiate these visits, only workers on sick leave, treating physicians or SIPs. During pre-return-to-work checkups, OPs are expected to identify barriers to returning to work and propose strategies to overcome them. This is a unique opportunity for OPs and treating physicians to collaborate concerning workers' situations. In the past, this type of visit has been underutilized by treating physicians for various reasons, including a lack of knowledge about this opportunity and a lack of trust in occupational physicians. Nonetheless, pre-return-to-work checkups have gained popularity in recent years among workers and their healthcare providers, as a consequence of promotional campaigns by the social security system's health branch. However, these checkups need to be planned well in advance to allow OPs to formulate return-to-work plans and reach agreements with employers and workers' supervisors.

The Healthcare System and the Role of Treating Physicians

Work disability prevention is poorly integrated with the French healthcare system, and treating physicians receive limited initial and continued medical education in this respect. Adversarial relations are regularly reported in the newsletters of medical unions between physicians working in the private sector and those in the social security system, and the extent of these adversarial relations is difficult to assess. For example, conflict may arise over a stabilization-assessment decision by an SIP if the worker's treating physician considers the decision premature. In the same vein, French OPs are regularly distrusted by treating physicians, who may consider OPs as advocates of employer interests to the detriment of workers. In such situations, the privacy of worker's medical information is invoked by treating physicians and OPs to justify noncollaboration in managing workers' cases.

However, in recent years, positive developments have been observed. OPs now have a better public image, particularly with regard to their role in the prevention of work disability and psychosocial hazards in workplaces during the 2009–2012 Eurozone financial crisis (Michiels et al., 2016). The number of pre-return-to-work consultations with OPs initiated by treating physicians has increased, which illustrates the growing tendency of healthcare providers to collaborate with occupational health services. This increased interest may be explained by promotional campaigns of the health branch of social insurance directed towards general practitioners and workers themselves, which include advertisements on the internet and information leaflets in treating physicians' waiting rooms.

The Role of Employers

Employers are required by law to protect workers' health, prevent occupational hazards, and provide job accommodations as requested by occupational physicians (OPs). However, enforcement of these obligations varies, depending on a number of factors. The influence of corporate culture is critical; it, along with the size and resources of the company, shapes quality of social relations in the workplace. Another important factor is the degree of integration commitment of OPs employed by large companies and their influence on the company's management and direction. There is a large difference between companies that are committed to work disability prevention, and companies where employees suffer from poor working and management conditions and where job accommodation is systematically denied.

There is currently a shortage of occupational physicians in France, resulting in the inability of some employers to fulfill their obligations in regards to medical follow-up of their workers. In such situations, workers lack access to occupational physicians and experience major difficulties when ill-health requires job accommodation. The OP population pyramid forecasts a dramatic acceleration of this shortage and difficulties in the short term (Dellacherie, 2008). Training of new OPs is impeded by the lack of popularity of this specialty among medical students, residents, faculties of medicine, and university hospitals. Training other physicians for OP qualification through continuing medical education could be a solution to the shortage. However, there are conflicting views between university instructors in occupational medicine, who strive to maintain high-level training, and other stakeholders (e.g., physician candidates, employers, labor-ministry staff), who would like to decrease the duration and content of the training. Last but not least, the number of university instructors in occupational medicine has continuously declined in recent years, lowering the research and training capacity of occupational medicine.

Work Disability Prevention Measures

As mentioned earlier, two work disability prevention measures are job accommodation and pre-return-to-work checkups with OPs. Another measure is gradual return to work. This measure is prescribed by the treating physician (general practitioner or specialist) and is intended to facilitate gradual return to work after a certain period of full-time sick leave. These prescriptions have to be jointly agreed to by SIPs, whose agreement is usually presumed, and by OPs, whose agreement takes place during pre-return-to-work visits. Employers can contest these prescriptions if they are able to prove that gradual return to work is incompatible with the company's work organization.

If the measures described above are insufficient to guarantee sustainable return to work and job retention, job-skills assessment and retraining for a different job may be necessary. For ill workers, these measures are initiated when workers are deemed unfit for their previous jobs, and no job accommodations are possible with the previous employer. For example, a truck driver with a permanent neurological impairment from sciatica will not be able to perform his usual job and will need to be retrained and placed in another job. Job-skills assessment and retraining is part of continuing professional education managed by employers and vocational-training organizations. Retraining and placement in new jobs usually requires skilled social workers and human-resources managers who are willing to identify which training and jobs are suitable for workers with particular medical restrictions. The OP's role at this stage is to provide as much information as possible about the workers' medical restrictions and their functional capacities, to facilitate the job transfer.

"Disabled Worker" Status and the Role of the "Disability Law"

In France, the federal legislation key to employment reintegration of workers with impairments related to illness or injury is what is commonly known as the "disability law."[10] According to this law, any employer with 20 or more workers must meet a quota of at least 6% of their employees being disabled workers, or face financial penalties. Formal disabled-worker status is an essential element of work disability policy in France. This status does not provide the worker with any direct financial benefit or formal protection against job termination for illness or injury. However, it gives the employer two important incentives to hire and retain workers with this status.

French law defines disability (*handicap* in French) as:

> Any limitation of activity or participation in social life incurred by a person in his or her environment, because of a substantial, prolonged or permanent deterioration of one or several physical, sensory, mental, cognitive or psychological functions, a polyhandicap, or a disabling health condition.

(author's translation)

Disabled-worker status is granted by authorities at the city or county level, on request of workers themselves, for a limited time (usually three to five years) (Labor code, Art. L5213–2). The mean waiting time for gaining disabled-worker status is about six months. The worker has to fill out a form and may receive help to do this from a social worker. Part of the form has to be filled out by the treating physician, and another part by the OP. Once disabled-worker status is granted, workers are not obliged to disclose it to current or prospective employers, or to occupational physicians. However, if workers require significant job accommodations, this disclosure is necessary in seeking financial support for the accommodations.

Financial penalties for not meeting the quota for employing people with disabled-worker status are an incentive for employers to hire and retain ill and injured workers. Financial penalties for not meeting the quota depend on the size of the company's workforce. In 2016 penalties charged for each missing disabled worker (Labor code, Art. L5212–1 to L5212–31) were €3,904 [US$4,663] for small companies (20–199 workers), €880 [US$5,828] for medium-sized ones (200–749 workers), and €5,856 [US$6,994)] for large companies (750 or more workers). In addition, an annual penalty of €14,460 [US$17,270] for each missing worker is imposed on companies that do not hire any disabled workers, irrespective of company size. All penalties are paid by employers to either a disability fund for the private sector or one for the public sector, and these funds promote employment and job retention of disabled workers. Private-sector employers have been covered by the disability law since it was passed in 1984, whereas public-sector employers have only been covered since the law's 2005 revision (Law No. 2005–102).

A second incentive for employers to hire and retain ill and injured workers is also financial. Any worker with disabled-worker status may benefit from specific measures intended to facilitate hiring and job retention, which are paid for by the two disability funds. The main measure is job accommodations (i.e., equipment, work organization) recommended by OPs. Other measures pertain to transportation from home to work, accessibility, and job retraining.

In France there is no better incentive for employers to prevent work disability than disabled-worker status. This status is the only way for employers to benefit from financing to accommodate workers with the status. However, disabled-worker status raises several points of concern. First, the symbolic meaning of the term *travailleur handicapé*[11] is far from neutral. Unlike English, French does not distinguish between 'handicap' and 'disability.' From the workers' point of view, the former label is primarily associated with feelings of low self-worth and stigmatization by others in their personal or professional environments. Consequently, few workers with limitations due to poor health apply for disabled-worker status, even though they may be entitled to it. A second point of concern applies to the many treating physicians who carry in their minds the stereotype of the wheelchair or the white cane and thus believe that disabled-worker status should be limited to the few workers with major mobility or sensory impairments. Consequently, they guide their ill patients away from seeking this status, which treating physicians, unlike OPs, consider a last resort. Although these divergent views about the symbolic meaning of disabled-worker status between treating and occupational physicians are reconcilable, the views may be a source of discomfort for patients or workers. Time and communication are needed between the treating and occupation physicians before agreement can be reached on the importance of this status as a job-retention strategy.

A third point of concern is the financial sustainability of the disability funds, in view of the increasing number of demands on them and a decrease in the revenues of both the public[12] and private[13] disability funds. The funds' revenues come from employers that do not comply with the disability law. As more employers comply with it, the funds' revenues are declining. In the private-sector fund, penalties from noncompliant employers decreased from €539 million [US$644 million] to €421 million [US$503 million] between 2010 and 2014. The decrease was even greater for the public-sector fund, where penalties decreased from €212 million [US$253 million] to €131 million [US$156 million] during the same period. Concurrently, the number of workers granted disabled-worker status increased by 40% between 2008 and 2011. These opposing trends clearly put the disability funds under strain and threaten their sustainability. Although the financing model of the disability funds may have been appropriate in past years, given the limited number of workers with major motor or sensory impairments, it now appears outdated, for various reasons. The broader definition of handicap in the disability law's 2005 revision increased the population of workers likely to be granted disabled-worker status, notably aging workers with musculoskeletal disorders. The increase in unemployment in France since 2008 has led to a greater importance for job retention, which has somewhat reduced the taboo associated with disabled-worker status. Finally, over time employers have become more aware of their legal obligation to meet the quota for hiring workers with disabled status and the penalties for not doing so, resulting in a reduction of revenue for the disability funds.

Recent Reforms

A reform of the labor code passed in September 2016[14] changed the legal context of France's occupational health system. Driving the reform were lobbying by employers to reduce their obligations; the government's neoliberal ideology and its consequent commitment to simplifying multiple regulations; the shortage of OPs; and controversy over the relevance of the "medical job fitness" concept.

The main consequence of the 2016 reform was a diminished role for OPs in the medical follow-up of workers. For most workers, the requirement to be examined by the company OP before hiring was eliminated. It was maintained only for a limited number of jobs considered high risk, such as jobs where workers are exposed to asbestos, lead, ionizing radiation, and biological and chemical hazards. Likewise, the concept of medical job fitness is maintained only for these so-called "high-risk jobs," and the requirement for medical-fitness certificates (i.e., fit notes) produced by OPs has been maintained. However, workers in high-risk jobs may be examined by other occupational health practitioners (i.e., nurses, medical residents, associate physicians who follow a curriculum in occupational health) between two periodical visits to OPs. For workers in non-high-risk jobs, OP follow-up has been replaced by an "information-and-prevention visit"[15] performed by OPs or other occupational health professionals. Workers now need to be medically examined every five years. For employees with disabled-worker status or who receive partial disability pensions, the initial information-and-prevention visit must be carried out by an OP; later visits may be carried out by other occupational health professionals.

All workers may still request medical consultations with their employer's OP at any time. The OP may still recommend job accommodations and other job transfers, whether or not workers' jobs are considered high risk. The consequences of the 2016 reform for work disability prevention are difficult to anticipate. For OPs, the reform will alleviate the burden of systematic visits and may free their time to focus on work disability prevention. On the other hand, less contact with OPs may result in delayed access for workers to work disability prevention if they do not themselves request consultations with their OPs.

Another part of the 2016 reform of the labor code, enforced on January 1, 2017, significantly changed the process followed when a worker or employer disagrees with an OP's fit note or recommended accommodations. Until 2017, such disagreements were settled by the regional Ministry of Labor office, with the possibility of appeal to the Ministry's national office. The worker's medical file was reviewed by an OP with the regional office's medical inspectorate, and the dispute-settlement process was free of charge for both workers and employers. The 2017 reform completely changed the process, from which the national and regional Ministry of Labor offices have now withdrawn. Since 2017, disputes are settled by local labor tribunals comprising representatives of employers and workers. The worker's medical file is reviewed by a medical expert, and the review is paid for by both the employer and the worker. Predictably, the reform has had negative consequences. One is aggravation of the power imbalance between workers and employers in settling disagreements. This major jurisdictional change, enacted by a socialist government in 2016, was driven by different but converging forces. The regional medical inspectorate was understaffed, and its OPs were overwhelmed by the number of disputes to be settled. In some regions, they were unable to fulfill their responsibilities, and this drove the state to remove their responsibility for settling disputes. Another driving force was the government's commitment to reduce its expenses, which led to the transfer of certain responsibilities to local authorities, the private sector, and individuals. Last but not least, taking a neoliberal view, France's employers lobbied for state disengagement from labor relations.

Concluding Remarks

There is no global, formal policy in France to improve work reintegration for people who have had to leave their jobs because of impairments due to illness or injury. A strong limitation to any future policy development is the lack of reliable statistics on job loss among workers deemed medically unfit for work by OPs and then not accommodated by their employers.

To achieve optimal work disability policy, France needs to (a) produce reliable statistics on job loss among workers with impairments from illness or injury; (b) train medical doctors (i.e., OPs and general practitioners) and employers in occupational health; and (c) require greater accountability from healthcare professionals, the social insurance system, and employers to ensure that their practice complies with regulations and guidelines in work disability prevention.

Notes

1. Reconnaissance de la qualité de travailleur handicapé.
2. Caisse Nationale d'Assurance Maladie des Travailleurs Salariés.
3. Code de la sécurité sociale.
4. In order to receive salary replacement in the case of non-work-related conditions, claimants must have worked for at least 150 hours during the three months before the sick leave.
5. Commission de conciliation amiable.
6. Tribunal des affaires de sécurité sociale.
7. Social security affiliation exceeds 12 months. Worked for pay more than 600 hours in the last 12 months.
8. Service de santé autonome.
9. Service de santé inter-entreprises.
10. Loi n° 2005–102 pour l'égalité des droits et des chances, la participation et la citoyenneté des personnes handicapées.
11. Handicapped worker.
12. Fonds pour l'insertion des personnes handicapées dans la fonction publique.
13. Association de gestion du fonds pour l'insertion des personnes handicapées.
14. Loi n° 2016–1088 du 8 aoÛt 2016 relative au travail, à la modernisation du dialogue social et à la sécurisation des parcours professionnels [Law no. 2016–1088 of August 8, 2016 regarding work, modernization of social dialogue, and the security of career paths].
15. Visite d'information et de prevention.

References

Centre of European and International Liaisons for Social Security. (2017). *The French social security system for salaried workers (general scheme)*. Retrieved from www.cleiss.fr/docs/regimes/regime_france/an_index.html

Chevreul, K., Berg Brigham, K., Durand-Zaleski, I., & Hernández-Quevedo, C. (2015). France Health system review. *Health Systems in Transition*, 17(3), 1.

Dellacherie, C. (2008). *L'avenir de la médecine du travail [The future of occupational medicine]*. Paris, France: Conseil économique et social [Economic and Social Council]. Retrieved from www.ladocumentationfrancaise.fr/rapports-publics/084000152/index.shtml

Grataloup, M., Massardier-Pilonchery, A., Bergeret, A., & Fassier, J. B. (2016). Job restrictions for healthcare workers with musculoskeletal disorders: Consequences from the superior's viewpoint. *Journal of Occupational Rehabilitation*, 26(3), 245–252. doi:10.1007/s10926-015-9609-y

Labor Code [Code du travail], Articles L4622–2, L4622–3, L5212–1 to L5212–31, L5213–2.

Law No. 2005–102 on equal rights and opportunities, participation and citizenship of persons with disabilities [Loi n° 2005–102 pour l'égalité des droits et des chances, la participation et la citoyenneté des personnes handicapées], Article 114 (passed 1984, modified 2005). Retrieved from www.legifrance.gouv.fr/affichTexte.do?cidTexte=JORFTEXT000000809647&categorieLien=id

Matsuda, S. (2012). A review of the French occupational health system—From the viewpoint of international comparison between France and Japan. *Asian Pacific Journal of Disease Management*, 6(2), 45–49.

Michiels, F., July, J., Poumeaud, H., Belhomme, V., & Forsse, C. (2016). Des risques psychosociaux à la qualité de vie au travail: quel rôle pour le service de santé au travail? [From psychosocial hazards to quality of working life: What role for occupational health services?] [conference abstract]. *Archives des Maladies Professionnelles et de l'Environnement*, 77(3), 560. doi.org/10.1016/j.admp.2016.03.479

Petit, A., Rozenberg, S., Fassier, J. B., Rousseau, S., Mairiaux, P., & Roquelaure, Y. (2015). Pre-return-to-work medical consultation for low back pain workers. Good practice recommendations based on systematic review and expert consensus. *Annals of Physical & Rehabilitation Medicine*, 58(5), 298–304. doi:10.1016/j.rehab.2015.08.001

Social Security Code [Code de la sécurité sociale], Articles L433–1 to L433–4. Retrieved February 1, 2018 from www.legifrance.gouv.fr/affichCode.do;jsessionid=BE5EECFE571C7C438E111F67D7FD5005.tplgfr22s_1?idSectionTA=LEGISCTA000006156130&cidTexte=LEGITEXT000006073189&dateTexte=20180615

Chapter 11

Work Disability Policy in Germany
Experiences of Collective and Individual Participation and Cooperation

Felix Welti

The Federal Republic of Germany (FRG) comprises 16 federal states. It is a member of the European Union (EU). In Germany, social security and labour law are under federal jurisdiction, whereas administration of the law is mostly a state or municipal responsibility. Five types of social insurance (pension insurance; sickness insurance; accident insurance; long-term-care insurance; and the federal employment agency) are administered by more than 100 distinct federal and state agencies, whose budgets total more than the federal budget. Most aspects of social security are regulated by the federal social code (SGB),[1] consisting of 12 books (SGB I–XII).

Germany signed ILO (International Labour Organization) Convention 159, Vocational Rehabilitation and Employment (Disabled Persons), in 1989 and the United Nations Convention on the Rights of Persons with Disabilities (CRPD)[2] in 2008. Germany had 82.2 million inhabitants in 2015. It had a federal budget of €327 [US$389] billion in 2017. In 2013, there were 38.8 million workers aged between 18 and 64. According to the participation report on the life situations of persons with impairments[3] in 2013 there were 12.8 million impaired people in Germany, comprising 15.8% of the population.[4] The impaired population was 5% among people aged 15 to 44, 19.3% from 45 to 64, 34.8% from 65 to 79, and 47.4% among people aged 80 and older. The number and proportion of impaired individuals have increased continuously, due to population aging.

The employment rate of all people with impairments aged between 18 and 64 (49%) is lower than that for the population as a whole (80%). Nevertheless, the employment rate of impaired people increased by 8 percentage points from 2005 to 2013. In that year, 55% of the nonemployed impaired people aged between 18 and 64 received a pension. Two thirds of employed impaired people, compared with three quarters of employed nonimpaired people, were employed full-time.

In 2013, 7.5 million people were classified as severely disabled. While most of them (4.7 million) were physically impaired, 357,000 were visually impaired, 316,000 had a hearing or speaking impairment, 546,000 were mentally impaired, and 299,000 had an intellectual impairment.

The greatest increase from 2005 to 2013 was among people with mental impairment (up 57%). Of all impairments, 85% were acquired from illness, 2% from accident, and 4% were from birth.

In 2014, 1.2 million severely disabled people were employed. The unemployment rate of severely disabled people was 13.4% in 2015, compared with 8.6% in the total population. Federal law obliges businesses to meet a target of 5% of their employees being severely disabled. In comparison, on average, 4.1% of corporate employees were severely disabled people in 2014. In the public sector, where the quota is 6%, 6.6% of employees were severely disabled. Outside the labour market, 300,000 disabled people, most of them intellectually impaired, were employed in sheltered workshops, which gives them access to social insurance. For workers in sheltered workshops, labour law, especially minimum-wage requirements, is generally not applicable.

Historical Development of Germany's Work Disability Policy

Roots in the Bismarckian System and Post-World-War-II Legislation

In the time of Chancellor Bismarck between 1881 and 1889, invalidity pension insurance,[5] sickness insurance,[6] and work accident insurance[7] were introduced. They were made responsible by law for providing medical rehabilitation to prevent invalidity pensions by preventing work disability. From the beginning, these social-insurance schemes were governed by elected boards of employers and insured workers. The agencies built rehabilitation clinics, often by the seaside or in the mountains, focusing on tuberculosis and other widespread chronic diseases.

In 1919, millions of young men returned to civilian life severely disabled after World War I. One of the first regulations of the new revolutionary government related to those men. Private companies and the public sector were obliged to employ severely disabled people. As well, employers could be forced to hire them. Special representatives within companies were to be elected, and firms were externally supported by a specific authority. A levy was implemented for companies that did not comply. People injured at work were soon included. Other disabled people remained outside the labour force and were supported by invalidity pension insurance. The cripples' welfare authority[8] was responsible for those who were born disabled or became disabled at an early age (Blumenthal & Jochheim, 2009).

In the FRG, these institutions were continued or else were restored after World War II. During the era of reconstruction and economic prosperity in the 1950s and 1960s, vocational rehabilitation in particular was greatly expanded through the pension-insurance agencies (being responsible for reduced-earning-capacity pensions as well as for old-age pensions), work-accident-insurance agencies, and the federal employment office. Medical rehabilitation of people outside the workforce remained the responsibility of the sickness-insurance administration. During the winter of 1956, a long, hard strike by metalworkers achieved a breakthrough: Employers under collective agreements were obliged to give employees six weeks of paid sick leave. Later, sickness pay was enshrined in law for all employers.

Toward a More Universal Disability Policy in the 1970s

The postwar era of disability policy ended in the early 1970s (Rudloff, 2003). At that point, to simplify the complex rehabilitation system, combining oversight of all the programs under one public agency was discussed. In 1969, the existing self-governed agencies, trade unions, and employer associations founded the federal joint committee for rehabilitation.[9] In 1974, coordination of the agencies was made obligatory by a new rehabilitation-framework law,[10] and the veteran-centered law was replaced by the severely disabled law.[11] The latter covered every disabled person, regardless of the cause of the disability. The quota system, levy for noncompliance, and government support for employers and employees financed out of the levy were kept.

From the late 1970s onward, the number of severely disabled people, people with reduced earning capacity taking early retirement, and rehabilitation increased, together with unemployment. Allowing early retirement was one of the government's strategies for handling unemployment and structural change in Germany's old industries, such as steel, coal mining, and shipbuilding (Behrend, 1992).

The German Democratic Republic (GDR) had a separate system under its severely disabled and rehabilitation laws, which, according to its different economic structure, focused on the responsibility of state-owned enterprises for the integration of disabled workers (Ramm, 2017). In 1990, at the time of German reunification, the FRG's system was implemented in what were now the six new states. In the system's initial years, many impaired people in the former GDR were unemployed and retired early.

Activation and Nondiscrimination Reforms Since the 1990s

In the late 1990s, there was a strategic turn in disability policy (Devetzi, 2015; Naegele, 2015; Reinhard, 2015). The EU had a stronger influence on social policies. Increasing the employment rate of older and impaired workers became an EU objective (Devetzi, 2011; Welti, 2008). Also, nondiscrimination on the grounds of age and disability was enforced by Council Directive 2000/78/EC (November 27, 2000), establishing a general framework for equal treatment in employment and occupation (European Community, 2000; Waddington & Lawson, 2009).

Until 2000, the occupational incapacity pension[12] related to the capacity for the specific individual profession in its criteria for pension eligibility. This was abolished, and the reduced-earning-capacity pension[13] was established with two new eligibility criteria related only to the overall labour-market situation and people's (a) inability to work more than three hours a day for fully reduced earning capacity and (b) inability to work more than six hours a day for partially reduced earning capacity (SGB VI, Section 43). Although the growth in new reduced-earning-capacity pensions decreased from nearly €280,000 in 1996 to €175,000 in 2015, the average age at which pensions start is still 52.

In 2001, the new rehabilitation framework law[14] (SGB IX) was passed to coordinate all public agencies dealing with rehabilitation and disability. These agencies now included the agency for the severely disabled, which was renamed the integration office,[15] and the social welfare authority[16] and youth welfare authority[17] at the municipal level.

The new law adopted the concept of disability in the World Health Organization's International Classification of Functioning, Disability and Health (ICF)[18] for rehabilitation, putting participation and self-determination at the center of legal disability terminology (Nebe, 2015; Welti, 2014).

The pension-insurance, sickness-insurance, and accident-insurance bodies now finance the process of gradual reintegration.[19] This means sick-listed workers return to work part-time under medical supervision, while still receiving social-insurance benefits. Employers are now obliged to complete a company reintegration management[20] procedure for every worker who is on sick leave for more than six (not necessarily continuous) weeks in one year (Düwell, 2011).

The elected representative boards of severely disabled employees inside each company were offered the opportunity under the new law to negotiate collective integration agreements[21] with their employers.[22] These agreements can be supported by the works council and moderated by the integration office (Nassibi, 2012).

In 2005, following recommendations of the Hartz Commission, the labour-market reforms reduced unemployment-insurance coverage for older workers from three years to one year, and closed one gateway to early retirement. The newly established Jobcenters now exert pressure on unemployed people and sanction them for noncompliance. As well, programs for complex, long-term vocational rehabilitation were reduced (Dornette et al., 2008).

In 2009, CRPD was adopted by Germany. Since then, disability policies have been discussed in the light of this international agreement, which includes a Right to Work (CRPD, Art. 27; Welti & Nachtschatt, 2018). In commenting on an individual legal case (*Gröninger v. Germany*, 2014, CRPD/C/D/2010), the Committee on the Rights of Persons with Disabilities, according to Article 34 of the CRPD, criticized the bureaucratic barriers in the German system of vocational rehabilitation. In its concluding observations in the initial report on Germany, according to

Article 35, paragraph 2 of the CRPD, the committee was concerned about segregation in the labour market and focused on the problem of sheltered workshops (United Nations, 2015, p. 8 (No. 49); Ritz, 2016).

Within the last few years, with employment rates increasing, some of the government's cuts to programs have been reversed. In 2012, unemployment insurance was prolonged for older workers. Reduced-earning-capacity pension benefits have risen slightly. The prevention law,[23] passed in 2015, required the sickness-insurance bodies to spend more money on workplace health prevention (Welti, 2015b). As for the pension-insurance bodies, their budget for rehabilitation rose slightly in 2014, and in 2016 they were made responsible for early-intervention, preventive rehabilitation to maintain work ability. The participation law[24] included reforms to the rehabilitation framework, scheduled to come into force in 2018. The definition of disability from the CRPD terminology was adopted by the participation law for SGB IX; it explicitly mentions environmental and attitudinal barriers (Welti, 2015a).

Dual Employer and Government Responsibility for Prevention of Work Disability

In Germany, both employers and government are responsible for the prevention and rehabilitation of work disability (Welti & Groskreutz, 2013a). Social insurance has been externalizing prevention and rehabilitation by making the pension- and accident-insurance bodies responsible for compensation and prevention of work disability. German social policy has, on the one hand, externalized solutions to social problems, shared responsibility with bigger units and, on the other hand, internalized solutions, giving responsibility back to society (Zacher, 2013). Laws benefiting severely disabled people are one example: The legislation reinternalized responsibility for social problems to businesses, because the situations after both world wars showed that no solution was possible without them. However, through employer levies, the integration office re-externalizes part of the costs of preventing and rehabilitating work disability. Later reforms rebalanced the responsibilities of government and employers.

Over the past 20 years there has been a new focus on employer responsibility. Early-retirement policies ended, and there was a tendency to cut social-insurance costs and contributions. Antidiscrimination laws were imposed on employers and, more recently, businesses developed more interest in securing skilled labour, due to an aging workforce and the prosperous economy.[25]

Employers' Responsibility for Health and Safety

Under EU law (Directive EEC/89/391; Directive EEC 91/383) employers have the main responsibility for workplace health and safety, which has been partially extended to workplace accessibility (Groskreutz & Welti, 2016). To fulfill these responsibilities, employers are both supported and controlled by the accident-insurance agencies. Together with the trade union representatives, business representatives comprise the self-governing boards of the accident-insurance agencies, which set security and prevention standards.

According to the Council Directive establishing a general framework for equal treatment in employment and occupation (European Community, 2000), also part of the EU framework, employers are responsible for reasonable accommodation as a part of nondiscrimination. Unequal treatment is only allowed if it is necessary because of the job profile. Employers are also obliged to take preventive measures against discrimination; for example, by colleagues (Fuerst, 2009; Kocher & Wenckebach, 2013).

In cases of temporary work incapacity and of rehabilitation, the employer is obliged to provide six weeks full salary. After six weeks of work incapacity in one year (not necessarily continuous) the employer is obliged to offer a reintegration management plan. This plan outlines an individual process of overcoming work disability, which involves the workplace's workers' council, the company representatives of severely disabled employees and, if necessary, the occupational physician, public rehabilitation agencies, and the integration office. Reintegration management already works well in larger companies, where it is enforced by binding agreements at the company level. However, reintegration is often not well managed in small or medium-size companies, especially if there is no workers' council (Welti et al., 2011). If an employer has not tried reintegration management, it is more difficult to dismiss a sick-listed worker if justification is required by a labour court acting on behalf of a worker's claim (Bundesarbeitsgericht, 2012; Kohte, 2008) or, in case of a severely disabled employee, when the dismissal has to be approved by the integration office (Bundesverwaltungsgericht, 2013).

The quota for employing severely disabled people, legally binding for all organizations with more than 19 employees, is now 5% for private businesses and 6% in the public sector. The levy in case of nonfulfillment depends on how far below the quota each employer falls: from €125 [US$149] to €320 [US$380] per month for every missing disabled employee, which is about 10% of the minimum average monthly salary. These levies finance the federal compensation fund[26] and the state-level integration office,[27] and totaled €550 [US$654] million in 2015 (less than 0.5% of the federal social budget). All of the levy revenue is spent on supports for the individual employment of severely disabled people. The specific use of the penalties is decided on with the participation of employers, trade unions, and disabled people's organizations (SGB IX, Sections 154–162).

Status as a severely disabled person is determined by the maintenance department,[28] another state-level agency. Severely disabled people are those who have been recognized as having 50% to 100% disability. People with 30% to 40% disability receive a status equivalent to severely disabled people from the federal employment agency if they cannot keep or get employment without this status. The degree system was derived from legislation covering war veterans and workers' compensation, where it is still used for calculating pensions. Medical assessment of the degree of disability is regulated in detail. In recent decades, there have been attempts to bring it closer to a modern concept of disability and, especially, to consider the barriers chronically ill and mentally disabled people face in gaining employment. For example, people with diabetes are now recognized as being disabled following different, participation-oriented, criteria than before, because of an initiative of the federal social court[29] (Bundessozialgericht, 2008; Knickrehm, 2008). This change in the concept of disability was driven by the ICF, the CRPD, and the Council Directive establishing a general framework for equal treatment in employment and occupation (European Community, 2000). The Court of Justice of the European Union (CJEU), in particular, has included people with chronic or long-term illness (Court of Justice of the European Union (CJEU), 2006) and extremely obese people within the scope of the court's antidiscrimination directive (CJEU, 2014), and the German federal labour court[30] recognized an HIV-infected worker without symptoms as disabled in the sense of the antidiscrimination law[31] (Aichele, 2016; Bundesarbeitsgericht, 2013).

Being recognized as severely disabled does not mean being incapable of work or entitled to a pension. On the contrary, in Germany this status was created to promote the employment of disabled people. But those with the status of severely disabled have the right to receive a full old-age pension two years earlier than other people.[32] Being recognized as severely disabled confers specific labour rights at work, especially the right to clearly defined reasonable accommodations and an extra five vacation days. The dismissal of a severely disabled worker has to be approved by the integration office, which may not be granted if the dismissal is caused by disability and a lack of accommodation. Being recognized as severely disabled also entitles employees and their employers to support for retaining employment from the integration office.

Government Responsibilities in Work Disability

Health and Safety

Government responsibility for health and safety in the workplace is shared between the state-level labour inspection[33] agencies and the accident-insurance bodies. In their responsibility for preventing occupational disease, they are supported by the sickness-insurance bodies.

Medical and Vocational Rehabilitation

The pension-insurance bodies are responsible for medical and vocational rehabilitation of nearly all employed people. In 2015, they had 1.4 million cases.

Most involved medical rehabilitation, and around 150,000 involved vocational rehabilitation. If the need for rehabilitation is caused by work accident or occupational disease, the work-accident-insurance bodies are in charge. In 2013, there were 14,230 cases of vocational rehabilitation. Vocational rehabilitation for people just starting their jobs is a mandate of the federal employment agency, which had 175,000 cases. These numbers have remained stable over the last few years for demographic reasons, as the baby-boomer cohort is part of the aging workforce.

Vocational rehabilitation includes personal and technical support for the employee (and also for their employer), education and training, workplace assistance, and mobility aids. Aids can include the cost of making a car accessible or a contribution to buying an accessible car. Although vocational rehabilitation is often carried out in institutions (www.bv-bfw.de; www.bagbbw.de), the trend now is to have it closer to employees' workplaces. Specific services in every county are provided for mentally and intellectually disabled people, for blind or deaf people, and for people with multiple disabilities.

For people who are not qualified for the general labour market, social-assistance agencies provide vocational rehabilitation in sheltered workshops. More than 300,000 people worked in sheltered workshops in 2016, and the number has increased in recent decades. Most workers in sheltered workshops are never brought into the general labour market and are paid below the legal minimum wage. This practice has been criticized (Trenk-Hinterberger, 2015) and may be inconsistent with EU law (CJEU, 2015). The federal participation law established a budget for work[34] (Nebe & Schimank, 2016; Schimank, 2016) for this group, a government subsidy for employers who permanently hire people who are not qualified for the general labour market, complemented with employment support consisting of personal and technical assistance (www.bag-ub.de).

In contrast to other European countries, medical rehabilitation in Germany is often carried out at in-patient treatment facilities far away from workplaces (Mittag & Welti, 2017). Consequently, the effectiveness of the current system is doubtful with regard to rehabilitation patients' outcomes for work ability and employment.

Payments and Pensions

If people are on sick leave for more than six weeks and less than 78 weeks, the health-insurance body pays a sickness benefit of about 70% of most-recent earnings. This benefit is also paid during gradual work reintegration, which can last up to six months. The employee's general practitioner or a specialist assesses incapacity for work and, only if in doubt, the common medical service of the sickness-insurance bodies will verify the assessment. Occupational physicians are normally not involved. The health-insurance body may request that employees receiving sickness benefits apply for rehabilitation through the pension-insurance body, within 10 weeks (SGB V, Sections 44–51).

In cases of longer or permanent earning incapacity, the pension-insurance bodies paid benefits to about 1.8 million people in 2015 (less than 5% of the workforce). Of those people, only 100,000 had partial earning incapacity. In 2015, 355,813 people applied for the earning incapacity pension, and 188,151 were approved.

Full earning incapacity (inability to work more than three hours a day) entitles applicants to a full pension and partial earning incapacity (three to six hours) to a half pension (SGB VI, Section 43). Earning incapacity is assessed by the social-medical service of the pension-insurance bodies, which is obliged to also assess whether rehabilitation is possible (SGB IX, Section 9). If it is, it takes priority over receiving a pension. Nevertheless, more than half of people receiving a pension have never received rehabilitation (Mittag, Reese, & Meffert, 2014). Some people are not impaired enough to be entitled to a pension but too impaired to find work. This is especially a problem in areas of higher unemployment, such as parts of eastern Germany (former GDR) and former industrial areas of western Germany (e.g., North Rhine-Westphalia). People in these regions have often been unemployed for a long time and subsist on basic jobseekers' assistance. Many of these long-term unemployed people have serious health problems.

Although the legal concept of a three-year, fixed-term pension is the norm (SGB VI, Section 102), in practice most pensions are extended until they transform into old-age pensions of the same amounts. As with the increase of people with severe-disability status, there has been a strong increase in mental impairment as a reason for receiving severe-disabled status: from 20.1% in 1996 to 42.9% in 2015. In the same period, musculoskeletal impairment as a reason decreased from 27.6% to 12.3%, maybe because similar problems are now categorized differently.

The amount of the pension benefit is related to individual contributions to the insurance body and the general pension level, which is related to the development of salaries as a whole. The reduced-earning-capacity pension benefit is calculated as if the person had contributed to the pension-insurance body at the same level as they did before becoming incapacitated, up to age 60. The age for the as-if contribution[35] recently increased to 62 and will rise to 65 in the next few years, which will slightly increase pension amounts.[36] After calculating an individual's earning-incapacity pension, 10.8% of its amount is then deducted. This will avoid these reduced-earning- incapacity pensioners being better off than old-age pensioners. Old-age pensioners, irrespective of their health conditions, have the opportunity to receive their pensions three years earlier, if they accept this deduction.

The level of earning-incapacity benefits has decreased in the last 15 years (Welti & Groskreutz, 2013b), because many people had low total contributions before they lost their earning capacity due to sickness and unemployment, and because the general pension-benefit level has been lowered. For old-age pensions, private or company pension plans have partially compensated this loss, which does not always include earning-incapacity risk. Overall, the average earning-incapacity pension is €730 [US$868]. The average new earning-incapacity pension starting in 2015 was €672 [US$799], which is below the 1996 level and below the level of basic social assistance. Being employed and earning money is restricted for earning-incapacity pensioners.

In the case of work injury or occupational disease, an accident pension is paid by the accident-insurance body. In 2014, 716,864 people qualified for it. The legally fixed level of accident pension benefits (SGB VII) is remarkably higher than the legally fixed level of general pension-insurance benefits (SGB VI). Injured workers are entitled to a payment of 80% of their most recent income for 26 weeks, after which they are compensated based on two thirds of their most recent income if they have full earning incapacity. Incapacity is measured by the degree of reduced work ability, which can range from 20 to 100 (SGB VII, Section 56).

If someone is incapable of earning but does not qualify for a pension, or if the pension does not cover the amount of basic social assistance (SGB XII), they can receive a means-tested subsistence allowance from their municipal government. In 2014, there were 487,258 people in this category.

Problems and Outlook for Work Disability Policy

Cooperation and Interaction Problems

The multitude of work disability actors in Germany leads to cooperation, interface, and interaction problems. At the federal and state levels, social insurance, state and local authorities work differently; they have to coordinate responsibilities at the interface and they have to cooperate and interact well with employers, workers, and disabled people's representatives.

Notably, there is no clear responsibility for employer support in the case where a sick or disabled worker is not recognized as severely disabled. Under the participation law, all public rehabilitation agencies are now obliged to have contact points for employers.

In the medical field, family doctors, who determine work incapacity, occupational physicians, who are responsible for workplaces, and rehabilitation specialists, who are mostly far from homes and workplaces, do not cooperate properly and do not follow a common plan (Deck, Träder, & Raspe, 2009; Feldes, 2016; Knülle, 2012).

Legislative reforms in 1974, 2001, and 2016 tried to deal with the lack of cooperation. In 2001, a reform tried to implement common service units for all government stakeholders at the local level (Shafaei, 2008). Legislative reform in 2016 dropped this concept, because public agencies had not complied. Now governments are trying to overcome cooperation problems via individual participation plans[37] (SGB IX, Section 19).

Reforming Approaches to Participation

Participation may be key to achieving better cooperation and more effectiveness in the German system of work disability prevention and rehabilitation. Rehabilitation is now called benefits for participation,[38] vocational rehabilitation is now called workplace participation,[39] and rehabilitation plans are called participation plans. The meaning of these new names can be understood in the broader sense of the ICF's definition of participation as "involvement in a life situation" (World Health Organization, n. d., p. 10) and sometimes in the sense of procedural and political participation (Hirschberg, 2011) stressed in the CRPD.

At the individual level, participation plans, obligatory since 2018 and involving disabled individuals in their own participation plan conferences[40] (Luik, 2014), are intended to bring together different actors and realize participative case management. A participation plan is to be drawn up in every case when two government rehabilitation agencies are involved (e.g., pension and health insurance) or when two kinds of benefit are being given (e.g., medical and vocational rehabilitation). If normal medical treatment is also involved, nearly every case should be subject to participation planning. The plan will not replace the decisions of the different agencies, but it should create a common basis for agencies' decisions. A participation plan also has to be drawn up if any insured person wants one.

Although there is no legal requirement yet to involve employers, workers' councils, elected representatives of severely disabled employees, general practitioners, occupational physicians or specialists in individuals' participation plans, these additions might be requested by rehabilitation agencies, which are instructed by law to involve these actors in the rehabilitation process.

At the company level, the latest reforms strengthened the requirement for electing representatives of severely disabled employees to promote accessible, inclusive workplaces and strengthen company plans and procedures for dealing with disability and long-term illness. Opinions of the elected representatives must be heard on all questions concerning severely disabled employees either individually or collectively, and, since 2017, disabled employees cannot be dismissed if they have not been heard (SGB IX, Section 178). The committee of severely disabled employees must be supported by the employer, who must pay their office and training expenses, and they are entitled to do committee work during working hours. The severely disabled representation[41] can be seen as a peer-support group for people with disabilities as well as participation of those concerned about work disability. This participative approach is becoming more and more accepted in the field of labour law (Düwell, 2016) and by employers and trade unions.

Within government agencies (e.g., the accident-insurance bodies), administrators design CRPD action plans, involving disabled people's organizations (DPOs), to become more accessible and participatory (Mehrhoff, 2014). The federal joint committee for rehabilitation (www.bar-frankfurt.de) has been mandated to foster participation through the involvement of DPOs in the committee's conceptual work and in creating joint regulations for rehabilitation agencies.

At the political level, the latest legislative reforms have involved DPOs. Their lobbying became nearly as influential as that of traditional players, especially trade unions and employers organizations. However, many of the DPOs are not very engaged in the specific field of work disability or they attend to only one of its aspects; for example, sheltered workshops. The long-standing DPOs, which developed from veterans' organizations, look more closely at issues such as old-age pensions or long-term care. Therefore, representatives of severely disabled employees, inside trade unions or independent of them, have become a voice for work disability issues in the political process, together with some business representatives advocating best practices and a newly defined economic interest in maintaining employees' work ability.

The advancement of new individual and collective political actors is not free from tension. DPOs and their issues have to find their place alongside trade unions and employer organizations in bipartite, self-governed institutions. For the new actors, there is a danger of participation overload. Accustomed to reacting to welfare-state initiatives, taking responsibility for policy development is not easy; it requires empowerment and training. To fill this gap, the participation law included a five-year, €50 million [US$59 million] package to promote independent peer counseling (Jordan & Wansing, 2016; Wansing, 2016). However, it is open to question how much the new peer-counseling structures will concentrate on work participation.

The new focus on participation of disabled people is also a challenge for science. Rehabilitation scientists in Germany have been used to communicating with traditional institutions, especially the pension-insurance agencies, which play a key role in distributing research grants and are entitled to fund research. So is the federal employment agency, which has its own research institute (www.iab.de). A shift in funding priorities from medical and functional outcomes to participation outcomes and, moreover, to involvement of disabled people in the research process, takes time. Not only that, rehabilitation science in Germany is still dominated by physicians and psychologists. But a new organization, alliance for participation research[42] (www.teilhabeforschung.bifos.org), consisting of scientists and DPOs, has been founded and has started discussing and lobbying on these issues (Farin, Anneken, Buschmann-Steinhage, Ewert, & Schmidt, 2012).

For the second time, the federal government has published a participation report on the situation of disabled people. The second report involves more sociological data and interpretations, and references the CRPD.

Recommendations to Address Challenges

In Germany's highly productive economy, more inclusive and accessible workplaces and labour-market conditions are needed.

The interface between employer and government responsibility should be more substantially defined. Small and medium-size businesses need better structured support for the employment of disabled people.

Employers' responsibility for sick-listed employees after the first six weeks of leave should be strengthened. It is still possible for an employer to ignore a sick-listed employee. Doing so allows the employer-employee relationship to gradually disintegrate. Instead, employers should take advantage of opportunities for gradual work reintegration.

Government agencies should improve cooperation of stakeholders in the work disability field, and they should determine more effective ways of interacting, especially between rehabilitation and professionals providing medical treatment. Occupational physicians could play a more important role.

Participation of individual sick-listed and disabled workers, and of their representatives inside and outside workplaces, could improve work disability policy and institutions, if these individuals and their organizations are empowered to participate.

Acknowledgments

The author thanks Oskar Mittag for recommendations and discussions that supported the writing of this chapter.

Notes

1. Sozialgesetzbuch.
2. See www.ohchr.org/EN/HRBodies/CRPD/Pages/ConventionRightsPersons WithDisabilities.aspx
3. Teilhabebericht.
4. All data in this section are from Drucksache 18/10940, 20/01/2017'. The earlier report is Drucksache 17/14476, 31/07/2013.
5. Invalidenversicherung.
6. Krankenversicherung.
7. Unfallversicherung.
8. Krüppelfürsorge.
9. Bundesarbeitsgemeinschaft für Rehabilitation.
10. Reha-Angleichungsgesetz.
11. Schwerbehindertengesetz.
12. Berufsunfähigkeitsrente.
13. Erwerbsminderungsrente.
14. Sozialgesetzbuch IX—Rehabilitation und Teilhabe behinderter Menschen.
15. Integrationsamt.
16. Sozialamt.
17. Jugendamt.
18. See www.who.int/classifications/icf/en/

19 Stufenweise Wiedereingliederung.
20 Betriebliches Eingliederungsmanagement.
21 Integrationsvereinbarungen.
22 These are now called *Inklusionsvereinbarungen* [inclusion agreements]. A variety of integration agreements can be viewed at www.rehadat-gutepraxis.de/de/integrationsvereinbarungen
23 Präventionsgesetz.
24 Bundesteilhabegesetz.
25 See www.unternehmensforum.org
26 Ausgleichsfonds.
27 Integrationsamt.
28 Versorgungsamt.
29 Bundessozialgericht.
30 Bundesarbeitsgericht.
31 Allgemeines Gleichbehandlungsgesetz.
32 The general age for old-age pension is rising continuously from 65 to 67. People born after 1946 received their pensions at the age of 65. People born after 1964 will wait until they are 67.
33 Arbeitsschutzbehörden.
34 Budget für Arbeit.
35 Zurechnungszeit.
36 Newly approved incapacity pensioners received, on average, €600 [US$714] in 2010 and €672 [US$799] in 2015.
37 Teilhabeplanung.
38 Leistungen zur Teilhabe.
39 Leistungen zur Teilhabe am Arbeitsleben.
40 Teilhabeplankonferenzen.
41 Schwerbehindertenvertretung.
42 Aktionsbündnis Teilhabeforschung.

References

Aichele, V. (2016). Die praktische Geltung der Menschenrechte. *Deutsche Richterzeitung*, pp. 342–347.
Behrend, C. (1992). *Frühinvalidisierung und soziale Sicherung in der Bundesrepublik Deutschland: Entwicklungsprozesse und Fallbeispiele*. Berlin, Germany: Deutsches Zentrum für Altersfragen.
Blumenthal, W., & Jochheim, K.-A. (2009). Entstehen und Entwicklung der Rehabilitation in Deutschland. In W. Blumenthal, & F. Schliehe (Eds.), *Teilhabe als Ziel der Rehabilitation: 100 Jahre Zusammenwirken in der Deutschen Vereinigung für Rehablitation e.V.* (pp. 11–30). Heidelberg, Germany: Deutsche Vereinigung für Rehabilitation.
Bundesarbeitsgericht. (2012, March 3). 1 ABR 78/10, BAGE *141*, 42.
Bundesarbeitsgericht. (2013, December 19). 6 AZR 190/12, BAGE *147*, 60
Bundessozialgericht (2008, April 24). B 9/9a SB 10/06 R.
Bundesverwaltungsgericht (2013, August 19). 5 B 47/13.
Court of Justice of the European Union. (2006, July 11). *Chacon Navas* [Spanish case] C-13/05.
Court of Justice of the European Union. (2014, December 18). *Kaltoft* [Danish case] C-354/13.

Court of Justice of the European Union. (2015, March 26). *Fenoll* [French case] C-316/13.
Deck, R., Träder, J.-M., & Raspe, H. (2009). Identifikation von potenziellem Reha-Bedarf in der Hausarztpraxis: Idee und Wirklichkeit. *Die Rehabilitation*, *48*(2), pp. 73–83. doi:10.1055/s-002-17442
Devetzi, S. (2011). Reforms of the incapacity benefits system in Europe. In S. Devetzi & S. Stendahl (Eds.), *Too sick to work? Social security reforms in Europe for persons with reduced earnings capacity.* (pp. 175–184). Alphen aan den Rijn, the Netherlands: Kluwer Law International.
Devetzi, S. (2015). Rechtliche Bestandsaufnahme im Rentenrecht: Der variable Übergang in den Ruhestand. In G. Igl, F. Welti, & M. Eßer (Eds.), *Alter und Beschäftigungen: Arbeitssituationen, Lebensentwürfe und soziale Sicherung der über 50-Jährigen* (pp. 67–74). Münster, Germany: LIT-Verlag.
Dornette, J., Rauch, A., Schubert, M., Behrens, J., Höhne, A., & Zimmermann, M. (2008). Auswirkungen der Einführung des Sozialgesetzbuches II auf erwerbsfähige hilfebedürftige Personen mit gesundheitlichen Beeinträchtigungen. *Zeitschrift für Sozialreform*, *54*(1), pp. 79–86.
Düwell, F. J. (2011). Zugang zum Arbeitsmarkt und Beschäftigungfähigkeit behinderter Menschen. *Vierteljahresschrift für Sozialrecht*, *29*(1), pp. 27–36.
Düwell, F. J. (2016). Welche Regelungen sind zur Sicherung der Rechte der Schwerbehindertenvertretungen geboten? Eine rechtspolitische Kontroverse. In U. Faber, K. Feldhoff, K. Nebe, K. Schmidt, & U. Waßer (Eds.), *Gesellschaftliche Bewegungen—Recht unter Beobachtung und in Aktion: Festschrift für Wolfhard Kohte* (pp. 47–71). Baden-Baden, Germany: Nomos.
European Community. (2000). European Equal Treatment Directive (2000/78).
Farin, E., Anneken, V., Buschmann-Steinhage, R., Ewert, T., & Schmidt, C. (2012). Diskussionspapier Teilhabeforschung. *Die Rehabilitation*, *51*(Suppl. 1), pp. 28–33. doi:10.1055/s-0032-1327691
Feldes, W. (2016). Versorgungslücken bei betrieblicher Wiedereingliederung psychisch Erkrankter: Vorschläge zu einem systemübergreifenden Schnittstellen- und Teilhabemanagement. *Soziale Sicherheit*, *65*(4), pp. 155–157.
Fuerst, A.-M. (2009). *Behinderung zwischen Diskriminierungsschutz und Rehabilitationsrecht: Ein Vergleich zwischen Deutschland und den USA*. Baden-Baden, Germany: Nomos.
Groskreutz, H., & Welti, F. (2016). Betriebliche Barrierefreiheit als Aufgabe der Schwerbehindertenvertretung. *Arbeit und Recht*, *64*(3), pp. 105–108.
Hirschberg, M. (2011). Partizipation: ein Querschnittsanliegen der UN-Behindertenrechtskonvention. *www.reha-recht.de, Forum D – Nr. 9/2011*. Retrieved from www.reha-recht.de/fileadmin/download/foren/d/2011/D9-2011_Partizipation_Querschnittsanliegen_UN-BRK.pdf
Jordan, M., & Wansing, G. (2016). Peer Counseling: Eine unabhängige Beratungsform von und für Menschen mit Beeinträchtigungen Teil 1: Konzept und Umsetzung. *www.reha-recht.de, Forum D – Nr. 32/2016*. Retrieved from www.reha-recht.de/fileadmin/user_upload/RehaRecht/Diskussionsforen/Forum_D/2016/D32-2016_Peer_Counseling_Teil_1_Konzept_und_Umsetzung.pdf
Knickrehm, S. (2008). Die Feststellung nach § 69 SGB IX im Lichte des "modernen" Behinderungsbegriffs. *Die Sozialgerichtsbarkeit*, *55*(4), pp. 220–227.
Knülle, E. (2012). Erhalt der Beschäftigungsfähigkeit: Reha als wichtiger Baustein. *www.reha-recht.de, Forum B – Nr. 3/2012*. Retrieved from www.reha-recht.de/

fileadmin/download/foren/b/2012/B3-2012_Erhalt_der_Beschaeftigungsfaehigkeit.pdf

Kocher, E., & Wenckebach, J. (2013). § 12 AGG als Grundlage für Ansprüche auf angemessene Vorkehrungen. *Soziales Recht*, *3*(1), pp. 17–28.

Kohte, W. (2008). Betriebliches Eingliederungsmanagement und Bestandsschutz. *Der Betrieb*, *20*(11), pp. 582–587.

Luik, S. (2014). Der Teilhabeplan—die Roadmap zum Reha-Erfolg: Plädoyer für eine gesetzliche Klarstellung. *Sozialrecht aktuell*, *18*(Sonderheft), pp. 11–17.

Mehrhoff, F. (2014). Behindertenrechtskonvention in der sozialen Sicherheit—Pflicht oder Kür? (Teil 1+Teil 2). *www.reha-recht.de, Forum D – Nr. 15/2014, Nr. 16/2014*. Retrieved from www.reha-recht.de/fileadmin/download/foren/d/2014/D15-2014_Behindertenrechtskonvention_in_der_sozialen_Sicherheit__Teil_1_.pdf; www.reha-recht.de/fileadmin/download/foren/d/2014/D16-2014_Behindertenrechtskonvention_in_der_sozialen_Sicherheit_Teil_2.pdf

Mittag, O., Reese, C., & Meffert, C. (2014). (Keine) Reha vor Rente: Analyse der Zugänge zur Erwerbsminderungsrente von 2005 bis 2009. *WSI-Mitteilungen*, *70*(2), pp. 149–155.

Mittag, O., & Welti, F. (2017). Medizinische Rehabilitation im europäischen Vergleich und Auswirkungen des europäischen Rechts auf die deutsche Rehabilitation. *Bundesgesundheitsblatt—Gesundheitsforschung—Gesundheitsschutz*, *60*(4), pp. 378–385.

Naegele, G. (2015). Altes und Neues zur Erwerbsarbeit Älterer: Mit besonderer Beachtung der betrieblichen Ebene. In G. Igl, F. Welti, & M. Eßer (Eds.), *Alter und Beschäftigungen: Arbeitssituationen, Lebensentwürfe und soziale Sicherung der über 50-Jährigen* (pp. 17–32). Münster, Germany: LIT-Verlag.

Nassibi, G. (2012). Die Durchsetzung der Ansprüche auf Schaffung behinderungsgerechter Arbeitsbedingungen: Betriebliches Eingliederungsmanagement und Beteiligung der Interessenvertretung. *Neue Zeitschrift für Arbeitsrecht*, *29*(13), pp. 720–725.

Nebe, K. (2015). Die stufenweise Wiedereingliederung: Sicherung der Erwerbsteilhabe durch komplementäres Arbeits- und Sozialrecht. *Die Sozialgerichtsbarkeit*, *62*(3), pp. 125–134.

Nebe, K., & Schimank, C. (2016). Das Budget für Arbeit im Bundesteilhabegesetz Teil 1: Darstellung der Entwicklung und kritische Betrachtung bis zur Befassung im Bundesrat. *www.reha-recht.de, Forum D – Nr. 47/2016*. Retrieved from www.reha-recht.de/fileadmin/user_upload/RehaRecht/Diskussionsforen/Forum_D/2016/D47-2016_Das_Budget_fuer_Arbeit_im_Bundesteilhabegesetz_Teil_1.pdf

Ramm, D. (2017). *Die Rehabilitation und das Schwerbeschädigtenrecht der DDR im Übergang zur Bundesrepublik Deutschland: Strukturen und Akteure*. Kassel, Germany: kassel university press. doi:10.19211/KUP9783737602990

Reinhard, H.-J. (2015). Ältere Beschäftigte im Fokus des Sozialversicherungsrechts: Rechtliche Bestandsaufnahme im Arbeitsmarktrecht. In G. Igl, F. Welti, & M. Eßer (Eds.), *Alter und Beschäftigungen: Arbeitssituationen, Lebensentwürfe und soziale Sicherung der über 50-Jährigen* (pp. 57–66). Münster, Germany: LIT-Verlag.

Ritz, H.-G. (2016). Teilhabe von Menschen mit wesentlichen Behinderungen am Arbeitsmarkt. *Behindertenrecht*, *55*(2), pp. 34–61.

Rudloff, W. (2003). Überlegungen zur Geschichte der bundesdeutschen Behindertenpolitik. *Zeitschrift für Sozialreform*, *49*(6), pp. 863–881.

Schimank, C. (2016). Das Budget für Arbeit im Bundesteilhabegesetz Teil 2: Öffentliche Anhörung und abschließende Beratung im Ausschuss für Arbeit und Soziales sowie 2. und 3. Lesung im Bundestag. *www.reha-recht.de, Forum D – Nr. 60/2016.* Retrieved from www.reha-recht.de/fileadmin/user_upload/ RehaRecht/Diskussionsforen/Forum_D/2016/D60-2016_Das_Budget_fuer_ Arbeit_im_Bundesteilhabegesetz_%E2%80%93_Teil_2.pdf

Shafaei, R. F. (2008). *Die gemeinsamen Servicestellen für Rehabilitation: Beratung und Unterstützung behinderter Menschen nach dem SGB IX.* Baden-Baden, Germany: Nomos.

Trenk-Hinterberger, P. (2015). Das Recht auf Arbeit im Kontext der UN-Behindertenrechtskonvention. In D. Stamatia & C. Jande (Eds.), *Freiheit— Gerechtigkeit—Sozial(es) Recht: Festschrift für Eberhard Eichenhofer* (pp. 652–670). Baden-Baden, Germany: Nomos.

United Nations. Committee on the Rights of Persons with Disabilities. (2015). *Concluding observations on the initial report of Germany*, CRPD/C/DEU/CO/1. Retrieved from https://documents-dds-ny.un.org/doc/UNDOC/GEN/G15/096/31/PDF/G1509631.pdf?OpenElement

Waddington, L., & Lawson, A. (2009). *Disability and non-discrimination law in the European Union: An analysis of disability discrimination law within and beyond the employment field.* Brussels, Belgium. doi:10.2767/49788

Wansing, G. (2016). Peer Counseling—Eine unabhängige Beratungsform von und für Menschen mit Beeinträchtigungen—Teil 2: Wirkfaktoren und Gelingensbedingungen. *www.reha-recht.de, Forum D – Nr. 59/2016.* Retrieved from www.reha-recht.de/fileadmin/user_upload/RehaRecht/Diskussionsforen/Forum_D/2016/D59-2016_Peer_Counseling_Teil_2.pdf

Welti, F. (2008). Work Activation and Rehabilitation of disabled people in Germany in the framework of European strategies: Problems of coherence and policy mismatch. In S. Stendahl, T. Erhag, & S. Devetzi (Eds.), *A European Work-First Welfare State* (pp. 145–156). Gothenburg, Sweden: Centre for European Research, University of Gothenburg.

Welti, F. (2014). Stichwort "Behinderung." In O. Deinert & F. Welti (Eds.), *Stichwortkommentar Behindertenrecht: Arbeits- und Sozialrecht. Öffentliches Recht. Zivilrecht. Alphabetische Gesamtdarstellung* (pp. 147–154). Baden-Baden, Germany: Nomos.

Welti, F. (2015a). Beeinträchtigung von Funktionen oder individueller Teilhabe? *Sozialrecht + Praxis, 25*, pp. 148–157.

Welti, F. (2015b). Das Gesetz zur Stärkung der Gesundheitsförderung und der Prävention—was bringt dieses Präventionsgesetz? *Gesundheit und Pflege, 5*(6), pp. 211–216.

Welti, F., & Groskreutz, H. (2013a). Non-public actors in social security in Germany. In F. Pennings, T. Erhag, & S. Stendal (Eds.), *Non-public actors in social security administration: A comparative study* (pp. 9–36). Alphen aan den Rijn, the Netherlands: Wolters Kluwer Law & Business.

Welti, F., & Groskreutz, H. (2013b). *Soziales Recht zum Ausgleich von Erwerbsminderung: Reformoptionen für Prävention, Rehabilitation und soziale Sicherung bei Erwerbsminderung.* Düsseldorf, Germany: Hans-Böckler-Stiftung. Retrieved from www.boeckler.de/pdf/p_arbp_295.pdf

Welti, F., Mahnke, C., Tauscher, A., Ramm, D., Seider, H., & Shafaei, R. (2011). *Betriebliches Eingliederungsmanagement in Klein- und Mittelbetrieben: Rechtliche Anforderungen und Voraussetzungen ihrer erfolgreichen Umsetzung.* Neubrandenburg, Germany: Hochschule Neubrandenburg.

Welti, F., & Nachtschatt, E. (2018). Equal rights of Persons with Disabilities to Work per Article 27 of the Convention on the Rights of Persons with Disabilities. In G. Wansing, F. Welti, & M. Schäfers (Eds.), *The Right to Work for Persons with Disabilities: International Perspectives* (pp. 51–86). Baden-Baden, Germany: Nomos.

World Health Organization. (n. d.). *International classification of functioning, disability and health (ICF)*. Retrieved February 15, 2018, from www.who.int/classifications/icf/en/

Zacher, H. F. (2013). *Social policy in the Federal Republic of Germany: The constitution of the social*. Berlin, Germany: Springer-Verlag. doi:10.1007/978-3-642-22525-3

Chapter 12

Keeping People at Work
New Work Disability Prevention Measures in Switzerland

Thomas Geisen

Workplace-related welfare policy has been dominated in recent decades by the principle of "getting people back to work." Since the turn of this century, however, a new principle has emerged: "keeping people at work." The new orientation focuses not on returning people to work after full medical treatment or a loss of employment but on new types of "activation" policies and practices.[1] This new work-activation-focused policy emphasizes prevention and early intervention, especially workplace safety and health promotion, in order to keep people at work.

Recent changes to the Swiss welfare state demonstrate this shift from "social investment" (Giddens, 1998, p. 99) to health promotion. With this shift, workplace health gained new importance and made employers more responsible for creating and maintaining healthy workplaces, promoting good health, and preventing work-related illness and injury. In Switzerland, this shift to health promotion occurred within the country's liberal tradition (Esping-Andersen, 1990). In this tradition, states appeal to companies' sense of social responsibility but do not force them to comply with policies using measures such as quotas for employing people with disabilities.

The new emphasis on keeping people at work reflects the great importance of work in modern societies, in which employment plays a key role in people's lives (Geisen, 2011a). Akabas and Kurzman (2005) emphasize that:

> to be part of a working group, recognized and appreciated by one's workmates, united with them whether by bonds or gripes or by general camaraderie, fulfills the ever-present human need to be accepted, supported, even to be authenticated by others.
>
> (p. 23)

Work is not simply a way to earn a living, it is also a "basic human activity" (Arendt, 1996) that connects workers to the human world and its objects, and also to other people. For Sigmund Freud, "work has a greater effect than any other technique of living in the direction of binding the individual more closely to reality; in his work he is at least securely attached to part of reality, the human community" (Freud,1930, quoted in Akabas & Kurzman, 2005, p. 22). Because of this world-binding effect, employment contributes greatly to well-being. Work endows people with self-esteem, a sense of belonging—to the workplace, the work team, the company—and dignity, because through work people care for themselves.

However, over their lifetimes, people also risk becoming unemployed, having a severe accident or illness, being obliged to devote more time to caring for children and other family members, and so on. In modern societies, welfare states have developed to support people facing such unforeseen and disabling situations. But, with one exception, Switzerland's workplace-safety legislation[2] and the social security system[3] focused on the ill or injured person but not on their workplaces or working conditions. In line with the principle of "individualization" (Wicki, 2001, p. 247), support is given only to people who are no longer able to participate in the labor force. Only with the most recent developments in welfare-state schemes, partly driven by international organizations (International Labour Organization (ILO), 2002; World Health Organization (WHO), 2007, 2011), have work and workplace integration been considered human rights, including for those with disabilities. In addition, workplace integration is increasingly perceived as crucial to the rehabilitation of employees after severe illness or accident (Organisation for Economic Co-operation and Development (OECD), 2013; Schubert et al., 2013). Especially for people with disabilities, work contributes much to maintaining a sense of continuity and coherence (Antonovsky, 1997) and of belonging within the life-world. There seems, then, to be no question that people with disabilities should have the right to work and equal access to the labor market. Nevertheless, in various European countries, including Switzerland, people with disabilities still struggle to regain access to the labor market after losing a job. Available Swiss figures comparing employment rates of people with disabilities with those of other people of working age show a gap of 12.6% (69% vs. 81.6%). The average gap in the EU28 countries is higher (18%) and in Germany higher still (22%) (Eurostat, 2014). That means that people with disabilities experience difficulties not only in accessing the labor market but also in retaining their jobs if they have severe illnesses or accidents.

A closer look at Swiss companies shows that they often have weak internal and external work disability and employee health support systems (Geisen, Lichtenauer, Roulin, & Schielke, 2008). Thus, employees often do not receive adequate professional support when they risk becoming ill or acquiring work-related or non-work-related disabilities. This is especially so for smaller companies; whereas, bigger companies have improved their employee supports in the last decade. The most recent data (Füllemann, Inauen, Jenny, Moser, & Bauer, 2017), which cover only companies with more than 100 employees, show that 23% have implemented complete corporate health-management strategies. These include (a) absenteeism and case management;

(b) corporate health plans; (c) corporate health promotion and employee surveys; and (d) workplace adaptation, HR-management and organizational development plans. In addition, 48% of companies have implemented most of these components, and 53% have implemented absenteeism and case-management schemes. Absenteeism management and case management are especially important in early intervention and professional support for employees at risk, and these supports can contribute to stabilizing their health (Geisen, 2011b; Harder & Scott, 2005). For employers, corporate health management contributes to safer workplaces and healthier workforces (Antonovsky, 1997; Bauer, 2005; Ulich & Wülser, 2009). Although companies in Switzerland are still reluctant to implement comprehensive corporate health management (Bauer, 2005), state policies have improved support for employers and employees in disability prevention.

This chapter shows how the most recent reforms to the Swiss welfare state have been implemented, and it discusses the reforms' impact on the health and social security of employees. The main argument is that, compared with earlier policies that removed injured or ill employees from work to recuperate and then returned them to work, recent policies bring the welfare state and social security measures closer to companies and workplaces, by requesting cooperation and support in keeping at work people at risk of severe illness or permanent disabilities.

Work Disability Prevention: A New Service in the Swiss Welfare System

Under Switzerland's liberal welfare state (Esping-Anderson, 1998), social protection and social support are neither comprehensive nor delivered by the government, as in social-democratic, northern European countries. Nor must social protection and social support be guaranteed by corporations, social partners, and the state, as in corporate-model central European countries, such as France and Germany (Esping-Andersen, 1998). Switzerland's liberal welfare model can be characterized as reluctant, because state regulations and programs were introduced only when people's capacities to deal with social challenges on their own became radically diminished and state support was considered indispensable (Wicki, 2001). So, although Switzerland was the first European country to enact a safety-at-work law, other social security laws were enacted much later than elsewhere in Europe. Switzerland is not only a reluctant but also a delayed welfare state (Wicki, 2001).

Swiss liberalism also influences the state's role in society; under liberalism, it should limit regulations to those needed to allow people to pursue their well-being and happiness, and it should not otherwise interfere in private affairs (Esping-Andersen, 1998). Under a liberal regime, welfare-related regulations focus more on individual needs than on practices in companies and organizations. This means that Swiss social policies encourage the employment of people with disabilities but do not enforce it—for example, through a quota system like Germany's (Niehaus, Magin, Marfels, Vater, & Werkstetter, 2008). Therefore, under Swiss social security legislation, the continued employment of people with disabilities depends on the will and commitment of employers. Employers are obliged neither by a quota system to hire people with disabilities, nor by strong legislation to retain employees who acquire work-related severe illnesses or disabilities. Due to its strongly liberal character, the Swiss welfare state is not likely to introduce stronger legislation or quota systems. Instead, the government encourages and supports companies' voluntary commitments to employ people with disabilities and take steps to prevent work-related illness and injury.

Voluntary commitments mean that companies change their policies only when public pressure or market-driven demand pushes them to prevent work disability and to develop corporate health-management programs. Such pressure was evident, for example, during political campaigns starting in 2006 to reform disability insurance. Companies were criticized for not offering enough job opportunities for people with disabilities, not retaining and returning to work employees with work-acquired disabilities, and not actively preventing illness. In response, major Swiss companies founded a network to improve workplace disability management (Kraft, Buffat, Baeriswyl, Egli, & Setz, 2013). This network developed into Compasso, a national agency to support employers on workplace disability and health issues (www.compasso.ch).

With regard to market-driven change, employee health is becoming more and more important for companies. Corporate health management has become an asset in the competition for qualified labor. That means that, in job interviews, candidates ask what health support is offered to employees, and the answer figures in whether they accept job offers (Geisen et al., 2016b). Therefore, even without state legislation or enforcement of improved employment for people with disabilities, Swiss companies are paying more attention to employee health.

Compared with other European countries, the employment rate among Swiss citizens with disabilities is quite high (Eurostat, 2014). However, an earlier study showed that only 8% of Swiss companies employ people with disabilities, although 23% report being willing to employ them but do not do so (Baumgartner, Greiwe, & Schwarb, 2004, pp. 255–260). The views and attitudes of Swiss employers play a crucial role in maintaining employment for people with work-related disabilities (Geisen et al., 2016a; Geisen & Harder, 2011). Among small and medium-sized companies in northwestern Switzerland, social responsibility and moral obligation are major reasons for employers to support employees through difficult health problems. These obligations are especially strong if the relationship between employee and employer has been a long and successful (Geisen, Kraus, Ochsenbein,

Schmid, & Studer, 2013). Employees often view support for company's supervisors, and health and disability-management staff, as crucial to preserving employability and smoothly functioning, productive workplaces (Geisen et al., 2013; Geisen et al., 2008; Geisen & Harder, 2011).

Recent developments show that the Swiss government is trying to develop more comprehensive measures that focus not only on individuals but also on workplaces. Disability-management research shows that early intervention greatly strengthens employability and job security (Geisen & Harder, 2011). This new work-activation approach (Bonoli & Natali, 2012) accompanies the principle of "demand and support," in which access to social benefits is tightened and their amount is reduced. Under the principles of activation and of demand and support, receiving social benefits comes with certain conditions; for example, requiring recipients to make sustainable efforts to return to work or participate in education and training programs. Here, social benefits are considered social investments (Giddens, 1998) in creating or restoring employability. Bonoli and Natali (2012) describe this social-policy shift over the past 20 years, "in virtually all European countries," as a process in which, for example:

> Unemployment compensation systems have been transformed from passive providers of replacement income into activation tools. New policies have emerged too, such as parental leave, child-care, and in-work benefits. Finally, the field of social policy is increasingly considered as part of a broader politico-economic settlement that can impact significantly on the functioning of a country's economy.
>
> (p. 5)

In the Swiss liberal welfare state (Esping-Andersen, 1990), however, the shift to more activating and demanding social policy was gradual. The Swiss welfare state has long been guided by the principle of covering basic needs with a minimum of social protection. The Beveridge liberal welfare state prescribed a system in which the government only supports people if they are no longer able to care for themselves, and such support should be minimal (Scharf, 2001, p. 47). In contrast to Switzerland, the Bismarck principles (Ziegelmayer, 2001, p. 64) are more salient to the corporatist and social-democratic welfare states elsewhere in Europe (Esping-Andersen, 1990). They attend to the needs of, for example, unemployed workers. The introduction of social-insurance schemes meant that workers' social status would be protected for a certain period, in which workers were unable to work because of severe injury, sickness, or unemployment (Kraus & Geisen, 2001). However, welfare states in the Western world represent unique systems that differ from the ideal types: liberal, corporatist, and social democratic—the "three worlds of welfare capitalism" (Esping-Andersen, 1990, pp. 26–27).

Of course, the development of European welfare states also depended on more general social and political developments. In the 1990s, especially during economic transformation and crises (e.g., in the Swiss chemical industry), introduction of early-retirement schemes and a rising number of disability-insurance claims helped resolve severe labor-market problems. Nonetheless, they also created new challenges for welfare states because of the growing number of people relying on welfare benefits. Welfare schemes experienced financial difficulties and, at the same time, companies began shifting responsibility for workers with health problems to the state welfare system. From a social security perspective, this development had the negative effect that companies could use the welfare system to replace workers with health problems and older workers, leaving them to rely on state benefits. In response, social-policy reforms since 2000 have adhered to two principles: (a) tightening access to social benefits and (b) introducing new schemes and measures in different policy areas not only to better support people in returning to work but also to strengthen workplace illness and accident prevention and to support ill or injured workers to stay at work (Geisen et al., 2016a; Moser, 2008). These reforms focus not only on supporting employees in need but also (in the case of disability insurance, for the first time in Switzerland) on helping companies and organizations deal with work-related health and disability issues, including severe illness and injuries.

Disability insurance[4] is the only social insurance that aims not only to help its members regain their employability and return to work but also to help companies improve disability prevention and manage existing health problems. Accident insurance,[5] corporate pension funds, daily-allowance and life-insurance plans have all introduced professional case management to support employees in returning to work. Through a sustainable reintegration process, these social and private insurance plans seek to improve the return-to-work transition of employees with work-related severe illnesses or injuries. Disability-insurance plans also assist employers, even those without employees currently on disability leave.

In 2003, the Swiss National Accident Insurance Fund was the first insurance company in Switzerland to introduce a case-management-based support structure for people with severe injuries. Over the next few years, the different daily-allowance insurance schemes and the other private insurance companies (e.g., offering life insurance) followed suit and introduced their own case-management support structures. This network of supports also includes employers' and supervisors' perspectives, and considers the workplace context; for example, workplace adjustment and workplace organization are key factors in return-to-work procedures. The case-management measures also contribute to the prevention of workplace disability. Companies thereby have access to disability-prevention schemes that serve both employees and employers. With this development, the dominant focus in return to work has shifted from employees to a broader one that considers the workplace an important factor in sustainable return-to-work programs. Where insurance companies provide professional case management,[6] the employer can also be sure that the return-to-work process for employees is conducted by professionals with expertise in reintegration counseling and health.[7] Professional case management has been defined as "a client-level strategy for promoting the coordination of human services, opportunities, or benefits. The major outcomes of case management are: (1) the integration of services across a cluster of organizations . . .; and (2) achieving continuity of care" (Moxley, 1989, p. 11). In structuring the support process, case management includes the following core elements: "outreach, screening and intake, comprehensive assessment, care planning, service arrangement, monitoring and reassessment" (Gursansky, Harvey, & Kennedy, 2003, p. 17). This systematic, professional approach is more likely to be efficient and effective than when the return-to-work process is solely the employee's responsibility. Research on disability management in Swiss companies shows clearly that employers see programs that support employees to return to work as successful, and that employees in need of such support value the schemes highly (Geisen et al., 2008).

Such innovative approaches to disability prevention by private and social insurance funds also lead to greater communication, cooperation, and coordination between insurers and employers. However, shifting the focus of disability prevention to include the employers' perspective and interests created challenges for both sides. New arrangements, practices, and structures were needed, as well as new competencies for disability-prevention professionals, including counseling skills and capacity to define processes for putting external supports in place. The more inclusive work disability prevention approach also required trust building, without which the new approach could not work. Research shows that motivation and commitment among both employees and employers is crucial to improving the work- and health-related challenges (Geisen, 2015; Geisen et al., 2008; Geisen et al., 2013;). A study of relationships between the disability insurance fund's offices and employers shows that these relationships have indeed improved, and that the enhanced cooperation contributes to reintegration of employees (Geisen et al., 2016a).

One of the most significant aspects of introducing work disability prevention schemes in private and social insurance providers is that employers and employees in small and medium-sized companies gain access to professional health support. Because of their size, these companies are not usually able to implement their own disability-prevention schemes (e.g., through comprehensive corporate health- management systems). In fact, in Switzerland, only about 23% of employers (large companies, governments, and institutions) have a company health-management system in place (Füllemann et al., 2017; Geisen, 2011b).

The disability insurance and daily-allowance insurance schemes provide the most important insurance support for work disability prevention in Swiss companies. The following section focuses on these insurance funds.

Case Management Support from Daily Sickness Allowance Insurance

The daily-sickness-allowance insurance scheme is part of Switzerland's liberal welfare state. It is a private fund, into which employers pay to be insured against employee sick-leave benefits. In Switzerland, the obligation to pay sick-leave benefits to employees is low at the beginning of someone's employment with the company but grows with their years of employment; for example, from one month in the second year to four months after 10–14 years, according to the Bern Scala (modeled on the Zurich Scala, one of the most used scales) (OECD, 2014). The employee must work a minimum of three weeks for the company and have a work contract longer than three months to be eligible. Although the insurance is not compulsory, to reduce their financial risk many of the bigger companies pay into it. But it is:

> not possible to estimate a coverage rate of daily sickness allowances among employees, since insurers only receive information on the total wage bill of the company. Nevertheless, from the 2009 Survey on Collective Labour Agreements it is known that 82% of the collective agreements covering at least 1,500 employees oblige companies to take out a collective insurance contract, which applies to about 22% of all employees in Switzerland . . . Another 13% of collective agreements recommend such collective insurance to its [sic] member companies.
> (OECD, 2014, p. 46)

For a maximum of three days' waiting time, the employer must continue to pay the salary of a sick or injured employee, after which the insurance company takes over and pays at least 80% of the salary, for at least 720 days over a period of 900 days.

Since the beginning of the 2000s and following the example of the the Swiss National Accident Insurance Fund, daily-allowance insurers have introduced new measures to support employers and employees in the return-to-work process. In the short term, the insurers want to reduce their immediate costs by shortening the delay in the return to work. In the long term, they want to ensure that the back-to-work process is of high quality and very effective. It is often argued that this leads to a win-win situation for the employer, the employee, and the insurance fund (Schmidt & Kessler, 2006). The aim is to achieve sustainability in the rehabilitation process and in the employee's return to work. In the beginning, the number of insurers offering case management to their clients (the insured employers) grew slowly, and case management became a marketing tactic for winning new clients. Since then, case management has become a standard service in the daily-allowance insurance industry. In supplying that service to companies, the insurance funds deploy not only their own case-management personnel, but they also work together with professional case-management-service providers. The advantage is that the insurer can better react to upturns and downturns, but the disadvantage is that the system becomes ever more complex, and more driven by files and reports. This increases the need for detailed and comprehensive case documentation.

On the insurer's side, interacting with case managers, employers, and employees requires new competences and qualifications to manage the varying claims and requirements. Because of this complexity, cost-effectiveness may be difficult to achieve for daily-allowance-insurance funds, which must act within the limits of the 720-day period in which they are obliged to cover the employee's wage. Work disability prevention practice shows that, in complex cases where case management is provided, some companies see this period as too short (Geisen et al., 2016b). A debate has begun about whether case management might not be better provided in the daily-allowance insurance field by contracting this function to outside consultants, because of potential conflicts of interest between insurers and insurance-company staff. Although there are no available data on this topic, it would appear that a great advantage of case management for work disability prevention is that professional intervention starts early, depending on the contract between the insurer and the company (e.g., after 30 days of sickness or accident leave).[8] In addition, according to the work disability literature, early detection and intervention are the most important factors in sustainable work disability prevention (Escorpizo, Brage, Homa, & Stucki, 2015; Harder & Scott, 2005; Loisel & Anema, 2013).

Work Disability Prevention and Management by Disability Insurance Schemes

After the Swiss accident-insurance and private daily-sickness-allowance insurance funds introduced work disability management schemes, the Swiss government followed suit in 2008 with its fifth reform of disability insurance.[9] With this reform, a new era began, in which the insurance culture changed from a pension and service-provision focus to an active focus on job retention and reintegration. At the core of this new policy was an early-identification and early-intervention scheme, whereby employees with serious health problems would be identified as early as possible by the employer or the employee's general practitioner,[10] and the disability insurer notified, so that disability insurer's case manager could contact the employee and employer.[11]

First, the case manager assesses the personal, health, and work situation of the employee. Based on that assessment, a decision is made whether to apply early-intervention measures to avoid severe disability and to secure workplace participation. Although employees' participation is voluntary, having a professional disability manager involved means that the support provided to employees will be directed to improving all aspects of their situations (e.g., ensuring that appropriate healthcare, household supports, and workplace adjustments are provided). An early return to work with a small workload that allows reintegration into workplace activities and coworker relationships plays a vital role in strengthening employee self-esteem and self-reliance. In the case of mental health problems, this is crucial to recovery. Return to work is planned according to the worker's progress, starting with a work trial, followed by work training, full recovery, and full (or reduced) labor-market participation. These steps should be achieved within a certain period.

From the very beginning of the return-to-work process, employment is seen as an important part of recovery. Early-intervention measures include workplace adjustment, qualification courses, job services, vocational counseling, social and vocational rehabilitation, and functional-capacity measurements. Such measures are not defined exclusively, because anything required to improve work capacity and avoid disability, including, for example, domestic help, should be considered. Although the costs of early-intervention measures are limited to CHF20,000 [US$20,000] per insured person, early intervention is crucial in preventing and managing work disability. It marks a change from general support and treatment policies to individual, case-specific assistance determined by specific needs. During the return-to-work process, the insurer's disability case manager is in contact not only with the employee but also with the employer, human resource manager, supervisor, general practitioner, work-team members, and others relevant to the employee's recovery. Based on the communication among and coordination of these different actors, support and additional resources are generated to effect recovery and return to work.

The government's fifth reform of disability insurance received a positive evaluation (Bolliger, Fritschi, Salzgerber, Züricher, & Hümbelin, 2012). The evaluators found that more people at risk of permanent disability came in contact with the disability-insurance system before they lost their employment, vocational reintegration happened more often and more quickly, and more people at risk of permanent disability returned to work, especially those with mental health problems (Bolliger et al., 2012).

Successful return to work depends on the full support and engagement of all actors involved. If not, the disability-management process is likely to fail. In companies where employers and employees commit to making disability management successful, it is more likely that good solutions can be found for difficult problems. And if no return to work is possible and the employee must leave the company, then there is still satisfaction that both sides tried their best. This is also a signal to other employees that the company will try its best to retain them should they face illness or disability (Geisen et al., 2008).

Conclusion

The Swiss welfare regime recently moved to incorporating work and workplace issues into disability prevention and rehabilitation measures. Work and workplaces are no longer seen as endangering health and therefore inimical to recovery. The latter perspective was mainly medically driven and dominated rehabilitation in Switzerland up to the early 2000s (Geisen & Harder, 2011; Harder & Scott, 2005; Loisel & Anema, 2013). The new perspective, work disability prevention and management, which was developed to counter the narrow medical model (Loisel & Anema, 2013), is a comprehensive approach that combines medical, social, and work-related aspects. In this new concept, work and workplaces are seen as crucial to well-being.

In Switzerland since the 2000s, the daily-allowance and disability-insurance funds have shifted their focus from providing pensions to work disability prevention and return to work. When employees face severe illness or accident, they often do not understand Switzerland's highly developed, elaborate health and social insurance system, and therefore employees do not get the support they need from that system. Part of the problem is the system's complexity, which makes it difficult for employees to navigate. Another problem is the employees themselves, who often do not seek medical advice early on for their health problems. Therefore, in complex cases, professional guidance for employees is very much needed, to ensure not only that they receive appropriate medical treatment but also to maintain employability and organize return to work. Often, neither employees, nor their employers, nor relatives or friends have the expertise to ensure the right care. Work disability prevention and management offer not only much-needed professional support that can be integrated into a company's internal structure, but also assistance from external service providers. Professional support is delivered within comprehensive case management, and the knowledge gained in managing cases produces organizational learning; for example, by changing company work processes to improve working conditions. However, professional support can only be efficient and effective if disability case managers are sufficiently educated and trained. Because work disability cases are becoming more complex and more work disabilities are related to mental health problems, work disability professionals need the highest possible qualifications.

In Switzerland, the field of work disability prevention is developing significantly through new measures introduced by the daily-sickness-allowance and disability-insurance funds. Through insurer-based disability prevention and management, professional services become more accessible to small and medium-sized companies, which dominate the Swiss economy. However, whereas disability case management has grown in recent years, employer support for work disability prevention and management is still limited. Yet, these programs have great potential for improving health. This will be an important challenge in the future, when workplaces will have to adjust to the aging workforce, skilled-labor shortages, and employees with physical- or mental health problems trying to return to work. Their potential can only be realized if work disability management professionals are not only qualified to oversee rehabilitation and return to work but are also able to contribute to organizational learning about employee health and disability prevention (Geisen, 2011b). Only by combining the expertise of professional case managers with organizational learning will knowledge of organizational needs during case management be produced and translated into further organizational development. In addition, there is an urgent need to introduce more comprehensive work-related supports and schemes in the private and social insurance programs and funds. Employers, especially, must become more involved in health, so that early identification and intervention of work-related health problems can improve and organizational development in health issues be supported. If employability is to be preserved and workforces are to be sustained, organizations' skill in "mindful change and organizational recognition" (Becke, 2014; Becke, Behrens, Bleses, Meyerhuber, & Schmidt, 2013, p. 21) must be improved.

This chapter has shown that the current Swiss system of work disability prevention and management is strongly driven by social and private insurance funds, which contribute to the new-welfare-state paradigm of "keeping people at work" through health promotion rather than through supplying social-investment policies for those not able to enter the workforce or those who have lost their jobs due to severe illness. In the new paradigm, employees' health conditions and workplace health issues gain new importance. However, Swiss companies are still insufficiently engaged in developing internal corporate health-management strategies; in many cases they use case-management services supplied by social and private insurance funds. This means that, although they offer case-management support to their employees, the companies themselves have no expertise in case management. If companies do not develop their own competence in health management, they will neither be able to make use of case-management data for corporate organizational learning, nor will they become competent partners with the insurance funds. Both case-management support and organizational learning are indispensable for effective, efficient communication, and cooperation, among the various actors involved in work disability. Without this double orientation, work disability prevention and management will not realize their full potential to support employees and to transform companies into healthier, more mindful organizations.

Notes

1 Implementation of the social-investment state and activation practices is often described as resulting from a shift from so-called welfare to workfare in the neoliberal transformation of European welfare states (see Bonoli & Natali, 2012; Lessenich, 2008).
2 The *Fabrikgesetz* [factory law] was introduced by the Swiss government in 1877, followed by the 1881 *Haftpflichtgesetz* [employers' liability law] (Wicki, 2001, p. 253).
3 The major elements of Switzerland's social security system are health insurance (introduced in 1912), accident insurance (introduced in 1918), old age and survivors' insurance (introduced in 1948), and disability insurance (introduced in 1960). These are the years in which the insurance came into being, not when the legislation was passed. The social insurance schemes are funded either equally by employees and employers (disability insurance at 0.7% of the income of each party; state pension at 4.2% of the income of each party; unemployment insurance at 1.1% of the income of each party) or by employers only (accident insurance premiums and sickness allowance insurance are based on the company's risk) (www.bsv.admin.ch/bsv/de/home/sozialversicherungen/ueberblick.html).
4 All employees are obliged to join state-regulated disability-insurance, accident-insurance, and corporate-retirement plans. Private companies offer daily-sickness-allowance and life insurance.
5 The state-regulated accident insurance plan checks that companies adhere to employment-protection regulations. Since 2003, the plan has also offered case management for injured workers.
6 Professional case management is a general procedure for structuring support processes and is applied in different fields, such as social work and healthcare. It is a comprehensive approach and differs from approaches such as disability management practitioner (DMP) certification, introduced and licensed by the Canadian organization NIDMAR (National Institute of Disability Management and Research) (www.nidmar.ca), founded in 1994. DMP certification has since been implemented in many other countries. Although the German Accident Insurance fund holds DMP certification licenses for Germany, Austria and Switzerland, in Switzerland this certificate plays no role in the qualifications of workplace disability managers. Professionals active in workplace disability prevention and management qualify as professional case managers through continuing-education programs offered by the Universities of Applied Sciences, mainly in schools of social work or of health sciences. Those courses are not NIDMAR-certified.
7 There is no overview available on the qualifications of case and disability managers in the daily-sickness-allowance and disability-insurance fields. Although many have backgrounds in psychology or social work, there are a range of other vocations, including recruiters, physiotherapists, technicians, and nurses. Before qualifying to work as case or disability managers, they must take extensive internal or external training in continuing education programs specializing in case management or disability management. External continuing-education courses are offered by the Universities of Applied Sciences in Switzerland. Internal courses are organized by employers.
8 Before the daily-sickness-allowance insurers introduced professional case management for their clients, return-to-work activities were the responsibility of employers. In the face of growing absenteeism rates, the insurers adjusted their premiums only according to the increased risk. At the beginning of the 2000s,

only a small proportion of the companies in Switzerland had company-level health-management strategies in place—many of which simply promoted occupational health and safety (Bauer, 2005)—and no professional, comprehensive, case-management schemes for employees (Geisen, 2011b, p. 20–21.). Because strong social security schemes in European welfare states provide social protection for a certain period, the focus on workplace health and disability has been fairly weak for a long time. Only the most recent developments promote the idea that early detection and early intervention help to avoid severe disabilities and illnesses.

9 See Bundesgesetz über die Invalidenversicherung (IVG) [Swiss federal law on disability insurance] (www.admin.ch/opc/de/classified-compilation/1959 0131/201709010000/831.20.pdf). The disability insurance fund was founded in 1960. The first two reforms to it, in 1967 and 1986, were directed at improving processes. A major organizational revision took place in 1991, when disability insurance functions were decentralized and the cantons took over implementation of the disability insurance law. In each of the 26 cantons, a disability insurance office opened. With the fourth reform of disability insurance in 2003, a regional medical service was introduced, so that each office had its own doctor for consultation (www.geschichtedersozialsicherheit.ch/institutionen/die-verwaltung-der-invalidenversicherung-iv/).

10 In general, health-related information is protected under Swiss privacy law, and an employer can only access it with agreement from the employee. The employer has the right to be informed by the general practitioner how the illness affects the employee's work capacities (e.g., lifting restrictions). Normally, information on the employee's limitations is more important to the employer than the illness diagnosis. Only with information on limitations can suitable work be identified so that the return-to-work process can begin.

11 Only larger companies in Switzerland employ occupational health physicians, particularly companies in industry, pharmaceutics, biotechnologies, etc., that deal with dangerous substances or have dangerous working conditions.

References

Akabas, S. H., & Kurzman, P. A. (2005). *Work and workplace: A resource for innovative policy and practice*. New York, NY: Columbia University Press.

Antonovsky, A. (1997). *Salutogenese: Zur Entmystifizierung der Gesundheit*. Tübingen, Germany: dgvt Verlag.

Arendt, H. (1996). *Vita activa: Oder vom tätigen Leben*. München, Germany: Piper.

Bauer, G. (2005). Gesundheitsmanagement im Betrieb: Entwicklungsstand und Entwicklungspotenzial in der Schweiz. *Managed Care: Schweizer Zeitschrift für Managed Care, Public Health, Gesundheits- und Sozialökonomie, 4*, 7–9.

Baumgartner, E., Greiwe, S., & Schwarb, T. (2004). *Die berufliche Integration von behinderten Personen in der Schweiz: Studie zur Beschäftigungssituation und zu Eingliederungsbemühungen*. Bern, Switzerland: Bundesamt für Sozialversicherungen.

Becke, G. (2014). *Mindful change in times of permanent reorganization: Organisational, institutional and sustainability perspectives*. Heidelberg, Germany: Springer.

Becke, G., Behrens, M., Bleses, P., Meyerhuber, S., & Schmidt, S. (2013). *Organisationale Achtsamkeit: Veränderungen nachhaltig gestalten*. Stuttgart, Germany: Schäffer-Poeschel.

Bolliger, C., Fritschi, T., Salzgerber, R., Züricher, P., & Hümbelin, O. (2012). *Eingliederung vor Rente: Evaluation der Früherfassung, der Frühintervention und der*

Integrationsmassnahmen in der Invalidenversicherung. Bern, Switzerland: Bundesamt für Sozialversicherungen.
Bonoli, G., & Natali, D. (2012). The politics of the "new" welfare state: Analysing reforms in Western Europe. In G. Bonoli & D. Natali (Eds.), *The politics of the "new" welfare state* (pp. 3–20). Oxford, UK: Oxford University Press.
Escorpizo, R., Brage, S., Homa, D., & Stucki, G. (Eds.). (2015). *Handbook of vocational rehabilitation and disability evaluation. Application and implementation of the ICF.* Cham, Switzerland: Springer.
Esping-Andersen, G. (1990). *The three worlds of welfare capitalism.* Cambridge, UK: Polity Press.
Esping-Andersen, G. (1998). Die drei Welten des Wohlfahrtskapitalismus: Zur Politischen Ökonomie des Wohlfahrtsstaates. In S. Lessenich & I. Ostner (Eds.), *Welten des Wohlfahrtskapitalismus: Der Sozialstaat in vergleichender Perspektive* (pp. 19–58). Frankfurt am Main, Germany: Campus.
Eurostat. (2014). Situation von Menschen mit Behinderung in der EU (press release). Retrieved from http://ec.europa.eu/eurostat/documents/2995521/6181596/3-02122014-BP-DE.pdf/be2aeb0e-fdd8-4c5b-be5b-27b6af37c2e7
Füllemann, D., Inauen, A., Jenny, G., Moser, P., & Bauer, G. (2017). *Betriebliches Gesundheitsmanagement in Schweizer Betrieben: Monitoring-Ergebnisse 2016. Gesundheistförderung Schweiz Arbeitspapier 40.* Bern, Switzerland: Gesundheitsförderung Schweiz.
Geisen, T. (2011a). *Arbeit in der Moderne: Ein Dialogue imaginaire zwischen Karl Marx und Hannah Arendt.* Wiesbaden, Germany: VS Verlag.
Geisen, T. (2011b). Workplace disability management as an instrument for human resources and organizational development. In T. Geisen & H. Harder (Eds.), *Disability management and workplace integration: International research findings* (pp. 13–26). Farnham, UK: Gower.
Geisen, T. (2015). Workplace integration through disability management. In R. Escorpizo, S. Brage, D. Homa, & G. Stucki (Eds.), *Handbook of vocational rehabilitation and disability evaluation. Application and implementation of the ICF* (pp. 55–72). Cham, Switzerland: Springer.
Geisen, T., Baumgartner, E., Ochsenbein, G., Duchêne-Lacroix, C., Widmer, L., Amez-Droz, P., & Baur, R. (2016a). *Zusammenarbeit der IV-Stellen mit den Arbeitgebenden.* Bern, Switzerland: Bundesamt für Sozialversicherungen.
Geisen, T., & Harder, H. G. (Eds.). (2011). *Disability management and workplace integration: New perspectives.* Farnham, UK: Gower.
Geisen, T., Hassler, B., Ochsenbein, G., Buys, N., Randall, C., Harder, H., . . . Dan, T. (2016b). *Demographic change and private sector disability management in Australia, Canada, China and Switzerland: A comparative study.* Olten, Switzerland: Fachhochschule Nordwestschweiz.
Geisen, T., Kraus, K., Ochsenbein, G., Schmid, M., & Studer, T. (2013). *Qualifizierung für Veränderung: Regionalstudie zur Kompetenz und Ressourcenentwicklung in Unternehmen.* Basel, Switzerland: Fachhochschule Nordwestschweiz.
Geisen, T., Lichtenauer, A., Roulin, C., & Schielke, G. (2008). *Disability Management in Unternehmen in der Schweiz.* Bern, Switzerland: Bundesamt für Sozialversicherungen.
Giddens, A. (1998). *The third way: The renewal of social democracy.* Cambridge, UK: Polity.
Gursansky, D., Harvey, J., & Kennedy, R. (2003). *Case management: Policy, practice and professional business.* New York, NY: Columbia University Press.

Harder, H. G., & Scott, L. R. (2005). *Comprehensive disability management*. Toronto, Canada: Elsevier.
International Labour Organization. (2002). *Managing disability in the workplace: ILO Code of Practice*. Geneva, Switzerland: International Labour Organization.
Kraft, E., Buffat, M., Baeriswyl, A., Egli, F., & Setz, M. (2013). *Evaluation Pilotprojekt FER—"Gesundheitliche Früherkennung und berufliche Reintegration."* Bern, Switzerland: Bundesamt für Sozialversicherungen.
Kraus, K., & Geisen, T. (2001). Einleitung. In K. Kraus & T. Geisen (Eds.), *Sozialstaat in Europa: Geschichte—Entwicklung—Perspektiven* (pp. 9–20). Wiesbaden, Germany: Westdeutscher Verlag.
Lessenich, S. (2008). *Die Neuerfindung des Sozialen: Der Sozialstaat im flexiblen Kapitalismus*. Bielefeld, Germany: Transcript Verlag.
Loisel, P., & Anema, R. J. (Eds.). (2013). *Handbook of work disability: Prevention and management*. New York, NY: Springer Science+Business Media.
Moser, J. (2008). *Der schweizerische Wohlfahrtsstaat: Zum Ausbau des sozialen Sicherungssystems 1975–2005*. Frankfurt am Main, Germany: Campus.
Moxley, D. P. (1989). *The practice of case management*. London, UK: Sage.
Niehaus, M., Magin, J., Marfels, B., Vater, G. E., & Werkstetter, E. (2008). *Betriebliches Eingliederungsmanagement: Studie zur Umsetzung des Betrieblichen Eingliederungsmanagements nach § 84 Abs. 2 SGB IX*. Köln, Germany: Universität Köln.
Organisation for Economic Co-operation and Development. (2013). *Psychische Gesundheit und Beschäftigung: Schweiz*. Bern, Switzerland: OECD.
Organisation for Economic Co-operation and Development. (2014). *Mental health and work: Switzerland*. Mental health and work. Paris, France: OECD.
Scharf, T. (2001). Sozialpolitik in Grossbritannien: Vom Armengesetz zum «Dritten Weg». In K. Kraus & T. Geisen (Eds.), *Sozialstaat in Europa: Geschichte, Entwicklung, Perspektiven* (pp. 43–62). Wiesbaden, Germany: Westdeutscher Verlag.
Schmidt, H., & Kessler, S. (2006). "Ability management": Erfahrungen in der Schweiz. In P. Löcherbach & W. R. Wendt (Eds.), *Case Management in der Entwicklung: Stand und Perspektiven in der Praxis* (pp. 192–208). Heidelberg, Germany: Economica.
Schubert, M., Parthier, K., Kupka, P., Krüger, U., Holke, J., & Fuchs, P. (2013). *Menschen mit psychischen Störungen im SGB II*. Nürnberg, Germany: Institut für Arbeitsmarkt und Berufsforschung.
Ulich, E., & Wülser, M. (Eds.). (2009). *Gesundheitsmanagement in Unternehmen: Arbetspsychologische Perspektiven*. Wiesbaden, Germany: Gabler.
World Health Organization. (2007). *Ottawa-Charta zur Gesundheitsförderung*. Verabschiedet von der Weltgesundheitsorganisation [WHO] am 21. November 1986 in Ottawa. Retrieved November 16, 2007, from www.euro.who.int/__data/assets/pdf_file/0006/129534/Ottawa_Charter_G.pdf
World Health Organization. (2011). *World report on disability*. Geneva: WHO Press.
Wicki, M. (2001). Soziale Sicherung in der Schweiz: Ein europäischer Sonderfall? In K. Kraus & T. Geisen (Eds.), *Sozialstaat in Europa: Geschichte, Entwicklung, Perspektiven* (pp. 249–272). Wiesbaden: Westdeutscher Verlag.
Ziegelmayer, V. (2001). Sozialstaat in Deutschland: Ein Systemwechsel? In K. Kraus & T. Geisen (Eds.), *Sozialstaat in Europa: Geschichte, Entwicklung, Perspektiven* (pp. 63–88). Wiesbaden: Westdeutscher Verlag.

Chapter 13

Disability Prevention Policies in Belgium
Navigating Between Scientific and Socioeconomic Influences

Philippe Mairiaux

After describing the main characteristics of the Belgian social security system, this chapter summarizes the various pathways that a sick-listed worker may follow in the system. Although attaining disability status is one of the possible outcomes, up to the end of the 1990s political interest and reforms focused on unemployment and healthcare costs, and sickness and disability remained in the background (Institut National d'Assurance Maladie-Invalidité [INAMI], 2014). Things have changed since then, and the chapter outlines three significant reforms relevant to disability prevention over the last 15 years:

- the 2004 launch of the multidisciplinary rehabilitation program for workers with back pain;
- the 2006 law on professional reintegration; and
- the 2011–2016 government back-to-work and reintegration-pathways projects.

The driving forces behind these reforms are discussed as well as the nature of the debates that took place between the various stakeholders before the reforms were legally enacted.

Belgium and its Social Security System

Belgium had a population of 11.3 million in 2017. This population is linguistically diverse: About 57% of Belgians speak Dutch, and the rest speak mainly French. About 11.5% of Belgium's inhabitants are of foreign nationality.[1] As in other European countries, Belgium's population is aging. In 2017 the median age was 41, and 18.3% of people were 65 or over; this proportion is predicted to rise to 22% in 2030 and 24% in 2040 (Statistics Belgium, 2017a).

Belgium is among the countries that established universal social security systems at the end of World War II. Before this war, state insurance was compulsory only for pensions, occupational diseases, and family allowances. The agreement, signed in 1944 by both the employers' federations and the trade unions, mandated that all social insurance, including unemployment, sickness, and disability insurance, become compulsory for all salaried workers and that the new social insurance system be managed equally by employer and trade union representatives. This agreement was also the beginning of the Belgian social-consultation model, in which the government tries to attain consensus among social partners before introducing reforms that could impact social policies, such as employment, health insurance, or pensions (Federal Public Service Social Security, 2016).

The components of the state insurance system are shown in Figure 13.1, together with the level of monthly levies on people's earnings, which are the base of its financing; complementary funding is provided by a percentage of the VAT receipts. Although some differences exist between the respective regimes for salaried workers, the self-employed, and civil servants, deductions on earnings are compulsory in each regime and are the basic condition for accessing benefits. These benefits (e.g., sickness, disability, and unemployment benefits, workers' compensation) are not means-tested, and their level is either a percentage of the beneficiary's salary or, for family allowances, determined by the number and age of their children. State insurance coverage is also offered to unemployed people and those on social assistance, even though they do not contribute to financing the system.

Within this system, healthcare insurance is administered by the National Institute for Health and Disability Insurance[2] (INAMI), which is under bipartite supervision. The Institute's structure was established in 1964, when the functions of the sickness and disability division and the healthcare division

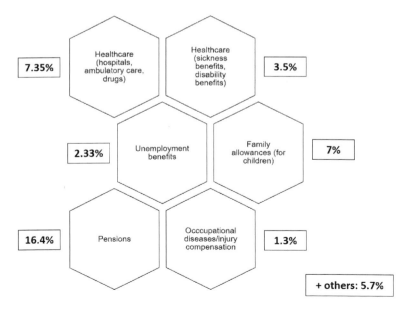

Figure 13.1 Main components of the Belgian social security system for salaried workers and monthly deductions from workers' gross salaries for each component.

were separated. Healthcare beneficiaries are partly reimbursed for ambulatory-care expenses and fully reimbursed for hospital expenses by sickness-fund federations supervised by INAMI (Federal Public Service Social Security, 2016).

Since 1964, the country's economic situation has obviously influenced the reforms described in this chapter. As with most industrialized countries, the 1974 oil crisis impacted Belgium's government debt. While the debt amounted to 65.9% of GDP in 1970, it increased rapidly after the oil crisis, to 109.4% in 1983 and 137.8% in 1993. The unemployment rate increased in parallel and reached 11% in 1983. During the 1990s, successive governments made drastic budget cuts, and some of these cuts aimed to contain healthcare costs; however, no specific cuts targeted sickness and disability insurance. Thanks to government cuts and some economic growth at the beginning of the 2000s, the unemployment rate fell to a record low of 6.1% in 2001 and government debt to 84% of GDP in 2007. Nonetheless, the 2008 financial crisis brought new budget deficits and job losses. In 2016, government debt stabilized around 106% of GDP and the unemployment rate at 7.8%, slightly lower than the EU27 average (8.5%). However, there were marked regional differences within Belgium between the Flanders region (< 5%) and the Walloon region (≥ 10%). The employment rate of people aged 20 to 64 (67.7%) remains lower than the EU27 average (71.1%) (Eurostat, 2017; Statistics Belgium, 2017b).

Pathway to be Followed by Sick-Listed Workers

Figure 13.2 illustrates the various steps that workers could go through (until December 2016) after receiving a sick note from a physician. Workers continue receiving full salary from the employer during either the first 14 days (for a blue-collar worker) or the first 30 days (for a white-collar worker). When the sick leave exceeds that period, workers are entitled to daily sickness benefits paid by state social insurance, at up to 60% of capped wages,[3] for up to 365 days. To get these benefits, the sick note has to be sent to the sickness fund for validation by a social insurance physician (SIP). This physician assesses the work incapacity of workers, either based on diagnostic criteria (if incapacity is due to a serious medical condition; for example, a neoplasm) or on a medical examination. To be accepted, the incapacity must represent at least 66% loss of earning capacity. During the first six months of sick leave, the assessment is made with reference to workers' usual jobs and, after six months, the assessment is made with reference to any job that workers might be able to get, based on their training and qualifications (Coordinating Law on health and disability insurance, 1994[4]).

At any time during sick leave, workers may decide to return to work (RTW) with either full or partial duties. Under the latter option, employees work part-time or with reduced productivity, providing that their employers agree, and they keep part of their sickness benefits. On returning to work, workers may also receive support from the company's occupational

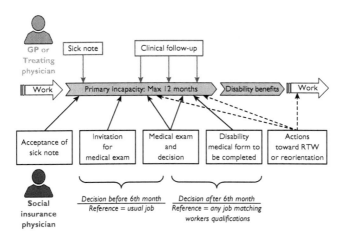

Figure 13.2 Pathway to be followed by sick-listed workers from the point of view of mandatory health insurance.

health physician (OP) in order to obtain a light-duty arrangement or receive workplace accommodations; however, the employer always has the final say in such matters.

If workers ultimately do not return to work, SIPs have the right to terminate their sick leave, taking into account the individuals' clinical status and jobs they might be able to do. Even though workers are still unfit for their usual jobs, they may be judged fit for other jobs. If that is the case, workers must then apply for temporary unemployment benefits through the National Employment Office[5] (ONEM). Workers on sick leave may also appeal an SIP's decision to a Labor Court free of charge; however, several months may elapse before judgments are rendered.

If the person's work incapacity is still recognized after 12 months, disability status will be awarded by the Medical Council for Disability,[6] a college of medical experts located within INAMI. With this status, benefits are calculated as a percentage of capped wages and vary from 40% to 65%, depending on the family situation (Federal Public Service Social Security, 2016). In 2014, disability benefits averaged €44.25 [US$53.28] a day for six days a week, roughly €1,150 [US$1,385] a month. For workers previously in low-paid jobs, disability benefits are thus lower than this average and often close to, or even below, the poverty level (€1,115 [US$1,343] a month for a person living alone). In 2015 the average time on disability benefits was 5.3 years for women and 6.15 years for men. Leaving disability status can result from the following events: death, reaching pension age, being denied the status by an SIP, or going back to work. In 2015 this last reason represented 4.25% of the total number of people on disability, a slight increase from 2006 (3.54%) (INAMI, 2017). In short, although Belgians generally consider disability status to be permanent and protective, it is in fact often associated with poverty and social isolation.

Establishment by Healthcare Insurance of a Multidisciplinary Rehabilitation Program for Low Back Pain Patients

In 2004, three legislative reforms were introduced through Royal Decree in a short period:

- On June 22, INAMI announced reimbursement criteria for a multidisciplinary back-rehabilitation program.
- On July 4, the Labor Ministry introduced a pre-return-to-work visit in occupational health legislation.
- On July 16, the Occupational Diseases Fund[7] (FEDRIS) launched a pilot project for back pain prevention among hospital nursing staff.

INAMI's multidisciplinary back-rehabilitation program offered any patient (worker or not) with serious back pain (more than six weeks) the opportunity to participate in two-hour group sessions involving physical reconditioning, back education, pain management, and ergonomic principles. The program had to be delivered by a multidisciplinary team (rehabilitation physicians, physiotherapists, clinical psychologists, and when possible ergonomists) and was aimed at preventing acute low back pain from becoming chronic. The Ministry of Health gave this program special attention and allowed each beneficiary to be reimbursed once in a lifetime. The Ministry's underlying message was to make patients aware that the program was a unique opportunity for learning how to actively manage back pain.

The FEDRIS back-pain prevention program was intended for nurses who had been off work due to nonspecific low back pain for at least four weeks but less than three months. This program aimed to promote early RTW by allowing workers to participate, free of charge, in the INAMI back-rehabilitation program and by also offering a financial incentive to their employers (€250 [US$297] in 2004, €420 [US$500] today) if they accepted an ergonomic analysis of the workers' tasks. At the start, both the INAMI and FEDRIS programs were designed to take into account the principles of the Sherbrooke Model, developed in Quebec by Loisel et al. (1997). In 2017, both programs were still offered; however, access to the FEDRIS program had been expanded in May 2007 to all workers, provided they are exposed to hazards of manually handling loads and/or whole-body vibration, as certified by their OP (Agence fédérale des risques professionnels [FEDRIS], 2017).

The pre-return-to-work-visit requirement allowed workers to meet with their OPs during sick leave. Such visits allowed OPs to identify barriers to RTW and to make contact with the workers' supervisors to discuss temporary work-task or workplace accommodations.

Although these three regulatory changes occurred almost simultaneously, they did not result from a remarkable coordination among three public agencies under the jurisdiction of different ministers. Nonetheless, this simultaneity suggests that these agencies were similarly influenced by new concepts and knowledge and perhaps shared a common awareness of the need to help people get back to work. These likely influences can be analyzed at a macro level, the political, and a meso level, each institution's management.

At the political level, a major change occurred as a result of the 1999 general election: A completely new coalition, involving the Socialist, Liberal, and Ecologist Parties, came into power with a strong reform agenda. Under the influence of Frank Vandenbroucke, the new Minister of Social Affairs (which included health), the concept of the active welfare state rapidly became a central element of the coalition's reform agenda. Mr. Vandenbroucke was a socialist and experienced politician, an economist who had just obtained a doctorate at Oxford University (Vandenbroucke, 2001). During his stay in England, he was deeply influenced by the works of Anthony Giddens, the ideological father of the "Third Way" (Giddens, 1998) of modernizing the welfare state. In this vision, there must be a balance between social rights and social duties for beneficiaries of the social security system. In addition, the safety net provided by the welfare state must be supplemented by activation policies; in other words, by policies that stimulate reintegration into work and avoid compensation benefits becoming unemployment traps. Rehabilitation programs that stimulate self-management by patients or workers obviously fit well within activation policies.

Within Belgium's health insurance, Mr. Vandenbroucke formed a €3.4 million [US$4.04 million] budget to support reform projects and asked the newly established advisory committee concerning health care for chronic diseases[8] to make recommendations for improving chronic-disease patients' access to appropriate care. In October 2000, a working group chaired by Dr. Boly, a senior SIP official who at the time was secretary of the Scientific Association of Insurance Medicine[9] (ASMA), submitted 11 recommendations for better management of chronic pain. Among these was the establishment of a limited number of multidisciplinary pain centers and, more notably, social integration and work retention strategies for chronic-pain patients. Thanks to clever lobbying by the Belgian Pain Society, the management of chronic low back pain soon became a priority in this new approach, which aimed to prevent subacute back pain from becoming chronic. For many stakeholders, however, the creation of specialized multidisciplinary pain centers, a third line of care, was a costly and inappropriate solution, as the intervention was very late!

The idea of earlier intervention, at a second line of care, began gaining ground in the spring of 2001, thanks not only to interpersonal relationships but to the support of a few leading rehabilitation physicians. On the scientific side, Dr. Boly, a respected adviser to Minister Vandenbroucke, had regular exchanges with Prof. P. Mairiaux, working in the Scientific Association of Occupational Health[10] (SSST). Dr. Vandenbroucke was thus aware that the Sherbrooke Model (Loisel et al., 1997) had been successfully applied to workers with back pain in a large steel company (Oblin & Mairiaux, 1997). On the clinical side, some rehabilitation specialists who had developed new active treatments for back pain in their respective centers successfully put the question of financing this type of earlier intervention on a meeting agenda of the Medical Technical Committee[11] (CTM), a high-level advisory body within INAMI in charge of updating the list of reimbursable healthcare benefits. The Committee members agreed to consider including the multidisciplinary back-pain program on the list. Mr. Vandenbroucke, with his research background, was quite happy to hear that the Sherbrooke-Model-like rehabilitation program was supported by strong scientific evidence. Hence, the project went ahead and, after more than two years of discussion, a final agreement was reached between INAMI, the sickness funds, the rehabilitation services, and the Minister about the rehabilitation program's budget and other components.

The context for the launch of the pilot FEDRIS program was somewhat different: It resulted from a consensus-building process between employers and trade unions within the bipartite management committee of FEDRIS. In March 2000, at the trade unions' suggestion, Minister Vandenbroucke asked the FEDRIS to examine the possibility of recognizing workers' low back pain as an occupational disease. In response, the FEDRIS set up two working groups, and a three-year discussion process (2000–2003) ensued about whether the government should compensate workers with back pain, and if so, how it should limit the expected costs. Should the money go instead to secondary prevention interventions? The two working groups eventually advocated for a combined approach: compensation only for lumbar-root syndrome, using restrictive exposure criteria, and considering more common back pain as a work-related occupational disease. For the former new compensation category, the FEDRIS would only subsidize prevention interventions and not grant disability benefits. During a special meeting of the FEDRIS management committee in January 2002, this combined approach was judged as socially responsible and respectful of workers' interests by both employers and trade unions. The main features of the program were eventually endorsed by the Council of Ministers in December 2003 and then published by Royal Decree in July 2004.

This story of the development of a significant innovation within the health insurance and occupational disease compensation systems reveals several influential factors:

- a government embracing the active welfare state;
- trade unions and employers reaching consensus about a socially balanced reform;

- a health minister with a marked interest in evidence-based policy;
- a trusting relationship between an influential SIP and an occupational health professor; and
- the support of a few dynamic clinicians for using available scientific evidence.

However, in sharp contrast to the importance given at the INAMI and FEDRIS programs' inception to the weight of science, it must be emphasized that no truly scientific study involving a control group has been initiated by INAMI or FEDRIS to assess the innovation's effectiveness for workers with back pain nor its cost-effectiveness. Although every year about 800 workers with back pain benefit from the FEDRIS program and an estimated 10,000 adults are reimbursed for participating in the INAMI program, besides the overall satisfaction of patients and the rehabilitation services, its actual impact is unknown.

A New Law on Work Reintegration (2006)

The active-welfare-state philosophy adopted by the Belgian government and the reform movement it initiated were key to modernizing Belgium's disability prevention policy. External factors were also influential: In 1996, an OECD report concluded that Belgian policies for allocating unemployment and disability benefits were purely passive and should be revised. This report was well known among senior managers in INAMI and the sickness funds. Hence, some sickness funds launched pilot projects between 2002 and 2006 to encourage participation of disability benefits recipients in the vocational rehabilitation programs funded by INAMI. At the time the participation rate was extremely low (1 participant/1000 recipients year). These pilot projects were quite useful in identifying access barriers to these rehabilitation programs and in recommending changes to the laws governing them.

In 2006, a new law introduced principles for organizing and supporting reintegration in several regimes of the social security system (State Journal, 2006). In health insurance, the new law reinforced existing options for supporting vocational rehabilitation programs that train workers for different jobs when they cannot return to their previous ones for health reasons. Later, in 2009, financial incentives were introduced to encourage workers to enter such programs and, at the end of the training, beneficiaries could keep receiving sickness benefits for six months in order to support their job search. The law expanded the role of SIPs: "Social-insurance physicians are also mandated to care for the social and work reintegration of the beneficiary on sick leave"[12] (State Journal, 2009, Article 89). Until 2006, the main role of SIPs was to verify sick notes issued by treating physicians, without any consideration of job-retention consequences. As a result of these legal reforms, the number of disability benefit recipients participating in vocational-rehabilitation programs increased from 435 in 2010 to 1,593 in 2013.

Successive Government Return-To-Work and Reintegration-Pathways Projects

After two governments (1999–2003 and 2003–2008) had actively pursued reforms of the social security system in order to adapt it to societal evolutions, reform slowed between 2008 and 2011, a period of great political instability. Meanwhile, however, accumulating data pointed to the need for new measures.

As shown in Figure 13.3, the average duration of sick leave increased between 2000 and 2013 (INAMI, 2016). A similar trend was observed for disability status. The number of disability-benefit recipients increased markedly from 1996 to 2015 among women, and moderately among men (see Figure 13.4). For both genders, the increase has accelerated in recent years. The INAMI annual reports show that, although the number of disability-benefit recipients totaled 175,766 in 1998, it increased to 269,499 in 2011 and to 347,808 in 2015. In 2015, the total corresponded to a disability rate (number of recipients divided by number of insured people) of 7.2% among men and 9.7% among women. In terms of costs, the increase was equally impressive: from €1.6 billion [US$1.9 billion] in 1998 to €6.4 billion [US$7.6 billion] in 2015, for cumulative costs of sickness and disability benefits. Remarkably, for the first time in Belgium's socioeconomic history, sickness and disability benefit expenses were higher in 2015 than unemployment benefit expenses (€6.2 billion [US$7.4 billion]) (ONEM, 2016).

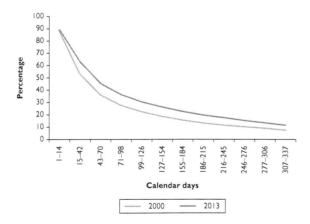

Figure 13.3 Change in the percentage of people remaining on sick-leave benefits during their first year of work incapacity. Y axis shows percentages of insured people. X axis shows days after receipt of sick note by the sickness fund.

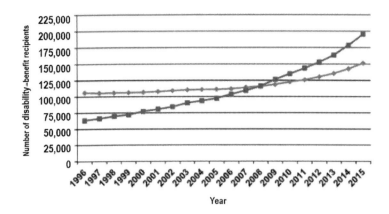

Figure 13.4 Change in the number of disability benefits recipients among salaried workers, 1996 to 2015. The line with diamonds represents men. The line with squares represents women.

From a policy point of view, this proves that it is as important to take action in the field of disability as it is in the field of employment.

Several factors could explain these trends in disability figures, and demographic changes are the most obvious (INAMI, 2017). As shown in Table 13.1, the proportion of working-age people (aged 20–64) in Belgium's population increased by 9.9% between 1996 and 2015. This proportional increase resulted mostly from a marked increase in the older age groups (over 40 years of age); in other words, among the age classes more prone to develop health problems. Although population aging is a major explanatory factor, it is not the only one. The number of people covered by sickness and disability insurance increased during the same period by 27.4%, a figure higher than the population increase. The increase in insurance coverage reflected an increase in the employment rate, greater among women (41.5%) than among men (16.1%). The steep increase among women was due to the progressive alignment of the legal pension ages for women and men between 1997 and 2009 (increasing from 60 to 65 years for women) and also to a proportional increase in the number of women participating in the labor market. However, if we control for women's increased pension age by considering only insured people under 60, the extraordinary increase in female disability benefit recipients (160.4%) can be only partly ascribed to the increased number of women covered by state insurance (34.8%) (INAMI, 2017).

So what could be the other explanatory factors? A growing number of studies point to the changing world of work and, more precisely, to the imbalance between the intensification of work demands (e.g., time pressure, emotional pressure, exposure to asocial behaviors) and resources that people

Table 13.1 Trends in the Belgian population 20 to 64 years old, 1996 to 2015

Age (years)	Men (% change)	Women (% change)	Total (% change)
20–24	+ 4.84	+ 5.44	+ 5.13
25–29	− 4.75	− 1.40	− 3.11
30–34	− 10.53	− 8.05	− 9.31
35–39	− 7.96	− 7.14	− 7.56
40–44	+ 4.65	+ 4.71	+ 4.68
45–49	+ 13.28	+ 12.87	+ 13.08
50–54	+ 50.47	+ 49.11	+ 49.79
55–59	+ 40.53	+ 37.23	+ 38.85
60–64	+ 24.14	+ 18.20	+ 21.05
Total 20–64	+ 9.72%	+ 10.02%	+ 9.87%

Note. INAMI (2017), p. 7.

have in facing these demands (e.g., control over own work, social support, participation in decision making). This imbalance, conceptualized in the Job Demands Resources model (Bakker & Demerouti, 2007), is known to generate chronic stress. This Job Demands Resources hypothesis is supported by the results of Belgium's national health survey (Van der Heyden & Charafeddine, 2015) and the 2015 European survey of working conditions (Lamberts et al., 2016), which both reported an increase in self-declared depression and anxiety, respectively, in the general population and the working population. The European survey also showed that, although job quality improved overall in Belgium, about 26% of workers are still in jobs whose quality was rated as either "heavy, repetitive, and inflexible" or of "poor value" (Lamberts et al., 2016, p. 124, Figure 4.1). These results seem to align with the INAMI data showing that two main disease groups contribute to granting of disability status: psychiatric disorders and musculoskeletal disorders. These two groups characterized 58.5% of disability benefit recipients in 2006, and by 2015 their proportion had increased to 65.6% (INAMI, 2017).

In December 2011, a more stable coalition government, headed by a socialist prime minister, came to power in Belgium. Given the growing number of people on sickness or disability benefits, it is understandable that the new government decided to appoint an adjunct minister in charge of return to work. The government created a task force whose aim was to design effective and practical measures to activate the growing number of people on sickness or disability benefits. The task force studied several reform options and was fortunately able to rely on a new driving force within the INAMI administration: In 2010, the director general of the sickness and disability division retired and was replaced by a much younger, dynamic person, Mr. Perl. As a result of the synergy between the adjunct minister and the INAMI administration, several cooperation agreements were signed in 2012 and 2013 between INAMI, the sickness funds, and the regional employment agencies to promote vocational training for workers on long-term sick leave or disability benefits. In 2013, the knowledge center for work incapacity[13] was also created within INAMI to monitor and analyze sickness and disability data and to support research on selected topics, such as work reintegration of workers with chronic pain and cancer survivors (Plasman et al., 2015).

Because the new government was only in power for a short time (December 2011–May 2014), it did not have time to introduce significant legislative reform with regard to disability prevention, except for two changes:

- By Royal Decree on April 12, 2013, the procedure for approving a partial RTW regime was simplified and made easier for workers.
- According to a law passed on December 26, 2013, employers could no longer use the reason of long-term sick leave to dismiss permanent employees.

While in power, the government had submitted other reform proposals for approval by the National Labor Council[14] (CNT-NAR), an advisory body composed of experts from the employer federations and trade unions. In February 2015, discussions within the Council resulted in the publication of an overview document (CNT-NAR, 2015), which delineated key elements of work reintegration that would need regulatory changes and suggested different options for addressing those elements. Meanwhile, however, general elections had taken place, and a new right-wing government had come into power in October 2014. The right-wing government's platform included two major reforms to ensure long-term sustainability of the social security system: raising the legal pension age to 66 years in 2025 and 67 years in 2030, and requiring a work-reintegration plan within the first three months of sick leave (Program Law, 2014). In addition, employers would pay the salaries of employees on sick leave for two additional months, to increase employers' accountability for retaining and reintegrating employees. The latter reform was audacious for a right-wing government and did not last long due to the furor of the employer federations, who argued that the reform would compromise the competitiveness of Belgian companies. After a few weeks of heavy lobbying, the government announced that this measure would be reexamined later!

As for the reintegration plan, government experts took some inspiration from reforms by the Norwegian government to curtail the expansion of disability benefit recipients. However, for the Belgian officials, important questions had to be answered:

- Who would be involved in the plan—only the sickness funds and their SIPs, or the labor ministry and the occupational health services as well?
- Which reintegration pathways would be proposed and for which categories of ill workers?
- How would the plan be financed?

The most sensitive question was of a more ideological nature: Should work reintegration involve "a stick behind the door"? In other words, should plans include penalties for workers unwilling to collaborate in their reintegration? There was heated debate between employers and some political parties, who were convinced that in any social benefits system there are always people who are prone to abuse and fraud. There was also opposition from trade unions and other parties, who were convinced that reintegration cannot be successful without voluntary cooperation of benefit recipients.

Throughout 2015, intense negotiations took place at several levels: within the CNT-NAR between social partners (employers and trade unions); within INAMI between the administration and the sickness funds; within the government between the ministers of social affairs and labor; and between the four political parties comprising the coalition government. In December 2015, the social partners agreed on allowing voluntary participation in reintegration pathways, at least during the project's initial phase. The government endorsed this agreement in principle, but that was not the end of the story.

Several months were needed to finalize the legal texts in 2016. Eventually, on November 24, two Royal Decrees were simultaneously published (State Journal, 2016): One defined the reintegration pathway within health and disability insurance, while the other organized a pathway inside the enterprise under the supervision of the OP. The reintegration pathways have been applied since January 1, 2017.

As can be seen when comparing the new scheme (Figure 13.5) to the previous one (Figure 13.2), the major change consisted of an early intervention in the sick-leave process. Within two months after the sickness fund receives the sick note, the SIP must carry out a quick scan of the case and classify the sick-listed person according to one of four categories (see Table 13.2). Individuals in Category 4 are referred to the OP at the company that employs them. This referral represents a major change of paradigm in the Belgian healthcare system.

In 1965, when every company, whatever its size, was legally required to engage an occupational health service, the requirement was designed to prevent, in most cases, the exchange of employee information between the treating physician or the SIP, and the OP, who is directly or indirectly paid by the employer and for that reason not considered independent. Although this view prevailed for half a century, fortunately attitudes are now changing. For instance, in 2010, the three scientific associations of, respectively, family physicians, SIPs, and OPs established a joint working group to discuss sick-leave management and in 2013 set up regional contact groups, the TRIOs. There appears to be growing consensus among physicians that patients/workers on sick leave for more than a few weeks benefit from good collaboration among and support from all three

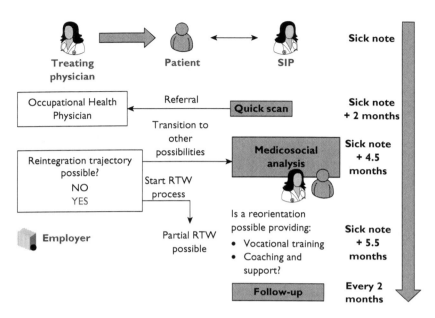

Figure 13.5 The new reintegration pathways introduced in health and disability insurance by Royal Decree on November 24, 2016

Table 13.2 Prognostic categories used by social insurance physicians to classify sick-listed workers during the QuickScan procedure

Category	Prognostic profile	Action to be taken
1	Good prognosis for RTW < 6th month	None
2	Very serious, noncurable medical condition. No reintegration possible	None
3	Serious but curable medical condition	Follow up every 2 months
4	Expected RTW difficulties could be met through temporary light work or assignment to other tasks	Refer to the occupational health physician and request reintegration pathway

professionals. Of course, in day-to-day practice, many of those physicians still harbor misconceptions about the role and personal ethics of some of their counterparts, and electronic tools for facilitating communication among physicians are not yet available. The paradigm change will thus take time to fully implement.

Conclusion

If the legislative introduction of reintegration pathways can be considered a great step forward in many ways, it also raises serious questions. Some are technical or logistical:

- Will it be possible for the sickness funds to implement the quick-scan procedure for so many sick-listed workers with a limited, and decreasing, number of SIPs?
- Will the predictive criteria of no spontaneous RTW to be used in the quick scan, currently under study by a team of university researchers (Goorts et al., 2017), be applicable to the whole population of sick-listed workers?

Other, more political, questions are currently the subject of heated debate; for instance, does it make sense to activate people toward work when there are not enough jobs for them or employers willing to reintegrate people with health limitations? Indeed, work reintegration involves not only medical issues, but it also interacts with the conditions of the labor market. In some municipalities of Belgium, especially in the Walloon region, the unemployment rate may exceed 20% of the working-age population (Institut wallon de l'évaluation, de la prospective et de la statistique [IWEPS], 2017). It is thus easier for employers not to reintegrate employees with health limitations or chronic diseases. Some analysts fear that this new reintegration policy is mostly aimed at cutting costs in the budget of sickness and disability insurance, and that it could eventually result in the exclusion of growing numbers of people from these sources of social security benefits and push them onto the safety net of last resort, social assistance.

Another heated debate at the government level and between social partners concerns the accountability of the various stakeholders. In its public communications, the government says it wants to balance responsibilities. On March 31, 2017, the Council of Ministers announced measures promoting the accountability of each category of stakeholders. The employers in companies employing at least 50 people will have to pay a penalty of €800 [US$951] for each reintegration plan they refuse to initiate without valid reasons. The insured workers will risk a 5% or 10% cut in their sickness benefits for one month if they do not properly collaborate with or if they reject the reintegration plan. This cut will not be permanent. With regard to physicians issuing sick notes, the government asked an advisory council of medical and administrative experts to develop guidelines for recommending sick-leave durations for the most frequent diseases, to be used by physicians when issuing sick notes.

Evaluation of the reforms is also under discussion. This evaluation needs to consider how to measure the specific impact of the reintegration-pathway reform on sickness and disability benefits payouts. It appears that many experts think that the various reforms since 2005 to progressively postpone and restrict workers' access to early-retirement schemes on one hand and, on the other, to more strictly control the actual availability of unemployed people to the labor market, have and are still having an unintended effect: increasing the number of disability benefit recipients. For example, before 2010–2011 if a masonry worker in his mid-50s with serious low back pain lost his job due to health limitations, it was relatively easy for him to get unemployment benefits or take early retirement. Now the employment office restricts its benefits to workers who still have work capacity, and most early-retirement schemes are only open to those over 60 or even 62. Therefore, the only exit is long-term disability. A detailed analysis of the interactions between these regimes, before and after the implementation of the reforms announced on March 31, 2017, is needed.

In conclusion, Belgium has made significant strides in preventing and managing disability over the last five years. It remains to be seen, however, what impact the most recent reform, reintegration pathways, will have on work-reintegration rates. Will the social value of this new initiative be offset (or not) by government cost-cutting objectives, ideological pressure favoring punitive policies, and the lack of effective incentives for employers to participate in reintegration?

Notes

1 Mainly from other European countries, Morocco, and Turkey.
2 Institut national d'assurance maladie-invalidité.
3 The ceiling was €138.62 [US$166.62] in June 2017.
4 Loi coordonnée relative à l'assurance obligatoire soins de santé et indemnités.
5 Office national de l'emploi.
6 Conseil médical de l'invalidité.
7 Fonds des maladies professionnelles–Fonds voor de beroepsziekten.
8 Comité consultatif en matière de dispensation de soins pour des maladies chroniques.
9 Association scientifique de médecine d'assurance.
10 Société scientifique de santé au travail.
11 Conseil technique médical.
12 Author's translation.
13 Centre d'expertise en matière d'incapacité de travail.
14 Conseil national du travail.

References

Agence fédérale des risques professionnels. (2017). *Programme de rééducation lombaire*. Retrieved from http://fedris.be/fr/victime/maladies-professionnelles-secteur-prive/programme-de-reeducation-lombaire

Bakker, A., & Demerouti, E. (2007). The Job Demands-Resources model: State of the art. *Journal of Managerial Psychology, 22*, 309–328.

Conseil National du Travail [National Labor Council]. (2015, February 24). *Plate-forme de concertation entre acteurs impliqués dans le processus de retour au travail volontaire de personnes présentant un problème de santé: Avant-projet de loi portant dispositions diverses en matière d'assurance indemnités et emploi* (Advice 1.923). Retrieved from www.cnt-nar.be/avis-2015.htm

Coordinating Law on Health and Disability Insurance [Loi coordonnée relative à l'assurance obligatoire soins de santé et indemnités] (Belgium), Art. 100 §1 (July 14, 1994).

Eurostat. (2017). *Employment and unemployment (Labour force survey)*. Retrieved from http://ec.europa.eu/eurostat/web/lfs/data/main-tables

Federal Public Service Social Security. (2016, January). *Social security: Everything you have always wanted to know*. Retrieved from https://socialsecurity.belgium.be/sites/default/files/alwa-en.pdf

Giddens, A. (1998). *The third way: The renewal of social democracy*. Cambridge, UK: Polity Press.

Goorts, K., Duchesnes, C., Vandenbroeck, S., Rusu, D., Du Bois, M., & Mairiaux, P. (2017). Is langdurig ziekteverzuim voorspeelbaar en meetbaar? *Tijdschrift voor Bedrijfs- en Verzekeringsgeneeskunde, 25*, 59–62.

Institut National d'Assurance Maladie-Invalidité. (2014). *L'assurance soins de santé et indemnités belge: Repères du passé, balises pour le futur*. Brussels, Belgium: Institut national d'assurance maladie invalidité.

Institut National d'Assurance Maladie-Invalidité. (2016). *Absentéisme en incapacité primaire: Analyse des facteurs explicatifs – période 2009–2014*. Brussels, Belgium: Institut national d'assurance maladie invalidité;.

Institut National d'Assurance Maladie-Invalidité. (2017). *Facteurs explicatifs de l'augmentation du nombre d'invalides – période 2006–2015*. Brussels, Belgium: Institut national d'assurance maladie invalidité.

Institut wallon de l'évaluation, de la prospective et de la statistique. (2017). *Indicateurs statistiques: Marché du travail*. Retrieved from www.iweps.be/indicateur-statistique/taux-dactivite-taux-demploi-taux-de-chomage-commune-calibres-lenquete-forces-de-travail/

Lamberts, M., Szeker, L., Vandekerckhove, S., Van Gyes, G., Van Hootegem, G., & Vereycken, Y. (2016, November). *La qualite de l'emploi en Belgique en 2015: Analyse sur la base de l'Enquête européenne sur les conditions de travail EWCS 2015 (Eurofound)*. Retrieved from www.emploi.belgique.be/moduleDefault.aspx?id=44596

Loisel, P., Durand, P., Esdaile, J. M., Suissa, S., Gosselin, L., Simard, R., Turcotte, J., & Lemaire, J. (1997). A population-based, randomized clinical trial on back pain management. *Spine, 22*, 2911–2918.

Oblin, P., & Mairiaux, P. (1997). Evaluation d'un programme intensif de revalidation pour travailleurs lombalgiques. *Archives des Maladies Professionnelles, 58*, 432–439.

Office National de l'Emploi [National Employment Office]. (2016, March). *Rapport annuel 2015 de l'Office National de l'Emploi: Vol. 2. Indicateurs du marché du travail et évolution des allocations*. Retrieved from www.onem.be/fr/nouveau/lonem-publie-son-rapport-annuel-2015

Plasman, R., Diallo, H., Pacolet, J., De Coninck, A., De Wispelaere, F., Vos, F., . . . & Perl, F. (2015). *Rapport annuel d'analyse sur l'incapacité de travail 2014*. Retrieved from www.inami.fgov.be/fr/publications/Pages/etude_incapacite_travail_collaboration_externes.aspx#.WbvuH4VOKUk

Program Law [Loi-programme] (Belgium) (December 19, 2014). Retrieved from www.etaamb.be/fr/loiprogramme-du-19-decembre-2014_n2014021137.html

State Journal. (2006, September 1). Loi portant des dispositions diverses en matière de maladies professionnelles et d'accidents du travail et en matière de réinsertion professionnelle (Belgium), Art. 71, Chapter 3.

State Journal. (2009, July 1). Loi portant des dispositions diverses en matière de maladies professionnelles et d'accidents du travail et en matière de réinsertion professionnelle (revised) (Belgium), Arts. 86–88, 89.

State Journal. (2016, November 24). *AR du 28-10-16 introduisant une section 6/1 (art. 73/1 à 73/11) dans l'AR du 28-05-03 : "Trajet de réintégration d'un travailleur qui ne peut plus exercer le travail convenu temporairement ou définitivement"* (Belgium).

Statistics Belgium. (2017a). *Statistiques et chiffres: Population.* Retrieved from https://statbel.fgov.be/fr/themes/population

Statistics Belgium. (2017b). Statistics and figures: Labour market. Retrieved from https://statbel.fgov.be/en/themes/work-training/labour-market

Van der Heyden, J., & Charafeddine, R. (2015). *Health and well-being, National Health Survey 2013* (Vol. 1, No. 1115). Brussels, Belgium: Scientific Institute of Public Health.

Vandenbroucke, F. (2001). *Social justice and individual ethics in an open society: Equality, responsibility and incentives.* Berlin, Germany: Springer-Verlag.

Chapter 14

Work Disability Prevention in the Netherlands
A Key Role for Employers

Angelique de Rijk

In 2016, the Dutch sickness-absence rate (for the first two years of absence) was just below 4%, and a modest 6% of working-aged people received disability benefits (Statistics Netherlands, 2017a; Statistics Netherlands, 2017b). These figures remained fairly stable during the previous decade. However, in 1979 the sickness-absence rate peaked at 10%, and in 1990 the disability-pension rate peaked at 14% (Aarts, de Jong, & van der Veen, 2002). The miraculous drops since then can only be understood in the context of (a) Dutch labor-market characteristics, (b) increased employer involvement in work disability policy development, and (c) failures of the generous disability benefit scheme introduced in 1967. Therefore, this chapter starts with a description of the current Dutch labor-market characteristics. Next, the chapter explains how Dutch employers have historically been involved to a much larger extent than employers in other countries in the development and implementation of sick-leave policy. The positive intentions of the game-changing disability benefit scheme of 1967 are explained. Then the chapter addresses the labor-market and policy developments in the 1980s and 1990s that paved the way for a new work disability scheme, covering sickness absence and long-term disability and introduced in 2004. The new system's most striking features are that Dutch employers are required to formulate action plans within 8 weeks of workers reporting sick and must pay at least 70% of the salary during the first two years of sickness absence. The reform's successes and challenges for the Netherlands are addressed. The chapter ends by discussing the transferability of the Dutch work disability system to other countries and its sustainability in the light of the four centenary-conversation questions asked by the International Labour Organization (2016).

Current Situation

The Netherlands is a constitutional monarchy with 17 million citizens as of 2016, a fairly high labor-participation rate and productive workforce, and an unusually high proportion of part-time workers, particularly among women.

Of the 17 million citizens, in 2016 almost 13 million were of working age (15–75), and 8.5 million participated in paid work for 12 hours per week or more. Thus, the labor-force participation rate as defined by Statistics Netherlands was 66% (Statistics Netherlands, 2017b). In terms of absolute labor participation (one hour per week or more), 75% of the working-age population aged 15 to 65 participated in paid work (Trading Economics, 2017a). This participation rate has been consistent for the past 20 years (Statistics Netherlands, 2017b; Trading Economics, 2017a).

Only 9 million people were effectively available for the labor market. Those not available were spouses whose partners had paid employment, those over 65 who were officially retired and, to a lesser extent, those receiving full disability benefits. In 2016 the unemployment rate was 6%, irrespective of hours previously worked per week (Trading Economics, 2017b).

The Netherlands is a champion of part-time work, a legal right that was initially introduced in the 1980s as a work-life balance solution. Almost half of employees work less than 36 hours per week, including three-quarters of employed women (recognizing their unpaid work at home). The average dual-earner family consists of a full-time working man and a woman working 16 to 24 hours per week (with the woman caring for children under 12 for two or three days per week) (Portegijs & van den Brakel, 2016). Only 4% of part-time-employed women would prefer to work full-time, an unusually low figure compared with other OECD (Organisation for Economic Co-operation and Development) countries (OECD, in Portegijs & Keuzekamp, 2008). Mothers would like to work a few more hours, particularly when children grow older, and women's careers are limited by part-time work (Portegijs & Keuzekamp, 2008; Portegijs & van den Brakel, 2016).

Working-age people in the Netherlands are quite productive, with about 6% receiving disability benefits and a two-year sickness-absence rate of approximately 4% (Statistics Netherlands, 2017a; Statistics Netherlands, 2017b).

Short History of Dutch Employer Involvement in Sickness Leave

Dutch employers have become extremely responsible for sickness-absence guidance and payment, as established in long-standing institutional arrangements. We can distinguish three areas of institutional arrangements:

- state and professional involvement with safe and healthy workplaces and the health of workers;
- income protection for disabled workers, strongly supported by tripartite institutions; and
- healthcare, which is strictly isolated from occupational healthcare and social insurance.

First, working conditions have been protected by laws since the 19th century; a labor inspectorate was already in place by 1899. The Netherlands Society of Occupational Medicine,[1] or NVAB, was founded in 1953 (Netherlands Society of Occupational Medicine, 2017). In 1959, a law recognized the profession of occupational physician and required that organizations with more than 750 workers have their own organized occupational health program (Wolvetang, Buijs, & van Oosterom, 1997).

Second, the Netherlands can be characterized as a corporatist welfare state (Eikemo & Bambra, 2008). Its foundation is a Bismarckian welfare state, based on social insurance providing earnings-related benefits for employees and financed by a mix of employer and employee contributions, or premiums. In contrast, Beveridgean social policy is characterized by universal (for all citizens without favoring employees) provision of benefits and financed by taxes (Bonoli, 1997). Some have characterized the Netherlands as a social-democratic welfare state (Anema, Prinz, & Prins, 2013; Esping-Andersen, 1990) on the basis of its level of expenditure on welfare. However, for the purpose of this chapter, we will focus on the historically grounded divisions of responsibilities, rather than the levels of investment within the system, in line with Bambra (2007). In the 20th century, a national network of employee insurance offices was developed in the Netherlands, financed by premiums paid by employers and employees and increasingly regulated by the state. These diverse offices never offered health insurance and focused only on income provision in case of work disability. This network evolved into one national Dutch Institute for Employee Benefit Scheme,[2] which was established in 2002 (Aarts, de Jong, & van der Veen, 2002).

A typical characteristic of the Dutch corporistic welfare state is its consultative economy (Labour Foundation, 2010). The consultative economy means that decision making and policy making are based on discussion, negotiation, and bargaining, especially where work and income are concerned (Labour Foundation, 2010). This culture has been officially institutionalized since the Labour Foundation[3] was established in 1945, just after World War II. This private national consultative body comprises Dutch employers' federations and trade-union confederations and is a bipartite organization based on parity (Labour Foundation, 2010), with, to date, influential spring and autumn consultation rounds with the government. In 1950, the Social and Economic Council of the Netherlands[4] was established, representing employers and employees, and including independent experts (who are called "Crown members") (Social and Economic Council of the Netherlands, 2015). This tripartite advisory body provides recommendations on request by the government or on its own initiative. These two bodies thus do make not policies but regularly advise the government, and their advice is influential in Dutch national policy making.

Employers thus pay directly, via premiums or extension of income, for a substantial part of the welfare state, which creates a larger sense of involvement in welfare than in a solely tax-based (Beveridge) system. Moreover, employer organizations and trade unions influence policy making at an early stage. Once developed, policies are well known to employers and employees, fit with their realities, and tend to be supported by most employers in the country, without large conflicts with employee interests. This typical Dutch incremental mode of policy development was carefully analyzed in the context of integrated healthcare for elderly citizens by Kümpers, van Raak, Hardy, & Mur. (2002). Also (although less emphasized), including experts in policy making supports the use of scientific evidence at the early stage of formulating policies.

Third, the Netherlands is characterized by its healthcare system being almost completely separate from occupational health and social insurance. Since 1903 treating physicians have been forbidden from writing sick notes for their patients. Other physicians (hired by employers or working for social insurance agencies) check the legitimacy of sickness absences and long-term disability. Since then, insurance medicine has been established as a profession, and the profession of occupational physician was officially established as early as the 1950s (Wolvetang et al., 1997). This separation of healthcare and occupational care from social insurance also encouraged employer involvement in work disability policy and practice (Prins & Bloch, 2001).

The Disability Benefit Scheme of 1967

With the introduction of the public disability benefit scheme,[5] in 1967 for all employees and in 1976 for all citizens, the Dutch welfare state was complete. The scheme covered long-term disability for the period after employment. This disability benefit scheme was linked to a sickness benefit scheme covering the first year of sickness absence, during which the employee was still employed. Both schemes did not fundamentally change until the first privatization of part of the sickness benefit scheme in 1996. The 1967 disability benefit scheme replaced diverse old laws, which only covered work risks for specific groups of employees, with a scheme that also covered social risks (not just consequences of workplace accidents) and thus loss of income due to all work disability (i.e., not being able to work due to a medical condition, regardless of its cause). The Netherlands was unique in not separating work injury from non-work injury in its disability benefit scheme. Also, the threshold for receiving benefits was only 15% loss of income, and the coverage increased incrementally, depending on the percentage of lost income, to a maximum of 80% of former income. The innovative and generous disability benefit scheme of 1967 was influenced overall by the notion of the rights to self-fulfillment and equality (Aarts et al., 2002).

Employees absent from work because of any sickness could apply for a sickness-absence benefit during the first year. During that year, the employee received healthcare treatment, and the legitimacy of their absence was monitored. Neither healthcare nor occupational health focused on restoring work ability.

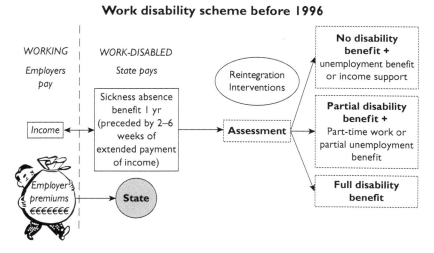

Figure 14.1 Dutch sickness-absence scheme before 1996

After one year of sickness absence earning ability, not work ability, was assessed to determine disability benefit eligibility (Aarts et al., 2002). If after one year of sickness absence an employee was not approved for the disability benefit scheme, unemployment benefits (via the Unemployment Insurance Act[6]) or income support[7] (a minimum income supplied by the state for those without income or possessions) were available. A partial disability benefit was also possible, which could be supplemented with unemployment benefits (see Figure 14.1).

Both the sickness-absence benefit and the disability benefit were financed by premiums paid by employers and employees. The premiums, in fact, also increased the employers' expenses on salaries. Most of the sickness-absence and disability benefit schemes were thus regulated and supplied by the government, but paid for by employers (see Figure 14.1).

Within the pre-1980 legislative framework, employers had ample opportunity to control sickness-absence and disability benefit costs. They could prevent sickness absence via the 1980 Working Conditions Act[8] and could perform medical examinations when hiring for jobs with high health risks. However, as will be explained below, legislation was not aimed at providing incentives for employers to reduce their sickness-absence and disability benefit costs. During the 1980s and 1990s, such incentives would gradually be introduced.

"Dutch Disease" in the Netherlands Economy and Work Disability Schemes During the 1980s and 1990s

Both the sickness-absence scheme and the disability benefit scheme became far more attractive to employees than had ever been expected. In 1979,

10% of those in paid jobs were not working and were receiving sickness absence benefits. This high sickness-absence rate resulted in a large number of employees applying for disability benefits after one year of sickness absence. In 1967, it had been expected that only 200,000 people would depend on disability benefits, but seven years later, more than 300,000 were on disability benefits. In 1980, the cost of these benefits was 4% of the GDP (Aarts et al., 2002).

However, at the beginning of the 1980s, the most important problem in the Netherlands was not the high sickness-absence rate and high number of disability benefit beneficiaries, but the deep economic crisis and unemployment. The term "Dutch disease" was coined in 1977 to explain a sharp decline in the Dutch economy following overreliance on natural gas resources discovered in 1959. As a consequence, domestic industries had been neglected, causing high inflation, a drop in investment, and a loss of global competitiveness (C. W., 2014).

As a response, the government, employer organizations, and trade unions entered into what was named the Wassenaar agreement[9] in 1982. Trade unions agreed to drop their insistence on frequent wage adjustments for inflation. Employer organizations agreed to offer a shorter working week, early retirement schemes, and part-time work. With these changes, company profits were restored and full employment could be realized. Despite the feeling of victory by the three parties over the agreement, the number of people receiving disability benefits increased. The first reason was the drop in available jobs due to economic recession, which allowed the government to loosen the disability benefit assessment policy. The reduced opportunities to find other jobs were taken into account when assessing access to the disability benefit scheme, which increased the number of recipients (Arents, Cluitmans, & van der Ende, 1999).

The second reason why the number of people receiving disability benefits increased without taking immediate measures was that the high disability benefit level was masked by another typical Dutch phenomenon: very low labor participation of women at that time. Although labor participation had generally and irrespective of gender dropped from 1975 to 1985, overall expenditures on social benefits were, relative to international norms, not exceptionally high. In 1985, 20% of the population depended on some benefit, which was average compared with 11 OECD countries. However, a large proportion of the population (35%) had no personal income (mostly married women), and only 45% of the working-age Dutch population (aged 15–64) had paid work (Arents et al., 1999).

In most Western countries, employment dropped because of the economic crisis in the early 1970s, while labor forces increased because the baby boomers began entering the labor market. In all countries, an increasing number of working-age people applied for disability benefits as an alternative to (massive) unemployment. However, this shift was more pronounced in the Netherlands. The proportion of older men (aged 55–64) who were employed dropped from a moderate 80.6% in 1970 to a striking low of 44.2% in 1997. This drop was explained primarily by the highly accessible disability benefit scheme. During this period, the proportion of older working men also dropped remarkably in Belgium, France, Finland, Germany, and Austria. Whereas in Germany and Austria disability benefit schemes also functioned as early-retirement schemes, the other countries had attractive early-retirement schemes (Aarts et al., 2002; Einerhand, Knol, Prins, & Veerman, 1995).

The third reason why work disability increased was a lack of cost awareness. The pay-as-you-go system, with employer-prepaid premiums, prevented both employers and employees from seeing the costs directly as theirs (Aarts & de Jong, 1998). The fourth reason was the striking lack of public expenditure for reintegration interventions (vocational rehabilitation), and thus low exit rates from the disability benefit scheme during the 1990s (Liedorp, 2002; Social and Economic Council of the Netherlands, 1991). Less than 0.01% of GDP was spent on reintegration interventions, compared with 0.4% in the United States, 0.10% in Sweden, and 0.15% in Germany and Switzerland (Aarts et al., 2002).

By 1990, a tremendous 14% of the Dutch labor force was on disability benefits. The prime minister used the words "The Netherlands is sick" (NRC Handelsblad, 1990), reflecting the contradiction between a prosperous country with highly educated citizens and excellent healthcare and the high number of people considered too ill to work (de Volkskrant, 1998). Finally, the state, employer organizations, and trade unions became fully determined to collaborate on this issue, affected by earlier positive experiences and new ideas about governance. During the 1980s, there was growing awareness that the state alone could not sufficiently influence social processes through strict legislation. Instead, legislation should only set the boundaries within which parties could operate, and other policy instruments, such as economic incentives, should be used (Liedorp, 2002). These new ideas, which parallel the "Third Way" (Giddens, 2001), introduced under the Clinton administration in the US and the Blair government in the UK, offered employer and employee organizations more room to influence policy.

In the Netherlands, this broadening of policy instruments resulted in a clear shift toward financial incentives for employers (Liedorp, 2002). This shift began in 1993, with sickness-absence premiums under the new Sickness Benefits Act[10] being tied to the short-term sickness rate of each organization. Next, in 1994, the government sickness-absence payment was replaced by a law mandating employers to pay at least 70% of the worker's salary during the first two (for small organizations) to six (for large organizations) weeks of sickness absence; after that, the government would take over sickness-absence payments. In 1996, the government sickness-absence payment was abandoned, and employers were mandated to pay at least 70%

of workers' salaries during the first year of work disability (Aarts et al., 2002; Liedorp, 2002). Finally, financial incentives to reduce long-term disability benefits were introduced in 1998. By then, employer premiums under the disability benefit scheme of 1967 were set according to the number of disabled employees in an organization (Liedorp, 2002). Until then, no measures had been taken to encourage return to work during the first year of sickness absence. The laws relied on employers taking responsibility themselves, prompted by financial incentives attached to preventing sickness absence and decreasing the length of sickness absences. Return-to-work interventions during sickness absence were offered by private occupational health companies, and private insurance companies who offered sickness-absence insurance to employers. Their packages came with preventive measures and return-to-work guidance to reduce the insurers' expenses.

Thus, during the 1980s and 1990s, legislation covering sickness absence and disability benefits gradually changed, with the aim of containing costs and providing incentives for employers to prevent sickness absence. At the same time, sick-listed employees also received job protection for one year. These changes in legislation were accompanied by research commissioned mostly by the government, although policy changes were often made too rapidly for their actual effects to be studied (Aarts et al., 2002).

By 2000, Dutch employers were held fully responsible for the implementation and financing of employee income protection during the first year of sickness absence. Still, the state was legally responsible for income protection of employees on sick leave. Only the legal framework had changed: the social insurance benefit was replaced by a statutory payment obligation. This change was supported by private insurers, who developed plans, with attractive premiums, that insured employers against the risk of paying sickness-absence benefits (Liedorp, 2002). These policy changes and the pace of change were totally different from other European countries with comparable economic characteristics. In Denmark, the threshold for disability benefit eligibility was higher, and participation in vocational rehabilitation was highly encouraged (Høgelund, 2003). In Sweden, employers were not required to pay sickness-absence benefits beyond the first two weeks (Liedorp, 2002). Compared with Belgium, more sickness-absence legislation was introduced in the 1980s and 1990s in the Netherlands, and it was also less permissive than the Belgian legislation (van Raak, de Rijk, & Morsa, 2005). The rapid changes in the Netherlands also constituted a drawback, as the new legislation on sickness-absence guidance to promote return to work could not be "internalized" by employees and employers. The legislation was not turned into a routine, which hampered use in practice (van Raak et al., 2005).

The New Work Disability Scheme in 2004

The new century brought with it two new laws: in 2002 the Gatekeeper Improvement Act[11] and in 2004 the Extended Payment of Income Act.

This resulted in a sickness-absence scheme that (a) obliged employers to pay at least 70% of the sick-listed employee's salary for two years (including job protection) and (b) via the gatekeeper improvement act, the requirement that employers, employees, and occupational physicians fulfill certain tasks during workers' absences to promote prompt reintegration into work. Simply stated, the two new laws meant that employers guided sickness absence and paid sickness-absence benefits directly (see Figure 14.2), thus regaining control over their expenses. Furthermore, employers, employees, and occupational physicians became the gatekeepers for access to disability benefits, in order to control the number of people receiving them. Thus, privatizing the first two years of sickness absence reduced the role of the state in controlling work disability.

Due to the "consultative economy," employers effectively contributed via bipartite and tripartite consultations to formulating these two new laws (Inspectie Werk en Inkomen, 2006). The trade unions agreed with the reforms because they no longer restricted protection of sick-listed employees' jobs to only twoyears (Høgelund, 2003). Extension of employers' payment to sick-listed employees for a maximum of two years has to be understood as the government trading employers' sickness-absence and disability benefit premiums for their payments to certain sick employees. These payments could be influenced by employers via prevention and reintegration interventions.

It is difficult to understand why the small- and medium-sized enterprises also agreed with the two new laws. Liedorp (2002) explained that, in 1996, when employers' payment of workers' sickness-absence benefits was

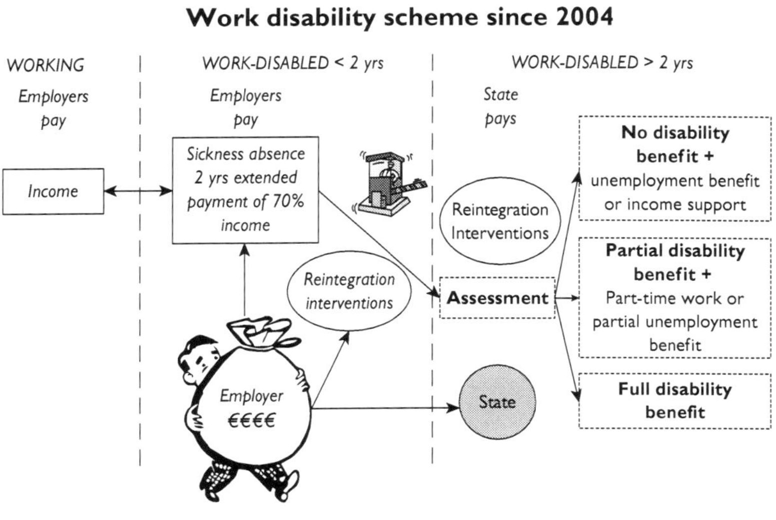

Figure 14.2 Dutch sickness-absence scheme since 2004

extended from two to six weeks, private insurance companies promised to offer employers attractive insurance rates to cover their risks of paying sickness-absence benefits. Moreover, sickness absence in small- and medium-sized enterprises has always been lower than in larger organizations (EurWORK, 2010).

Employers Pay For and Guide Sickness Absence

The combination of employers paying for and guiding sickness absence was thus considered self-evident in the Netherlands. The Gatekeeper Improvement Act was developed to address the lack of early intervention and cooperation by employers during sickness absence. Hertogh, Putman, & Urban (2001) analyzed how sickness absence for mental health problems, the most common reason for sickness absence, was in fact a "one-way-ticket to a disability benefit" (p. 11). Other Dutch studies revealed a similar lack of cooperation in return to work during the first year of sickness absence (de Rijk, van Raak, & van der Made, 2007; van Raak et al., 2005). The Gatekeeper Improvement Act of 2002 was expected to change this pattern, due to three main measures: (a) employers and occupational physicians became gatekeepers for entering the disability benefit scheme, (b) employers, employees, and occupational physicians now have responsibilities under the Act for the steps listed below during periods of sickness absence, and (c) these responsibilities are checked by the social insurance agency and, if necessary, sanctioned (e.g., with benefit reductions for employees or fines for employers) (OECD, 2007; Reijenga, Veerman, & van den Berg, 2006). The following steps must be followed during a sickness absence:

1   The employee contacts the employer on the first day of sickness absence.
2   Within six weeks, a certified occupational physician, hired by the employer, has to provide an analysis of the work (dis)ability problem.
3   Within eight weeks, the employer and employee formulate a reintegration plan, including work modifications and gradual return to work.
4   If the employee is not reintegrated after one year, the employer is obliged to offer a suitable job in another organization (in practice, this is often facilitated by a reintegration agency).
5   If the employee is not reintegrated after two years, the employee can apply to the social insurance agency for disability benefits.

From an international perspective, it might still be difficult to understand why employers so easily accepted their responsibility for ill employees for a period of two years. It is important to note that, immediately after introduction of the Gatekeeper Improvement Act in 2002, the one-year employer obligation seemed arbitrary. Moreover, policy makers increasingly focused on an incentive structure that promoted participation in paid work rather than income protection (OECD, 2007) and concluded that more than a year of exploring work modifications, other jobs within the organization, and jobs elsewhere was needed to prevent entry into the disability benefit scheme. It was expected that extending employer payment of sickness-absence benefits for another year would reduce the number of disability benefit beneficiaries. Meanwhile, new plans for stricter thresholds for entering the disability benefit scheme were being prepared. Thus, employers expected that lower disability benefit premiums would outweigh the extended period of sickness-absence payments.

Successes in the New Work Disability Scheme

The new work disability system promoted by the Gatekeeper Improvement Act and the Extended Payment of Income Act had immediate, significant effects. Sickness absence dropped and, since the Act on extended wage payment included job protection and most employees worked under permanent contracts in the first decade of this century, the drop implies that more employees kept their work and income. This drop was related to the number and type of actions taken during the period of sickness absence, also confirming the effectiveness of the new act. Moreover, the health of employees returning to work did not deteriorate (Inspectie Werk en Inkomen, 2006). Further, the number of new disability benefit claimants dropped from 8.4 per 1,000 employees in 2004 to 4.5 per 1,000 employees in 2006 (Jehoel-Gijsbers & Linder, 2007). As a result of both economic development and the new legislation, expenditures for sickness absence and disability benefits decreased remarkably, as shown in Figure 14.3 (OECD, 2010).

Compared with other countries, the Netherlands' drop in new disability benefit claimants was large (OECD, 2010). The relationship between the drop in new sickness-absence and new disability benefit claimants was also stronger than in other countries, confirming the gatekeeper role of the new Act (OECD, 2010). Although the largest decrease in sickness absence had already taken place in the 1980s, due to the economic crisis and reduction in physically harmful jobs (Einerhand et al., 1995), these figures confirm the contribution of the Gatekeeper Improvement Act to increasing return-to-work rates during sickness absence without harming employees' health.

It soon appeared that the Gatekeeper Improvement Act was particularly successful in reducing sickness absence in formerly underserved populations, specifically women and immigrants (Jehoel-Gijsbers & Linder, 2007). Apparently, the Gatekeeper Improvement Act and the Extended Payment of Income Act stimulated employers in sectors offering precarious and demanding work, such as cleaning, to offer the same guidance and standards of sickness absence already present in sectors employing traditional white male breadwinners. The gatekeeper improvement act's flexibility regarding

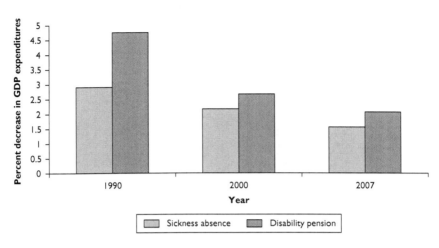

Figure 14.3 Drop in sickness-absence and disability-pension expenditures, as a percentage of GDP. Based on data from Table 2.1 in OECD (2010), Sickness, disability and work: Breaking the barriers. A synthesis of findings across OECD countries.

changing reintegration plans allows employees to try new opportunities for returning to work if an initial option fails. This flexibility is important, as a Canadian study showed how fixed reintegration plans hamper, rather than encourage, return to work, because the course of illness is often capricious and unpredictable (Maiwald, Meershoek, de Rijk, & Nijhuis, 2013).

Challenges with the Dutch Work Disability Scheme

Despite its clear success, the Gatekeeper Improvement Act is not a magic solution. Hoefsmit, de Rijk, Houkes, & Nijhuis (2013) showed that the Act does not remove distrust between employers and employees, particularly not during the second year of sickness absence when employers' tolerance in accepting their employee's sickness absence often expires. Further, Hoefsmit, Boumans, Houkes, & Nijhuis (2016) and Hoefsmit, Houkes et al. (2016) demonstrated that employers are still in need of additional, more detailed roadmaps. In cases of conflict between employers and employees, the Gatekeeper Improvement Act does not decrease, and might even extend, the length of sickness absence (Inspectie Werk en Inkomen, 2006). In addition, if mental health problems that lead to sickness absence are caused by workplaces, the Act does not support effective return to work, as shown by Verdonk, de Rijk, Klinge, & van Dijk-de Vries, A (2008). In these cases, requiring sick-listed employees to wait a year before switching to another workplace is unnecessarily long.

A further challenge is that employers and occupational physicians might not have the time and financial resources to adequately support employees on sickness absence (Her Majesty's Dutch Medical Association, 2016; Social and Economic Council of the Netherlands, 2014). Small- and medium-sized companies, especially, complain about the risk of paying employees sickness-absence benefits for the extra year, and the state secretary for Social Affairs and Employment expressed concern about the potential for employers to select healthier employees (Ascher, 2016). Due to the separation of occupational health and healthcare, employers cannot rely on support from healthcare services. Moreover, effective and fast treatment of work disability is not available in the case of conditions requiring large amounts of care and medication (Prins & Bloch, 2001).

While the Gatekeeper Improvement Act and the Extended Payment of Income Act favor disabled people who are already employed, other disabled groups of working age are underserved. The acts favor insiders, not outsiders. First, the Gatekeeper Improvement Act is seldom applied to sick unemployed people or those who work for temporary agencies (Inspectie Werk en Inkomen, 2006).

Second, due to the hesitancy of employers to hire people with health problems (even though selection on the basis of health is officially forbidden), the number of unemployed disabled people has increased. Even with the earlier changes in legislation, when employers became directly responsible for an additional six weeks of employee sickness-absence benefits, this hesitancy was observed (Høgelund, 2003). In the Netherlands, the gap in employment rates between disabled and nondisabled people is among the largest in Europe (Eurostat, 2014). These unemployed disabled people have a relatively high risk of poverty. Although about a quarter of unemployed, working-age, disabled Dutch people are poor, only 5% of nondisabled unemployed people are. Poverty is less prevalent among Dutch unemployed disabled people than in, for example, the United Kingdom (35.4%) and Belgium (35.7%) but far more prevalent than in, for example, France (17.1%) and Sweden (18.2%) (Eurostat, 2015). This is also related to the increased threshold for receiving disability benefits (35% loss of earning capacity instead of 15%) after 2004. The number of people with work disability who are not receiving disability benefits (but, instead, temporary unemployment benefits or income support) and who are not finding work has thus increased in the last decade (Statistics Netherlands, 2017b).

Third, in the Netherlands, self-employed people are not covered in cases of sickness absence and disability, except by income support. Depending on their age, family situation, other income, and assets, income support adds from 70% to 100% of minimum wage. The self-employed population is relatively large in the Netherlands, comprising about 10% of those with paid work (Social and Economic Council of the Netherlands, 2010).

Is the Dutch Work Disability System Transferable to Other Countries?

A major drawback of the Gatekeeper Improvement Act and the Extended Payment of Income Act is, thus, that they favor employees, who are the only group that is guaranteed to receive 70% of their former income over two years of work disability and whose jobs are protected. This insider/outsider phenomenon, related to the Dutch Bismarckian welfare state, should not be transferred to other countries. The question as to whether the Gatekeeper Improvement Act can be transferred at all can be answered with a "Yes, but." As explained above, this Act is highly beneficial for the group it was meant to serve (employees), and it seemed to be particularly good at providing those who were traditionally underserved regarding sickness-absence guidance (Jehoel-Gijsbers & Linder, 2007). But even for employees, the Act will only be effective if:

- the organization has a sense of urgency about reducing sickness absence;
- occupational physicians are available, who are trained to translate disease into functional limitations that can be communicated to employers without harming employees' privacy; and
- the necessary skills, or even culture, for multidisciplinary cooperation are available among employers, occupational physicians, and other stakeholders, such as treating physicians.

It is doubtful that the Extended Payment of Income Act could be transferred to other countries. Requiring that employers directly pay sickness-absence benefits for two years is only possible in the context of a corporatist welfare state, a consultative economy, and protection of employees' jobs when they are on sick leave. However, encouraging employers to take some financial responsibility for sick leave will certainly help reduce the length of sickness absence.

The Issue of Sustainability

To conclude, the two acts are highly effective for the group they were designed to serve, and their effectiveness was enabled by sociopolitical and economic developments in the Netherlands over the past five decades. However, the acts' sustainability is questionable; it depends on whether employers can still be given a key role when the labor market becomes more diverse, flexible, and unstable.

In 2017, the Social and Economic Council of the Netherlands published a memorandum, entitled "The Future of Work in the Netherlands," in reaction to the four centenary-conversation questions asked by the International Labour Organization (2016):

1   Work and Society: What role will work have in our society over the next century?

    According to the memorandum, an important challenge will be to increase the relatively low labor-participation rate and hours worked per week of low-skilled women and immigrants.
2   Decent Jobs for All: How do we guarantee employment and employee protection over the next century?

    Globalization and technologization can offer chances to improve the quality of work but can also threaten basic work values. Specific to the Netherlands, says the memorandum, is the increase of flexible employment relationships that differ from those for permanent employees. The two acts are not applied to sick unemployed people and those who work for temporary agencies (Inspectie Werk en Inkomen, 2006), and the acts do not cover the situation of employees with temporary contracts that end during the first two years of sickness absence. Equal opportunities need to be provided for low- and high-skilled citizens, and the government has to provide an appropriate interpretation of the concept of solidarity across citizens.
3   The Organization of Work and Production: How will production processes change, and what effect will this have on employment and employee protection?

    According to the memorandum, new risks for sickness absence might develop among employees not able to keep up with the high pace of change in production processes.
4   The Governance of Work: How do we exercise governance over work, nationally and internationally?

    According to the memorandum, globalization should not lead to a downward spiral in employment and social security of employees.

These four areas of new developments imply that, increasingly, Dutch employers are confronted with unpredictable costs and employees with unpredictable risks, while the government has to better protect vulnerable workers and small employers, and find new ways to create solidarity. The Dutch consultative economy will be challenged and has to find ways to develop a more universal welfare state; that is, a welfare state with the same provisions for all citizens irrespective of having (had) an employer or not, one that upholds human rights and enables fulfilling jobs for all working-age adults. Although the consultative economy will help find answers through its integration of diverse perspectives, Dutch employers will not likely play the key role in the welfare state that they did in recent decades.

Notes

1   Nederlandse Vereniging voor Arbeids- en Bedrijfsgeneeskunde.
2   Uitvoeringsorgaan Werknemers Verzekeringen.

3 Stichting van de Arbeid.
4 Sociaal-Economische Raad.
5 Wet op de ArbeidsOngeschiktheidsverzekering.
6 Werkloosheids Wet.
7 Bijstand.
8 Arbeidsomstandighedenwet.
9 Akkoord van Wassenaar.
10 Ziektewet.
11 Wet Verbetering Poortwachter.

References

Aarts, L. J. M., & de Jong, P. R. (1998). *Privatization of social insurance and welfare state efficiency. Evidence from the Netherlands & United States.* Paper presented at the 2nd International Research Conference on Social Security, Public versus Private Provision Session, Jerusalem, January 25–28, 1998.

Aarts, L. J. M., de Jong, P. R., & van der Veen, R. (2002). *Met de beste bedoelingen: WAO 1975–1999—Trends, onderzoek en beleid.* [With the best intentions: disability benefit scheme 1975–1999—Trends, research and policy]. Doetinchem, the Netherlands: Elsevier.

Anema, J. R., Prinz, C., & Prins, R. (2013). Sickness and disability policy interventions. In P. Loisel & H. Anema (Eds.), *Handbook of work disability: Prevention and management* (pp. 357–371). New York, NY: Springer Science+Business Media.

Arents, M., Cluitmans, M. M., & van der Ende, M. A. (1999). *Benefit dependency ratios: An analysis of nine European countries, Japan and the US.* Rotterdam, the Netherlands: Nederlands Economisch Insitituut.

Ascher, L. (2016). *Advies aanvraag SER Langdurige werkeloosheid en loondoorbetaling bij ziekte* [Call for advice from the Social and Economic Council on long-term unemployment and extended payment of income during sickness absence].

Bambra, C. (2007). Going beyond the Three Types of Welfare Capitalism. Regime theory and public health research. *Journal of Epidemiology and Community Health, 61*, 1098–1102.

Bonoli, G. (1997). Classifying welfare states: A two-dimension approach. *Journal of Social Policy, 26* (3), 351–372.

C.W. (2014, November 5). What Dutch disease is, and why it's bad. *The Economist.* Retrieved from www.economist.com/blogs/economist-explains/2014/11/economist-explains-2

de Rijk, A., van Raak, A., & van der Made, J. (2007). A new theoretical model for cooperation in public health settings: The RDIC-model. *Qualitative Health Research, 17*(8), 1103–1116.

de Volkskrant. (1998, December 23). *WAO van crisis naar crisis* [Disability benefits from crisis to crisis]. Amsterdam, the Netherlands: de Volkskrant. Retrieved from www.volkskrant.nl/archief/wao-van-crisis-naar-crisis~a466964/

Eikemo, T. A., & Bambra, C. (2008). The welfare state: A glossary for public health. *Journal of Epidemiology and Community Health, 62*(1), 3–6.

Einerhand, M. G. K., Knol, G., Prins, R., & Veerman, T. J. (1995). *Sickness and invalidity arrangements. Facts and figures from six European countries.* The Hague, the Netherlands: Ministerie van Sociale Zaken en Werkgelegenheid [Ministry of Social Affairs and Employment].

Esping-Andersen, G. (1990). *The three worlds of welfare capitalism.* New Jersey, NJ: Princeton University Press.

Eurostat (2014). *Employment rate of persons aged 15–64, by country and disability definition, 2011.* Retrieved from http://ec.europa.eu/eurostat/statistics-explained/index.php/File:Employment_rate_of_persons_aged_15-64,_by_country_and_disability_definition,_2011_(in_%25).JPG

Eurostat. (2015). *People at risk of poverty, severely materially deprived 2013.* Retrieved from http://ec.europa.eu/eurostat/statistics-explained/index.php/File:Table_1_People_at-risk-of-poverty,_severely_materially_deprived_2013.png

EurWORK. (2010). *Absence from work – Netherlands.* Retrieved from www.eurofound.europa.eu/observatories/eurwork/comparative-information/national-contributions/netherlands/absence-from-work-netherlands

Giddens, A. (Ed.). (2001). *The global third way debate.* Cambridge, UK: Polity Press.

Her Majesty's Dutch Medical Association. (2016). *Zorg die werkt* [Care that works]. Utrecht, the Netherlands: KNMG.

Hertogh, M. W., Putman, L. S., & Urban, K. L. (2001). *Enkeltje WAO: De gebrekkige begeleiding van werknemers met psychische klachten tijdens het eerste ziektejaar* [One-way ticket to disability benefit: Inadequate support of Dutch employees with mental health complaints during their first year of sickness]. Breukelen, the Netherlands: NYFER.

Hoefsmit, N., Boumans, N., Houkes, I., & Nijhuis, F. (2016). A process evaluation of a return-to-work intervention to improve cooperation between sick-listed employees and their supervisors (COSS). *Work, 55,* 593–603.

Hoefsmit, N., de Rijk, A., Houkes, I., & Nijhuis F. (2013). Work resumption at the price of distrust: A qualitative study on return to work legislation in the Netherlands. *BMC Public Health, 13,* 153.

Hoefsmit, N., Houkes, I., Boumans, N., Noben, C., Winkens, B., & Nijhuis, F. (2016). The effectiveness of an intervention to enhance cooperation between sick-listed employees and their supervisors (COSS). *Journal of Occupational Rehabilitation, 26,* 229–236.

Høgelund, J. (2003). *In search of effective disability policy: Comparing the developments and outcomes of the Dutch and Danish disability policies.* Amsterdam, the Netherlands: Amsterdam University Press.

Inspectie Werk en Inkomen [Labor and Income Inspectorate]. (2006). *Wet verbetering Poortwachter: Een overzicht van ontwikkelingen op het terrein van de wet verbetering poortwachter* [Gatekeeper Improvement Act: an overview of the developments related to the Gatekeeper Improvement Act]. Amsterdam, the Netherlands: IWI.

International Labour Organization. (2016). *The future of work centenary initiative.* Retrieved from www.ilo.org/global/topics/future-of-work/WCMS_448448/lang--en/index.htm

Jehoel-Gijsbers, G., & Linder, F. (2007). Ontwikkelingen in omvang van ziekteverzuim en WAO-instroom [Developments in the sickness-absence rate and influx into disability benefits]. In Jehoel-Gijsbers (Ed.), *Beter aan het werk: Trendrapportage ziekteverzuim, arbeidsongeschiktheid en werkhervatting 2007* [Better at work: trend report on sickness absence, disability benefits, and return to work 2007]. The Hague, the Netherlands: Social Cultural Planning Office.

Kümpers, S., van Raak, A., Hardy, B., & Mur, I. (2002). The influence of institutions and culture on health policies: Different approaches to integrated care in England and the Netherlands. *Public Administration, 80*(2), 339–358.

Labour Foundation. (2010). *Labour Foundation in brief*. The Hague, the Netherlands: Labour Foundation.

Liedorp, M. (2002). *Twintig jaar ziekteverzuim- en arbeidsongeschiktheid: Het dilemma tussen sturingsbehoefte en sturingsmogelijkheden* [with summary in English]. [Twenty years of government policy on absenteeism due to illness and disability: the dilemma between the wish to control and the limits of governance]. (Unpublished doctoral thesis). Utrecht University, Utrecht, the Netherlands.

Maiwald K., Meershoek A., de Rijk A., & Nijhuis F. (2013). How policy on employee involvement in work reintegration can yield its opposite: Employee experiences in a Canadian setting. *Disability and Rehabilitation, 35*(7), 527–37.

Netherlands Society of Occupational Medicine. (2017). *NVAB, the Netherlands Society of Occupational Medicine*. Retrieved from www.nvab-online.nl/english/english

NRC Handelsblad. (1990, December 1). Is Nederland ziek? [Is the Netherlands sick?]. Retrieved from www.nrc.nl/nieuws/1990/12/01/is-nederland-ziek-6948778-a461409

Organisation for Economic Co-operation and Development. (2007). *Sickness and disability schemes in the Netherlands: Country memo as a background paper for the OECD Disability Review*. Paris: OECD. Retrieved from www.oecd.org/social/soc/41429917.pdf

Organisation for Economic Co-operation and Development. (2010). *Sickness, disability and work: Breaking the barriers. A synthesis of findings across OECD countries*. Paris: OECD. Retrieved from www.oecd.org/publications/sickness-disability-and-work-breaking-the-barriers-9789264088856-en.htm

Portegijs, W., & Keuzenkamp, S. (2008). *Nederland deeltijdland* [The Netherlands, part-time country]. The Hague, the Netherlands: Social Cultural Planning Office.

Portegijs, W., & van den Brakel, M. (2016). *Summary emancipation monitor*. The Hague, the Netherlands: The Netherlands Institute for Social Research & Statistics Netherlands.

Prins, R., & Bloch, F. S. (2001). Social security, work incapacity and reintegration. In Bloch, R.F. & Prins, R. (Eds.), *Who returns to work & why? A six-country study on work incapacity & reintegration* (International Social Security Series, Vol. 5). New Brunswick, NJ: Transaction.

Reijenga, F. A., Veerman, T. J., & van den Berg, N. (2006). *Onderzoek evaluatie Wet verbetering Poortwachter* [Research evaluation of Gatekeeper Improvement Act]. The Hague, the Netherlands: Astri.

Social and Economic Council of the Netherlands. (1991). *Advies ziekteverzuim en arbeidsongeschiktheid: Advies over het beleid ten aanzien van ziekteverzuim en arbeidsongeschiktheid voor de staatssecretaris van Sociale Zaken en Werkgelegenheid* [Advice on the policy regarding sickness absence and disability benefit for the secretary of state for social affairs and employment]. The Hague, the Netherlands: Social and Economic Council of the Netherlands.

Social and Economic Council of the Netherlands. (2010). *SER-advies ZZP-ers in beeld* [Social and economic council advice: self-employed in the picture]. The Hague, the Netherlands: Social and Economic Council of the Netherlands.

Social and Economic Council of the Netherlands. (2014). *Advies Betere zorg voor werkenden: Een visie op de toekomst van de arbeidsgerelateerde zorg* [Advice on better care for workers: vision of the future of occupational healthcare]. The Hague, the Netherlands: Social and Economic Council of the Netherlands.

Social and Economic Council of the Netherlands. (2015). *The power of consulation*. The Hague, the Netherlands: Social and Economic Council of the Netherlands.

Social and Economic Council of the Netherlands. (2017). *The future of work in the Netherlands*. The Hague, the Netherlands: Social and Economic Council of the Netherlands.

Statistics Netherlands. (2017a). Laagste ziekteverzuim in horeca [Lowest sickness absence in hotel and catering industry]. Retrieved from www.cbs.nl/nl-nl/nieuws/2017/27/laagste-ziekteverzuim-in-de-horeca

Statistics Netherlands. (2017b). *Trends in the Netherlands 2017*. The Hague: Statistics Netherlands. Retrieved from www.cbs.nl/-/media/_pdf/2017/44/trends_in_the_netherlands_2017_web.pdf

Trading Economics. (2017a). *Netherlands employment rate, 1992–2017*. Retrieved from https://tradingeconomics.com/netherlands/employment-rate

Trading Economics. (2017b). *Netherlands labor force participation rate, 1998–2017*. Retrieved from https://tradingeconomics.com/netherlands/labor-force-participation-rate

van Raak, A., de Rijk, A., & Morsa, J. (2005). Applying new institutional theory: The case of collaboration to promote work resumption after sickness absence. *Work, Employment & Society*, *19*(1), 141–152.

Verdonk, P., de Rijk, A., Klinge, I., & van Dijk-de Vries, A. (2008). Sickness absence as interactive process: Gendered experiences of young higher educated women with mental health problems. *Patient Education and Counselling*, *73*, 300–306.

Wolvetang, H., Buijs, P. E., & van Oosterom, A. (1997). *Arbeids- en bedrijfsgeneeskunde: Historie, ontwikkeling en doelstelling* [Occupational medicine: history, development and objectives]. In H. Wolvetang, P. E. Buijs, & A. van Oosterom (Eds.), *Handboek Bedrijfsgezondheidszorg* [Handbook of occupational medicine] (pp. A1-1/1–A12/16). Groningen, the Netherlands: Wetenschappelijke uitgeverij Bunge.

Chapter 15

The Rise and Fall of Income Replacement Disability Benefit Receipt in the United Kingdom
What Are the Consequences of Reforms?

Ben Barr and Philip McHale

The United Kingdom (UK) has a population of over 65 million, 63% of whom are of working age (16–64 years old). The population is aging, with increases in the over-65 population seen over the past 40 years and projected to continue (Office for National Statistics, 2017). Importantly, there are major geographical imbalances, with the UK having larger regional differences in gross domestic product (GDP) per capita than any other European country (Eurostat, 2017). Large areas of the UK, such as the north and the southwest of England, and Wales, experienced economic shocks with the decline in mining and heavy industry in the 1980s and 1990s, and these deindustrialized areas have lower incomes and employment and higher levels of disability than the rest of the UK.

Since the 1970s, the number of people out of work in the UK because of a disability has increased sharply. By 1995, around 7% of the workforce were in receipt of out-of-work income-replacement disability benefits,[1] costing 1.6% of GDP (Banks, Blundell, & Emmerson, 2015; Organisation for Economic Co-operation and Development (OECD), 2010). In this chapter, we outline the potential reasons for this increase, and reforms since 1995 that aimed to reduce the numbers of people receiving disability benefits and increase the employment of disabled people.

The strategy of successive governments has been to characterize this as an employment rather than a disability problem. Interventions have focused on reducing disincentives to work by reducing access to disability benefits and their income-replacement rates and on improving the employability and job-search behavior of disabled people through welfare-to-work programs. Increasingly, participation in these programs is one of the conditions of receiving benefits. We outline some of the potential impacts of these reforms—both positive and negative—and briefly discuss alternative approaches for both supporting the employment of disabled people and preventing poverty among disabled people out of work.

The Rise in Disability Benefit Receipt in the UK

In most Organisation for Economic Co-operation and Development (OECD) countries, disabled people are less likely to be employed than nondisabled people.

The reasons for this are complex and include barriers related to impairments, inaccessible workplaces, discrimination, and the clustering of disability with other barriers to employment, such as low education and skills (OECD, 2010). Disabled people are also at greater risk of poverty because of these lower levels of employment and the costs associated with disability. To address this issue, most OECD countries have developed social-protection systems that provide income-replacement benefits to people who cannot work due to disability.

Since 1971, there have been a number of income-replacement disability benefit schemes in the UK. These are all nationally administered, with benefits generally paid at a flat rate, although before 1995 there was a component that depended on prior earnings. People who have paid sufficient National Insurance contributions are not means-tested. A separate scheme known as the Industrial Injuries Disablement Benefit (IIDB), introduced in 1948, is available for people who become ill or are disabled because of an accident at work or due to recognized occupational diseases (Department for Work and Pensions, 2017b). The relatively narrow eligibility criteria for IIDB means that claimants under this scheme have remained small compared with those of the main income-replacement disability benefit scheme. Individuals who claim IIDB remain eligible to claim other income-replacement benefits, and the value of payments is based on the degree of disablement. For relatively short-term sickness absence, employers are obliged to pay a minimum allowance, known as Statutory Sick Pay, for the first 28 weeks of sickness absence. For simplicity, we use the term "disability benefits" in this chapter to refer to the main income-replacement disability benefit schemes in the UK.

The first disability benefit scheme, Invalidity Benefit (IvB), was introduced in the UK in 1971. Individuals on IvB also received the earnings-related Additional Pension and an age-related addition that was payable at higher rates for people disabled at younger ages (B. Bell & Smith, 2004). The following two and a half decades saw a rapid escalation in the number of people claiming this benefit, from 250,000 in 1978 to 2.5 million in 1995 (Figure 15.1). Similar increases in disability benefit recipients also occurred in many other OECD countries (OECD, 2010).

To understand subsequent reforms, we first explore the reasons for the large pre-1995 rise in claimant numbers. A number of potential explanations have been put forward. First, the obvious explanation would be that the rise reflected an increase in the number of people with physical and mental impairments. Some commentaries have rejected this explanation, pointing out that population health has improved over this time with increased life expectancy (McVicar, 2008). Some descriptive studies, however, report that the number of people reporting disability did increase substantially (B. Bell & Smith, 2004; Faggio & Nickell, 2005). As can been seen in Figure 15.2, the prevalence of people reporting that they had a work-limiting disability increased by around 50% between 1984 and 1996 and has remained fairly

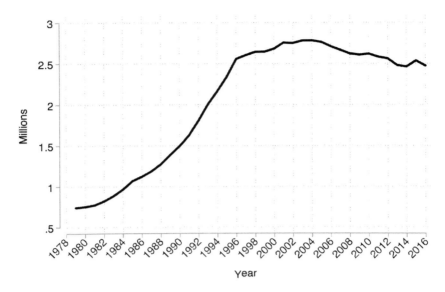

Figure 15.1 Number of people receiving main earnings-replacement disability benefits, 1978 to 2016.

constant since then. Other surveys produce higher estimates, suggesting that the prevalence of reported disability in the working-age population doubled during this time (Burchardt, 2000). The relationship, however, between self-reported disability and the number of people claiming disability benefits is complex. Although it is possible that increased disability led to an increase in people claiming benefits, several authors suggest that self-reported measures may be biased, as people receiving disability benefits may exaggerate impairments to "justify" their benefit receipt (Benítez-Silva, Buchinsky, Man Chan, Cheidvasser, & Rust, 2004; Kreider, 1999). It is also possible that there was increased clinical recognition of certain conditions, such as musculoskeletal and mental health conditions, between 1984 and 1996. This increase in diagnosis could have led to an increasing number of people being defined as disabled and accessing disability benefits.

Most of the literature explaining the increase in disability benefit claimants in the US has concluded that economic conditions played a more important role than health-related factors (McVicar, 2008); however, the situation in the UK is less clear. The 1980s and 1990s in the UK were periods of economic volatility, including two recessions with two peaks of high unemployment. Disney and Webb (1991) found that increases in unemployment were associated with increases in disability benefit receipt, although the levels of receipt did not decline again when unemployment fell (Disney & Webb, 1991). The increases in unemployment and increases in disability benefit receipt during this time were particularly concentrated

Disability Benefit Receipt in the UK 245

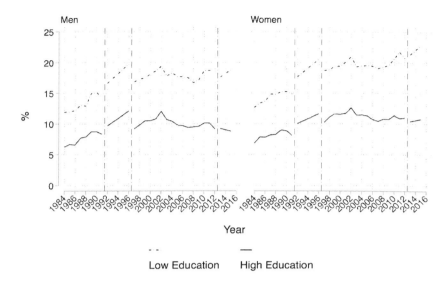

Figure 15.2 Percentage of men and women aged 20 to 59 reporting a health problem that limits the kind of paid work they can do, by educational group.

in areas of the UK that experienced rapid decline in mining and heavy industries in the 1980s and 1990s. These were industries with relatively high levels of poor health, and people in these areas with chronic ill-health and impairments may have been the first to lose their jobs and the least likely to be rehired (Beatty, Fothergill, & Macmillan, 2000). As we can see in Figure 15.3, the disability/employment gap (between the employment of disabled people and the rest of the population) increased during this time, indicating that the employment prospects for disabled people declined relative to the nondisabled population. This decline in the employment prospects of disabled people could also have reflected changes in the types of jobs available in the labor market. Analysis of the British Household Panel Survey found that people in occupations characterized by low control were more likely to exit employment onto disability benefits. Therefore, the increase in the prevalence of low-control jobs could, in part, explain the rise in disability benefit receipt (Baumberg, 2014).

Although there is substantial evidence that these economic trends contributed to the increase in the number of people claiming disability benefits, the mechanisms producing this effect remain unclear (McVicar, 2008). It could be that adverse economic conditions caused an increase in the prevalence of poor health or that they differentially affected the employment of people with chronic health problems. Another possibility is that people who would otherwise have been employed in better economic times tended to take up disability benefits rather than unemployment benefits.

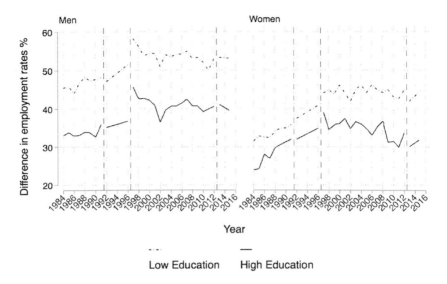

Figure 15.3 Trends in the disability/employment gap.

Many studies, particularly those in the US, have argued that the increase in people claiming disability benefits was due to increases in (a) demand for disability benefits from the loss of jobs in the labor market and (b) "supply" of disability benefits from relaxed eligibility and assessment criteria and increased income-replacement rates (the benefit amount relative to average wages) (McVicar, 2008). A systematic review of studies from five OECD countries (UK, Canada, Denmark, Sweden, and Norway) found that changes in eligibility and assessment criteria for disability benefits tended to have little effect on the employment of disabled people, while increased replacement rates did have a small negative effect on employment (Barr et al., 2010). In contrast to the US, however, disability benefits amounts in the UK declined from around 25% of average wages in the 1970s to 15% in 1995 (Banks, Emmerson, & Tetlow, 2014). Therefore, this decline itself is unlikely to explain the rise in disability benefits (McVicar, 2008). Others have argued, however, that the higher amount paid in disability benefits relative to unemployment benefits and the increased restrictions and conditions applied to unemployment benefits in the 1980s (McVicar, 2008), along with the relaxation of assessment criteria for disability benefits (B. Bell & Smith, 2004), may have contributed to more people claiming disability benefits.

It is therefore likely that the increase in people claiming disability benefits in the UK reflects the decline in jobs in areas of heavy industry. This may have led to an increase in health problems in these areas. Changes in the labor market may have further reduced the chances that people with chronic health problems returned to and stayed at work. Disability benefits provided

Disability Benefit Receipt in the UK   247

a relatively accessible source of income for the increasing numbers of people out of work with health problems.

Most studies of the increase in benefit claimants have assumed that this was a policy failure, suggesting that it excluded people from the labor market. Another interpretation is that it reflected improved social-protection coverage for an expanding group of disabled people at high risk of poverty. During the 1980s and early 1990s, there was a large increase in income inequalities and poverty in the UK across most population groups. Between 1985 and 1996, however, although poverty increased among disabled people, this increase was lower than among nondisabled people. The percentage of disabled people in the bottom fifth of the income distribution also fell substantially (Burchardt, 2000). It is possible that the expansion of disability benefits during this time may have partially mitigated the increased poverty risk among disabled people.

The Policy Response

Many OECD governments have become concerned about the rising number of people receiving disability benefits and have sought to develop policies

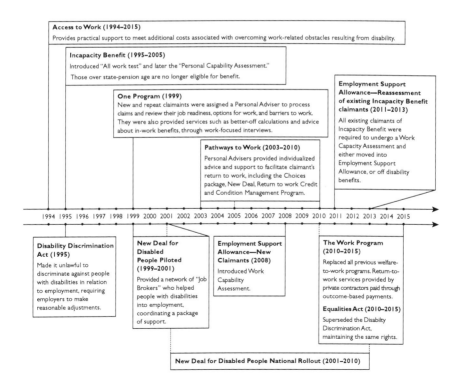

Figure 15.4 Policy changes regarding UK earnings-replacement benefits for disabled people and welfare-to-work programs, 1994 to 2016.

to enable more people to enter and stay in employment (Organisation for Economic Co-operation and Development, 2003). In the UK, the policy response has largely conceptualized the issue as an employment rather than a disability problem. Policies have focused on reducing disincentives to work by reducing income-replacement amounts and access to disability benefits, while improving the employability and job-search behavior of disabled people. See Figure 15.4 for a summary of policy changes over time.

Changes to the Benefit System

In 1995, IvB was replaced with a new benefit called the Incapacity Benefit (IB). While a claimant's eligibility for IvB had been assessed based on information provided by the claimant's family doctor about whether they could undertake their usual work, eligibility for the new IB was determined through an All Work Test carried out by a government-approved doctor, who assessed the claimant's ability to carry out *any* work (Border, 2012). IB was paid only to those under the state pension age (65 for men and 60 for women at the time) and the earnings-related component was removed. In 2000, the disability-assessment process was further tightened, and in 2001 the generosity of the benefit was further reduced (Banks, Blundell, Bozio, & Emmerson, 2011).

Although the growth in new disability benefit claims stopped with these reforms, the number of existing claimants remained high. In 2008, further reforms introduced another new disability benefit, Employment and Support Allowance (ESA). ESA replaced IB for all new claimants, while existing claimants continued to receive IB. The main change with the introduction of ESA was a stricter assessment process and greater requirements for benefit claimants to prepare for employment or risk losing their benefits. Eligibility for ESA is assessed through the Work Capability Assessment (WCA), a functional-abilities checklist that uses a point-based system to distinguish three groups of people:

1 Those judged to be fit for work, who are not eligible for ESA.
2 Those who could return to work with further support, who are eligible for ESA but are required to take actions to prepare for work (called the work-related activity group).
3 Those assessed as unable to return to work, who are eligible for ESA but are not obliged to undertake work-related activity (called the support group).

In 2010, the UK government initiated a major program to reassess all 1.5 million existing IB claimants, using the WCA. A private contractor carried out the assessments on behalf of the Department for Work and Pensions. Following reassessment, claimants were either moved off IB if found to be fit for work or, if not, transferred to ESA. Further changes to ESA were introduced in 2012, with the benefit becoming means-tested for those in the work-related activity group for more than one year. In 2017 the ESA's value was cut for new claimants by 30%, from around £100 (US$133) per week to £70 (US$93) per week, reducing it to the level of unemployment benefits (Department for Work and Pensions, 2016a).

Welfare-to-Work Programs

Alongside the above-described changes to the disability benefit system, several welfare-to-work programs have been introduced that have provided job-search assistance, training, and education to support disabled people moving into employment.

In 1999, the One Advisory Service was introduced to integrate employment and benefit services. Claimants of benefits were assigned a personal adviser who would process the benefits claim and assess employability through a work-focused interview. Claimants were required to attend these interviews or risk losing part of their benefits (Clayton et al., 2011).

The New Deal for Disabled People (NDDP) was piloted from 1998 to 2001 and then extended nationally from 2001 to 2010. This voluntary initiative provided Job Brokers who offered various forms of employment support, including vocational advice, individual action plans, job-search support, financial advice, and training opportunities (Clayton et al., 2011).

In 2003, another new program, Pathways to Work (PtW), was introduced to support IB claimants in finding work. The scheme was mandatory for all new IB claimants and included an expanded support package: work-focused interviews, support for managing health conditions, and financial support for those returning to low-paid work. These supports augmented the existing support available through the NDDP. PtW was implemented on a much larger scale than were previous initiatives. Between 2003 and 2010, 1.25 million people received support through this program (Clayton et al., 2011).

In 2011 PtW, NDDP, and all other welfare-to-work programs in the UK were replaced by a new initiative called the Work Programme. The main difference between this program and previous initiatives was that private contractors provided it through a payment-by-results framework. While contractors were free to design programs as they saw fit, the payments they received depended on the number of clients who entered employment (Johnson, 2013).

Disability Rights Legislation and Workplace Accommodations

The Disability Discrimination Act (DDA) was introduced in 1995 to protect the rights of disabled people and prevent discrimination. In 1996 the employment provision was added, making it illegal for employers to treat individuals unfavorably due to disability and requiring employers to make reasonable accommodations to remove potential barriers that an employee may encounter due to their disability. The DDA was superseded in 2010 by the Equality Act, which maintained the same rights but further clarified the definition of disability (UK Government, 2010).

To support employers removing barriers and to support disabled people in employment, the government introduced the Access to Work scheme in 1994. This scheme provides disabled people with financial or practical support to help them overcome barriers to employment. This support includes communication support, aids and equipment, support workers, and travel support (Department for Work and Pensions, 2017a). The effectiveness of this scheme has been limited by low levels of uptake, particularly among the groups most likely to leave employment due to disability (Department for Work and Pensions, 2016b). Uptake is highest among people from higher managerial and professional occupations, public-sector workers, younger individuals, and those with mobility or sensory impairments. Despite mental health disability being the most common reason for claiming income-replacement benefits, there is a significant underrepresentation of such individuals among Access to Work beneficiaries (Clayton et al., 2012).

The Consequences of the Policy Response

This section focuses on the employment, poverty, and health consequences of the policies discussed in the previous section.

The Effect of Policy Changes on Disability Benefit-Claimant Numbers and the Employment of Disabled People

The increasing trend in the number of people receiving out-of-work disability benefits leveled off after 1995 (see Figure 15.1), and at the same time so did the disability/employment gap (see Figure 15.3). There is some evidence that the disability benefit reforms in 1995 contributed to both the change in the trend in disability benefits and the change in the trend in the employment prospects of disabled people at that time (B. Bell & Smith, 2004; Faggio & Nickell, 2005). This was also the year, however, that the UK economy entered a period of stable economic growth and rising general employment, which probably also contributed to the lower number of disability benefit claimants.

Since 2003, the number of claimants has slightly declined (around 12% between 2003 and 2016). The disability/employment gap, as measured by the Labour Force Survey, has also narrowed slightly—but largely just for people with more education (see Figure 15.3). Other surveys, including the General Household Survey and the Health Survey for England indicate, however, that the disability/employment gap widened slightly during this time (Baumberg, Jones, & Wass, 2015). It is not easy to disentangle any effect of policy reforms since 2003 from broader labor-market trends. However, given that one would expect reforms to disability benefits to have a greater impact on low-educated groups, because of the higher proportion of these people on disability benefits (Banks et al., 2015), the fact that the disability/employment gap has not changed for low-educated groups since 2003 (see Figure 15.3) does not provide strong evidence for an employment effect from the reforms.

One study investigating the impact of the eligibility reassessment between 2011 and 2013 of 1.5 million long-term claimants for disability benefits concluded that the reassessment had not led to an increase in employment for disabled people but, instead, had probably just moved some, particularly people with mental health problems, off disability benefits and onto unemployment benefits (Barr, Taylor-Robinson, Stuckler, Loopstra, Reeves, Wickham, et al., 2015). Similarly, another systematic review found that tightening the eligibility criteria for disability benefits tended to shift people onto other out-of-work benefit schemes rather than into employment (Barr et al., 2010).

Evaluations of the welfare-to-work interventions implemented since 1995 provide some limited evidence that these interventions, especially NDPP and PtW, may have helped some participants back into work (Clayton et al., 2011). These programs, however, tended to focus on disabled people who were closest to the labor market, and it is not clear how effective they were for people with more complex problems. The payment-by-results model of the Work Programme seems to have exacerbated this focus, incentivizing providers to pick participants who were most likely to return to work at the expense of individuals most in need of support, to maximize success and thus funding (Johnson, 2013).

The reforms to the disability benefit system and related welfare-to-work programs seem to have only had, at most, a limited impact on the employment of disabled people. This raises the question about the effects of other policies aimed at influencing employers and the work environment. Studies investigating the introduction of antidiscrimination legislation have found no significant impact on employment for disabled people and that such legislation was associated with worsening employment opportunities among certain groups (D. Bell & Heitmueller, 2009; Pope & Bambra, 2005). Similar results have been found in other countries (Acemoglu & Angrist, 2001). Although there is generally positive evidence internationally for the impact of workplace accommodations, in the UK there has been less emphasis on policies to reduce workplace barriers to the employment of disabled people and greater focus on the individuals themselves.

The Effect of Welfare Reforms on Poverty and Health

As noted above, the primary objective of disability benefits is to provide social protection to people who cannot work due to disability. Analysis of the impact of these welfare reforms, therefore, needs to assess their impact on poverty and welfare as well as on employment. Although the number of people receiving disability benefits has fallen slightly since 1996, expenditure on these benefits has fallen more (Banks et al., 2015). This is largely because the average generosity of benefits has declined, with an increasing proportion of claimants facing means testing. The current value of disability benefits in the UK is well below the level estimated to be required for healthy living, and proposed reforms are due to further reduce their value (Department for Work and Pensions, 2016a; Marmot, 2010).

Therefore, there has potentially been a reduction in both the coverage and adequacy of the main income-replacement disability benefit scheme. To our knowledge, there are no empirical investigations into the impact of UK welfare reforms on poverty among disabled people. Figure 15.5 shows the trend in poverty of disabled and nondisabled people out of work between 1994 and 2014. At the beginning of this period, disabled people out of work were less likely to be poor than nondisabled people out of work, potentially reflecting the protective effect of disability benefits. It should be noted, however, that the calculations of poverty in Figure 15.5 do not include the extra costs incurred by disabled people. Poverty among disabled people out of work has, however, been increasing rapidly, while it has remained constant for nondisabled people out of work. This suggests that, even if the reforms of recent years have increased the employment of disabled people,

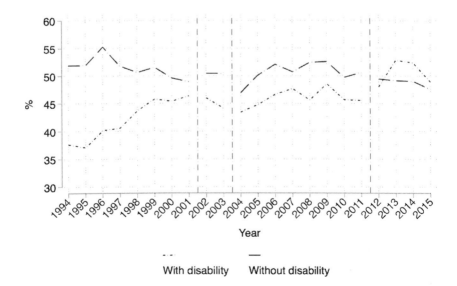

Figure 15.5 Trends in poverty among disabled and nondisabled people out of work, aged 20 to 59.

they may have also increased poverty risk among disabled people who have remained out of employment.

In recent years, there have also been increasing reports that welfare reforms have negatively impacted population health, particularly mental health. Several anecdotal reports and surveys describe individuals who rely on the disability benefit system experiencing deterioration in their mental health (Iacobucci, 2014). A study investigating the process of reassessing eligibility of long-term disability claimants found that reassessment was associated with an increase in suicides, self-reported mental illness, and prescriptions for antidepressants (Barr, Taylor-Robinson, Stuckler, Loopstra, Reeves, & Whitehead, 2015).

Discussion and Conclusion

The analysis outlined above shows that, in the UK during the 1980s and 1990s, there was a large increase in people reporting disabilities and a decline in their employment prospects. This coincided with a large increase in people receiving income-replacement disability benefits. After 1995, this trend leveled off, and there has been a small decline in the number of claimants since 2003. The disability/employment gap has narrowed slightly, but this has largely been just for disabled people with higher levels of education. Although the 1995 reforms may have helped prevent the continued rise in disability benefits and had positive employment effects, the policies implemented since then appear to have had little or no impact on the employment of disabled people. There has, however, been an increase in poverty among disabled people out of work since 1996 and evidence that recent reforms to disability benefits have adversely affected mental health, potentially increasing impairment.

It is clear that current reforms to the disability benefit and employment systems in the UK are not achieving the objectives of either improving the employment prospects of disabled people or preventing poverty among disabled people who are out of work. It is likely that achieving both of these objectives will require further changes to the disability benefit system and the employment support that is provided for disabled people.

Improving the employment prospects of disabled people and preventing poverty will both require a number of changes in approach. First, eligibility for disability benefits will need to realistically reflect the opportunity that different groups of disabled people have of actually entering employment. Debates about the nature of disability over a number of decades have recognized that it is not simply a set of objectively measured impairments, but depends on the way society is organized and the restrictions this places on disabled people (Baumberg, Warren, Garthwaite, & Bambra, 2015). Whether a given level of impairment results in disability will depend on a number of factors unrelated to impairment, including workplace conditions, education and skills, and the local labor market. The UK is relatively unusual in not taking into account these social factors when assessing eligibility for disability benefits. A fairer approach would be to develop a real-world assessment that considers functional impairments alongside social factors that influence ability to work (Baumberg et al., 2015). There are international examples of such assessments, such as in the Netherlands, Sweden, Denmark, Canada, and the USA. In Denmark, for example, the assessment is carried out by a social worker and accounts for issues other than health, such as skills, experience, interests, and job preferences. All the examples have administrative problems; however, they provide evidence that real-world assessment is achievable (Baumberg et al., 2015).

Second, disability benefits will need to be provided at a level that can prevent poverty among disabled people out of work. Reviewing the value of disability benefits may help ensure that they provide a decent standard of living. Disability benefits can be compared with national poverty lines, average household consumption, average household income, national minimum income, or other objective measures of the minimum standards for healthy living. Disability benefits also need to be properly indexed to inflation to ensure their value does not erode over time. The adequacy of disability benefits should take into account the cost of healthcare, housing, education, and social services and the extent to which these costs are subsidized. Additional cash benefits and/or services should also be provided to cover the extra costs of living with impairments (Saunders, Barr, McHale, & Hamelmann, 2017).

Third, evidence-based employment support will need to target employers as well as disabled people. There is growing evidence indicating the components of employment support that are likely to improve employment of disabled people. Multicomponent disability-management programs that (a) include workplace accommodations (Clayton et al., 2012); (b) address health-related barriers to employment alongside vocational training; and (c) are coordinated between employers, health specialists, psychologists, social insurance case-workers, and other professionals, are likely to be effective (Franche et al., 2005; Hillage et al., 2008). Earlier intervention to prevent loss of employment and promote return to work is likely to be more effective than support that occurs later (Black & Frost, 2011). At present, the available evidence has not been sufficiently implemented in the UK's main employment-support programs. The support that is available often comes too late, does not include all the components outlined above, and is not coordinated between the main actors involved.

Effective reform of the UK's employment and disability system will need to focus on the dual objectives of improving the employment prospects of disabled people and preventing poverty among disabled people who are out of work. Effective reform will also require establishing fairer real-world disability assessments, ensuring adequate benefit levels, and implementing evidence-based approaches to support disabled people moving into employment.

Note

1 Income-replacement disability benefits in the UK are paid to people of working age who are assessed as unable to work due to disability. The purpose of the benefit is to provide income to disabled people who are not able to receive income through employment.

References

Acemoglu, D., & Angrist, J. D. (2001). Consequences of employment protection? The case of the Americans with Disabilities Act. *Journal of Political Economy*, *109*(5), 915–957.

Banks, J., Blundell, R., Bozio, A., & Emmerson, C. (2011). *Disability, health and retirement in the United Kingdom*. Cambridge, MA: National Bureau of Economic Research. Retrieved from www.nber.org/papers/w17049

Banks, J., Blundell, R., & Emmerson, C. (2015). Disability benefit receipt and reform: Reconciling trends in the United Kingdom. *Journal of Economic Perspectives*, *29*(2), 173–90. doi:10.1257/jep.29.2.173

Banks, J., Emmerson, C., & Tetlow, G. C. (2014). *Effect of pensions and disability benefits on retirement in the UK*. Cambridge, MA: National Bureau of Economic Research. Retrieved from www.nber.org/papers/w19907

Barr, B., Clayton, S., Whitehead, M., Thielen, K., Burström, B., Nylén, L., & Dahl, E. (2010). To what extent have relaxed eligibility requirements and increased generosity of disability benefits acted as disincentives for employment? A systematic review of evidence from countries with well-developed welfare systems. *Journal of Epidemiology & Community Health*, *64*(12), 1106–1114. doi:10.1136/jech.2010.111401

Barr, B., Taylor-Robinson, D., Stuckler, D., Loopstra, R., Reeves, A., & Whitehead, M. (2015). "First, do no harm": Are disability assessments associated with adverse trends in mental health? A longitudinal ecological study. *Journal of Epidemiology & Community Health*, *70*(4), 339. doi:10.1136/jech-2015-206209

Barr, B., Taylor-Robinson, D., Stuckler, D., Loopstra, R., Reeves, A., Wickham, S., & Whitehead, M. (2015). Fit-for-work or fit-for-unemployment? Does the reassessment of disability benefit claimants using a tougher work capability assessment help people into work? *Journal of Epidemiology & Community Health*, *70*(5), 452. doi:10.1136/jech-2015-206333

Baumberg, B. (2014). Fit-for-Work—Or work fit for disabled people? The role of changing job demands and control in incapacity claims. *Journal of Social Policy*, *43*(2), 289–310. doi:10.1017/S0047279413000810

Baumberg, B., Jones, M., & Wass, V. (2015). Disability prevalence and disability-related employment gaps in the UK 1998–2012: Different trends in different surveys? *Social Science & Medicine*, *141*, 72–81. doi:10.1016/j.socscimed.2015.07.012

Baumberg, B., Warren, J., Garthwaite, K., & Bambra, C. (2015). *Rethinking the Work Capability Assessment*. London, UK: Demos. Retrieved from www.demos.co.uk/project/rethinking-the-work-capability-assessment/

Beatty, C., Fothergill, S., & Macmillan, R. (2000). A theory of employment, unemployment and sickness. *Regional Studies*, *34*(7), 617–630. doi:10.1080/00343400050178429

Bell, B., & Smith, B. (2004). *Health, disability insurance and labour force participation*. London, UK: Bank of England. Retrieved from http://papers.ssrn.com/sol3/papers.cfm?abstract_id=641161

Bell, D., & Heitmueller, A. (2009). The Disability Discrimination Act in the UK: Helping or hindering employment among the disabled? *Journal of Health Economics*, 28(2), 465–480. doi:10.1016/j.jhealeco.2008.10.006

Benítez-Silva, H., Buchinsky, M., Man Chan, H., Cheidvasser, S., & Rust, J. (2004). How large is the bias in self-reported disability? *Journal of Applied Econometrics*, 19(6), 649–670. doi:10.1002/jae.797

Black, C., & Frost, D. (2011). *Health at work—An independent review of sickness absence in Great Britain*. London, UK: Department for Work and Pensions. Retrieved from www.gov.uk/government/publications/review-of-the-sickness-absence-system-in-great-britain

Border, P. (2012). *Assessing capacity for work*. London, UK: Parliamentary Office of Science and Technology. Retrieved from http://researchbriefings.parliament.uk/ResearchBriefing/Summary/POST-PN-413

Burchardt, T. (2000). *Enduring economic exclusion: Disabled people income and work*. York, UK: Joseph Rowntree Foundation. Retrieved from www.jrf.org.uk/report/enduring-economic-exclusion-disabled-people-income-and-work

Clayton, S., Bambra, C., Gosling, R., Povall, S., Misso, K., & Whitehead, M. (2011). Assembling the evidence jigsaw: Insights from a systematic review of UK studies of individual-focused return to work initiatives for disabled and long-term ill people. *BMC Public Health*, 11(1), 170. doi:10.1186/1471-2458-11-170

Clayton, S., Barr, B., Nylen, L., Burström, B., Thielen, K., Diderichsen, F., . . . Whitehead, M. (2012). Effectiveness of return-to-work interventions for disabled people: A systematic review of government initiatives focused on changing the behaviour of employers. *The European Journal of Public Health*, 22(3), 434–439. doi:10.1093/eurpub/ckr101

Department for Work and Pensions. (2016a). *Improving lives: The work, health and disability green paper*. Retrieved from www.gov.uk/government/consultations/work-health-and-disability-improving-lives

Department for Work and Pensions. (2016b, December 21). *Access to Work: Statistics on recipients*. Retrieved September 7, 2017, from www.gov.uk/government/collections/access-to-work-statistics-on-recipients--2

Department for Work and Pensions. (2017a, February 28). *Access to Work: Factsheet for customers*. Retrieved September 5, 2017, from www.gov.uk/government/publications/access-to-work-factsheet/access-to-work-factsheet-for-customers

Department for Work and Pensions. (2017b, March 30). *Industrial Injuries Disablement Benefits: Technical guidance*. Retrieved June 26, 2017, from www.gov.uk/government/publications/industrial-injuries-disablement-benefits-technical-guidance/industrial-injuries-disablement-benefits-technical-guidance

Disney, R., & Webb, S. (1991). Why are there so many long term sick in Britain? *The Economic Journal*, 101(405), 252–262. doi:10.2307/2233816

Eurostat. (2017). *GDP at regional level: Statistics explained*. Retrieved September 15, 2017, from http://ec.europa.eu/eurostat/statistics-explained/index.php/GDP_at_regional_level

Faggio, G., & Nickell, S. (2005). *Inactivity among prime age men in the UK*. London, UK: Centre for Economic Performance. Retrieved from http://eprints.lse.ac.uk/19912/

Franche, R.-L., Cullen, K., Clarke, J., Irvin, E., Sinclair, S., Frank, J., & Institute for Work & Health (IWH) Workplace-Based RTW Intervention Literature Review Research Team. (2005). Workplace-based return-to-work interventions: A systematic review of the quantitative literature. *Journal of Occupational Rehabilitation*, 15(4), 607–631. doi:10.1007/s10926-005-8038-8

Hillage, J., Rick, J., Pilgrim, H., Jagger, N., Carroll, C., & Booth, A. (2008). *Review of the effectiveness & cost effectiveness of interventions, strategies, programmes & policies to reduce the number of employees who move from short-term to long-term sickness absence & to help employees on long-term sickness absence return to work*. Brighton, UK: Institute for Employment Studies. Retrieved from www.employment-studies.co.uk/resource/review-effectiveness-cost-effectiveness-interventions-strategies-programmes-policies-reduce

Iacobucci, G. (2014). GPs' workload climbs as government austerity agenda bites. *BMJ*, 349. doi:10.1136/bmj.g4300

Johnson, R. (2013). The Work Programme's only success is at "creaming and parking." *The Guardian*. Retrieved from www.theguardian.com/commentisfree/2013/feb/20/work-programme-success-creaming-parking

Kreider, B. (1999). Latent work disability and reporting bias. *The Journal of Human Resources*, 34(4), 734–769. doi:10.2307/146415

Marmot, M. (2010). *Fair society, healthy lives: The Marmot review*. London, UK: University College London. Retrieved from www.parliament.uk/documents/fair-society-healthy-lives-full-report.pdf

McVicar, D. (2008). Why have UK disability benefit rolls grown so much? *Journal of Economic Surveys*, 22(1), 114–139. doi:10.1111/j.1467-6419.2007.00522.x

Office for National Statistics. (2017). Overview of the UK population. Retrieved September 7, 2017, from www.ons.gov.uk/peoplepopulationandcommunity/populationandmigration/populationestimates/articles/overviewoftheukpopulation/july2017

Organisation for Economic Co-operation and Development. (2003). *Transforming disability into ability policies to promote work and income security for disabled people*. Paris, France: OECD. Retrieved from www.oecd.org/els/emp/transformingdisabilityintoability.htm

Organisation for Economic Co-operation and Development. (2010). *Sickness, disability and work: Breaking the barriers*. Paris, France: OECD. Retrieved from www.oecd-ilibrary.org/content/book/9789264088856-en

Pope, D., & Bambra, C. (2005). Has the Disability Discrimination Act closed the employment gap? *Disability and Rehabilitation*, 27(20), 1261–1266. doi:10.1080/09638280500075626

Saunders, M., Barr, B., McHale, B., & Hamelmann, C. (2017). *Key policies for addressing the social determinants of health and health inequities*. World Health Organization Health Evidence Network Synthesis Report, 52. Copenhagen, Denmark: WHO Regional Office for Europe.

UK Government. (2010). *Definition of disability under the Equality Act 2010*. Retrieved April 18, 2017, from www.gov.uk/definition-of-disability-under-equality-act-2010

Part 4

Challenges and Opportunities for Work Disability Policy

Chapter 16

Science, Politics, and Values in Work Disability Policy
A Reflection on Trends and the Way Forward

Ellen MacEachen and Kerstin Ekberg

Work disability policy is a complex arena. It draws together policies and programs geared to people who are injured, ill or impaired (either temporarily or permanently), in order to foster engagement in the labor force. At stake is how the state can best support work-disabled people by providing a mix of employment services and benefits for unemployment, along with sickness and disability absences from work. Questions arise about when support is needed, how much, for whom, and for how long.

The social, economic, and historical contexts of different countries can drive how problems are seen and what solutions seem possible. A political reality is that policies are driven by social contracts, which are social expectations and tolerance within a society that help explain and justify its legal, political, and economic structures (Lessnoff, 1990; Paz-Fuchs, 2011), and so policies are inherently value-laden. As noted by Deborah Stone, "all disability insurance systems are about figuring out who deserves society's help" (Van Ostaijen & Jhagroe, 2015, p. 129). Embedded within policies are assumptions about the targets of policy (e.g., that groups of people are worthy or unworthy of resources (Altreiter & Leibetseder, 2015)) and about the motivations and behavior of benefit claimants (Springer, Haas, & Porowski, 2011). A task for policy analysis is to expose and disentangle value assumptions embedded in policy.

This volume focuses on work disability policy in the context of the work-activation agenda that began in the 1990s, as elaborated by the Organisation for Economic Co-operation and Development's (OECD) series on sickness, disability, and work OECD, 2010). In these and related documents, activation policies are described as tools that provide support and incentives for people to search for and find jobs that lead to self-sufficiency and independence from public-support benefits (OECD, 2013). Activation documents use the language of "mutual obligations," meaning that state supports, such as disability- and income-support benefits, are "conditional upon people's efforts to regain self-sufficiency" (OECD 2013, p. 8). The activation agenda has been controversial. Although OECD documents celebrate activation as contributing to greater social integration for people with work disabilities, some see activation as the state retreating and abandoning support for vulnerable populations (Raffass, 2017). Ultimately, considerations such as rising benefit costs can drive activation policies (Belin, Dupont, Oulès, Kuipers, & Fries-Tersch, 2016; OECD, 2010).

All of the countries addressed in this book adhere to activation to some degree in their health and disability policies, and most have had many years to develop and fine-tune these policies to create the desired activation effects. In different ways, these countries have all been moving toward policies that promote early return to work and buttress labor-market reintegration.

An important context for consideration of values in work disability policy is how work disability policy plays out in cause-based and comprehensive welfare systems. Although few systems are completely one or the other, a key distinction is that, in comprehensive systems, illness and disability benefits are paid from general tax revenues while, in cause-based systems, benefits (such as for illness and accidents related to work), are paid directly or indirectly by employers (Bonoli, 1997). These distinctions influence the implementation of work disability and activation policies, as they shape the types of pressures, including financial incentives, applied to employers and workers in relation to the use of benefits and implementation of work-reintegration programs. The distinction between cause-based and comprehensive systems has been overlooked in OECD analyses; for instance, they did not include workers' compensation programs in cause-based systems, despite their very significant costs and relationship to work disability (Lippel, Chapter 4, this volume).

This final chapter synthesizes the others in this volume. We dig at the values and trends in work disability policies, including workers' compensation policies, as they are described in the 13 countries across North America, Europe, Australasia, and China addressed in this volume. First we review two work-activation strategies common across jurisdictions, tightening the inflow of benefit recipients and facilitating employment outflow. Then we turn to particular activation strategies: introduction of part-time-leave benefits, timing of early return to work, duration of benefits, and vocational rehabilitation and work reintegration. We then identify new roles and practices that have arisen in the context of activation-oriented work disability policies. These are changes to the role and influence of employers and healthcare providers, and attempts within jurisdictions to coordinate disjointed work disability programs. The chapter concludes with a reflection on value assumptions embedded in policy, key gaps in work disability policy, and the way forward.

Tightening the Inflow of Benefit Recipients and Enhancing Job Readiness

An important backdrop to the activation agenda is the rising cost of social security benefits across advanced economies, viewed by some analysts as unsustainable (Burkhauser & Daly, 2012; OECD, 2010), together with concerns about the impact on these costs of an aging workforce (Belin, Dupont, Oulès, & Kuipers, 2016). To tackle this problem, a common policy approach across jurisdictions has been to reduce the inflow of people onto benefits and facilitate their outflow to employment by enhancing supports for vocational rehabilitation and job placement.

Restricting access to benefits has been a key strategy used to reduce the inflow of disability-benefit claimants (Beatty & Fothergill, 2015; Gais & Weaver, 2002). For instance, since the 1990s, American states have introduced stricter workers' compensation eligibility criteria, including more stringent time limits for securing information, and have also cut benefit levels (Dembe, Chapter 3, this volume; Speiler & Butler, 2012;). Stricter eligibility criteria were also introduced in the UK, beginning in 1995, to reduce amounts paid for benefits (Barr & McHale, Chapter 15, this volume), and the same year in New Zealand (Duncan, Chapter 6, this volume). Sweden also restricted disability-benefit eligibility in 2006 and reduced the duration of sick leave (Ståhl & Seing, Chapter 8, this volume). In Germany, the maximum duration of unemployment benefits was reduced to one year in 2005 (Welti, Chapter 11, this volume). Embedded in this tightening eligibility for income-support benefits is an assumption that high claim rates are, at least in part, due to some people being attracted to receiving benefits but not really needing them.

In an interesting countertrend, there may be some broadening of conditions eligible for disability benefits coverage, specifically mental health conditions. Although these conditions have surpassed musculoskeletal conditions as the leading reason for work disability pensions in many jurisdictions (MacEachen et al., 2017), recognition of mental illness as a work-related injury has been patchy. In the US, there is considerable variation at the state level in workers' compensation coverage of psychological injuries (Wise, 2016). Workers' compensation systems in Australia recognize mental-health impairment as an eligible condition for benefits but the New Zealand accident insurance fund does not (Duncan, Chapter 6, this volume). In Canada, work-related mental health has been increasingly recognized by workers' compensation boards. The Quebec workers' compensation system recognized psychosocial hazards and injury in 2000 (Lippel, Vézina, & Cox, 2011). The Ontario workers' compensation system recognized chronic mental stress as compensable in 2018 (Workplace Safety and Insurance Board (WSIB), 2017), following a tribunal ruling that non-recognition of work-related chronic stress infringed on workers' rights to equality, as guaranteed by the Canadian Charter of Rights and Freedoms (Workplace Safety and Insurance Appeals Tribunal (WSIAT), 2014).

Policy changes to reduce the inflow of disability-benefit claimants have been increasingly accompanied by efforts to increase the outflow of people to the labor force, in the form of state support to help people develop skills or find jobs. For instance, the UK's welfare-to-work programs began providing job-search assistance, training, and education in the 1990s (Bambra, Whitehead, & Hamilton, 2005). Such activation-oriented policies draw attention to the role of claimants and align with the OECD's "mutual obligations" model (OECD, 2013), which emphasizes claimants' obligation to seek and accept employment. A challenge with tightening claimant inflows and the duration of benefits, and the assumption that these approaches nudge people into employment, is that we know little about receptivity of the labor market or the quality of jobs into which people are nudged. In the OECD's (2013) report, *Activation Strategies for Stronger and More Inclusive Labour Markets in G20 Countries*, the topic of job quality is almost absent. The report only briefly mentions a "division between standard and nonstandard forms of employment" and a "related trend toward income inequality in many countries" (p. 12). Labor-market analysts note that activation policies lead many benefit recipients to take low-wage, unstable jobs that do not offer good career prospects or lift them out of poverty (Goldberg & Green, 2009; Martin, 2015; Raffass, 2017). This trend raises the following value and research questions: When workers return to work or re-enter the labor market, is this a return to decent jobs or to insecure, short-term employment? Should workers be required to accept jobs under their skill levels? More needs to be said about whether policies should drive workers toward any job, regardless of quality, or whether, instead, policies should advance decently paid, sustainable employment.

In some jurisdictions, such as New Zealand's accident insurance system (Duncan, Chapter 6, this volume), Sweden's social insurance system (Ståhl & Seing, Chapter 8, this volume), and Ontario's workers' compensation system (MacEachen, Kosny, Ferrier, Lippel et al., 2012), job-search-and-placement policies have been relatively passive. In these jurisdictions, increasing the outflow of beneficiaries to the labor force involves assessing employability in relation to jobs on the labor market, regardless of whether jobs are available. This potential mismatch places responsibility for reintegration solely on individuals.

Although policy makers across jurisdictions have taken similar activation approaches (i.e., tightening benefits inflow and facilitating outflow through skill-building and employment supports), their strategies for implementing work activation policies have varied, driven by the sociolegal conditions and economic contexts for work disability policy in each country. Key strategies observed in the chapters in this volume are the introduction of part-time sick-leave benefits, timing of early return to work, duration of work disability benefits, and the structure of vocational rehabilitation and work reintegration.

Part-Time Sick-Leave Benefits

Across jurisdictions, different approaches underlie the structure of state sick-leave benefits; that is, whether the leave must be an all-or-nothing (full-time) work absence or, instead, part-time with concurrent part-time employment. Part-time sick leave policy is an approach that has been growing across jurisdictions. For instance, Germany introduced part-time sick leave in 2000 (Welti, Chapter 11, this volume), Finland in 2007 (Martimo, Chapter 9, this volume), and Belgium in 2013 (Mairiaux, Chapter 13, this volume).

Behind part- or full-time sick leave approaches are guiding assumptions about accommodation and recovery. Part-time sick leave allows people who are unable to work full-time to work for parts of the day or week. This support allows workers to retain labor-force attachment (Belin, Dupont, Oulès, Kuipers, & Fries-Tersch, 2016). However, other systems, such as the Ontario Disability Support Plan in Canada retain an all-or-nothing approach to work disability leave.[1] This approach may also be guided by a concern that a part-time return-to-work policy could attract more disability claimants at greater cost for the state. However, in Sweden, where part-time sick leave has been in place since 1955, cases of partial sick leave do not differ in the duration of work absence, and fewer part-timers transfer to disability pensions (Försäkringskassan, 2008), both of which lower costs to the state.

Timing of Early Return to Work

Across the jurisdictions covered in this volume, the beginning of official work incapacity and employment-reintegration planning has varied widely. At one extreme, the waiting period during which employers continue to pay the salaries of injured or ill workers before the state-benefits system kicks in is zero days. For instance, in many Canadian provinces, workers' compensation systems pay income-replacement benefits to workers beginning with the first day that they miss work due to work-related injury or illness. In other jurisdictions, state benefits are introduced somewhat later. For instance, in Sweden, employers pays workers' salaries for the first two weeks (Ståhl & Seing, Chapter 8, this volume), and German employers pay for the first six weeks of temporary work incapacity (Welti, Chapter 11, this volume).

These different designs for the timing of the start of work-incapacity benefits prompt different timings for mechanisms to support workers' return to work after illness or injury. A key feature of work disability policy is the notion that early return to work, before full recovery, is physically and mentally rehabilitative for workers (not to mention cost-effective for employers and the state) (MacEachen, Chapter 1, this volume). However, the optimal operationalization of earliness is not clear. Work disability research has shown that early return to work does not necessarily cause harm to workers and, in some cases, reduces recovery time (Gensby et al., 2012; Viikari-Juntura, Kausto, Shiri, Kaila-Kangas, & Takala, 2012). However, there is no evidence that identifies whether employment reintegration is more or less rehabilitative for workers if they return to work one day or two, four, or six weeks after their injury or illness. Nonetheless, there is some evidence that very early returns can harm worker recovery (Lippel, 1999; MacEachen, Kosny, Ferrier, & Chambers, 2010). Jurisdictions where the policy mechanisms to begin return to work begin after some time away, rather than immediately, provide leeway to workers. Embedded in these approaches is time for workers to seek healthcare, and to adjust to and manage their illnesses or impairments before returning to work.

Duration of Work Disability Benefits

Questions can be raised about the period for which employers should be financially responsible for workers when they are work-disabled. Returning to the case of Canadian provinces, the experience-rated premiums that employers pay in cause-based workers' compensation systems impose financial penalties on employers for each day a worker is absent for work-caused illness or injury. The same system also provides rebates to employers with very low worker-absence rates. This approach has prompted perverse employer behaviors, such as suppression of claim reporting (Rappin, Wuellner, & Bonauto, 2016; Shannon & Lowe, 2002) and rushing workers back to work before they are ready. In such cases, very prompt work return is not necessarily incited by employers' attitude that work is rehabilitative (Waddell, Burton, & Aylward, 2008) but, rather, a blunter concern with workers' compensation premium costs and rebates (Lippel, 1999; MacEachen et al., 2010).

At the other extreme is the Netherlands, where employers are responsible for their workers' salary for two years following illness, injury, or impairment. This requirement provides employers with a great deal of control over sickness claims and their management. These employers have strong direct financial incentives to bring their workers back to work, as they must pay their salaries for the long term, whether they work or not. However, unlike the Canadian workers' compensation system, when Dutch workers are on sick leave, their employers' expenses are limited to lost wages and productivity. Employers do not incur the added daily financial penalties in the form of insurance surcharges that are imposed by experience-rated workers' compensation systems. Indeed, as explained by de Rijk (Chapter 14, this volume), Dutch employers accepted this responsibility because they preferred it to the previous system, where premiums had paid for sickness-absence benefits and disability pensions.

Related to the issue of work disability benefits' duration is the question of whether employers and the state should have limited liability for benefit duration and costs. In some jurisdictions, such as Queensland, Australia, some disability-income-support benefits are time- and cost-limited. Workers' compensation benefits paid to workers end after five years or after a maximum amount payable,[2] whichever comes first (WorkCover Queensland, 2018). In other jurisdictions, disability benefits are time-limited but not cost-limited. For instance, in Belgium, workers can receive benefits equal to 60% of capped wages for up to one year (Mairiaux, Chapter 13, this volume), and, in Switzerland, workers can receive a daily allowance for up to two years (Geisen, Chapter 12, this volume). In Ontario, Canada, and also China, there is no time or cost limit[3] to workers' compensation or disability benefits in cases of severe work-limiting permanent impairments. Workers can receive benefits until age 65, when retirement pensions begin (WSIB, 2018a).

Lump-sum payments to workers provide a way of limiting benefit duration entirely, and this is an approach increasingly being used, for instance, in Australia (Safe Work Australia, 2014), China (Shan, Chapter 7, this volume), and the United States (Hunt & Barth, 2010). Lump-sum payments can be attractive to government administrators, as they settle the amounts paid to workers, reduce transactions with them, and often involve a partial or full release of the employer and insurer from further liability for the injuries. However, the benefit of such payments to workers is questionable. Claimants may agree to them without the knowledge or bargaining power to reach a fair settlement (Hunt & Barth, 2010), and temporary financial windfalls may discourage workers from resuming work after injury, thereby creating later financial hardship (Guest & Drummond, 1992).

Placing a cap on the duration or cost of illness and disability benefits requires presumptions about the context and the worker. It may be assumed that an adequate social safety net will catch the worker at the end of the limited benefit-payment period or, where there is no adequate safety net, that people with ongoing illness or injury are undeserving of further state or employer support. These assumptions raise questions about values: How far are the state and employers liable for the conditions that led to the worker's disability? What is owed to the worker? Taking the example of Queensland, Australia, workers who reach the end of their workers' compensation benefits will then be placed into a means-tested social security system that is far less generous than workers' compensation (Grant, Chapter 5, this volume). Likewise, the end of sickness benefits in comprehensive systems can also lead to less generous unemployment or social welfare benefits. However, in most countries there is scarce data on how many people are transferred between benefits or to social welfare from disability benefits.

Vocational Rehabilitation and Return to Work

Since the 1990s, activation-oriented policies have focused on bringing workers back to work as early as possible after sickness or injury. In this context, vocational rehabilitation, which once focused mainly on workers through such programs as improving their training and job readiness, have increasingly broadened to include measures that require the participation of other stakeholders, including employers and physicians. However, the commitment required of these stakeholders varies. For instance, in some jurisdictions such as Switzerland, the social-security insurer helps employers reintegrate sick-listed workers by providing them with support, including professional case management (Geisen, Chapter 12, this volume). In Sweden (Ståhl & Seing, Chapter 8, this volume), reintegration policy requires that employers be active but provides little or no a financial stimulus to prompt their active engagement.

As such, although these policies identify a role for employers in the work reintegration of sick-listed workers, this role is not always strongly reinforced in practice. As well, the obligations of employees can be unclear. In contrast, in Belgium, employers who do not initiate reintegration plans face fines (Mairiaux, Chapter 13, this volume). In cause-based workers' compensation systems, employers also face penalties. They are expected to adapt workplaces and workers' tasks or work hours until workers are fully fit to resume their former duties, and financial sanctions (via experience-rated insurance premiums) are imposed on employers for workers who do not return to work. Although these sanctions prompt many employers to engage in early-return-to-work activities, they have also prompted cost-avoidance behaviors that can harm worker health, as described further in the section below.

In other jurisdictions, reintegration policies and programs draw in a range of stakeholders. In the Netherlands, the law requires that employers, workers, and occupational physicians collaborate. Employers must offer work modifications and opportunities for gradual return to work (de Rijk, Chapter 14, this volume). In Germany, when a worker takes more than six weeks of sick leave in one year, the employer is required to initiate a company reintegration-management plan (Welti, Chapter 11, this volume). In other countries, such as Finland, France, and Belgium, active work reintegration involves workplace visits by occupational physicians (Martimo, Chapter 9, this volume; Fassier, Chapter 10, this volume).

The integration of vocational rehabilitation and return to work within a comprehensive policy framework, as suggested by Belin, Dupont, Oulès, and Kuipers (2016) in their European Agency for Safety and Health at Work report, provides a basis for improved coordination mechanisms for the involved stakeholders. However, activation policies in comprehensive systems often do not address reintegration after the early work return. This can leave workers struggling to manage their limited functionality when they are not fully fit for work. Although return to work after sick leave may require temporary or permanent workplace accommodations to avoid illness or injury relapse, policies in many countries do not cover accommodations, with the possible exception of jurisdictions that allow modified work hours or part-time sick leave. As well, many countries limit the duration of vocational rehabilitation, and work-disability policies often do not cover workers who are temporary employed.

Fairness to Employers

As activation-oriented work-disability policies have developed, the role and responsibilities of employers have also evolved. Interestingly, a new discussion has opened up about fairness to employers in a terrain whose focus was previously on fairness to workers; for example, through ensuring adequate worker support during unemployment, injury or illness. Fairness to employers is mentioned in the chapters in this book on Sweden and Belgium, where the authors note that government proposals to increase employers' financial responsibility for work disability costs were withdrawn following employer protest (Ståhl & Seing, Chapter 8, this volume, Mairiaux, Chapter 13, this volume). As described below, in Canada and New Zealand, fairness to employers is highlighted as a reason for continuing the experience rating of workers' compensation premiums.

Experience rating is designed to hold firms responsible for their employees' accident and illness records, as opposed to each employment sector paying the same insurance premium. At first glance, experience rating appears to enhance employer accountability, as employers are financially penalized for health-related worker absence within their own firms. However, experience rating of workers' compensation premiums, introduced in Canada in the early 1990s, brought with it new problems of unfairness to workers. This is because, when employers have a financial incentive to reduce their costs associated with reported claims, they can play the system to their benefit. This game includes not reporting injuries and requiring that workers return to work before they are ready (MacEachen et al., 2010; MacEachen, Lippel et al., 2012; Mansfield et al., 2012). Indeed, after experience rating was introduced in Canada, new private-sector companies emerged to assist, and even encourage, employers to fight the cost of workers' injury claims, in exchange for representatives' fees (Ison, 2013). These new companies have, in turn, created work for appeals courts, lawyers, and worker representatives.

In Ontario, the Chair of the 2012 Workplace Safety and Insurance Board Funding Review concluded that experience rating posed a "moral crisis" (p. 81) because of harms to workers resulting from perverse financial incentives encouraging employers to not report workers' injury and illness claims (Arthurs, 2012). Upon receipt of this assessment, the workers' compensation board swiftly initiated a second review, which produced a report focused on fairness to employers. This second report noted that any move to adjust experience-rating arrangements must be one that "employers accept as fair and reasonable" and that involves employers "paying their 'fare share' of the costs" (Stanley, 2013, p. 2). This meant that employers should continue to pay only for the worker injury rates that they report as occurring within their firm, rather than a set sector rate.

New Zealand introduced experience rating for work-related accidents and injuries in 1992. It was inserted into the country's no-fault accident compensation scheme (ACC), which previously had not distinguished between accidents and illness caused and not caused by work. As described by Duncan (Chapter 6, this volume), experience rating introduced fault into the ACC. Although experience-rated insurance premiums have well-recognized problems in terms of fairness to workers, New Zealand policy makers' justification for introducing experience rating was to be "fair to the people [employers] who pay levies and tax that support ACC" (Provost, 2013). In addition, since 2000 larger "accredited employers" who meet certain criteria have been allowed to manage their employees' work-related claims in house in return for reduced premiums (Duncan, Chapter 6, this volume; Department of Labour, 2000).

In the Netherlands, employers are wholly experience rated, as they pay directly for their own costs of worker injury and illness. Since 2004, they have been fully responsible for the costs of employee health for two years, regardless of work relatedness. As with New Zealand's accredited employers, this responsibility can be financially advantageous to employers. However, putting responsibility on Dutch employers has not come without its own problems for fairness to workers. Studies have shown that, under these conditions, Dutch employers sometimes avoid hiring workers who may incur health costs, such as those with health conditions or an unhealthy appearance (Koning & Lindeboom, 2015; Oorschot, 2002).

It is ironic that, at the same time as this conversation about employer fairness has entered work-disability policy discussions, employers have been retreating from their traditional role in society as providers of income security and benefits. Trends associated with globalization and flexible markets show that employers increasingly avoid hiring permanent employees (Kalleberg, 2011) and more and more often hire labor through limited-term contracts (Broughton et al., 2016). As such, employers appear to be ambivalent stakeholders in work disability policy. As de Rijk (Chapter 14, this volume) asks: Is a strong role for employers viable as the labor market becomes more diverse and flexible?

Healthcare Gatekeeper Politics

The role of healthcare providers as gatekeepers to sickness and disability benefits has also evolved since activation policies began in the 1990s. Chapters in this volume suggest that healthcare providers are increasingly accountable to employers and government-benefit providers, and less directly accountable to workers, as patients and benefit claimants. With some exceptions, the key gatekeepers have been claimants' family physicians. For instance, in Australia, despite pressure from physiotherapists, only family physicians can provide sick notes (Johnston & Beales, 2016). Exceptions are countries such as Belgium, where social-insurance physicians play this role, and the Netherlands, where occupational physicians are the gatekeepers to state benefit systems.

An interesting trend across work-disability systems is the reduced authority of family physicians to provide access to work-disability benefits. One approach has been to allow only certain healthcare providers aligned with the state or the employer to have the final word on an individual's work capacity and eligibility for benefits. In the UK, this change occurred with the 1995 move to allow only government-approved doctors to assess eligibility for Incapacity Benefit (Barr & McHale, Chapter 15, this volume). In New Zealand, a similar move to stricter medical assessments also came in 1995, with a shift to work incapacity being assessed by government-designated doctors only (Duncan, Chapter 6, this volume).

Another approach that has reduced family physicians' gatekeeper role is broadening the range of healthcare providers who can assess sickness, while leaving the last word on applicants' eligibility for benefits with work-disability-benefits insurers. For instance, in Ontario, Canada, any member of a regulated health profession (e.g., nurses, physiotherapists) can provide sick notes for the purpose of workers' compensation benefits (WSIB, 2018b). In the US, independent medical exams by physicians are typically ordered by insurers (Dembe, Chapter 3, this volume) and, in Canada, workers' compensation authorities increasingly use internal medical consultants to provide illness or injury evidence (Kosny et al., 2016). This evidence from state-contracted and so-called independent physicians is included in workers' claim files, which may also include assessments by family doctors and other health professionals. Insurance case managers, who do not usually meet claimants in person and are not normally medically trained, are then the party to make final decisions about which medical assessments to accept in the process of accepting or denying a worker's claim (Kosny et al., 2016).

With this gatekeeper shift to designated and preferred doctors, and with moving eligibility decision making to insurance case managers, comes a change in assumptions about the role and value of healthcare providers. Whereas physicians were once gatekeepers to social security systems ostensibly based on their competence, diagnostic skills, and the ethical standards of their profession, now the terrain appears to be increasingly political. Indeed, in some work-disability systems, family doctors have been cast as unreliable worker advocates. For instance, in Kosny et al.'s (2016) study of Canadian physicians' role in the return to work of injured and ill workers, physicians were cast by workers' compensation case managers as "advocates" who would do "what the patient wanted," rather than what was medically indicated (p. 11).

With this discursive shift, the focus has turned away from gatekeepers having adequate medical training or diagnostic ability and toward the official alignment of healthcare professionals with employers or the state. This is especially apparent in the case of independent medical examiners, who assess workers' impairment and ability to work without extensive knowledge of the workers, sometimes only via a "paper review" without ever having met workers directly (Kosny, MacEachen, Ferrier, & Chambers, 2011).

The healthcare providers' gatekeeper role becomes particularly contentious in cause-based jurisdictions. In these systems, healthcare providers must not only certify that there is an injury or illness, but they must go a step further to decide whether it is caused by the worker's job. This is a particularly difficult call to make when health conditions are multifactorial or slow in developing, as is the case for back pain or psychological injury. Under such ambiguous conditions, and where the worker's health condition may lead to costs for the employer or the benefits provider, there can be strong pressure on employer- or state-aligned healthcare providers to determine that the condition was not work related (Kilgour, Kosny, McKenzie, & Collie, 2014a; Klienfield, 2009).

Another development in work-activation policies that limit sickness-leave duration is growing tension between family and social-insurance physicians. For instance, Fassier (Chapter 10, this volume) describes strain between treating physicians and social insurance physicians in France, as the latter can override the former's assessment of work ability. As well, both do not trust occupational physicians, who are seen as employer advocates. Likewise, Stratil, Rieger, and Völter-Mahlknecht (2017) note low levels of cooperation and communication between German general practitioners, occupational-health physicians, and rehabilitation physicians, not only because they do not trust each other but also because of a concern that occupational physicians may have conflicts of interest due to their relationship with employers.

Coordination for Activation

A challenge facing work-disability policy in many jurisdictions is how to bridge siloed social-support programs and coordinate agencies that deal with employment, rehabilitation, health, and disability. As noted by Grant (Chapter 5, this volume), transaction costs arise when systems are discontinuous, contradictory, or poorly implemented. The state incurs transaction costs in terms of service duplication, inefficiency, and pull on extra resources such as appeals courts and multiple medical assessments needed to prove eligibility for benefits. The costs to workers are failure to access needed benefits, and mental harm related to frustrating and adversarial encounters with benefit systems (Kilgour, Kosny, McKenzie, & Collie, 2014b).

Extensive cooperation is required between different parties for work disability management (MacEachen, Clarke, Franche, & Irvin, 2006; Ståhl, Svensson, Petersson, & Ekberg, 2010). Within jurisdictions, parties such as sickness-absence officers, social-security-system actors, employers, workers, and different kinds of doctors must share information and collaborate (MacEachen et al., 2006). The various parties must have time to meet and develop trusting interactions, and must share common points of reference (Franche, Baril, Shaw, Nicholas, & Loisel, 2005). Within a country, coordination can become complex when it crosses different levels of services and benefits; for instance, state and federal levels. As well, not all workers may be eligible for the same sickness-absence programs. Programs can differ depending on whether workers are employed in the private sector, public sector, agricultural sector, military, or maritime transport (Grant, Chapter 5, this volume; Shan, Chapter 7, this volume; Dembe, Chapter 3, this volume). In most countries, one jurisdiction cannot require changes in the others or coordinate work disability policy.

A lack of coordination among systems can lead to cost-shifting and downloading of responsibility from one program to another. For instance, when one system, such as workers' compensation, tightens eligibility requirements, this can lead people to apply for benefits under other systems, such as social security (Parolin & Luigjes, 2018; Stapleton, 2013). As well, contradictions arise where claimants may be considered able to work by one authority but in need of full income support by another (Duncan, Chapter 6, this volume). Lippel (Chapter 4, this volume) aptly demonstrates how Canadian workers access different benefits and treatments depending on their provincial location, type of employment, and cause of disability. In the worst case, lack of coordination can lead to workers simply falling through system cracks and not accessing healthcare and income support at all. For instance, workers in China who move from the countryside to the city for work cannot access illness or injury support because they are not officially registered in the urban jurisdiction (Shan, Chapter 7, this volume).

This challenge of coordinating work disability systems to better support activation policies has been the focus of important reforms in some jurisdictions. Australia created a National Disability Insurance Scheme, which replaced the fragmented state and federal disability schemes, in 2016. Germany is another jurisdiction that has made significant efforts to coordinate work disability programs. As early as 1974, it developed a rehabilitation framework that coordinated all agencies dealing with rehabilitation and disability. In 2001, the rehabilitation-coordination framework was renewed, adopting a common definition of disability (Welti, Chapter 11, this volume). This common disability definition is a particularly interesting move. In jurisdictions where each benefit program has its own definition of disability, the differences hamper communication and transition across agencies and create an enormous amount of miscommunication and paperwork for physicians and other parties (Kosny et al., 2011). Germany instituted a further reform in 2016 to create cooperation across stakeholders, and again in 2018 revised its cooperation approach due to stakeholder noncompliance with the previous one (Welti, Chapter 11, this volume). The successive German reforms show that, even when there is strong commitment to legislate and implement work disability coordination and cooperation, solutions are not always simple.

It is worth considering that achieving system coordination is not necessarily an end in itself. That is, coordination is not always positive for all stakeholders. In some cases, although systems may become more integrated, integration may create inequality by assigning greater control to one party over another. Barr and McHale (Chapter 15, this volume) describe how the merger of the UK's unemployment and benefit services submerged disability under the broader reconceptualization of unemployment. They note that the newly dominant focus on unemployment may divert resources needed to address work disability related to mental health, which is now the most common reason for claiming earnings-replacement benefits.

Finland and the Netherlands provide additional examples of coordination that has shifted a greater degree of control to one party. In these countries, coordination has been implemented through employers. In the Netherlands, as described above, worker health is the responsibility of employers for two years from the start of the sickness or injury. This arrangement has given employers a great deal of control over work-disability costs and management, as they employ the occupational physicians who certify work absence and they are also the party to manage workers' rehabilitation plan. In Finland, occupational health services are also provided within work organizations. Employers can arrange these services by employing occupational physicians and other occupational healthcare staff internally or buying the services from a public health center, private medical center, or an association of employers. Occupational physicians bridge the workplace and healthcare systems by collaborating with other healthcare providers, social security, employment, and social-services staff (Martimo, Chapter 9, this volume). The strategy of putting work-disability coordination under the control of employers assumes that employers are fair players. As such, this strategy may work best when labor relations are positive. Where they are not or the labor force is low-skilled and easily replaceable, or where temporary employment contracts dominate, giving employers this degree of control may disadvantage some workers (Seing, MacEachen, Ståhl, & Ekberg, 2015).

In Germany, the Netherlands, and Finland, where work-disability policy coordination has been achieved, an important context is the countries' tradition of tripartite consultation: between government, employers, and labor organizations. Each country has well-organized employer and labor organizations. The Dutch describe their "consultative economy" as characterized by decision and policy making based on discussion, negotiating, and bargaining between employer federations and trade unions (Social and Economic Council, 2015). As de Rijk (Chapter 14, this volume) argues, tripartite consultation creates an environment without policy surprises in which all parties have had their say. In Germany, cooperation frameworks draw together self-governed agencies, trade unions, and employer associations (Welti, Chapter 11, this volume). In Finland, trade unions and employer organizations have traditionally been heavily involved in the evolution of social security (Martimo, Chapter 9, this volume).

These examples of countries where work-disability system coordination occurs raise questions about the quality of organization and exchange that is needed for successful stakeholder coordination. In countries where workers are not well organized, such as the US, where the private-sector unionization rate is only 6.5% (Bureau of Labor Statistics, 2017) and Canada, where it is only 15% (Statistics Canada, 2018), labor representation at a tripartite bargaining table will be inadequate. In any case, as both Dembe (Chapter 3, this volume) and Lippel (Chapter 4, this volume) note, there appears to be no political will to coordinate work disability systems in the US or in Canada. However, a starting point, as Dembe notes, could be the development of a common definition of disability across major social-security programs.

Key Gaps in Work Disability Policy and the Way Forward

In this chapter, we discussed work disability issues and trends raised in the other chapters in this volume. The activation agenda's optimistic goal has been to bring people into the labor force who might otherwise be unemployed or living on disability benefits. Furthermore, this agenda has fostered return-to-work programs that limit sick-leave duration and provide more vocational-rehabilitation and job-support programs. A socially and economically integrated population is a laudable goal, especially in some jurisdictions where individuals are caught in so-called benefit traps that restrict workers' ability to work, even when they are ready and willing to do so (Stapleton, O'Day, Livermore, & Imparto, 2006).

However, with all policy shifts come a variety of consequences. In this chapter, one of our aims was to expose the value assumptions embedded in activation-oriented work disability policies and to note practices that have arisen in conjunction with their implementation. Our synthesis included work disability policies across both comprehensive and cause-based social-security systems, and noted particular tensions resulting from each of these arrangements. We questioned policy assumptions about worker needs and behavior, the responsibility of employers and extent of their roles, the authority and political affiliation of healthcare providers, and the extent of the state's obligation to those who are unable to work due to illness, injury, or impairment. At stake is what is kinds of support people with illness, injury and disability most need, and how political decisions are framed about who deserves society's support. A key question is whether work-disability systems are sufficiently sensitive and coordinated to properly identify and support the needs of people when they are not fully integrated into the labor force.

Across international work disability policies, several issues stand out as upcoming challenges. These are the problems of labor demand, uneven access to benefits and vocational-rehabilitation support, and mental health disability.

Labor Demand

Work-disability policy currently focuses on moving people away from benefits and toward seeking employment by providing vocational training and job coaches. An embedded assumption in activation-oriented work-disability policy is that there is a receptive labour market for people who seek jobs. However, work-disability policies generally do not address the problem of labor demand. As noted by Mairiaux (Chapter 13, this volume), in an environment where there are not enough jobs for all people seeking employment, are activation policies realistic?

Essentially, once the state has reduced claimants' sickness benefits, provided them with vocational training, and coached them to seek work, these claimants may still be unable to secure employment. This is not surprising in open labor markets, where employers may choose to hire able-bodied workers rather than disabled and retrained workers.

Some countries (e.g., France and Germany) have imposed quotas that require employers to hire people formally recognized as significantly disabled, but these quotas focus only on workers with severe impairment. What needs to be addressed within activation strategies is the employment receptivity of people without formal labels such as "significant and permanent disability." This population includes workers who face employment barriers because of social marginalization related to being older, unskilled, disabled, experiencing mental or other chronic illness, or the long-term unemployed. Accordingly, some analysts note that activation policies do not suit all economic conditions and recommend that, when labor demand is not buoyant, eligibility criteria for benefits should be more flexible (Martin, 2015).

Uneven Access to Work Disability Benefits and Services

In a context of growing income inequality within countries (Atkinson, 2015), unequal access to work disability benefits and services becomes a stark issue. When benefits are structured to serve people who have left full-time, permanent employment, then precariously employed workers, such as those who have been able to access only part-time employment or short-term contracts, are rendered particularly vulnerable: they fall to the edges of eligibility for social-welfare supports (International Labour Organization, 2016; Standing, 2011). Furthermore, the growing population of self-employed and freelance workers is not well addressed in many systems, including the growing number working in the so-called sharing economy

(International Labour Organization, 2016; PricewaterhouseCoopers, 2015). Essentially, work disability benefits tend to support people in permanent jobs who become ill or impaired, but they are less available for those who are more marginally employed.

Uneven access to work disability services and benefits for employed workers and nonemployed people (or, in the case of New Zealand, between those disabled by accidents and other causes) is a related problem. In many jurisdictions, people who experience work disability in the course of employment have better access to vocational rehabilitation, and their income-support benefits are often much higher than those for people who are work-disabled but not employed. This is another structure that appears to force a wedge between those who are well-established in the labor market and those who are precariously employed.

Mental-Health Disability

Despite mental disorders being the most common reason for sick leave in most countries (MacEachen et al., 2017), many jurisdictions still do not accept them as a work-related disability, and return-to-work programs generally focus on physical impairments. Excluding mental health from work-related disability may be partly due to requirements for so-called objective biomedical measures and diagnoses in assessing work capacity. Mental health claims are difficult to clinically assess because of the uncertainty of diagnosing them and predicting when someone with a mental illness or psychological injury can return to work (Brijnath et al., 2014). The difficulties establishing clinical criteria may be one reason for policy makers' reluctance to accept mental health disability as a work-related disorder. Nonetheless, this growing problem needs to be addressed, particularly the complexities of reintegrating workers with mental health disorders, including social stigma, chronicity, and variable illness patterns.

Going forward, it is critical for researchers, analysts, and policy makers to attend to the bigger picture of both the politics and the science of work-disability policy. Although scientific evidence is useful for decision making, it can be based on non-naturalistic conditions or exclude relevant sociopolitical conditions. Many examples in this volume show how science and politics together shaped how jurisdictions developed their approaches to work-disability policy. Although costs have undoubtedly spurred many activation-oriented work-disability policies, less often considered is the fundamental issue behind all work-disability approaches: the values that are embedded in these policies and that guide how they are implemented. These values reveal countries' changing social contracts and the willingness of their policy makers and citizens to apply resources in an inclusive and thoughtful way to supporting the engagement of work-disabled people in the labor force.

Notes

1 Benefits are structured to encourage workers not to work. If they do earn income (over $200 in a month), their income support is reduced (www.mcss.gov.on.ca/en/mcss/programs/social/odsp/info_sheets/employment_supports.aspx).
2 www.worksafe.qld.gov.au/laws-and-compliance/workers-compensation-laws/workers-compensation-benefits-including-qote
3 However, most benefit plans, including Ontario's, have a ceiling on weekly insurable earnings.

References

Altreiter, C., & Leibetseder, B. (2015). Constructing inequality: Deserving and undeserving clients in Austrian social assistance offices. *Journal of Social Policy*, *44*(1), 127–145.

Atkinson, A. B. (2015). *Inequality: What can be done?* Boston, MA: Harvard University Press.

Arthurs, H. (2012). *Funding fairness: A report on Ontario's Workplace Safety and Insurance System*. Retrieved from www.wsib.on.ca/cs/groups/public/documents/staticfile/c2li/mdex/~edisp/wsib011358.pdf and www.wsib.on.ca

Bambra, C., Whitehead, M., & Hamilton, V. (2005). Does "welfare-to-work" work? A systematic review of the effectiveness of the UK's welfare-to-work programmes for people with a disability or chronic illness. *Social Science and Medicine*, *60*, 1905–1918.

Beatty, C., & Fothergill, S. (2015). Disability benefits in an age of austerity. *Social Policy & Administration*, *49*(2), 161–181.

Belin, A., Dupont, C., Oulès, L., & Kuipers, Y. (2016). *Safer and healthier work at any age—Final overall analysis report*. Luxembourg, Luxembourg: European Agency for Safety and Health at Work. Retrieved from https://osha.europa.eu/en/tools-and-publications/publications/safer-and-healthier-work-any-age-final-overall-analysis-report-0/view

Belin, A., Dupont, C., Oulès, L., Kuipers, Y., & Fries-Tersch, E. (2016). *Rehabilitation and return to work: Analysis report on EU policies, strategies and programmes*. Bilbao, Spain: European Agency for Safety and Health at Work. Retrieved from https://osha.europa.eu/en/tools-and-publications/publications/rehabilitation-and-return-work-analysis-eu-and-member-state

Bonoli, G. (1997). Classifying welfare states: A two-dimension approach. *Journal of Social Policy*, *26*(3), 351–372.

Brijnath, B., Mazza, D., Singh, N., Kosny, A., Ruseckaite, R., & Colli, A. (2014). Mental health claims management and return to work: Qualitative insights from Melbourne, Australia. *Journal of Occupational Health*, *24*, 766–776.

Broughton, A., Green, M., Rickard, C., Swift, S., Eichhorst, W., Tobsch, V., . . . Tros, F. (2016). *Precarious employment in Europe: Part 1, patterns, trends and policy strategy*. Brussels, Belgium: European Parliament, Directorate-General for Internal Policies. Retrieved from www.europarl.europa.eu/RegData/etudes/STUD/2016/587285/IPOL_STU(2016)587285_EN.pdf

Bureau of Labor Statistics. (2017). Union membership rate 10.7 percent in 2016. Washington, DC: Bureau of Labor Statistics. Retrieved from www.bls.gov/opub/ted/2017/union-membership-rate-10-point-7-percent-in-2016.htm

Burkhauser, R. V., & Daly, M. C. (2012). Social security disability insurance: Time for fundamental change. *Journal of Policy Analysis and Management, 31*(2), 454–461.
Department of Labour, New Zealand. (2000). *Framework for the Accredited Employers Programme.* Retrieved from www.legislation.govt.nz/regulation/public/2000/0111/latest/DLM5330.html
Försäkringskassan [Swedish social insurance agency]. (2008). *Deltidssjukskrivning: En registerstudie över utvecklingen 1995–2006* [Social insurance report]. Stockholm, Sweden: Försäkringskassan. Retrieved March 18, 2018 from www.forsakringskassan.se/wps/wcm/connect/3de6b1b7-4e00-40e5-81b3-75b40bddeffe/social forsakringsrapport_2008_12.pdf?MOD=AJPERES
Franche, R. L., Baril, R., Shaw, W. S., Nicholas, M., & Loisel, P. (2005). Workplace-based return-to-work interventions: Optimizing the role of stakeholders in implementation and research. *Journal of Occupational Rehabilitation, 15*(4), 525–542.
Gais, T., & Weaver, R. K. (2002). *State policy choices under welfare reform* (Policy Brief No. 21). Washington, DC: The Brookings Institution. Retrieved from www.brookings.edu/wp-content/uploads/2016/06/pb21.pdf
Gensby, U., Lund, T., Kowalski, K., Saidj, M., Jørgensen, A.-M. K., Filges, T., . . . Labriola, M. (2012). *Workplace disability management programs promoting return to work: A systematic review.* Oslo, Norway: Campbell Collaboration. Retrieved March 18, 2018 from www.campbellcollaboration.org/library/workplace-based-disability-programmes-promoting-return-to-work.html
Goldberg, M., & Green, D. A. (2009). *Understanding the link between welfare policy and the use of food banks.* Retrieved from www.policyalternatives.ca/sites/default/files/uploads/publications/National_Office_Pubs/2009/Link_Between_Welfare_Policy_and_Food_Banks.pdf
Guest, G. H., & Drummond, P. D. (1992). Effect of compensation on emotional state and disability in chronic back pain. *Pain, 48,* 125–130.
Hunt, H. A., & Barth, P. S. (2010). *Compromise and release settlements in workers' compensation: Final report.* Kalamazoo, MI: W. E. Upjohn Institute for Employment Research. Retrieved from http://research.upjohn.org/cgi/viewcontent.cgi?article=1181&context=reports
International Labour Organization. (2016). *Non-standard employment around the world: Understanding challenges, shaping prospects.* Geneva, Switzerland: International Labour Organization. Retrieved from www.ilo.org/global/publications/books/WCMS_534326/lang--en/index.htm
Ison, T. G. (2013). Reflections on workers' compensation and occupational health & safety. *Canadian Journal of Administrative Law and Practice, 26,* 1–22.
Johnston, V., & Beales, D. (2016). Enhancing direct access and authority for work capacity certificates to physiotherapists. *Journal of Manual Therapy, 25,* 100–103.
Kalleberg, A. L. (2011). *Good jobs, bad jobs: The rise of polarized and precarious employment systems in the United States, 1970s to 2000s.* New York, NY: Russell Sage Foundation.
Kilgour, E., Kosny, A., McKenzie, D., & Collie, A. (2014a). Interactions between injured workers and insurers in workers' compensation systems: A systematic review of qualitative research literature. *Journal of Occupational Rehabilitation, 25*(1), 160–181. doi:10.1007/s10926-014-9513-x
Kilgour, E., Kosny, A., McKenzie, D., & Collie, A. (2014b). Healing or harming? Healthcare provider interactions with injured workers and insurers in workers'

compensation systems. *Journal of Occupational Rehabilitation, 25*(1), 220–239. doi:10.1007/s10926-014-9521-x

Klienfield, N. R. (2009, March 31). Exams of injured workers fuel mutual mistrust. *The New York Times.* Retrieved from www.nytimes.com/2009/04/01/nyregion/01comp.html

Koning, P., & Lindeboom, M. (2015). The rise and fall of disability insurance. *Journal of Economic Perspectives, 29*(2), 151–172.

Kosny, A., Lifshen, M., Tonima, S., Yanar, B., Russell, E., MacEachen, E., ... Cooper, J. (2016). *The role of health-care providers in the workers' compensation system and return-to-work process: Final report.* Toronto, Canada: Institute for Work & Health. Retrieved from www.iwh.on.ca/sites/iwh/files/iwh/reports/iwh_report_role_of_health-care_providers_in_rtw_2016.pdf

Kosny, A., MacEachen, E., Ferrier, S., & Chambers, L. (2011). The role of health care providers in long term and complicated workers' compensation claims. *Journal of Occupational Rehabilitation, 21*(4), 582–590. doi:10.1007/s10926-011-9307-3

Lessnoff, M. H. (Ed.) (1990). *Social Contract Theory.* Oxford, UK: Basil Blackwell.

Lippel, K. (1999). Therapeutic and anti-therapeutic consequences of workers' compensation. *International Journal of Law and Psychiatry, 22*(5–6), 521–546.

Lippel, K., Vézina, M., & Cox, R. (2011). Protection of workers' mental health in Québec: Do general duty clauses allow labour inspectors to do their job? *Safety Science, 49*(4), 582–590.

MacEachen, E., Clarke, J., Franche, R. L., & Irvin, E. (2006). Systematic review of the qualitative literature on return to work after injury. *Scandinavian Journal of Work Environment and Health, 32*(4), 257–269.

MacEachen, E., Du, B., Bartel, E., Ekberg, K., Tompa, E., Kosny, A., Petricone, I, Stapleton, J. (2017). Scoping review of work disability policies and programs. *International Journal of Work Disability Management, 12*, e1. doi:10.1017/idm.2017.1

MacEachen, E., Kosny, A., Ferrier, S., & Chambers, L. (2010). The "toxic dose" of system problems: Why some injured workers don't return to work as expected. *Journal of Occupational Rehabilitation, 20*(3), 349–366.

MacEachen, E., Kosny, A., Ferrier, S., Lippel, K., Neilson, C., Franche, R., & Pugliese, D. (2012). The "ability" paradigm in vocational rehabilitation: Challenges in an Ontario injured worker retraining program. *Journal of Occupational Rehabilitation, 22*, 105–117. doi:10.1007/s10926-011-9329-x

MacEachen, E., Lippel, K., Saunders, R., Kosny, A., Mansfield, E., Carrasco, C., & Pugliese, D. (2012). Workers' compensation experience-rating rules and the danger to workers' safety in the temporary work agency sector. *Policy and Practice in Health and Safety, 10*(1), 77–95.

Mansfield, L., MacEachen, E., Tompa, E., Kalcevich, C., Endicott, M., & Yeung, N. (2012). A critical review of literature on experience rating in workers' compensation systems. *Policy and Practice in Health and Safety, 10*(1), 3–25.

Martin, J. P. (2015). Activation and active labour market policies in OECD countries: Stylised facts and evidence on their effectiveness. *IZA Journal of Labor Policy, 4*(4), 1–29.

Organisation for Economic Co-operation and Development. (2010). *Sickness, disability and work: Breaking the barriers—A synthesis of findings across OECD countries*. Paris, France: OECD.
Organisation for Economic Co-operation and Development. (2013). *Activation strategies for stronger and more inclusive labour markets in G20 countries: Key policy challenges and good practices*. Paris, France: OECD. Retrieved from www.oecd.org/els/emp/G20-2013ReportActivation.pdf
Oorschot, W. V. (2002). Miracle or nightmare? A critical review of Dutch activation policies and their outcomes. *Journal of Social Policy, 31*(3), 399–420.
Parolin, Z., & Luigjes, C. (2018). *Incentive to retrench? Institutional moral hazard among federal & state social assistance programs after welfare reform*. Antwerp, Belgium: Herman Deleeck Centre for Social Policy. Retrieved from www.centrumvoorsociaalbeleid.be/sites/default/files/CSBWorkingPaper1802.pdf
Paz-Fuchs, A. (2011). *The Social Contract Revisited: The Modern Welfare State*. Retrieved from www.fljs.org/files/publications/Paz-Fuchs-SummaryReport.pdf
PricewaterhouseCoopers. (2015). *The sharing economy*. Retrieved from www.pwc.com/us/en/technology/publications/assets/pwc-consumer-intelligence-series-the-sharing-economy.pdf
Provost, L. (2013). *Accident Compensation Corporation: Using a case management approach to rehabilitation*. Wellington, New Zealand: Controller and Auditor-General. Retrieved from www.oag.govt.nz/2014/acc-case-management/docs/acc-case-management.pdf
Raffass, T. (2017). Demanding activation. *Journal of Social Policy, 46*(2), 349–365.
Rappin, C. L., Wuellner, S. E., & Bonauto, D. K. (2016). Employer reasons for failing to report eligible workers' compensation claims in the BLS survey of occupational injuries and illnesses. *American Journal of Industrial Medicine, 59*(5), 343–356.
Safe Work Australia. (2014). *Key workers' compensation information, Australia*. Retrieved from www.safeworkaustralia.gov.au/system/files/documents/1702/key-workers-compensation-information-2014.pdf
Seing, I., MacEachen, E., Ståhl, C., & Ekberg, K. (2015). Early-return-to-work in the context of an intensification of working life and changing employment relationships. *Journal of Occupational Rehabilitation, 25*(1), 74–85. doi:DOI 10.1007/s10926-014-9526-5
Shannon, H., & Lowe, G. S. (2002). How many injured workers do not file claims for workers' compensation benefits? *American Journal of Industrial Medicine, 42*, 467–473.
Social and Economic Council. (2015). The power of consultation: The Dutch consultative economy explained. Retrieved from www.ser.nl/~/media/files/internet/talen/engels/brochure/informatiebrochure-power-consultation-en.ashx
Speiler, E. A., & Butler, J. F. (2012). The lack of correspondence between work-related disability and receipt of workers' compensation benefits. *American Journal of Industrial Medicine, 55*, 487–505.
Springer, J. F., Haas, P. J., & Porowski, A. (2017). *Applied Policy Research: Concepts and Cases*. New York, NY: Routledge.
Ståhl, C., Svensson, T., Petersson, G., & Ekberg, K. (2010). A matter of trust? A study of coordination of Swedish stakeholders in return-to-work. *Journal of Occupational Rehabilitation, 20*(3), 299–310.

Standing, G. (2011). *The precariat: The new dangerous class*. New York, NY: Bloomsbury Academic.

Stanley, D. (2014). *Pricing Fairness: A Deliverable Framework for Fairly Allocating WSIB Insurance Costs*. Retrieved from www.wsib.on.ca/cs/groups/public/documents/staticfile/c2li/mdex/~edisp/wsib011280.pdf

Stapleton, D. C., O'Day, B. L., Livermore, G. A., & Imparto, A. J. (2006). Dismantling the poverty trap: Disability policy for the twenty-first century. *Millbank Quarterly, 84*(4), 701–732.

Stapleton, J. (2013). The "welfareization" of disability incomes in Ontario. *Toronto, Canada: Metcalf Foundation*. Retrieved from https://metcalffoundation.com/wp-content/uploads/2013/12/Welfareization-of-Disability-Incomes-in-Ontario.pdf

Statistics Canada. (2018). *Unionization rates falling: Canadian megatrends*. Retrieved from www.statcan.gc.ca/pub/11-630-x/11-630-x2015005-eng.htm

Stratil, J. M., Rieger, M. A., & Völter-Mahlknecht, S. (2017). Cooperation between general practitioners, occupational health physicians, and rehabilitation physicians in Germany: What are problems and barriers to cooperation? A qualitative study. *International Archives of Occupational and Environmental Health, 90*(6), 481–490.

van Ostaijen, M., & Jhagroe, S. (2015). "Get those voices at the table!" Interview with Deborah Stone. *Policy Science, 48*, 127–133.

Viikari-Juntura, E., Kausto, J., Shiri, R., Kaila-Kangas, L., & Takala, E. (2012). Return to work after early part-time sick leave due to musculoskeletal disorders: A randomized controlled trial. *Scandinavian Journal of Work, Environment & Health, 38*(2), 134–143.

Waddell, G., Burton, A. K., & Aylward, M. (2008, May/June). A biopsychosocial model of sickness and disability. *The Guides Newsletter*.

Wise, E. A. (2016). Psychological injuries, workers' compensation insurance, and mental health policy issues. *Psychological Injury and Law, 9*(4), 283–297.

WorkCover Queensland. (2018). *Weekly compensation*. Retrieved from www.worksafe.qld.gov.au/rehab-and-claims/support-and-benefits/weekly-compensation

Workplace Safety and Insurance Appeals Tribunal. (2014). Decision No. 2157/09, 2014 ONWSIAT 938 (CanLII) — 2014-04-29. Toronto, Canada: Workplace Safety and Insurance Appeals Tribunal. Retrieved from www.canlii.org/en/on/onwsiat/doc/2014/2014onwsiat938/2014onwsiat938.pdf

Workplace Safety and Insurance Board. (2017). *WSIB chronic mental stress policy consultation summary*. Toronto, Canada: Workplace Safety and Insurance Board. Retrieved from www.wsib.on.ca/WSIBPortal/faces/WSIBDetailPage?cGUID=WSIB070670&rDef=WSIB_RD_ARTICLE&_afrLoop=602409173489000&_afrWindowMode=0&_afrWindowId=null#%40%3FcGUID%3DWSIB070670%26_afrWindowId%3Dnull%26_afrLoop%3D602409173489000%26rDef%3DWSIB_RD_ARTICLE%26_afrWindowMode%3D0%26_adf.ctrl-state%3D1ahtdpootr_4

Workplace Safety and Insurance Board. (2018a). *Benefits for loss of earnings*. Toronto, Canada: Workplace Safety and Insurance Board. Retrieved from www.wsib.on.ca/WSIBPortal/faces/WSIBDetailPage?cGUID=WSIB014536&rDef=WSIB_RD_ARTICLE&_afrLoop=513591078679000&_afrWindowMode=0&_afrWindowId=1add39dv6g_1#%40%3FcGUID%3DWSIB014536%26_afr

WindowId%3D1add39dv6g_1%26_afrLoop%3D513591078679000%26
rDef%3DWSIB_RD_ARTICLE%26_afrWindowMode%3D0%26_adf.
ctrl-state%3D1add39dv6g_29

Workplace Safety and Insurance Board. (2018b). When to report an injury or illness to the WSIB. In *Injury or illness reporting at WSIB*. Toronto, Canada: Workplace Safety and Insurance Board. Retrieved from www.wsib.on.ca/WSIBPortal/faces/WSIBArticlePage?fGUID=835502100635000330&_afrLoop=616105651953000&_afrWindowMode=0&_afrWindowId=null#%40%3F_afrWindowId%3Dnull%26_afrLoop%3D616105651953000%26_afrWindowMode%3D0%26fGUID%3D835502100635000330%26_adf.ctrl-state%3D1ahtdpootr_104

Index

Page numbers in **bold** refer to tables.
Page numbers in *italic* refer to figures.
Page numbers followed by *n* refer to notes.

1967 Dutch benefit scheme 226–7
1970s German social security systems 173
1980s & 1990s Dutch economy & work disability schemes 227–30
1990s German social security systems 173–5
2004 Dutch work disability scheme 230–7
2015 to 2017 Swedish activation policies 131–8

Abenhaim, Lucien 20
absence *see* work absence
access to work 59, 154, *247*, 250, 271, 276–7
accidents 10, 51–67, 88–100, 142–6, 150–4, 159–60, 171–82
accommodation 5–6, 11, 265, 268; Belgium 208–10; Canada 59–64; Finland 146–7; France 160–9; Germany 176–8; Sweden 126–7; United Kingdom 249–50; United States 40–1, 43
ACFTU *see* All-China Federation of Trade Unions
activation 3–12, 261–4, 267–77; Belgium 210, 215, 219; Germany 173–5; Sweden 125–38; Switzerland 189–93, 201*n1*
aging populations 6–8, 73–6, 88–9, 93–4, 142, 205, 242, 263
AIA *see* Automobile Insurance Act
Alberta Workers' Compensation Board Review Panel 65
All-China Federation of Trade Unions (ACFTU) 113

All Work Test *247*, 248
AMA Guides to the Evaluation of Permanent Impairment 44
Americans with Disabilities Acts 6, 31, **35**, 39–40
Anema, Johannes 21
asbestos **36**, 153, 168
The Association of Workers' Compensation Boards of Canada (2005) 23
Australia: cause-based systems 10, 72–84, 263, 266–7, 269–70, 273; New Zealand's accident scheme 93, 96–7, 99
Automobile Insurance Act (AIA) 60

back pain/problems 4, 272; Australia 74; Belgium 205, 209–12, 220; France 159–61; Sherbrooke Model 18–22; United States 37, 45, 46*n6*
Barr, Ben 11, 242–55
Belgium 11, 205–20, 265, 267–70
benefits 4–7, 261–78; Australia 72–83; Belgium 206–20; Canada 50–68; China 103–7, **110**, 113, 116; Finland 142–51, 154–5; France 160; Germany 174–5, 178–81; Netherlands 223–36; New Zealand 89–99; Sherbrooke Model 18, 23; Sweden 125–38; Switzerland 193–6; United Kingdom 242–55; United States 31–46
Berecki-Gisolf, J. 51
Beveridge policy 159, 193, 225–6
Bismarckian approaches 11, 159, 172–3, 193, 225, 236

Black Lung Benefits Act 36
bounded rationality 125, 136
British Household Panel Survey 245
bullying 53

Canada: cause-based social security systems 10, 50–68, 263–7, 269, 271, 273, 275; Sherbrooke Model 18–20, 23–5
Caron case Supreme Court ruling 59, 64, 68n3
case management, Switzerland 191, 194–202
case studies, Canada 52–66
cause-based social security systems 9–11, 18–20, 23–5, 29–121, 262–73, 275, 277; Australia 10, 72–84, 263, 266–7, 269–70, 273; Canada 10, 50–68, 263–7, 269, 271, 273, 275; China 10, 103–18, 267, 273; New Zealand 10, 88–100; United States 10, 31–47, 267
center-left government, Sweden 131–4, 137
center-right government, Sweden 129–31, 135–7
Centers for Disease Control and Prevention 43
certification 105, 116, 143–6, 168
China 10, 103–18, 267, 273
chronic conditions: Australia 73–4; Belgium 209–10, 215–16, 219; Canada 53–4, 58–61, 65–6; Germany 172, 177; New Zealand 91; Sherbrooke Model 21; United Kingdom 245–6; United States 37–8, 41
Clay, F. J. 51
Collie, A. 51
compensation systems 3, 10, 262–73; Australia 10, 72–84; Belgium 206, 210–12; Canada 10, 50–68; China 103–18; Finland 143–4, 151–3; France 160–1; Germany 175–7, 180; New Zealand 10, 88–100; United States 31–9, 41–7
comprehensive social security systems 10–11, 123–255, 262–70, 272–7; Belgium 11, 205–20, 265, 267–70; Finland 10, 141–55, 265, 268, 274; France 10–11, 158–69, 268, 272, 276; Germany 11, 171–84, 263, 265, 268, 272–4, 277; Netherlands 11, 223–38, 266, 268, 270, 274; Sweden 10, 125–38, 263–5, 268–9; Switzerland 11, 189–202, 267–8; United Kingdom 11, 242–55, 263–4, 274
congenital disorders, New Zealand 91, 99
Convention on the Rights of Persons with Disabilities (CRPD) 171, 174–5, 177, 181–2, 183n2
cooperation experiences 61–3, 171–84, 191, 195, 200, 215–17, 272–4
Cornell University's Employment and Disability Institute 41–2
corporate health management 190–2, 195, 200
costs 4–7, 262–74, 277; Australia 72, 78–80; Belgium 211–14, 219–20; Canada 59, 64–6; China 110, 116; Dutch systems 229–30, 237; Finland 141, 143–6, 148–55; Netherlands 227–30, 237; New Zealand 89–94, 97–100; Sweden 126–7, 134; Switzerland 196–8; United Kingdom 242–3, 254; United States 31–3, 38–9, 44–5
courts 59, 64, 68n3, 78, 81, 113–14, 177–8, 208
crime 53–61, 64–7, 91
CRPD see Convention on the Rights of Persons with Disabilities
Cultural Revolution, China 104

daily-sickness-allowance insurance schemes 196–7
damages claims 72, 77, 79
Dembe, Allard E. 10, 31–47
demographic issues 5–9, 52–4, 72–3, 76, 88, 103, 158, 178, 214
depression see mental health conditions
Directives 144, 173, 176–7
Disability Affected Life Years 74
disability determination see eligibility
Disability Discrimination Act 247, 249–50
Disability Support Pensions (DSP) 76, 81–2
discrimination: Australia 72, 77–9; Canada 52, 65; Finland 154; Germany 173–7; New Zealand 91–3, 97–100; Sweden 126–7; United Kingdom 243, 247, 249–51
dispute settlement 168–9
drug overdoses 42–3
DSP see Disability Support Pensions
Duncan, Grant 10, 88–100
Dupuis, M. 18–19
"Dutch disease" 227–30

Index

EAP *see* Employee Assistance Programs
EARN (The Employer Assistance and Resource Network on Disability Inclusion) 41
earnings/income: Australia 80; Belgium 206–9; Canada 51–68; China 113; Finland 141–3, 148–53; France 159–61; Germany 172–5, 178–80; New Zealand 94–5; Sweden 126; United Kingdom 243–4, *247*, 248; United States 32
economic trends 3–12; Australia 73–4, 79; Belgium 205–20; Canada 51, 57–60, 63–7; China 103–7, 112–13, 117–18; Finland 141–2; Germany 172–5, 182–3; Netherlands 224–38; New Zealand 89–92, 96–100; Sweden 127, 135–6; Switzerland 189, 193–4, 200; United Kingdom 242, 244–6, 250; United States 40
education 40–2, 53, 60, 163–5, 193, 199, 243–6, 249–51, 253–4
EI *see* Employment Insurance
Ekberg, Kerstin 261–78
eligibility: Australia 72, 76–7, 80–4; Belgium 208–9; Canada 51–2; China 105, 116, 118*n*2; Finland 146, 148–52; France 162; Germany 176–7; New Zealand 88–9, 93–6, 98; United Kingdom 243, 246–8, 251, 253–4; United States 31–8, 44, 46
Employee Assistance Programs (EAP) 42
Employee Pensions Act 148
The Employer Assistance and Resource Network on Disability Inclusion (EARN) 41
employers: Australia 79–81; Belgium 205–11, 216–20; Canada 50–2, 56–68; China 104–18; Finland 141–55; France 158–69; Germany 172–83; Netherlands 11, 223–38; New Zealand 89–93, 96–100; Sherbrooke Model 19–20, 24; Sweden 126–34, 137; Switzerland 189–202; United Kingdom 243, 250–1, 254; United States 31–3, **35**, 39–46
Employment Insurance (EI) 50–1, 61
employment support 38, 178, 249, 253–4, 264
Employment Support Allowance *247*
Employment and Support Allowance (ESA) 248–9

Equalities Act *247*, 250
ESA *see* Employment and Support Allowance
European Agency for Safety and Health at Work 144, 268
evidence comparisons/interpretations 7–10, 265–6, 271, 277; Australia 74–5, 80–4; Belgium 212; New Zealand 93, 96–9; Sherbrooke Model 22–5; Sweden 135–8; United Kingdom 245, 250–4
experience rating 24, 98–9, 154–5, 266, 268–70
Extended Payment of Income Act 230–7

fairness issues 269–71
The Family and Medical Leave Act (FMLA) **35**
Fassier, Jean Baptiste 10–11, 158–69
fédérale des risques professionnels [FEDRIS] 209–12
Federal Employees Compensation Act 36
federal jurisdictions: Australia 72, 76–84; Germany 171–3, 176–82
federal programs: Canada 50–1, 67; United States 31–42, 44–6
Federal Republic of Germany (FRG) 11, 171–84
federal social code (SGB) 171, 174–6, 179–81
FEDRIS *see* fédérale des risques professionnels
Feuerstein, Michael 21–4
Finland 10, 141–55, 265, 268, 274
fitness 11, 162, 167–8
FMLA *see* The Family and Medical Leave Act
France 10–11, 158–69, 268, 272, 276
Freud, Sigmund 189–90
FRG *see* Federal Republic of Germany

gatekeeper politics 134, 230–7, 270–2
Geisen, Thomas 11, 189–202
General Household Survey 250–1
Germany 11, 171–84, 263, 265, 268, 272–4, 277
Giddens, Anthony 210
"gig" economy/workers 6, 39, 73
Gluckman, Peter 24
government: Australia 72, 76–84; Belgium 205–7, 210–20; Canada 50–4, 67; China 104–7, 112, 116; Finland 141–6, 154–5; France 158–9,

167–8; Germany 171–83; Netherlands 225–31, 237; New Zealand 90–4; Sherbrooke Model 21; Sweden 125–38; Switzerland 191–8; United Kingdom 242, 248–50; United States 31–2, 36–7, 40, 43, 45
Grant, Genevieve 10, 72–84
Gröninger v. Germany, 2014 174–5

harassment 53, 59–61
Hartz Commission 174
healthcare providers/services: Australia 72, 77–8; Belgium 205–12, 217; Canada 51–2, 57, 61–3, 67; China 104, 107; Finland 142–6, 150, 153–5; France 158–68; gatekeeper politics 134, 230–6, 270–2; Netherlands 224–7, 229, 235; New Zealand 89, 100; Sherbrooke Model 19–20; Sweden 125–7, 132–4; United Kingdom 254; United States 31, 37, 45–6
Health Insurance Act 141, 146, 154
health promotion, Switzerland 189, 191, 200
health and safety 10, 24, 81, 91, 144–5, 175–80
Health Survey for England 250–1
history: Germany 172–5; Netherlands 224–6; New Zealand 88–91
human rights 59–61, 64, 77–9, 83, 92, 190, 237

ICF *see* International Classification of Functioning
IIDB *see* Industrial Injuries Disablement Benefit
illnesses & sickness 3, 5, 261, 263–8, 270–7; Australia 72–84; Belgium 205–20; Canada 50–68; China 104, 112, 116, 118; Finland 141–8, 152–5; France 159–65; Germany 171–83; Netherlands 223–37; New Zealand 89, 91–9; Sherbrooke Model 20; Sweden 125–38; Switzerland 189–94, 196–202; United Kingdom 243; United States 31–4, 36–9, 42–6
ILO *see* International Labour Organization
immigrant workers 53–4, 59–66
INAMI *see* Institut National d'Assurance Maladie-Invalidité
incapacity benefits: Australia 74–83; Belgium 207–8, 213, 216; Germany 174–80; New Zealand 91–4, 97–9; United Kingdom 248–9; United States 31, 37–9, 41–2, 46*n*2
income protection/security 4–6, 270; Australia 72, 77, 79–82; Netherlands 224–5, 230, 233; Sweden 126, 130; United States 31, 39
income replacement, UK 242–55
Industrial Injuries Disablement Benefit (IIDB) 243
inequities 72, 83, 91–3, 153–4, 247
injuries: Australia 72–84; Canada 50–68; China 103–18; Finland 152–4; Germany 171–82; New Zealand 10, 88–100; Sweden 126, 131; Switzerland 189–96; United Kingdom 243; United States 31–46
Institut National d'Assurance Maladie-Invalidité (INAMI) 205–18
insurance/insurers: Australia 72, 77–81; Belgium 205–19; Canada 50–1, 60–1, 64–8; China 107–18; Finland 141–55; France 159–61, 164, 169; Germany 171–82; Netherlands 224–7, 230–2; New Zealand 90–2, 99–100; Sherbrooke Model 19–20; Sweden 125–38; Switzerland 192–202; United Kingdom 243, 254; United States 31–4, 36–40, 44–7
integration programs 5, 9–10, 262, 264–6, 268, 277; Belgium 205, 210, 212–20; Netherlands 227, 229, 231–4; Sweden 125, 127–31; United States 31, 38, 40–2, 45
International Classification of Functioning (ICF) 174, 177, 181
International Labour Organization (ILO) 99, 144, 171, 190, 223
Invalidity Benefit (IvB) 243, 248
IRSST *see* Research Institute of the Quebec Workers' Compensation Board
IvB *see* Invalidity Benefit

Job Capacity Assessments 81–2
Job Demands Resources model 215
job transitions, Sweden 126, 129–37

knowledge centres 216

Labor code 162–3, 166–8
Labor Contract Law in 2008 107, 115
Labor Law of the PRC, 2009 107

Labour Force Survey 250–1
laws: Australia 72–84; Belgium 205, 207, 212–13, 216; China 105–15; France 165–8; Germany 171–82; Netherlands 225–7, 229–37; United States 31, 33, 35, 39, *41*, 43–4
LeBlanc, F.E. 18–19
legislation: Australia 72–84; Canada 50–64; Germany 172–5, 177, 180–2; Netherlands 227, 229–37; New Zealand 90–4, 99; United Kingdom 249–50; United States 31, 43–4
legitimacy of injuries 38–9, 97
LHWCA *see* Longshore and Harbor Workers' Compensation Act
liberalism 67, 91, 167–9, 189–96, 210
Lind, James 23
Lippel, Katherine 10, 50–68
Loisel, Patrick 9
Longshore and Harbor Workers' Compensation Act (LHWCA) **36**
long-term disability 38–46, 75–6, 79, 81–3, 148–52, 223, 226, 230
low back pain 18–19, 160–1, 209–12, 220
lump-sum payments 44, 59, 72, 80, 109, 160–1, 267

MacEachen, Ellen 3–12, 261–78
McGill-Melzack (MGM) pain score 20
McHale, Philip 11, 242–55
Mairiaux, Philippe 11, 205–20
"malingering," 18, 97
Manifest Grants 81–2
Martimo, Kari Pekka 10, 141–55
means-tested support 51–2, 91–3, 97, 99, 249, 252
Medicaid program **35**
medical assessments 94–6, 105, 118*n*2
medical rehabilitation 142, 150–1, 172–3, 177–8
Medicare program **35**, 38, 78
mental health conditions 8, 263, 265, 272, 274, 276–7; Belgium 215; Canada 53–4, 58–61, 65; China 105, 116; Finland 149–50, 153; Germany 171–2, 177–9; Netherlands 232–4; New Zealand 89, 91, 96, 99–100; Sherbrooke Model 22; Sweden 126–7, 130; United Kingdom 243–4, 250–1, 253; United States 42–3
MGM *see* McGill-Melzack pain score

migrant workers 112, 116
motor-vehicle accidents 51–67
musculoskeletal disorders 22, 45, 74–5, 130, 149–51, 153, 244, 263

Nachemson, Alf 18
National Disability Insurance Scheme (NDIS) 79
National Employment Office (ONEM) 208, 213
National Employment Standards (NES) 78
National Institute for Health and Disability Insurance 205–18
National Insurance contributions 243
NDIS *see* National Disability Insurance Scheme
needs-based benefits 92, 97
negligence 32, 67, 72, 77, 79, 93
neoliberalism 67, 91, 167–9
NES *see* National Employment Standards
Netherlands 11, 21, 223–38, 266, 268, 270, 274
New Deal for Disabled People *247*, 249
New Mexico 38
New Zealand 10, 24, 88–100, 263–4, 269–71, 277
no-fault systems 10, 32, 51, 54, 67, 77, 80, 88–100, 108
non-work-related conditions 54, 91, 97, 103, 105, 113–16, 159–60, 190, 226

Occupational Accidents, Injuries and Diseases Act 152
occupational disease *see* work-related conditions
Occupational Diseases Fund 209–12
Occupational Health Care Act 142, 144, 147, 154
occupational health services/systems 10, 141–55, 158–69, 216–19, 224–7, 230–6
occupational physicians (OP) 159, 162–9, 208–10, 217, 225–6, 231–6
OECD *see* Organisation for Economic Co-operation and Development
The Official Disability Guidelines (ODG) 44
One Advisory Service 249
ONEM *see* National Employment Office
One Program *247*
Ontario, Canada 54, 58–9, 61–8, 263–5, 267, 269, 271

Index

OP *see* occupational physicians
opioid medications 42–3
Organisation for Economic Co-operation and Development (OECD) 261–4; Australia 73, 79; Canada 50; Finland 142, 153–5; Netherlands 224, 232–4, 238; Sweden 127–8, 136; Switzerland 190, 196; United Kingdom 242–3, 246–7

pain *see* back pain
part-time sick leave 127, 143–5, 264–5, 268
Pathways to Work 247, 249, 251
pensions 6, 263–7; Australia 76, 81–2; Belgium 205–8, 214–16; Canada 50–1, 57–8, 60, 64–5; China 104, 115; Finland 141–3, 146–54; France 160–1; Germany 171–82; Netherlands 223–4; Sweden 128–9, 134; Switzerland 194, 197–9; United Kingdom 243, 248–50, 252
People's Republic of China (PRC) 105–7, 115
positionality 9
poverty 11, 264; Belgium 208–9; China 104, 116; Netherlands 235; New Zealand 92, 98; United Kingdom 242–3, 247, 250–4
PRC *see* People's Republic of China
Prime Minister's Science Advisory Committee 24
prostheses 91, 110
Protection of Disabled Persons of 2008 105–6
Act on the Protection of Privacy in Working Life 143
provincial authorities 50–4, 67
Public Employment Service 155

quality of life 21, 73
Québec Automobile Insurance Act 60
Quebec, Canada 51, 54–68, 263
quota systems 78, 165–7, 172–3, 176, 189, 192, 276

reforms: Belgium 205–16, 219–20; China 104–5, 115, 117; Finland 141, 151, 154; France 167–8; Germany 173–5, 180–2; Sweden 125–38; United Kingdom 242–55

Regulation on the Employment of the Disabled (2007) 106, 118
Regulation on Work-Related Injury Insurance 107–9, 112
rehabilitation 262–8, 272–7; Belgium 205, 209–13; Canada 52–67; China 105, 109–10, **114**, 116–18; Finland 141–55; Germany 171–83; Netherlands 229–30; New Zealand 88–100; Sherbrooke Model 18–21, 24; Sweden 126–37; Switzerland 190, 196, 198–200; United Kingdom 249, 254; United States 32–3, 38, 43–4
reintegration programs *see* integration programs
Research Institute of the Quebec Workers' Compensation Board (IRSST) 18–20
re-training 165–6
return to work 5–9, 262, 264–71, 275–7; Australia 72, 80–2; Belgium 207–10, 212–18; Canada 51–68; China 103, 109–18; Finland 146, 154; France 160–5; New Zealand 89–90, 95–100; Sherbrooke Model 9, 19–25; Sweden 125–8, 138; Switzerland 193–202; United States 38, 40–5
rights: advocacy movements 4–5; Australia 77–9, 83; China 109–13; Finland 154; Germany 174–5; human rights 59–61, 64, 77–9, 83, 92, 190, 237; United Kingdom 249–50
de Rijk, Angelique 11, 223–38
Royal Commission on Compensation for Personal Injury 89–92, 96–100
Royal Decrees 216–18
rural China 103–5, 107–8, **114**, 116–18

safety: health and 10, 24, 81, 91, 144–5, 175–80; US work related injuries 44–5
Safe Work Australia 72, 75, 81–2, 93, 96, 267
SAMHSA *see* Substance Abuse and Mental Health Services Administration
scurvy 23
Seing, Ida 10, 125–38
sexual assault 53–4, 59–61, 91
SGB *see* federal social code
Shan, Desai 10, 103–18
Sherbrooke Model 9, 209–11

short-term disability 38–40, *41*, 42, 45, 142–3, 176
sickness *see* illnesses & sickness
Sickness Impact Profiles (SIP) 20
SII *see* Social Insurance Institution of Finland
SIP *see* Sickness Impact Profiles; social-insurance physicians
social code books 171, 174–6, 179–81
social contracts 4, 8, 12, 261, 277
social-democratic government 129, 135–6
Social Insurance Acts 126
Social Insurance Institution of Finland (SII) 142–52, 155
social-insurance physicians (SIP) 159–65, 207–12, 216–19
socialism, China 103–4, 107, 113
Social Security Disability Insurance (SSDI) 31–4, 36–8, 45–6
Spitzer, Walter 18–19
SSDI *see* Social Security Disability Insurance
SSI *see* Supplemental Security Income
Ståhl, Christian 10, 125–38
standards 61, 78, 104–5, 108–9, 112, **114**, 176
Standing Committee of the National Congress 108, 118*n*6
state agencies, Germany 171, 173, 176, 180–2
state jurisdiction, Australia 72, 76–83
state monopolies, New Zealand 90–1
state programs, United States 31–46
Statistics Canada 50, 60, 275
Statutory Sick Pay 243
stick approaches 52, 65–6
stigmatization issues 5–6, 66, 166, 277
students 52–61
Substance Abuse and Mental Health Services Administration (SAMHSA) 42
Supplemental Security Income (SSI) 32–5, 46*n*1
Supported Living Payments 88
Supreme Court of Canada 59, 64, 68*n*3
Supreme People's Court (2004) 113–14
sustainability, Dutch policies 236–7
Sweden 10, 125–38, 263–5, 268–9
Switzerland 11, 189–202, 267–8
system complexity 6–7
system goals 37–40

temporary workers 126, 143–4
territorial jurisdictions 72, 76–80, 83
tort actions **36**, 44, 72, 77, 79, 90, 107, 113–14
trade unions *see* unions
transitional change, Sweden 126, 129–37
trauma 37, 109
Trevethick v. Ministry of Health (2008) 92
tribunals 52, 61, 78, 263

UK *see* United Kingdom
unions: Belgium 206, 211, 216–17; Canada 67; China 113; Finland 141, 154; Germany 173, 176–7, 181–2; Netherlands 225–31; Sherbrooke Model 19–21; Sweden 126, 134
United Kingdom (UK) 11, 242–55, 263–4, 274
United States (US) 10, 31–47, 267
universal accident schemes 10, 88–100
urban China 103–5, **114**, 116–18
US *see* United States

Vandenbroucke, Frank 210–11
veterans **35**, 141, 173, 177, 182
vocational rehabilitation 262–8, 272–7; Belgium 212–13; Finland 142, 146–53; Germany 171–5, 177–8, 181; Netherlands 229–30; New Zealand 88–99; Sherbrooke Model 18–21, 24; United Kingdom 249, 254; United States 43–4

Waddell, Gordon 18
wage-replacement systems 32, 39, 46, 52–4, 61, 65
Wassenaar agreement 228
WC *see* workers' compensation
WCA *see* Work Capability Assessment
welfare-to-work programs 242, *247*, 249, 251, 263
"well-being services" 150
Welti, Felix 11, 171–84
WHO *see* World Health Organization
WIIF *see* work-related injury insurance fund
"Woodhouse Report" 89–92, 96–100
work ability 128–33, 138, 146–8, 154
work absence 4–5, 261, 264–6, 269, 272–4; Australia 75; Canada 51, 56, 61, 66; Finland 143, 146–8; France 159; Netherlands 223–37; Sherbrooke

Model 19, 24; Sweden 127–38; Switzerland 190–1; United Kingdom 243; United States 40–1; *see also* illnesses & sickness
work activation *see* activation
Work Capability Assessment (WCA), UK 248
work-capacity assessments 88, 94–6, 106–10, 114–16
workers' compensation (WC): Australia 10, 72–84; Belgium 206, 210–12; Canada 50–68; New Zealand **36**, 63, 89; US cause-based systems 31–9, 41–7
Workplace Safety and Insurance Act (WSIA) 61–2, 263
Workplace Safety and Insurance Board (WSIB) 61, 63, 66, 263, 267, 271
work principle, Sweden 127, 130, 132–5, 138

The Work Program *247*, 249, 251
work-related conditions: Australia 73–84; Belgium 209–12; Canada 53–63; China 103–18; Finland 142–6, 150–4; France 158–69; Germany 172–3, 178, 180; Netherlands 226; New Zealand 10, 88–100; Sweden 126, 131; Switzerland 189–96; United Kingdom 243; United States 31–46
work-related injury insurance fund (WIIF) 107–13, 116–18
World Health Organization (WHO) 174, 177, 181, 190
World War I 172
World War II 4, 141, 172–3, 205–6, 225
WSIA *see* Workplace Safety and Insurance Act
WSIB *see* Workplace Safety and Insurance Board

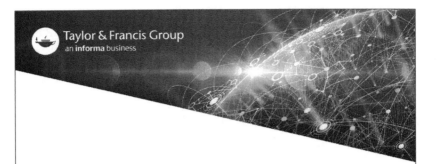

Taylor & Francis eBooks

www.taylorfrancis.com

A single destination for eBooks from Taylor & Francis with increased functionality and an improved user experience to meet the needs of our customers.

90,000+ eBooks of award-winning academic content in Humanities, Social Science, Science, Technology, Engineering, and Medical written by a global network of editors and authors.

TAYLOR & FRANCIS EBOOKS OFFERS:

- A streamlined experience for our library customers
- A single point of discovery for all of our eBook content
- Improved search and discovery of content at both book and chapter level

REQUEST A FREE TRIAL
support@taylorfrancis.com